SEEDTIME OF REFORM

SEEDTIME
OF REFORM

American Social Service and Social Action
1918–1933

CLARKE A. CHAMBERS

Ann Arbor Paperbacks
THE UNIVERSITY OF MICHIGAN PRESS

TO JOHN D. HICKS AND GISELA KONOPKA

whose scholarship in history and social work led the way, and whose friendship provided encouragement and inspiration

PREFATORY NOTES

"Perhaps you may ask, 'Does the road lead uphill all the way?' And I must answer, 'Yes, to the very end.' But if I offer you a long, hard struggle, I can also promise you great rewards."

—Grace Abbott, Commencement Address, the New Jersey
College of Women, June 1934

WRITING at the end of what assuredly had been a frustrating decade for social reformers, Donald Richberg recalled in 1929 the fighting faiths that had driven the prewar generation to attempt nothing less than a sweeping transformation of American life. "My generation was spoiling for a fight with the ancient enemies of progress — the self-satisfied. It was sick and tired of pot-bellied politicians; tired of bankers and business men preaching a one-day-in-seven version of the Golden Rule. It wanted to get religion, but not in churches patronized by thieves. So when T. R. located Armageddon and the band played marching hymns, we put on shining armor and went out to 'battle for the Lord.'" The Great War, he believed, began the wholesale destruction of hope, plundered his generation of its "spiritual heritage." Beyond that, progressivism, he saw in 1929, had rested on certain shaky premises: that the line between right and wrong could be clearly drawn; that given the chance, the people would act wisely; that upon the foundation of informed and enlightened opinion responsible officials could build constructive reform. The postwar decade had laid bare the insufficiency of these principles: what was right and what was wrong more frequently required the test of scientific analysis than of popular opinion; "the People can't vote right unless they have the capacity for right judgment"; as for public officials, they followed "propaganda or prejudice" as often as responsible opinion and "neither know what is right, nor how to do it." All was not in vain, however; constructive achievements had been won; and, he concluded: "It is altogether possible that the oncoming generation may do the same." [1]

Witnesses there were, in great legions, to bear testimony to the postwar disenchantment with the progressive reform urge which had moved that earlier era. John Haynes Holmes, devout and devoted crusader for all good causes, summarized in 1927 his discontent: "Up to 1914 all things had seemed possible here in America. It was a stupendous under-taking — to subdue the power and arrogance of organized capitalism and remould it to the democratic patterns of the rights of man." But now all that was gone. "We have no confidence any more — no confidence that we were ever justified in having confidence! . . . Our people are fat, corrupt, contented. But we are slaves just the same." With rare un-charitable bitterness, Holmes blamed the rout of fine promise upon "the fat materialism of a corrupt age." [2]

In mid-decade Frederic C. Howe's *Confessions of a Reformer* set off a series of commentaries by "pre-war radicals" on the oppressive climate of the twenties. Some saw apathy and boredom as root responses; others suggested that war had consumed the moral energies of the people and that a respite from crusading was now required; others found progres-sive dreams deficient, lacking in realism, too hopeful of society's con-version to justice; others blamed the decade's "money madness," the defilement of ideal by material plenty; still others noted that progres-sivism was dead of its own success — by achieving so many of the re-forms it had sought, it had worked itself right out of a job. Stuart Chase complained that progressivism had proved "inept because its moral judgments took the place of sound analysis." Norman Thomas said the nation was "drunk with prosperity" (presumably as with bad gin). "The old reformer," he continued, "has become the Tired Radical and his sons and daughters drink at the fountain of the *American Mer-cury*. They have no illusions but one. And that is that they can live like Babbitt and think like Mencken." [3]

The distinguished contributors to this symposium, put together in the *Survey*, offered varied, and often vague, assurances. Many called for a new radicalism that would form an alliance with the working class and strive for economic reconstruction before political reform. Some counseled patience and a willingness to explore new avenues of diag-nosis and cure: the world was more complex than many had imagined and more resistant to change; new tactics and a new spirit were there-fore in order. At least one "pre-war radical," Charlotte Perkins Gilman, expressed relief "in being free from the work demanded by various 'causes' now won or temporarily in abeyance, and able at last to write and lecture on my own lines of social philosophy." But her response was unusual; others were eager to re-enlist in some cause. "New times will produce new causes," predicted William Allen White. And Ray S.

Baker echoed that hope — that a new earth "cannot at once, overnight, be shaped to our ideas of perfection, is no cause for sickly disillusionment, but for new enthusiasm and new effort." If only the socialists among them displayed any clear sense of direction, the others, while disappointed with the postwar collapse of reform, were still hopeful that the old fighting spirit could be revived.

It is curious that this particular group, at that particular moment, did not explicitly take up the issues that the *Survey* magazine itself, under the imaginative editorship of Paul U. Kellogg, had been exploring ever since the armistice of 1918 — the deprivation of civil liberties and of freedom of speech, the denial of first-class citizenship to persons of colored skin, industrial exploitation, the growing commercialization of culture, urban congestion, slum housing, insecurity of employment, dependency in old age. In response to these problems, new programs were being elaborated and new concepts of social reform were being created. That reform was not dead but for the moment quiescent, that the cause of progress was not moribund but merely catching its breath was not immediately apparent to those who were caught up in day-to-day frustration and sometimes demoralized by what seemed to be irrevocable defeats. The passing of time would indicate that new lines of action were being tried out in the confused twenties. Not all of them would prove fruitful of ultimate success; but there was a larger validity and viability to the reform impulse in the Golden Years than most participants then realized and than most critics and scholars have since acknowledged.

This study began as an essay at discovering what happened to the reform impulse in American life in the years between the end of World War I and the inauguration of Franklin D. Roosevelt. Students of American liberalism have traditionally treated the Great War as the end of reform and the decade between armistice and panic as a great hiatus; historians, concerned with the continuity of reform, have tended to discount the decade of "normalcy and reaction," and to leapfrog over it, often clumsily, from the backs of T. R. and Woodrow Wilson to the back of F. D. R.

Then came Henry F. May's provocative essay on "Shifting Perspectives on the 1920's," with its implied invitation to join in a re-evaluation of that decade's history, and Arthur S. Link's bold question "What happened to the progressive movement?" "[P]erhaps it is high time that we discard the sweeping generalizations, false hypotheses, and clichés that we have so often used in explaining and characterizing political developments from 1918 to 1929," he wrote. "Perhaps we should try to see these developments for what they were — the normal and ordinary political behavior of groups and classes caught up in a swirl of social and economic change. When we do this we will no longer ask whether the progressive movement was defunct in the 1920's. We will ask only what happened to it and why." [4] Professor Link offered a few tentative answers; others had already engaged themselves, searching again for answers to that question. Paul Carter, Robert M. Miller, and Donald B. Meyer explored the social role of the Protestant churches in the interwar era, while Aaron I. Abell told the story of the social action programs of American Catholicism; Irving Bernstein related the social history of labor during the "lean years," 1920–1933; Joseph Dorfman carried through his exhaustive study of the economic mind in American civilization in two encyclopedic volumes which summarized the careers and scholarship of every notable figure in economic thought, both academic and nonacademic, during the years 1918–1933; Al Smith, a political link between Wilson and Roosevelt, found a lively biographer in Oscar Handlin, while Fiorello H. La Guardia's remarkable career commanded the attention of two able scholars, Arthur Mann and Howard Zinn; D. Joy Humes traced the significance of Oswald Garrison Villard, "liberal of the 1920's"; James Shideler, Gilbert Fite, John D. Hicks, and Theodore Saloutos threw new light on farm protest movements; Bernard Bellush, Frank Freidel, Daniel Fusfeld, and Arthur M. Schlesinger, Jr., traced the early career of Franklin Roosevelt and thereby the origins of much of the New Deal; William Leuchtenburg and John D. Hicks offered new summary evaluations of the significance of what earlier had been known as "the era of wonderful nonsense."

Still there were gaps in the story, and where they had been filled there was the need for reinterpretation. Two aspects of the 1920's particularly came to engage my attention — the role of voluntary reform associations of concerned but disinterested citizens, and the role of social welfare leaders and social service agencies. What were they thinking and doing during the Golden Years of the Jazz Age? To their story I turned, drawing upon the research of others when it seemed relevant, adding research of my own when the inclusion of supplementary evidence seemed expedient. I have not wished to retell the story that others have told so well — of the decline and revival of the social gospel, for example, or of farm organization protest, or of organized labor. Where these narrative analyses have impinged upon my own central concerns, I have taken the liberty of borrowing from them (always with profound gratitude for the labors of other workers in the vineyard). But it was never part of my intent to attempt an over-all synthesis of all aspects of all reform movements in the interwar years. I wished merely to set forth my own partial evidence on certain reformers and reform associations whose activities had been relatively neglected by other scholars, to tell my own limited (but I hope not insignificant) story, and to let it go at that. As for professional social work, my primary interest was in the social action dimension of its diverse programs and not in its service functions as such; my attention focused upon what Porter Lee called the "cause" rather than the "function" aspects of social welfare, although it became my conviction that · the latter often gave rise to the former and that the two were as often mutually supportive as competitive or antagonistic. To have explored extensively the service activities of professionally oriented welfare agencies, both local and national, would have led to a book vastly different from this one. Such a study desperately needs doing; I have not attempted it here.

I was moved by primitive curiosity, then, to find out what had happened — this on the hunch that there was much more to the story of reform and welfare in the 1920's than had yet been revealed. I was moved equally by the desire to test, however inadequately and partially, that hoary hypothesis (and boast) that voluntarism in America was the mark of a democratic, open, fluid, pluralistic society. The vigor of voluntary associational activity is the measure of a dynamic and free society, it is said. Voluntary associations offer to the individual in a highly mobile and impersonal society a sense of place and the psychological rewards of participation; they "distribute and diversify power and influence" and protect society against "inflexibility and stagnation." [5] The tradition of voluntarism fragments power, provides unnumbered laboratories for social experimentation, makes possible the elaboration of new lines of social policy without the necessity of resorting to partisan politics as the only means of social action. In the realm of social welfare, one expert has concluded, the persistence of mutual, neighborly assistance through private agencies has provided ". . . research, experimentation, initiation of new programs, stimulation of community interest, plugging the gaps left by government, offering flexibility of services and assisting local communities to meet their unique problems in ways that cannot be undertaken by centrally administered public services." [6] Through the multifold institutions of a plural society the consent of the governed may be earned; or, to state the reverse proposition, they may be the means for clarifying the common issues of a society and for engineering a fresh consensus of social policy that the body politic may then implement.

That's a rather large order! And there were many critics who bewailed what they witnessed as the decline of voluntary associational activity as society tended toward consolidation, unification, depersonalization. Where everything was organized, what chance was there to save the individual from oppressive and coercive forces quite beyond his power singly to resist? With the triumph of big business, big labor, big agriculture, and big government, how was the general welfare to be promoted? With the heaviness of organization weighing down upon the intimate social groups in which he lived, how were new modes of organization and new lines of action to be initiated, tested, expanded or abandoned?

If no ultimately valid and big answers to these big questions are easily to be had, at least the game was worth the search. My interest was drawn, therefore, to an exploration of the role of voluntary associations and their leaders in social reform and social service movements. Of the thousands to be pursued, I could glance at no more than relatively few and hope that those few were among the more significant and representative.

Perhaps I have stated my purposes extravagantly. So I conclude on a more simple note — I wished to provide a partial answer to the question of what happened to the reform impulse between the New Nationalism and the New Freedom, on the one hand, and the New Deal on the other; I wished to study the role of voluntary associations and their leaders in the years of normalcy.

There is a caveat, ancient and true, in the historical guild, against setting a Mormon to writing Mormon history; but I am reminded of the legendary story of the Mormon graduate student who, when challenged on his capacity to handle a topic of Mormon history objectively, replied to the implied criticism: "Sir, do you suppose that anyone who is *not* a Mormon can write an impartial account?" I am, of course, a "Mormon," so to speak. If my natural parents were good, solid, but liberal Republicans, I am also the child of the 1930's and the New Deal; neither heritage do I wish to deny or reject. That I am a participant in the work of the Christian Social Relations Commission of my home parish, a member of the Urban League, and a precinct worker for Minnesota's Democratic senators may sufficiently summarize my moral commitments and political engagements. So baldly to note is not to confess an elaborate faith — to do so here would hardly be appropriate; it is merely to warn the reader at the very outset that I make no pretense of ivory-tower impartiality. That I have suppressed no evidence goes without saying. I have tried to let the historical record speak directly, and I have tried not to let my predispositions twist and distort my findings. I have necessarily sought to impose upon ever-chaotic events an analysis of motives and consequences, preferring more often than not to let my evaluations be implicit in the narrative. At many points I have run the calculated risk of attempting to record events as they must (or may) have seemed to participants or observers at the time.

True scholarship demands self-discipline; it may call for intellectual asceticism. It may also involve, however, the capacity imaginatively to project oneself into the points of view and value systems of others. Two settlement house leaders who enter my story of social reform and welfare movements — Robert A. Woods and Albert J. Kennedy — had this in mind when they noted that understanding required acceptance and involvement as well as objective observation. Understanding, they wrote, is acquired "not only by alertness but by sympathy. Only those who can go among men and women with affection can understand the tissue of objective causes and inward motives which bind people together. Scientific disinterestedness calls for, not the separateness of the observer, but suspended judgment in the midst of action." [7]

The historian can never live with those whom he studies, of course, in the same sense that a settlement resident can live with his neighbors. But he can experience vicariously their lives, their hopes and their frustrations, their insights and their passions, witness their virtues and their frailties. The historian must be able to play both the role of disinterested observer, the man from Mars, and that of one who is engaged (in the French sense of *engagé*). The one without the other may lead to history that is either inaccurate or sterile.

Others will judge the degree to which I have balanced the two and thus approximated the impossible ideal. I can say only that the gathering and weighing of evidence was often a painful and exhausting task and that I came to live with the subjects of this study with profound affection.

C. A. C.

St. Paul, Minnesota
June 1963

SCHOLARS incur debts that simple acknowledgment cannot begin to repay. However lonely the historian may be in the process of research and writing, whatever his ultimate personal responsibility, he is supported at every moment of his professional life by a host of colleagues whose own work and advice are vital to his very existence. Some of these are numbered among his best friends (and his most severe critics). Others, however, he may know only through their books and articles from which he has gathered evidence, borrowed leads, and garnered hypotheses. The most exhaustive and complicated of footnote and bibliographic citations can never possibly take note of the influences of their studies upon his own thought and writing; a general statement of thanksgiving for the existence of this community of scholars will have, therefore, to suffice.

There are librarians and archivists too numerous to list who ferret out materials the historian would otherwise miss. I am especially grateful for courtesies granted me at the Library of Congress, the New York Public Library, the New York School of Social Work, the Franklin D. Roosevelt Library, the Library of Swarthmore College, the Newberry Library, the Chicago Historical Society, the Women's Archives of Radcliffe College, the Wisconsin and the Minnesota Historical societies, and the libraries of the University of Minnesota and the University of California at Berkeley. I enjoyed the support of sympathetic chairmen and colleagues — Herbert Heaton, John Bowditch, Harold C. Deutsch, Hyman Berman, Timothy L. Smith, and John B. Wolf — who did so much to promote my efforts. Theodore C. Blegen, dean of the Graduate School at the University of Minnesota, arranged financial assistance for travel and research and provided encouragement and good sound advice as well. An entire year free of teaching and administrative burdens was provided by a sabbatical leave from the University of Minnesota, and by fellowship grants from the General Service Foundation and the Co-operative Foundation, both located in St. Paul, Minnesota; to John Musser and to Arthur J. Smaby go my special thanks. I am grateful also for the hospitality extended by the History Department of the University of California at Berkeley, whose guest I was during the academic year 1961–1962; in the stimulating environment there, and with the free time so generously afforded, the writing of the manuscript went forward much faster and better than would otherwise have been possible.

Critics of research-in-progress papers I gave at professional conferences offered insights and warnings which opened up new lines of inquiry and saved me from (some) errors. At one time and another I benefited from conversations with Roy Lubove, Allen Davis, Alfred Romasco, and Vaughn Bornet. Early drafts of the manuscript were read in whole or in part by friends and colleagues in history, social work, and American Studies. Charles G. Cleaver gave it a rigorous going-over on matters of both substance and style; James Leiby, Gisela Konopka, Ralph and Muriel Pumphrey, Rachel Marks — social-welfare historians — stole time from busy lives to examine and criticize the manuscript; John C. Farrell advised me on the sections dealing with the settlement movement. Jeanne Sinnen, senior editor of the University of Minnesota Press, provided invaluable suggestions on style, structure, organization, and interpretation, as well as attending to a myriad of editorial details. Lucky the author who can rejoice in an editor as able, cheerful, and conscientious as she. They will all recognize the fruits of their efforts in this book; they will note as well, I fear, where stubbornness kept me from acting upon their good advice; for however great the assistance and contributions of others, the final responsibility is, of course, mine.

Parts of this book first appeared in article form; and I wish to thank the following journals for their original interest in publishing the findings of my research and for permission now to draw from their publications: "FDR, Pragmatist-Idealist: An Essay in Historiography," *Pacific Northwest Quarterly*, 52:2 (April 1961), pp. 50–55; "Creative Effort in an Age of Normalcy, 1918–33," *The Social Welfare Forum, 1961* (New York: Columbia University Press, 1961), pp. 252–271; and "Social Service and Social Reform: A Historical Essay," *Social Service Review*, 37:1 (March 1963), pp. 76–90.

C. A. C.

1

GREAT EXPECTATIONS: HOPES DEFERRED

"The war has not destroyed man's faith; it has renewed our faith in mankind — renewed it, strengthened it, justified it. . . . By the war the spirit of man has been transformed, society has been reorganized, and the world reconstructed."

— Mrs. I. P. Lampson of the American Federation of Teachers
to the Women's Trade Union League Convention, 1919

"'Don't argue with the East wind,' says J. R. Lowell, 'put on an overcoat!' The women's organizations put on raincoats and stood in the deluge, never swerving one inch from their Federal cycle of ideas, but hardly one of our special bills ever passed in all the eight years that I worked in Washington. We labored, we kept the broader faith, Nation-wide action for Nation-wide evils, but we made no headway in the tepid, torpid years. However, we at least kept the faith — which is more than most of the men did."

— Mrs. Elizabeth H. Tilton, Massachusetts reformer,
in her manuscript autobiography

THE American nation entered World War I in the same exuberant spirit with which during the Progressive Era it had crusaded for the reconstruction of society at home. Woodrow Wilson set the tone, and it is likely that he was supported by a broad national consensus. The German submarine threatened the security of the United States; the submarine also challenged certain clear rights of neutrals, put American lives and property in jeopardy, assaulted national honor. For Wilson, however, acceptance of the known horrors of modern warfare could be justified only if war were now made the instrument for achieving a larger justice in international affairs, for releasing humanity from the burdens of militarism and autocracy. Dissenters from this consensus there were — many social reformers opposed war because it demanded violent and coercive means that were certain to corrupt humane and democratic goals — but it may safely be assumed that most Americans shared Wilson's exhilaration. If the premises upon which the Wilsonian policy rested could be implemented, progress toward the winning of that ancient dream of brotherhood, justice, and peace would be assured. In the midst of the second great contest of arms, in 1940, Lewis Mumford, social critic of the interwar era, recalled the enthusiasm with which his generation had enlisted in the great crusade to make the world safe for democracy: ". . . we expected that at the end of that fierce and rancorous conflict, in which other men had been engaged for four searing years, the beat of angels' wings would at once be heard in the sky and concord and brotherly love would immediately settle over the earth."[1]

In this hopeful context, social reformers continued to labor for the uplift of society at home, even as the holocaust of war increasingly consumed the nation's energies, and to plan bold programs for the postwar world. Victory found reform groups ready to strike forward at once to realize peace and security in the world, progress and reform at home. Progressive goals, postponed by war, were now quickly to be won. Every reform association gathered its resources for the great day coming. At war's end, associations like the National Consumers' League and the Women's Trade Union League, to mention only two, could draw upon a generation of experience in seeking to reconstruct American society; their leaders had been schooled in the pioneering years just before and after the turn of the century. To trace briefly the quality and force of reform in the prewar era is to clarify its role in the postwar years and to introduce the individuals and the groups that will figure so largely in the story to be unfolded here.

The National Consumers' League (NCL), with its state and city affiliates, took its traditional place at the head of the advance guard. Its commander was the woman who had been its secretary since its founding in 1899, the indomitable Florence Kelley. Organized in response to the proliferation of social problems that had accompanied the revolutionary transformation of the nation into a highly mechanized, industrialized, and urbanized society, the league had enlisted the support of good solid middle-class women and men in its crusade against industrial malpractices and against the unreasonable exploitation of the labor of women and children. Like other progressive associations with which it was allied, the Consumers' League placed its faith in the intelligence and good will of the American people and in their desire to right social wrongs, a conviction that Frances Perkins later summarized as the belief "that if the people knew the facts about inhuman working conditions and the neglect of children, they would desire to act morally and responsibly."[2] And so the league deliberately had worked through research and study, publicity and propaganda, to educate the public to the sources and consequences of social evil.

League leaders, in a typically progressive manner, had relied equally on education and moral exhortation to achieve their ends. To the degree that the league was Florence Kelley and she the league — for thirty-three years, until her death in 1932, she dominated its every action — moral passion was as much its characteristic as cool, pragmatic realism. How like a "raging furnace" she had been, Mrs. Kelley confessed to an associate in 1925, and "consumed with burning indignation."[3] "Her work started invariably with investigation, proceeded to a report and recommendation," wrote Frances Perkins of her old friend; by sheer force of character she kept her associates loyal to the cause, inspired them by her example and by her dedication, best described as religious. "This woman effected basic changes in American life by her brilliant analysis of the need of social advance, by her selfless dedication, by her grueling research and her reliance on facts, and by her courage and sense of personal responsibility."[4] This said in retrospect at mid-century by one who helped put into national effect what Florence Kelley had pioneered.

Careless of her own comfort and appearance — dressed "always in black, no stays" — but never careless of the needs of others, Mrs. Kelley was at once a woman not to be put down or denied and a woman willing to step aside when the interests of friends were to be served.[5] To an old friend from Hull House days, Mary Rozet Smith, Jane Addams' most intimate associate, she wrote in 1919 of her decision to accompany Miss Addams on a world peace errand to Switzerland: "My going was an act of faith, not of conviction. When anyone asked why I was going I said 'To black J. A.'s boots and lug her suitcases.' Of course, I was quite useless."[6] All who knew her rejoiced in her vigor and loyalty, and shared her fatigues and frustrations. She was — in the words of her associate and biographer, Josephine Goldmark — an "impatient crusader," critical of mind, sharp of tongue, demanding from others the same wholeness of devotion and investment of energy that she herself ever demonstrated. She was a John the Baptist "crying in the wilderness," reported Mary (Molly) Dewson, another of that band of woman reformers whose careers culminated in the New Deal.[7] Working with Florence Kelley in the interests of reform promised a challenge and an adventure. Furthermore, perhaps, it promised a sense of purpose and engagement to women in a community that ordinarily denied them full participation because of their sex.

As for the Consumers' League it found devoted leaders in addition to Mrs. Kelley, in other settlement and social workers (Grace and Edith Abbott, Jane Addams, Josephine and Pauline Goldmark, Alice Hamilton, Julia Lathrop, Lillian Wald, for example); in philanthropic-minded women of substance and wealth (Emily Balch, Josephine Shaw Lowell, Maud Nathan, Eleanor Roosevelt); and in professional and academic men (Newton D. Baker, Louis Brandeis, John Graham Brooks, John R. Commons, Arthur Holcombe, Paul U. Kellogg, John H. Lathrop, John A. Ryan). State leagues in Massachusetts, New

York, Pennsylvania, and Illinois enjoyed early success; not far behind were accomplishments in Connecticut, Oregon, California, Minnesota, and Wisconsin. Hoping at first that noncoercive means would be sufficient to persuade employer groups to take the initiative in reducing child labor and in providing better wages and conditions, particularly for women employees, the league had advanced quickly into the field of legislative action, advocating use of the police power of the state to achieve their goals where publicity and persuasion had proved inadequate. In alliance with other, like-minded associations, and in some cases with the support of organized labor, the league secured local ordinances and state statutes which restricted child labor, regulated safety and sanitation conditions, established maximum hours and minimum wages for women workers. The league exerted influence, as well, for pure food and drug legislation and compulsory school attendance laws, and worked for woman suffrage and for measures protecting infant and maternal health.

Its single most significant contribution to the cause of prewar reform was undoubtedly its success in winning judicial acceptance of the constitutionality of maximum-hour legislation. This victory was recorded in the 1908 *Muller v. Oregon* decision, which set a precedent for substantial enlargement of the power of the state to regulate private property and contract. Mrs. Kelley together with Josephine Goldmark had done the empirical research for the presentation of the case in which abundant evidence was set forth that women workers suffered physical and moral harm from excessive hours of labor; Louis Brandeis had provided the legal argument, in the soon to be classic brief which bore his name.

When the constitutionality of minimum-wage legislation for women was questioned, the Consumers' League again seized the legal initiative, Felix Frankfurter substituting for Brandeis who joined the Supreme Court in 1916. However, the *Stettler v. O'Hara* decision of 1917, which affirmed the legality of an Oregon statute by a tie vote of four to four (Brandeis abstaining), proved to be an ambiguous and tenuous victory.

By 1917, when the progressive movement was transformed into a world crusade, the Consumers' League and its allies could look back with satisfaction, nevertheless, at the series of social advances it had helped to secure. And in a spirit of determination and confidence, at its first meeting following the armistice, the Executive Committee of the National Consumers' League pledged its cooperation with all other national and international associations "to regain the ground lost for our industrial ideals during the past four years." It stressed the need to establish international standards for labor, and proclaimed its intent to carry forward an intensive campaign in the states for legislation on minimum wages and child labor. These measures constituted old, unfinished business; new was the resolve to work for prompt enactment of compulsory health insurance at the state level of government.[8] In national convention assembled, a year later, with Newton D. Baker, Wilson's secretary of war, presiding, the full body of delegates hammered out a Ten-Year Program for reform. Goals for national political action included enlargement of the regulatory power of the federal government particularly in the consumer goods industries. The delegates endorsed the creation of government fact-finding boards to gather and publicize full information during strikes — this in the hope that enlightened public opinion would serve to encourage settlements both reasonable and just. They urged the passage of a child-labor bill for the District of Columbia as a means by which national standards could be established that the states might emulate. Approved in principle were decent wages, maternity insurance, and "compulsory industrial insurance against sickness." The heart of the NCL's Ten-Year Program was, however, the determination to win by state action strict regulation of the conditions under which women labored in industry. To the winning of these goals, in state and nation, the Consumers' League buoyantly set forth.[9]

The Women's Trade Union League (WTUL), which drew its funds and its members from many of the same sources as the Consumers' League, had long worked in tandem harness with the latter on behalf of legislation which would protect women and children in industry. If anything its programs had been more drastic and aimed at a broader reconstruction of American life than the NCL's, even though its president, Margaret Dreier Robins, a philanthropic lady of independent means, gentle and compassionate, never quite matched the controlled fury of Florence Kelley, well-born but an incorrigible fighter. That Mrs. Robins, who lived for years with her husband Raymond in a slum neighborhood, remained a Republican to the end of her days and that Mrs. Kelley was an avowed (if nondogmatic) socialist seemed to influence the relative tones of their respective associations but little. The WTUL sought the winning of industrial rights equally through trade union organization and through political action; the Consumers' League depended upon legislative action and worked essentially through publicity, propaganda, and lobbying activity. The Consumers' League was supported, in its local and state chapters as in the national organization, by women and men of wealth, education, and leisure. The Trade Union League enjoyed much the same patronage, but in addition there was active participation by young women drawn from the ranks of labor. From the beginning Mrs. Robins was determined to raise up leaders from the trade union movement, and when she felt it was feasible to resign as president, in the mid-1920's, she arranged for her successor to be an industrial worker, one who knew what it was to labor in shop or factory.[10] As early as 1919 the Board of Directors of the Trade Union League numbered but two members who were not workers — Mrs. Robins and her sister Mary Dreier; the others, nine in all, represented trade union members. Understandably, the WTUL tended to reflect a more radical point of view, not only in regard to labor legislation itself but toward all related issues of economic and social concern, than did the Consumers' League, whose membership was more genteel and more respectable. Florence Kelley might know in her bones what the daily problems of labor and poverty truly were; she lived most of her adult life either at Hull House in Chicago or at the House on Henry Street on the Lower East Side, New York. Her colleagues, however, were not so directly in contact with life as it was lived along the margin of need; they were business and professional men and their wives, public servants, reformers by conviction and conversion not by pressing circumstance.

Organized in 1903, the Women's Trade Union League had quickly joined the progressive movement to remedy the industrial evils of exploitation: long hours and low pay, abominable conditions of employment, the hazards of accident and ill health. Settlement house workers were prominent in leadership in the early years, but the alliance of compassionate women of wealth and trade union leaders soon took over. In the WTUL's program to stimulate the organization of women into trade unions, Mrs. Robins and others like her reached out to the general public, explained the problems, demonstrated the needs, raised strike funds from sympathetic citizens, retained legal counsel, and if necessary put up the bail for women arrested on the picket line. The league provided assistance in a number of strikes among the textile, clothing, and needle trades, and in the Chicago stockyards; but it feared that to throw the full burden for remedying the inequities of employment upon the women workers themselves was to risk "the cruel and primitive method of revolution." To this, an early editorial in the league's official paper continued, "the only alternative is for the whole community through cooperative action to undertake the removal of industrial wrongs and the placing of industry on a basis just and fair to the worker."[11]

Political action, then, was required along with trade union activity to secure better conditions, a decent wage, a limit on hours, and the legal right to organize and bargain without harassment. Mrs. Robins saw working women seeking, through the league, to "redeem that promise 'of the more abundant life' which is the pledge of our religion and our constitution."[12] Samuel Gompers, whose support was sometimes more verbal than actual, declared in a speech before the group in 1905 that the purpose of the league was not charity but assistance in order that working women "could be helped to help themselves." Vigorous applause met his concluding statement that workers sought "less charity and more rights."[13] The league evolved a concept of major importance, that of a "living wage" which would be sufficient to provide not only for the immediate needs of food, clothing, and shelter, but for education and recreation as well, and enough to cover the unpredictable but certain hazards of unemployment, sickness, and old age. When the battle for minimum-wage laws fell short of achieving this goal, the league would turn to social insurance as the means to win security.

The war years saw the WTUL advancing its program on every front. Working together with other interested groups, the league won in July 1918 the establishment of a Woman in Industry Service within the Department of Labor as part of the effort to mobilize the home front for maximum efficiency. High standards of hours, wages, and conditions were secured, by writing these principles into government contracts rather than by congressional legislation. Directed by Mary Van Kleeck, who was assisted by Mary Anderson, the Woman in Industry Service was able, in the brief months of its existence, to achieve many of the guarantees toward which the WTUL had long been working. With the war's end it was possible, after a great deal of lobbying, to get this service established as a permanent Women's Bureau whose procedures were primarily those of investigation and publicity, whose powers were few, but whose weight of authority in the making of policy recommendations proved to be substantial. Mary Anderson, Swedish immigrant who had been discovered and pushed forward by the WTUL, took over as first director of the new bureau, a position she held until her retirement in 1944.

The Women's Trade Union League, pleased with its success in the war years, moved into the postwar era confident that goals already won could be consolidated and that a rapid extension of its reform program was feasible; the time had now come to implement democracy's victory with appropriate steps toward the establishment of industrial democracy. Taking its cue from Mrs. Robins — who declared early in 1919 that "self-government in industry, as in politics, is essential to a free people" — the league set forth a program for social reconstruction. All the old plans were stated again: equal pay for equal work, one day's rest in seven, a prohibition on night work, the eight-hour day, the abolition of child labor. Beyond these traditional goals, the league posited the need for a living wage and for the participation of women workers in setting industrial standards. The desirability of public ownership of utilities and natural resources was declared. The importance of preserving civil rights, free speech, and the right to assembly received notice. The league capped its reconstruction program with a plea for a system of "social insurance without profit against unemployment, sickness, and accident including industrial diseases and injuries, providing for maternity benefits, old age and invalidity pensions."[14]

The annual convention of the league, meeting in June 1919, carried away with an enthusiasm bred of postwar hope, went still further. In the field of foreign affairs it railed against the injustices of the Treaty of Versailles but heartily endorsed the Covenant of the League of Nations, demanded the withdrawal of troops from Russia and the recognition of the Soviet Union, and suggested the propriety of applying the principle of self-determination to Ireland. At home it pledged itself to make the good fight for health insurance and for "public ownership, and workers' control of all public utilities, including mines, packing houses, grain elevators, as well as the means of transportation and communication."[15]

Other associations shared the apparent conviction of the Women's Trade Union League and the National Consumers' League that the moment was propitious for the completion of unfinished reform business and the launching of new programs for the reconstruction of the social life of the nation. The American Association for Labor Legislation (AALL) had crusaded, since its founding in 1906, for the inauguration of government programs, at state and national levels alike, which would protect workmen and their families against the hazards of industrial employment. The association, which had grown from an original membership in 1906 of around two hundred to over three thousand by 1919, had been particularly effective in securing the adoption of workmen's compensation laws. The AALL was the creature of John B. Andrews, who served throughout its entire history as its executive secretary, and of his wife, Irene Osgood Andrews. A student of John R. Commons', Andrews was the joint author with his mentor of several studies, and he exerted an influence that reached out into many other reform groups.

Like most other voluntary associations, the AALL's policies were elaborated and implemented by a mere handful of concerned persons including many who were on the committees and boards of other reform groups as well. For example, the association's president in 1918 was Samuel McCune Lindsay, who had long served the National Child Labor Committee and in 1923 would be named its chairman. The association's vice presidents included Jane Addams and Lillian Wald of settlement house fame, along with William H. Childs, Robert W. De-Forest, Felix Warburg, and Rabbi Stephen S. Wise, all active in a variety of welfare groups. Among others on the Executive Committee were John Mitchell, by 1918 a senior statesman of the labor movement, and Margaret Dreier Robins, who initiated the reconstruction program of the AALL, endorsed in December of 1918.

The association had been active throughout the last year of the war in helping to establish uniform standards for labor in regard to hours, wages, and conditions. Now, with peace established, the association announced its intention to consolidate labor's wartime gains, especially those measures which women workers had so recently won. The AALL promised to press for effective prohibition of child labor and for the establishment of the principle of the minimum living wage for women. In addition the association warned of the economic problems that the adjustment to peacetime production would create and urged an enlarged federal employment service, government regulation of private agencies, and coordinated public works programs as partial remedies for the maladjustments that the transition surely would bring. Beyond that, the AALL agreed to step up its campaign for insurance against industrial accidents and occupational diseases, and to place a new emphasis on working out new programs for social security — government insurance against sickness, unemployment, and old age.[16]

The National Child Labor Committee (NCLC), too, shared the conviction of the reform groups generally, that the coming of peace promised a great forward surge of reform. Its hopes seemed to be justified by the recent success in winning national child-labor legislation after a generation of agitation. Established in 1904, the committee had, like so many other reform associations, arisen out of the activity of settlement house workers, in this case out of a special committee on child labor formed in 1902 by the New York Association of Neighborhood Workers. Aiming first at the establishment of regulations at the state level of government, it won striking (if always partial) reforms throughout the industrial North and West; but children engaged in agricultural labor off the family farm and children generally in the southern states received little if any statutory protection. The need for comprehensive national action if effective standards were to be applied where the exploitation of child labor was most severe was soon made clear, and during the Wilson administration, with some constitutional misgivings, Congress passed the Keating-Owen Act of 1916 providing for federal regulation of the labor of children engaged in the mining or manufacture of goods that entered the flow of interstate commerce. Although it had not fixed national standards stringent enough to meet the desires of the NCLC, and although its administrative procedures of joint state and federal government enforcement were unevenly applied, the law generally established — in the brief months it was enforced — a prohibition on the labor of children younger than fourteen years and a maximum eight-hour day with no night work for children aged fourteen to sixteen.

It wasn't long before the constitutionality of the statute was challenged, however, and in June 1918 the Supreme Court, divided five to four, knocked down the law as null and void on the grounds that Congress had clearly exceeded its powers under the commerce clause by interfering in an area of local regulation reserved to the states. The proponents of regulation rushed immediately to fill the vacuum created by the court's action. By December of 1918 a new bill had been proposed and passed by Congress providing for a 10 per cent tax on commodities entering interstate commerce upon which children had worked. The NCLC had been assured by its legal advisers that use of the tax power, while an awkward device, was probably constitutional. The new law was endorsed, moreover, by representatives of the Consumers' League, the American Federation of Labor, and the United States Children's Bureau. In 1922 the Supreme Court would find this method, too, null and void on the grounds that it involved an unreasonable invasion of powers reserved to the states, but for the moment proponents of national action felt secure enough in the accomplishment to plan still more ambitious programs to remedy the multiple evils of child labor.[17]

The deliberations of the National Child Labor Committee in 1918 and 1919 demonstrated its determination to strike out boldly on new paths of social and political action. The tightening up of prohibitions and regulations, at both state and national levels, was to be encouraged as a matter of course. But such measures, it was believed, were clean-up tasks, important but no longer crucial now that the federal government was in the field. To leaders of the NCLC the war had revealed how debilitating of the national strength were lack of education, denial of opportunity, poor standards of health. If the committee was to be true to its traditional concern for the health and welfare of the entire community, and now for its strength as well, a massive assault on all forms of social deprivation was in order. Prohibition of the most obnoxious forms of labor exploitation was essential, but not in itself enough. Nothing less than concern for the whole field of child welfare would now suffice. Publicity and education would have to be stepped up, for the "letter of the law" rested upon the "edict of community custom."[18] The NCLC called for a national effort to uplift the standards of education. Federal aid to education, particularly to poorer states, would offer a positive alternative to employment in factory, field, and mine by making schooling more attractive. More broadly, the committee recognized that it would have to concern itself with the complex problems of juvenile delinquency in both urban centers and rural areas, and with housing and recreation and human conservation generally.

Humane concern for the plight of the working child — what Felix Adler, who devoted his life to the cause, called the "infinite pity of it" — must be supported, moreover, by a hard analysis of the facts as scientific management demonstrated them: shorter hours, better conditions, the employment only of mature and able workers paid off in higher efficiency and lower labor costs.[19]

Early in 1919, to signal the shift in strategy from an attack in force on a single point of the enemy's line to a cordon attack all along the line, the committee changed the name of its official publication from the *Child Labor Bulletin* to *The American Child*. In an early issue of the renamed journal, Wiley Swift evidenced the committee's new concern for the broad field of child welfare: "For the sake of the child and for the sake of the country, there must be education in and for health, efficiency, good living, good homes, good community life."[20]

From their origins in the 1890's, settlement houses had played a crucial role in pioneering economic, social, and political reforms. There was hardly a reform that the residents of the houses had not either initiated or supported. The Child Labor Committee, the Women's Trade Union League, the Consumers' League had grown out of settlement workers' concerns. The settlements had provided a home base of operation for these associations, and had furnished leadership for the American Association for Labor Legislation as well.

It had been motives of social service that had often compelled pioneer settlement residents to go and live with the disinherited who were crowded into the squalid slums of the nation's bursting cities. Overwhelmingly of middle-class and professional background, often from families of substantial means, well-educated, mostly of native-born, Anglo-Saxon, Protestant inheritance, these young men and women had gone down to the slums not so much to uplift the poor as to share with them their daily lot.[21] Concerned about the schisms that were dividing America in the latter years of the nineteenth century, the settlement pioneers sought to reconcile class to class, race to race, religion to religion. In an age that required the written word to inform the socially privileged how the other half lived, it was essential that the gulf between the classes be bridged so that the former unity and coherence of society might be restored through the enlargement of mutual understanding. Did the alien ways new immigrants brought with them from southern and eastern Europe seem to threaten subversion of American traditions and debasement of American values? Then somehow the immigrant must be shown the peculiar genius of the American way; then somehow America must be taught the cultural enrichment it stood to gain from new immigrant contributions. Did strange customs of worship — of Jew and Roman Catholic — seem to threaten the presumed homogeneity of the nation's religious commitment? Then interpretation here, too, was required. Did the acceleration of social change find the generations estranged? Then the settlement workers would labor to restore effective communication between the old and the young, between parent and child.

The settlements claimed to deal in brotherhood, not philanthropy; their spirit was fraternalistic rather than paternalistic. Robert A. Woods and Albert J. Kennedy — settlement pioneers in Boston and New York — spoke to these points when they stressed the need for the resident to seek understanding as much through involvement as through intellectual alertness. Jane Addams — Saint Jane to many of her disciples, and to some of her detractors who used the designation ironically — stood upon the same working principle. The settlement worker, she said in 1905, learned not alone from firsthand observation and the compiling of evidence but from sharing the common lot of the disinherited; the resident must "have genuine sympathy and continued relations with those who work day after day, year after year." Through a shared life, the settlement workers could come in time, not to speak for the slum dwellers, but to help them "express themselves and make articulate their desires."[22] Only as the residents identified themselves with the "ill-favored and ill-assorted" would they be accepted, and with acceptance become "the leaven to permeate and transform" the neighborhood, through the neighborhoods the community, and through communities the nation.[23]

Steeped in nineteenth-century Christian humanitarianism, many settlement leaders expressed their motives in words and tones familiar to a Bible-reading and Bible-believing generation. They echoed the cries for social justice of Old Testament prophecy, and took seriously the redemptive power that Christ released in the New. With the boldness of Amos or Jeremiah they proclaimed the injustices of labor exploitation and political corruption; they decried the denial of opportunity, and described feelingly the oppressive weight of poverty. When frustrated, defeated, despondent, they could take heart from the expected fruits of their witness. They sought not "righteousness" for a "scattered few," but "a more abundant life for all."[24] Through renunciation and service they sought to reconcile the separated. By losing their own private lives they hoped to find meaning and purpose for living. They longed to win through to "human brotherhood, without requiring either the disclosure or invasion of the subtle reserves of personality which makes the religious approach to man at best so difficult."[25] They spoke of their mission to mediate, to redeem, to transform through "moral imagination" and through the "propaganda of deed."[26] Not all settlement leaders were explicitly moved by religious convictions, of course, and in some cities there was mutual suspicion between church and neighborhood workers; but many centers were launched by institutional churches and the religious metaphor tended to be employed by the devout and the doubters alike.

The settlements, perforce, were driven to the propaganda of deed by the nature of the environment in which they resided. A day's visit, a year's residence showed clearly what the problems were and what needed to be done. Jane Addams rang the changes, in 1906: "Insanitary housing, poisonous sewage, contaminated water, infant mortality, the spread of contagion, adulterated food, impure milk, smoke-laden air, ill-ventilated factories, dangerous occupations, juvenile crime, unwholesome crowding, prostitution, and drunkenness are the enemies which the modern city must face and overcome would it survive." [27] So the settlement workers went to work. They opened up day nurseries and kindergartens for the children of working mothers. They offered courses of instruction in personal hygiene and child care, in domestic science. With Lillian Wald, on the Lower East Side, New York, in the lead they established a visiting nurse service: delivered babies, urged such standards of personal cleanliness as were reasonable amongst general squalor, comforted those who were dying of tuberculosis, tried to quarantine communicable diseases. They encouraged the establishment of clubs for boys and girls, whose ends were both recreational and educational. Through clubs for men and women they sought to release poor immigrants from the bondage of illiteracy, customs ill-suited to urban slum living, and ignorance of American ways. They set up lending libraries, public baths, little backyard playgrounds. They collected money to send slum children to country camps for a week or two of relief from the oppressive summer heat and dirt that weighed down the natural exuberance of youth.

All these were actions designed to establish certain minima for a decent existence. To meet other needs the settlements and neighborhood houses organized cultural activities which dealt "in the maximums, rather than the minimums of human desire." [28] Classes in needlecraft, cooking, weaving, and sewing were added to the evening program in the houses; for young boys and young men there were special classes in carpentry, printing, bricklaying, and other practical crafts. Courses in pottery, ceramics, water colors, and oils were soon added, and instruction in vocal and instrumental music. Bands and orchestras were organized, as well as choruses and glee clubs. Amateur theatricals, at the House on Henry Street and at Hull House, and folk festivals and plays set loose the creative impulses of drama. All these activities, wrote Woods and Kennedy, aimed not only at the uplifting of vocational skill but at the uplifting of cultural taste as well. The applied arts fostered "accuracy, neatness, order, perseverance, initiative," and a sense of property (good bourgeois qualities, it might be noted). The finer arts made possible a fuller life, a "gentler" life.[29]

Still there was unfinished work. The settlements, by themselves, could no more than nibble at problems whose solutions, if they were to be more than partial and inadequate, required concerted action of the entire community. The settlements persuaded municipal administration to apply "public resources to meet a great body of new collective needs." [30] Having pioneered new programs and proved their efficacy, settlement workers, together with their allies, moved in on city hall to demand massive and coordinated efforts from the city fathers. They petitioned for, and often won, the setting aside of land and space for parks and playgrounds. They pleaded for better streets, regular garbage collection, more efficient sewage systems, programs of public health and sanitation. They encouraged the public schools to establish kindergartens and to provide afternoon and evening classes in the trades and arts for both youth and adults. They persuaded libraries and art museums to remain open at times convenient to common laborers. To private and public agencies they turned over the burden of providing relief funds to cover family emergencies. Graham Taylor, speaking to the 1915 conference of the National Federation of Settlements, summed it up: "The transference of social function to the community is in line with the constant policy of the settlements to find by losing, to gain by giving, to subordinate institutions to causes; to experiment, demonstrate, dare to fail, and, in success, to turn over to public control whatever the community can do better on a larger scale." [31]

And still the problems persisted. One line of action was clear — the settlements would have to enter the political arena, first in local government but soon at the state and national levels as well, in order to win regulation or eradication of all those social evils that remained. And so many settlement leaders — a fraction of the movement, perhaps, but a saving remnant — sought out their natural allies and launched frontal attacks of political action. They advocated municipal ordinances for the regulation of housing and sanitation. They lobbied for the strict regulation or prohibition of child labor, and for minimum-wage and maximum-hour legislation for women workers. They joined the crusade for woman suffrage in order that women might be more effective in the "housekeeping" areas of public life. They argued for the establishment of special courts for juvenile offenders. They publicized the principle of workmen's compensation, and this effort would lead many of them by the end of the Progressive Era to embrace the cause of social insurance. Having learned with Jane Addams that "private beneficence is totally inadequate to deal with the vast numbers of the city's disinherited," they endorsed every move to enlarge the responsibility of government to care for dependent citizens whose needs arose out of social rather than individual deficiencies.[32]

Then came the war in Europe and the long, tortured debate over America's proper role in the world. A good number of the most prominent settlement leaders — including "beloved lady" Jane Addams and Lillian Wald, whose belovedness was sometimes tempered by the astringent quality of her personality — became pacifists. Others — most notably Robert Woods and Albert Kennedy — favored America's entrance into the war on the side of the democracies. Mary Kingsbury Simkhovitch, then president of the National Federation of Settlements, on the very eve of the awful decision, April 2, 1917, was moved to explain her break with Jane Addams on this issue in a public letter: "America cannot hold aloof . . . it cannot stand apart, but must rather die that the world may live." [33]

Whatever stand the settlement leaders took toward the war — and Jane Addams was a painfully lonely woman by 1918 — the settlements themselves turned, as always, to the business at hand. Working together with their traditional allies in the Consumers' League and the Women's Trade Union League, they agitated for the construction of protective labor standards by contract and by state and national legislation. They supported wartime drives against organized prostitution and the liquor traffic. They labored — often futilely and against great odds — to create a climate favorable to the welcoming into the community of southern Negroes, attracted to northern cities by wartime industries. They tried to protect their immigrant neighbors, many of whom were classified as enemy aliens, from official and unofficial harrying. The settlements assisted in draft registration, in drives for war relief, and in campaigns to save food and fuel. They encouraged their neighbors to plant victory gardens and themselves ran day nurseries for children of working mothers. Families made dependent by the departure of a husband or father for military service were somehow cared for or put in touch with agencies which could supply their immediate and pressing needs.

Although the war was accompanied by persecution of and intolerance toward those who did not cheerfully accept the war and all that war demanded, although civil liberties were put in jeopardy, although the war stirred up much that was hateful and spiteful, although the sacrifices extorted by war were often uneven, with the burdens thrown on those least able to bear them, settlement leaders were generally hopeful that the fruits of victory might include the opportunity to strike through to new high plateaus of civilization. Robert Woods witnessed the "social dynamic" unleashed by war and hoped that in the postwar world that energy would be channeled toward social reconstruction. The "nation organized for righteousness," he proclaimed, must continue its "vast organism of service, of fellowship, of creative power." If the nation could be mobilized for war against autocracy and militarism, it could be mobilized for war against degrading poverty and injustice.[34] So while Jane Addams turned her attention to the causes of peace, the reconstruction of wartorn Europe (friend and foe alike), and international cooperation, other settlement leaders bore in again on the need for social reconstruction in neighborhood, community, and nation.

Neither task was an easy one. When Jane Addams, immediately after the armistice, called for a just peace in response to an appeal from a group of German women, she received some messages of warm praise and support, but more warning her (as one did): "These are the women who spit on our soldiers, who carried water to our wounded only to pour it on the ground before their suffering eyes. . . . Remember they are the mothers of Huns."[35] When she proposed drastic and sweeping programs for broadening social democracy, cries of radicalism were raised.

Wiser in the peculiar ways of humanity than before the war, but still little daunted, the settlement workers, like other reform groups, set about in the immediate postwar world to pick up where they had left off, to implement their hopes for social reconstruction. Preliminary to the annual convening of the National Federation of Settlements in 1920, Charles C. Cooper, director of Kingsley Association in Pittsburgh, visited settlements in New York, Chicago, Cleveland, and Minneapolis to sound out sentiment on the great issues of the day. In a long letter to Jane Addams he summarized his observations. "In the great War, and in the troubled years that followed," he wrote, "the settlement had its measure of failure." But so, too, did all institutions of American life. Everywhere he found a profound sense of lingering shock that civilization could have fallen into "such a devastating war." Pessimism he found, and uncertainty, but a desire to act as well, a will to strike forward again. Pleading with Jane Addams to strike a new note for advance, he concluded: "We do not need new machinery but a clearing of vision, a deepening of conviction, and a new consecration of life. . . . We need a call to a new service along the old lines." [36]

The East Aurora settlement conference of 1920 did indeed attempt to pick up old lines of action and apply them with renewed vigor. Settlements, it was agreed, would continue to pioneer new kinds of service and would seek to accelerate the turning over of programs of proven efficacy to other private and public agencies. The issue deemed most crucial, however, was that of inadequate and insufficient housing. No one knew better than settlement workers the cost that society paid for crowded quarters, lack of privacy, and primitive sanitation. The delegates discussed various remedial actions: effective enforcement of housing ordinances, slum clearance, the building of model tenements by public or cooperative agencies. They stated the need for some kind of community subsidy for low-cost housing. They also stressed the need for enlarged and improved parks and playgrounds as part of a general attack on the evils of urban living. [37]

Elsewhere, settlement workers returned to their old labors of social reform and social service. In Chicago and New York they recognized the need to receive Negro migrants from the rural South and to educate them to urban and northern ways. Settlements everywhere sought to counter the rise of juvenile delinquency, which was not unrelated to the general dislocations of the war years, with educational and recreational programs, summer vacation outings, and organized sports. In supporting the causes of civil liberties, world peace, and international cooperation many settlement workers followed the example of militant action set by Jane Addams and Lillian Wald. Settlement workers played a major role in the formation of the American Civil Liberties Union in January of 1920. They took up the pleas for establishment of industrial standards, for decent wages, for regulation of working conditions, and for recognition of the right of labor to organize and to bargain collectively. In all these areas, settlement workers must take the lead, wrote Lillian Wald to Albert Kennedy in 1919, in putting into action "the moral social impulses" of the community, for settlement workers knew the "people as people, and not as abstractions." [38]

If their enthusiasm had been dampened by war, the settlements were still determined to fight the good fight; other social work and reform groups shared to a larger degree the confidence of the Women's Trade Union League, the National Consumers' League, the Child Labor Committee, and the American Association for Labor Legislation. Edward T. Devine, writing the lead editorial in November 1918 for the *Survey* magazine (the semiofficial journal of the social work profession), had expressed confidence that reconstruction of the world would proceed apace in the weeks and months following the armistice. Wartime efforts, he insisted, proved that the nation, mobilized for peace and reform, could win victories over poverty and disease and social injustice. The benefits and burdens of wartime had been democratically shared; the tax structure had been broadened at its base and sharply increased at its apex, and continuation of this tax policy in the postwar era could raise the money essential to the winning of the national purpose of reform. War had led the nation to accept labor unions and the processes of collective bargaining as viable instruments of achieving industrial peace and progress. Women workers had risen to the challenges of war; they had earned the right to participate fully in the economic and political life of the nation. War had required the mobilization of volunteer service for national strength; those efforts could now be harnessed to community welfare. The moment for reconstruction was at hand. [39] In the spring of 1919, Devine was still writing in the same vein, calling for a "drive for social reconstruction." This was no time for timidity, he exhorted, but for boldness of concept and will. The goals of health and security, production for use, municipal planning, social harmony were there to be won if only a concerted community effort were made. [40]

In this spirit a National Conference on Social Agencies and Reconstruction, held in late November of 1918, established a special committee to recommend to professional associations of social workers a program for postwar reconstruction. Devine was appointed to this committee as were other outstanding social workers and reformers — C. C. Carstens, Samuel McCune Lindsay, L. A. Halbert, and Arthur J. Todd. The committee's report, submitted in May of 1919, set forth the need for advance all along the line and at every level of national life. It called for an extension of wartime insurance and pension systems; for federal aid to education and the establishment of a Cabinet Department of Education; for the establishment of a Cabinet Department of Public Health to carry through national welfare programs in the areas of housing, accident prevention, disease eradication, and health insurance; for the conservation of natural resources and the reclamation of waste lands; for the legislative establishment of industrial standards; for city planning and government loans for home building; for the creation of a Cabinet Department of Public Works; and for the protection of civil rights.[41]

Church groups, too, joined in the wholesale pronouncements on reform. The Federal Council of Churches of Christ in America, meeting in May 1919, brought its famous social creed of 1912 up to date. The new program warned against the use of violent means, which seemed to be the alternative if orderly reform were not achieved. Specifically, the council declared labor's right to participate in management and to earn a just wage had first claim on industry; and it called for demobilization and for economic equilibrium, an expanded federal employment service, public works, land settlement, and a "guarded extension" of insurance to cover the hazards of unemployment, accident, ill health, and old age. Women in industry were deserving of particular protection, for homemaking and motherhood were their highest calling; minimum-wage legislation, an eight-hour day, and equal pay for equal work were, therefore, included in the program. The rights to decent housing, to free speech, and for Negroes the right to equality before the law and the right to participate fully in the life of the community were all spelled out.[42] The statement of the Methodist Episcopal Church on social reconstruction contained many of the same proposals.[43] The report of the National Catholic War Council (several months later, in September 1919, to be renamed the National Catholic Welfare Council) spoke boldly to the glaring injustices of industrial life and proposed legislation ensuring a living wage and setting minimum wages, guarantees of the right of labor to organize and bargain collectively, maintenance of the tax on products produced by child laborers, and (until increases in wage rates made this unnecessary) establishment of social insurance against sickness, accident, invalidism, and old age.[44] The statement on social justice of the Central Conference of American Rabbis, issued in July 1920, departed only in minor detail from these other programs, and added a plea for anti-lynching legislation and for continued unrestricted admission of immigrants to the United States.[45]

Everywhere there were great expectations and the desire to pick up old unfinished business and carry it quickly to completion. With measures long central to progressivism finally nailed down, it was clear that reformers and the associations they directed were eager to advance toward new goals. Most notable of the new programs now receiving wholehearted endorsement was that of social insurance. Precedents for insurance schemes could be traced back to Louis Brandeis' electrifying speech before the National Conference of Charities and Correction in 1911, to its incorporation the following year in the report of the Committee on Standards of Living and Labor of that conference, and to its subsequent endorsement by Theodore Roosevelt's Progressive party; research on and agitation for social insurance could be traced back to the writings of Mabel L. Nassau, Henry R. Seager, and Isaac M. Rubinow. Whereas social insurance had once been a peripheral ideal, however, it was now, in the immediate postwar era, put forth as of primary and immediate concern.

Here and there were doubters, men and women whom the war experience had tipped off balance. Here and there were reformers who sensed even as early as 1918, when their colleagues were looking toward the future with confidence, that a new age was being born, an age less hospitable to rational planning, social justice, peace. Increasingly a sense of uneasiness and anxiety crept into the deliberations of those busily engaged in drafting blueprints for social reconstruction.

Faith, hope, and charity; and the most necessary of these was hope. But the hopes of many had been shattered in the months that followed the armistice. Peace, peace, the prophets cried; and there was no peace. Lillian Wald, traveling in Europe in the spring of 1919, wrote home of the persecution of the Jews in eastern Europe, of the fear of proletarian revolution that paralyzed the will, of mass discontent, and of renewed antagonism between nations and classes.[46] Committed to peace and collective security, many reformers were torn by their desire to see the League of Nations established with the United States a leading member, and their knowledge that the treaty itself contained gross injustices that the league would have to accept and enforce. The long and bitter debate in the United States Senate over ratification of the Treaty of Versailles, and with it the Covenant of the league, was a spectacle not likely to strengthen the sanguine expectations of internationalists and pacifists.

At home, in the meantime, demobilization proceeded helter-skelter with little direction or guidance. Prices shot up; wages and salaries and farm income did not. Labor went out on strike. A walkout in Seattle evolved into a general strike just short of class struggle. The strike of the Boston police came close to anarchy. Workers in coal and railroads and steel walked out and were beaten back by the combined power of employers, the press, and in some cases the government. An interchurch committee, chaired by the Methodist Bishop Francis J. McConnell, mover of all good causes, prepared an elaborate analysis of the steel strike with recommendations for its resolution. Its efforts at reconciliation were ignored and rejected. Belatedly, the President of the United States, utterly fatigued by his efforts to salvage the League of Nations, called an industrial conference for October 1919. To it came representatives of labor, management, and the public. A proposed resolution declaring the right of labor to organize and bargain collectively, more vague than the labor delegates had originally suggested, received endorsement from representatives of labor and the public but was rejected out of hand by the employer representatives. Without this minimal agreement on principle, labor felt it had nothing to gain from further deliberations and so withdrew its delegates. And that was the end of the conference.[47]

The Red Scare, coming on the heels of wartime hysteria, took its toll of reform energy as well. Wartime syndicalist acts were, in the postwar years, turned against dissenters of many kinds. Patriotic associations drew up lists of citizens suspected of disloyalty. Teachers were required to take oaths attesting to their loyalty before contracts were renewed. Aliens suspected of disloyalty were rounded up and deported. Reform proposals were labeled pro-German or pro-Russian, and for the time the designation was enough to assure their defeat. In New York, the newly formed League of Women Voters lashed out against what its members saw as deliberately misleading statements of the New York League for Americanism and the Associated Industries of New York, which attacked as radical any constructive welfare measure. These tactics, they complained, made a "reasoned adjustment" of social issues all but impossible.[48]

Many reform associations found it difficult in 1919 and 1920 to raise funds from private solicitation. Lillian Wald confided to her old and dear friend Lavinia Dock the troubles she faced: "Confidentially, my political attitude is making some of our generous friends uneasy and one of our largest givers — nearly $15,000 a year — has withdrawn because I am 'socialistically inclined.' Poor things; I am sorry for them — they are so scared. It is foolish since, after all, counting things in the large and wide, I am at least one insurance against unreasonable revolution in New York."[49]

A keynote address at the December convention of the Child Labor Committee in 1918 had warned that "After every great war there has been a lapse in morale, a tendency for people to relax."[50] By 1920 it was painfully and abundantly clear that the slump had materialized. To maintain a fighting edge in the midst of social unrest proved everywhere difficult. The war had uprooted men and women not only from their homes but from established ways. John A. Fitch reported to the Association for Labor Legislation, in December 1919, that never before had he witnessed such "fear and suspicion of the aims and motives of organized labor." The sentiment now, he said, was for "suppression, rather than understanding."[51] To a settlement worker in Philadelphia it seemed that life was oriented toward finding ways and means to win a larger personal share of the material abundance that America promised. The search made for cynicism and distrust: ". . . *everyone trusts in riches but few trust the rich.*"[52] Another social worker listed the troubles he saw daily: the "cynical failure" of the peace, soaring prices, unemployment, talk of democracy but deprivation of civil liberties. "My neighbors are frightened, suspicious, resentful and restless. Any wonder?"[53]

When Elizabeth H. Tilton left community work in Massachusetts and joined the legislative lobby of the National Congress of Mothers in the nation's capital, early in 1922, she was warned that she would be "appalled" at the "selfishness" of great statesmen who sought nothing but "notoriety" in order "to get elected another time." After eight frustrating years of testifying in favor of welfare legislation she put down her private thoughts in the words quoted at the beginning of this chapter. Mrs. Tilton was a nervous, anxiety-ridden soul, given to alternating moods of exuberance and depression; if her expression was frequently extravagant, she had, nevertheless, an often shrewd insight into the tone of events in which she was caught up. Her personal frustration in the "tepid, torpid" years of the 1920's may be accepted as accurately reported.[54]

It may be added, however, that a small band, a Gideon's army, kept the faith, working through little voluntary associations, operating on a shoestring. Up and down the country they wandered, lecturing, writing, studying, exhorting. They converged on city councils, on state assemblies, and on Congress to testify and to witness to their beliefs. Rebuffed, reviled, ridiculed, they kept the faith. Turned back again and again, they began to pioneer new methods and posit new goals. Out of defeat was born the desire to seek out new paths of reform, new roads to Zion. Out of frustration was born social imagination. By the end of the decade, new devices for social reconstruction, devices that anticipated much of the central program of the New Deal, had been elaborated. The high enthusiasm with which some had predicted immediate reconstruction of American society at the end of the war proved not justified, but neither were the years of the twenties the wasteland for reform that they have frequently seemed.

THE CRUSADE FOR CHILDREN

"Whoso loves a child loves not himself but God; whoso delights a child labors with God in his workshop of the world of hearts; whoso helps a child brings in the Kingdom of God; whoso saves a child from the fingers of evil sits in the seat with the builders of cities and the procurers of peace."

— Attributed to Julia Lathrop, 1918, by Catheryne Cooke Gilman

"Will it [the 1930 White House Conference on Child Health and Protection] face the fact that children toil because their fathers find no work? Because their fathers are in the bread-lines? Because fathers are killed and disabled in mines and mills? Because, in brief, American industry does not yet pay its social costs?"

— Florence Kelley, "Challenge of the Working Children,"
Friends Intelligencer, 22 November 1930

PROBABLY no segment of the progressive crusade engaged more fully the moral energies of reformers than the battle against the exploitation of children in mine, factory, street, and field. There was something peculiarly vicious and un-American in a system that squeezed a profit from the labor of tender hands. Child labor hardened the natural gentleness of childhood into premature callousness. Children who labored from sunup to sundown in cotton mill or coal pit or beet field were denied the opportunities of education to which all children, rich or poor, had an inherent right. Daily labor, too early and too long, blighted the mind, shriveled the spirit, corrupted the character of souls precious to a democratic nation as to God. If God's vengeance could be trusted, certainly He would judge with righteous wrath those who stole childhood from the children of the nation. So it seemed to Felix Adler and Owen R. Lovejoy, to Gardner Murphy, Florence Kelley, and Margaret Dreier Robins, to Senator Albert J. Beveridge who first moved for national action, to Woodrow Wilson whose belated conversion to the cause swept aside constitutional scruples and made possible federal action in 1916 to control this unconscionable evil.

By the terms of the Keating-Owen Act standards of regulation were applied across the nation. It will be remembered that when by a narrow margin of one vote the Supreme Court, in 1918, found these to be in violation of Article X of the Constitution, an invasion of the police power reserved to the several states, Congress responded at once with the imposition of a 10 per cent tax on the commodities in interstate commerce of mining and manufacturing firms that employed children. Effective as of April 1919, the second child-labor act remained in force until, in May of 1922 in *Bailey v. Drexel Furniture Company*, it too was overturned by the Supreme Court. All forms of federal action, apparently, were null and void.

As the nation emerged from war into the dawn of peace, however, reformers generally felt assured that their goal had been secured. It remained to strengthen the enforcement of the law, to win higher standards in the more enlightened states, and to persuade the laggard states (particularly in the South) to emulate their example by establishing standards above the national minima. If they kept the pressure on, never relenting a moment, they felt that higher standards would gradually evolve until the injustice of child labor was eradicated once and for all.

With confidence in the right, the National Child Labor Committee and its allies embarked, in the immediate postwar years, upon new phases of work designed to enrich the life of children everywhere. The committee which had, over the years, displayed the "regularity of a morality, the enthusiasm of a religion" must now stress research, careful study, the less dramatic but equally effective working out of new and elaborate plans which would create opportunities for the children of the disinherited to share in the opportunities that America had always promised.[1] Owen Lovejoy struck this new note for the committee in 1919 when he declared that the elaboration of constructive programs in every field of health, recreation, and education was now essential to "the development of all the children of the nation into healthy, intelligent, moral, efficient men and women — competent as American citizens."[2] Raymond G. Fuller, one of the committee's staff, designated the shift in policy as one leading away from mere "social amelioration" toward "social construction." "Pity and tears" were all right in their day but now "humanitarianism and patriotism" could be "harnessed together" in constructive pursuit of positive welfare.[3] Another spokesman for the committee, Gertrude Folks, emphasized public responsibility for constructive measures. "Our public schools," she said, "our juvenile courts, our playground centers, our public health nursing . . . everything which goes to determine what kind of a man the child will become is a concern of the State."[4]

With time, the rationale for the NCLC's new policy became more sophisticated. From the typewriter of Raymond G. Fuller, particularly, poured articles elaborating the new themes. Child labor, he came to insist, had to be understood "as an effect of causes, and not merely as a cause of effects."[5] Family poverty, parental ignorance, lack of social opportunity drove children to mine and mill. Premature labor in turn led to poverty, ignorance, and apathy being willed to still another generation. "The children of grown-up child laborers are born to child labor and all that it means."[6] The only way to break the self-perpetuating cycle was ceaselessly to attack with every means available all along the line. If poverty caused child labor, let the sources of poverty be rooted out by workmen's compensation and mothers' pensions. If schools failed to offer fulfillment for the work instincts of children, let the schools depart from sterile academicism and offer attractive and practical programs in crafts and sports and applied arts. Compulsory attendance laws would never work unless the schools themselves satisfied the needs of childhood and prepared the child for life. Vocational guidance and training together with curricular reform were demanded.

Beyond all that, Fuller led the committee to recognize that justification for a diversified attack could properly rest upon a "new reverence for childhood," a guarantee of the right of every child "to have a childhood, and to enjoy it fully." The committee should seek stricter enforcement of prohibitory and regulatory laws, yes; it should endorse all measures aimed at the elimination of poverty, by all means; and it should encourage constructive alternatives to child labor, particularly in the fields of education and recreation. But in addition, he urged, the committee should open new lines of research in order that the objectives of a full and normal childhood might be defined. Modern psychology, he said, showed that "neither in body nor mind is the child a miniature adult." The special psychic needs of children required investigation. The child's need for play was biologically rooted; his need for constructive and creative accomplishment was instinctual. Society's mandate was to find appropriate, nonexploitive work for children so that they would not be tempted by the unrewarding drudgery of the jobs open to child labor. The right of the child to his childhood must become the committee's primary concern. "Not an unoccupied childhood . . . but a well occupied childhood" was the goal.[7]

By the same token, the Child Labor Committee determined to advance in a spirit more scientific than sentimental. It had always relied upon the gathering and analysis of hard factual evidence, of course, and the traditional appeal to moral sentiment was hardly discarded in the postwar decade; but a shift in emphasis is clearly discernible. Studies indicated that by 1920, although the employment of children in street trades, in tenement trades, in textile and tobacco industries persisted, their primary employment was in agriculture, off the family farm. Thus the census of 1920, taken when the second child-labor act was still in effect, indicated that of all children, aged ten to sixteen, gainfully employed (well over a million boys and girls), 60 per cent were engaged in agricture, 17 per cent in manufacturing and mining, 14 per cent in trade and clerical positions. Because the census that year was taken in January, in the slack season for agricultural employment, the figures for rural child labor were assumed to be low. If the number of gainfully employed children aged ten through fifteen is taken as a percentage of all children in that age bracket, the state of Mississippi had the highest figure for 1920, 25 per cent. Eight other southern states had percentages ranging from 12 to 24. Of the top twelve states only two — Rhode Island with 13 per cent and Massachusetts with 9 — fell outside the South. These being the crude facts, the Child Labor Committee found it expedient to accelerate its studies of rural child labor and to evolve policies that would have an impact upon rural life. When Felix Adler of New York resigned as chairman of the board, in 1921, after seventeen years in that position, David Franklin Houston from Texas, who had served as President Wilson's secretary of agriculture, was elected in his place essentially in order to give the committee added authority in speaking to the evils of rural, southern child labor.

The Child Labor Committee, and its associates in the Consumers' League, the Women's Trade Union League, and the League of Women Voters, counted many substantial, if still partial, gains in the three or four years following the armistice. As long as the federal child-labor-tax act remained in force, minimum employment standards were enforced in every section of the nation. Even in the South, where minimum standards adopted during the first wave of reform (1903–1915) had been weakly enforced, amendments to state laws had been secured after 1916 which brought it closer in line with the rest of the nation. To a larger degree in the South than in the rest of the nation the initiative came from disinterested citizens, largely professional men and their wives; the workers themselves were unorganized and inarticulate.

The committee considered every step forward in schooling a victory for its own program, for illiteracy and child labor were interdependent. As with education, so also with health. In 1920 the committee gave office space and clerical assistance to the newly formed Child Health Organization until it was on its feet. It also played a part in helping to organize the Council for Co-ordinating Child Health. Every advance in improved wages, public health, recreation, child care, and vocational training was marked up on the asset side of the ledger by the committee, even though its direct contribution in these fields was relatively slight. The improvements were moderate enough, but the committee and its friends were more than holding their own.

Then, in 1922, came the *Bailey v. Drexel Furniture Company* ruling. Proponents of federal action were stunned: a generation of crusading nullified by the only nonelective branch of the national government. Owen Lovejoy's report to the NCLC's Board of Trustees, which held that although the ruling was a disappointment it might have a "salutary effect on the public mind" by making it clear that the battle was yet to be won, was barely convincing even to Lovejoy.[8] At any rate he suggested a new attack. In May, immediately after the decision, he asked the board to consider the possibility of working for a constitutional amendment. Although more members of the board favored this course of action than opposed it, the latter group included Julia Lathrop, chief of the Children's Bureau, who felt that 1922 was an "unfavorable time" to press for still another amendment. "I have been astonished to find the popular distaste for governmental activity," she reported, and recommended a "Fabian policy." [9]

Florence Kelley reacted to the court ruling and to the indecisiveness — as she saw it — of the board of the Child Labor Committee, on which she still served as a director, with a vehemence that arose out of long impatience with what were, she felt, reactionary and irresponsible judges and pussyfooting reformers.[10] If anything in the world was wrong, the exploitation of children was wrong. Mrs. Kelley's flutelike voice took on an edge, more sharp steel than silver, as she scolded her colleagues. The strategy of advancing on the broad front of constructive measures — education, recreation, welfare — had now to be set aside. The time had come to join battle again. But, she fumed, the Child Labor Committee was stalling and delaying. The board was a "shadow of its former self," Mrs. Kelley wrote to Newton Baker, chairman of her own organization, the Consumers' League. Paul Warburg and Felix Adler were no longer there to support her efforts.[11] Some other group would have to assume leadership where the Child Labor Committee had defaulted, for there was, in her view, but one course of action open — amendment of the federal Constitution explicitly to authorize

Congress to enact national child-labor regulations. State action, she knew, would not do except as a supplement to federal action.[12]

The trouble was, as Florence Kelley soon discovered, not everyone saw the need as clearly as she nor could the varied associations with a concern for child labor be brought to agree on a single line of action. The American Federation of Labor, in national session soon after the *Bailey* decision, had been carried away, for the moment at least, by Senator Robert M. La Follette's proposal for a constitutional amendment to limit the power of the Supreme Court to review congressional statutes. But it was not clear what the AFL would propose, or what course it would pursue, although its good intentions were evidenced by Gompers' leadership in establishing a Permanent Conference for the Abolition of Child Labor not many months after the *Bailey* decision.

Florence Kelley waited impatiently for constructive action. Her letters to friends in the League of Women Voters (Mrs. Maud Wood Park and Marian Parkhurst), to her colleagues in the Consumers' League, to constitutional experts whose legal judgment she respected (Felix Frankfurter and Ernst Freund) sizzled with indignation. Gompers, she reported, thought the process of amendment was "inevitable, while deploring the necessity." The Child Labor Committee, she complained, "has defaulted all leadership in this crisis, and the A. F. of L. is the infelicitous banner bearer for children." To Edward P. Costigan, the league's closest friend in Washington, she wrote: "We must certainly get disentangled from the leadership of Mr. Gompers. It is worse than anything I had imagined. Whether the futility is caused by incompetence or chicanery the net result is the same, and is intolerable."[13]

Mrs. Kelley was able to bring Newton Baker around to her point of view, but her board proved to be as divided as the Child Labor Committee on the expediency of the amendment procedure. The board refused, by a tie vote of five to five, to endorse the draft amendment proposed by its secretary; but it authorized her to work out an amendment in consultation with other allied associations. These allies, in Florence Kelley's view, included most notably the League of Women Voters, the WTUL, the YWCA, and the Woman's Christian Temperance Union.

Summer became fall, and still no agreement on a proposal could be reached among the many separate organizations, which seemed united on but the single principle that the employment of children was an abhorrent evil. The Permanent Conference for the Abolition of Child Labor was unable to come up with a specific proposal acceptable to other groups. Neither was the Child Labor Committee, whose concern for protecting the prerogative of the several states to act concurrently with the federal government kept it from endorsing any proposal which seemed to concentrate all power in organs of the central government. The Child Labor Committee's chairman, David F. Houston, was apparently opposed to any measure which threatened to encroach upon the states' constitutional prerogatives. His resignation in February 1923, and the subsequent election of Samuel McCune Lindsay as chairman of the board, cleared the way for more forthright action; but by that time it was too late for Congress to act and it would not convene again until December.

Given these circumstances the National Consumers' League chose to work through a special subcommittee on child labor of the Women's Joint Congressional Committee, a "holding company" group which had been established in 1920 to unify the efforts of women's reform associations in seeking welfare legislation. Florence Kelley was a member of the subcommittee; so, too, was Matilda Lindsay for the Trade Union League, Marian Parkhurst from the League of Women Voters, and Mary Stewart of the National Federation of Business and Professional Women's Clubs; they were joined later by representatives sent by the YWCA, the General Federation of Women's Clubs, the National Congress of Mothers, and the Parent-Teachers Association.

Proponents of some kind of federal action remained, however, divided into several camps, and each camp, in turn, was splintered many ways. Lack of coordination and lack of centralized leadership led to delay and confusion and spiteful feelings all around. The AFL, together with the Child Labor Committee, was generally more aware than other groups of the problem of securing ratification of an amendment unless rather explicit guarantees of local action were set forth in it. On the other hand Florence Kelley interpreted every move to make the amendment politically more palatable as a sellout to reactionary politicians or selfish employers. Old friends urged upon her the need for moderate action. Alice Hamilton, for example, citing her agreement with Felix Frankfurter (knowing that Mrs. Kelley valued his legal advice above all others), insisted that the movement proceed along two fronts — state action and federal amendment. "Many states, especially the southern ones, will be so unwilling to submit to interference from Washington that they will hasten to get a law of their own in hopes of staving it off," she predicted. Florence Kelley accepted this position, verbally at least, adding that action on both levels would have to be aggressive in character; but throughout 1923 she remained adamant in her refusal to countenance any weakening of language in the proposed amendment.[14]

When, in April 1923, the Supreme Court found against the constitutionality of minimum-wage legislation for women in the *Adkins* decision, Mrs. Kelley was certain that a turning point in the history of social reform had been reached. To compromise now was surely to knuckle under to the forces of reaction. Throughout 1923 her distrust of jurists and legalists made her ever more inflexible in her dealings with spokesmen for other associations. Pursuing a course that lacked the wholehearted support of her board, her energies sapped by the arguments following the *Adkins* decision, she reacted with suspicion to every gesture of conciliation. She labeled the Child Labor Committee's suggestion that the constitutional amendment grant "concurrent" power to both federal and state government as legally ambiguous, "radical and disastrous."[15] When overtures were made in June 1923 toward resolving differences in wording of the various amendment proposals by the establishment of an unofficial committee to be composed of Matthew Woll for the AFL, Ethel Smith for the WTUL, and herself "representing all the rest of the United States and the Universe" (she wrote a friend), Mrs. Kelley walked around the offer suspiciously and finally asked to be forgiven from joining. The offer was stacked against her, she believed, two to one for the granting of "concurrent" power.[16]

Leaders of the Child Labor Committee gave way no more than did Florence Kelley. Samuel McCune Lindsay and Owen Lovejoy won endorsement of their point in an official resolution, accepted by the Board of Trustees in October 1923, that the proposed amendment should grant "power to establish minimum standards that will reserve to the states the right to exceed such standards and to enact laws for the prohibition of child labor, not inconsistent with Federal legislation."[17] An elaborate explanation of this position followed in a lengthy letter to all members of the Board of Trustees and the Advisory Committee. The NCLC insisted upon the clear granting of "concurrent" power in order to make certain, beyond all reasonable doubt, that the central government would never pre-empt all authority in this legislative field. The real battle would be not in Congress but in the states. Unless the states were absolutely assured of a "concurrent" power, they would hesitate and hold back; the whole movement would miscarry and utterly fail.[18] In its public statements the Child Labor Committee continued to stress the constructive side of its total program, hoping thereby to alleviate the anxieties of those who feared that statutory prohibitions would deny the right and duty of children to help with family chores in the home or on the farm. Although opposed to child labor, the committee stated its belief in the efficacy of "children's work . . . in work with a purpose — work which trains for useful manhood and womanhood. We do not believe that children should be idle." [19]

With proponents of a child-labor amendment publicly divided on its wording (and privately often at each other's throats), and with no direction forthcoming from the White House, Congress was understandably reluctant to move. But 1924 was an election year, the progressives were threatening independent third-party action again, and liberals in both parties were weary of fruitless debate. The states would have the final authority to accept or reject, in any case. So an amendment was finally agreed upon by Congress for submission to the states which granted the substance of power to the federal government while protecting the prerogative of the several states, even though the word "concurrent" was not employed. Section 1 of the proposed amendment authorized Congress "to limit, regulate and prohibit the labor of persons under eighteen years of age." Section 2 stated simply: "The power of the several States is unimpaired by the article except that the operation of State laws shall be suspended to the extent necessary to give effect to legislation enacted by the Congress." The acceptance of Florence Kelley's view that the age limit should be eighteen, not sixteen as some proposed, was scored as a winning point for her side. The Child Labor Committee counted the second section to its advantage since the states were thus left free to establish regulations above the national minima, and since the demands of political expediency were satisfied by the protection afforded the states.

The delay remained a source of considerable concern to Florence Kelley and her associates. Forty-two state legislatures had met in 1923, only thirteen would convene in 1924. Favorable action by the necessary three-quarters of all states could not be expected until 1925 at the earliest. The federal government would not be able to legislate until its 1926 session.[20] Still, with the passage of the amendment by comfortable margins in both houses of Congress, Mrs. Kelley's spirits lifted. "With 44 legislatures in session in 1925," she wrote to an old friend, "we ought to achieve ratification within a year from now."[21] Others were not so hopeful. The Child Labor Committee settled down to work for ratification, even though it feared that the times were not auspicious and considered the procedure of amendment clumsy at best. An article in the *Survey* magazine prophesied: "The familiar bogeys . . . of states' rights, the prohibition analogy, the grasping bureaucrats of Washington, the sacred right of the 17-year old farmer boy to pick blueberries on the hill, and all the rest — will no doubt troop from state capital to state capital to do their worst."[22]

The *Survey's* observations may have been half in jest, but within weeks of the passage of the amendment by Congress proponents of ratification were forced to recognize that parody was uncomfortably close to the truth. Jane Addams forwarded to Florence Kelley a letter she had received from Alonzo B. See of the A. B. See Elevator Company in New York, which complained that ratification of the amendment would keep American boys from healthy and wholesome labor, deprive them of their "manliness and self-respect," and turn the country into "a vast kindergarten." Professional reform leaders he dismissed as "sentimental people" who made a "good living" out of agitation.[23] By autumn, Florence Kelley was writing plaintive letters to her friends complaining that the amendment was being misrepresented as a measure to forbid young girls to wash the family dishes and young boys to "drive the cows to pasture."[24]

Although opponents of the amendment did not really settle down to a serious campaign until it had been passed along to the states, they had made known their views when it was under debate in Congress. Manufacturers' associations testified that hard labor was character-building, that states' rights and personal liberty were at stake. Some argued that the amendment would upset the delicate balance between central and local government; and one representative of an industrial association, who had proclaimed the preference of his group for effective state action, when challenged to cite a single measure for the regulation of child labor which his association had endorsed, could not supply the details. A group called the Sentinels of the Republic was joined by the Women Patriots, the Citizens' Committee to Protect Our Homes and Children, the Moderation League of Pennsylvania, and other such organizations in decrying this Bolshevik plot to nationalize the nation's children, to destroy the home, to centralize government. The opposition of the National Association of Manufacturers, with its state affiliates, and the *Southern Textile Bulletin* undoubtedly carried more weight. Most ominous, to those whose lifelong work was tied to effective reform, was the opposition of the bloc of farm lobbyists led by the American Farm Bureau Federation.

Anticipating opposition to the amendment throughout rural America, the Child Labor Committee had voted, early in February 1924, "temporarily [to] discontinue its studies of rural child labor in order not to prejudice rural communities against the proposed amendment." Publication of reports already prepared on child labor in the Nebraska sugar-beet enterprise and in the cotton fields of Texas was to be postponed.[25] The committee had then set about in the spring and summer to broaden its appeal and widen its base of support. Social workers, educators, public officials, ministers, labor leaders, and wherever possible representatives from the American countryside were drawn into the campaign. To those who protested that the law could never legislate morality, citing the obvious weaknesses of the prohibition amendment in that regard, Eduard C. Lindeman, speaking under the auspices of the committee, replied that the law was not only the embodiment of community sentiment, but could also be made to play a "creative role" in persuading the community to move forward to "a new standard of living." [26] By autumn, the Child Labor Committee had prepared for distribution to Farm Bureau associations and county agents of the Extension Service throughout the country a pamphlet designed to allay the fear that the amendment, if ratified, would deprive farm boys and girls of the right and duty to help with the family chores. The amendment, this leaflet made clear, did not automatically outlaw the labor of children under eighteen years of age. It involved no prohibition on housework or chores. It merely authorized Congress to regulate the employment of children in factory and mine, and as migrant agricultural laborers. Congress could be trusted to implement the amendment cautiously and wisely. It was unlikely that Congress would be moved arbitrarily to prohibit all kinds of labor in all kinds of industries without very careful attention to the specific needs of particular enterprises. No reflection on the integrity of the Supreme Court was intended, the pamphlet continued; but the hard fact remained that national action was required to meet a national disgrace.[27]

By the end of summer each reform association was conducting its own drive for ratification. Together they formed a special coordinated group which they titled Organizations Associated for Ratification of the Child Labor Amendment. Mrs. Arthur C. Watkins, of the Parent-Teachers Association, was named as chairman; Julia Lathrop served as vice chairman; and Marguerite Owen, from the League of Women Voters, was its secretary-treasurer. Serving on its steering committee were representatives from the Women's Trade Union League (Rose Schneiderman and Nelle Swartz), the Consumers' League (the redoubtable Florence Kelley), the American Association for Labor Legislation (Irene Osgood Andrews), and the National Child Labor Committee (Owen Lovejoy and Wiley Swift), plus other interested individuals without associational affiliation. The *ad hoc* association was as clumsy in action as it was in title. It did serve as a clearinghouse for information; but its attempts to coordinate strategy were not notably successful.[28] The real work would have to be done by the member associations and by their local affiliates in the several states.

The first contest came in Massachusetts, where the several reform groups enjoyed substantial strength and where they could draw upon decades of experience.[29] They proved unequal to the task. The President of the United States, but a few years earlier governor of the state, remained cool and silent, although he had endorsed the amendment when it had been before Congress. The National Association of Manufacturers and the Associated Industries of Massachusetts leaped into the fray with the cry that the amendment was Bolshevik-inspired. A special Citizens Committee for Protection of Our Homes and Children (financed and controlled by textile and shoe manufacturers, the Women's Trade Union League charged) warned of the threat of still another governmental invasion of the privacy and sanctity of the home. When William Cardinal O'Connell saw a threat to parental discipline in the amendment, Mayor James M. Curley of Boston, candidate for governor, found it expedient to agree. An "advisory referendum," in the regular November elections, brought out nearly 700,000 "No" votes to fewer than 250,000 "Aye."

The opposition of the Roman Catholic hierarchy in Massachusetts was undoubtedly the crucial factor in the nearly three-to-one popular rejection of the referendum, although a growing reaction against the consequences of the Eighteenth Amendment may have had some bearing on the reluctance to embrace the proposed Twentieth. The Roman Catholic Church, however, was not of one mind on the issue. The Bishops' Program of Social Reconstruction, in whose formulation Father John A. Ryan had played the major role, had endorsed federal child-labor legislation along with other national welfare measures. As director of the Social Action Department of the National Catholic Welfare Conference and as a member of both the Child Labor Committee and the Consumers' League, Ryan had thrown his influence on the side of the amendment soon after the *Bailey* decision. Following his lead, the National Conference of Catholic Women had endorsed ratification as did the 1924 Catholic Conference on Industrial Problems. Edward Keating, original co-sponsor of the first federal bill in 1916, was a Roman Catholic as was Senator Thomas J. Walsh of Montana, one of the most vociferous of the amendment's many prominent proponents. But the main body of the hierarchy and many laymen stood opposed. Some argued — as did their non-Catholic counterparts — that the amendment threatened government invasion of the home. A more serious threat, potentially at least, was seen concerning the Church's role in education. There was a move in many parts of the nation to retard parochial school education; in some states legislation was pending which would require the attendance of all children in the public school system. The Roman Catholic community, always aware of its minority status, was extraordinarily sensitive to every move of the Protestant majority in the 1920's, whether the issue was education or immigration restriction or welfare measures, which in any way seemed to challenge its values or its programs. The *Catholic Charities Review*, the *Catholic World*, and *Catholic Action* might argue that the child-labor amendment in no remote way implied an interference with education, but to other Catholic organs, associations, and leaders it appeared that any enlargement of the powers of national or state government constituted a potential encroachment upon the Church's prerogatives. William Cardinal O'Connell had been pointing to the dangers inherent in political centralization for many years; the child-labor amendment was another bit of evidence of a pernicious trend in American life. If ever the amendment had a chance in Massachusetts, Cardinal O'Connell's pastoral letter of October 1924 quickly scotched it. Father Ryan soon thereafter conceded defeat, not only in Massachusetts but in the nation.

By the end of January 1925, six states had joined Massachusetts in rejecting the amendment — Georgia, Kansas, North Carolina, Oklahoma, South Carolina, and Texas. Reformers took heart from the affirmative action of Arkansas, Arizona, and California. Success or failure now hung on New York where the reform associations, strong there as nowhere else in the nation, had reason to hope for forthright support from the governor, one of their own, Alfred E. Smith. The American Association for Labor Legislation, meeting in December 1924, was so thoroughly convinced that the child-labor amendment, together with a maximum-hour bill for women workers, would carry the state legislature with ease that it determined to stress other reforms that were less certain of passage.

Perhaps there was still reason to hope; but unease rather than confidence marked the reform temper as the associations prepared for what they saw as the decisive battle. Felix Adler, whose official retirement from the Child Labor Committee had in no way lessened his concern, noted with dismay the mounting fear and even panic with which the amendment was being received. Respectable and conservative gentlemen had always stood for this reform; what now had gone wrong? The prohibition analogy he rejected. To suggest that there was a parallel between the liberty of private behavior and the social liberty to exploit children was preposterous; but he had to recognize that many people were apparently being moved by such a fraudulent argument. Charges of Bolshevism and nationalization of the nation's youth seemed even more outrageous; yet there they were. His pragmatic suggestion that citizens test their fears against the actual experience under the federal laws of 1916 and 1918 went largely unnoticed.[30] William L. Chenery attributed opposition primarily to the consideration that wartime regulations had "left many people cold to any extension of national control." But he, too, had to admit that irrational reactions played a larger role in the rise of anxiety.[31] The Child Labor Committee traced opposition to fear of federal invasion of states' rights, to fear that Congress would prohibit all child labor up to the eighteen-year permissive limit, but also to the careless charges of Bolshevism brought against the measure.[32] Even Florence Kelley began to despair of expecting a rational and considered debate on the real merits of the amendment. "Is there any living

Democrat in this state, beside the Governor and the State Department of Labor who is right on the Children's Amendment . . ." she asked of Frances Perkins. Was there not someone who could persuade the press — Herbert Bayard Swope and Walter Lippmann — to rally the forces for ratification? If the *World* — "owned and edited by 'liberal' Jews" — joined Cardinal O'Connell "against the children" there was no hope.[33]

The blow came early in January 1925, when Governor Smith, stating his personal approval of ratification, recommended that the measure be submitted to the people in referendum. Florence Kelley raged — the governor had "gone over to the enemy."[34] The New York State Assembly, no more eager for a showdown than the governor, failed to act upon the proposed referendum. And so the proposal died. Henry F. Pringle, author of an exposé on the evils of child labor, wrote the epitaph for the movement in a letter to his own paper, the *World*, whose editors had opposed ratification: "The fact of the matter is that I haven't much faith in the States. I don't think they are entitled to their 'rights' when they fail to exercise them."[35]

The Child Labor Committee knew at once that the New York Assembly's failure to act virtually eliminated all chance for favorable action in the state in the near future. Proponents of the amendment lacked the resources to carry on a lengthy and costly campaign; the climate of opinion was unfavorable. An alliance of industry, upstate conservative Republicans, and the Catholic hierarchy could not be overcome. To risk repeating the disastrous events in Massachusetts was foolhardy.[36] From the Valley of Democracy, William Allen White wrote his concurring advice: "We are in a slough of reaction. It is the height of folly to push humanitarian measures at this time and give their opponents the prestige of defeat. . . . It was grotesque folly to try it in Kansas."[37] Samuel McCune Lindsay quickly saw that the "popular tide" was running against ratification. His recommended course of action was endorsed at once. The committee would continue to cooperate with all other associations seeking ratification, but was to avoid a referendum at all costs. Its major effort would focus on persuading the several states to act through legislation rather than ratification. This new strategy would smoke out all those who were now publicly on record in favor of state action as opposed to national. "This plan is vital as it forces the opposition to prove their willingness to take care of their own problem or else acknowledge the need of a national standard."

"Our devotion is always to the cure of the patient," Lindsay concluded, "not to the specific remedy." [38] The Child Labor Committee settled down for a long and hard struggle. Owen Lovejoy rejoiced that the logic of "Democracy and Christianity" was on the side of the exploited children; nevertheless, he said, it was well to advance forewarned — "We will have to combat disbelief, apathy and tremendous business antagonism." [39]

Florence Kelley, recalling the extraordinary efforts that ratification of the woman-suffrage amendment had required, proposed now to follow the same procedures to victory — incessant publicity and the use of petitions to make obvious the need for constructive action. The time was not appropriate to submit to a referendum in New York; but a petition signed by 100,000 leading citizens might turn the tide. Not many associations proved eager, however, as Mrs. Kelley reported to her board, to take such action as might "call forth a renewal of the mad onslaught of the 1924 political campaign, injuring the prestige of all organizations that were backing the amendment." [40] The reluctance of the Child Labor Committee to get involved in a time- and nerve-consuming campaign was, to the impatient Mrs. Kelley, evidence of its "rabbit-hearted" leadership. George W. Alger, chairman of the New York State Child Labor Committee, was finally persuaded to lend his signature, she wrote, but only after twelve members of the national board of the YWCA, including Mrs. John D. Rockefeller, Jr., agreed to sign the petition. Getting Matthew Woll of the AFL lined up, she felt, was nothing less than a miracle. Sidney Hillman and John Haynes Holmes proved to be valuable allies; and the Consumers' League got agreement from over one hundred civic groups to distribute petitions. But by February 1927, after nearly two years of frenzied activity, barely 10,000 signatures had been secured. [41]

In the meantime other associations, the Women's Trade Union League most notably, kept up the fight. Ethel Smith, the league's chief lobbyist, devoted a great deal of her time to working with other women's associations in promoting publicity favorable to ratification and to the passage of state legislation. Progress, however, had to be measured in minor achievements. It was helpful to expose a southern Farmers' States Rights League as an agency controlled by southern cotton mill owners, but revelations were rarely followed by positive action. By June 1925 the WTUL had been forced to the unhappy conclusion that opposition to the amendment constituted opposition to any effective regulation, local, state, or national.[42]

The conclusions to which the Child Labor Committee were driven were no more hopeful. Every attempt to find allies for state action among those groups whose avowed purpose was to block federal intervention in local affairs failed without exception. What saddened Owen Lovejoy most, however, was "the extent to which the children themselves were forgotten in the debates." [43] Over a million children under the age of sixteen continued to labor in field and factory. A rigid age minimum of fourteen years was enforced in but eight states; only sixteen states prohibited night labor. Less than half the states in the Union required educational or health certificates for children seeking employment.[44] In the city tenements the labor of boys and girls was sweated; the textile industry and the canning industry remained primary places of employment. In the sugar-beet fields of Colorado and Idaho children spent long hours stooped over the tough and ugly plants. On long, hot summer days in the fields of Mississippi and Texas, young children went to the fields at sunup with their parents and picked the bolls of cotton into long gunny sacks they dragged along the rough ground. Medical doctors summed up the costs of ill health in child labor: chronic fatigue, a high incidence of tuberculosis, heart strain, curvature of the spine, permanent injury to bone and muscle. Long monotonous labor, uninterrupted by school or play, contributed to anxiety, nervousness, insomnia, and disintegration of the child's personality. These evils, in turn, led eventually, but directly, to "delinquency, dependency, or an ineffective and purposeless life." Premature labor of children at adult tasks hurt the child; it also weakened "the foundation of the social structure itself." [45]

When Professor Wilson D. Wallis of the Department of Anthropology at the University of Minnesota wrote that child labor in America was more brutal than any found in savagery or among "ruder peoples," the Child Labor Committee picked up his statement and gave it wide publicity. Everywhere else in the world, Wallis observed — among the American Indian tribes, in Africa, in the South Seas — children were "allowed to live their own lives." Only in America were millions of children denied their inherent right to "full development." [46] A classic stanza of reform doggerel made the same point:

> No fledgling feeds the father bird,
> No chicken feeds the hen —

No kitten mouses for the cat,
  This glory is for men.
We are the Wisest, Strongest Race —
  Loud may our praise be sung!
The only animal alive
  That lives upon its young.[47]

By decade's end the Child Labor Committee could count but six states as having ratified the amendment — Arkansas, Arizona, California, Wisconsin, Montana, and Colorado. Samuel McCune Lindsay marked the twenty-fifth anniversary of the committee's life by recalling its origins: "It is a striking commentary on our times that at first the committee was not incorporated, for the reformers of the early days of the new century believed its task would soon be accomplished once the American public was informed of the facts. The public has been informed — and child labor persists."[48] By the end of the 1920's, crusaders were falling back upon Sarah Cleghorn's bitterly ironic quatrain:

The golf links lie so near the mill
  That almost every day
The little children may look out
  And see the men at play.[49]

When Lovejoy resigned as executive secretary of the Child Labor Committee early in 1926, his assistant, Wiley Swift, was asked to fill the vacancy in an acting capacity. Swift, born and trained in the South, represented the most cautious wing of the committee. His first course of action was to retrench, to cut back on field work and research, to transfer to other agencies, whenever possible, the costs of local campaigns. The crusading phase of the committee's work had passed, he believed. "From now on," he wrote in 1927, "the movement will be more gradual and necessarily less spectacular. A little here and a little there is the way we shall inch up to better things."[50]

Opposition to Swift's cautious and credulous policies gathered force. Lillian Wald within the committee, Grace Abbott and Maud Wood Park outside, had from his appointment expressed concern lest Swift's new line lead to a surrender of all they had together championed.[51] Gertrude Folks Zimand, daughter of Homer Folks, for many years secretary of the New York State Charities Aid Association and for many years on the Child Labor Committee's board, was brought onto the executive staff, and her position proved to be far more militant than Swift's. To Mrs. Zimand, research and publicity would never suffice; the weight of the law would have to be brought to bear upon those who persisted in practices of exploitation which ran counter to every moral precept and social need. "Law makes morals as morality makes laws," she wrote in 1928. "Outlawry by legal statutes will in time ripen into outlawry by community custom." [52] By 1931, Wiley Swift, who was never honored with more than the title of "acting" secretary, was no longer on the committee's staff. Courtenay Dinwiddie, a more aggressive soul, took his place, and the committee was free again to strike forward without internal dissension.

Only the saintly or those with a robust sense of perspective can survive the experience of being out of step with the march of events without losing equanimity of spirit. Proponents of child-labor reform, in the tepid years of the 1920's, were frequently jostled off balance and upset. Disappointment was their daily diet. Beaten back, in campaign after campaign, some reform leaders seized the expedient of compromise and accommodation. A few took the line of most resistance. Florence Kelley would have been happy to have won a few more victories than she did, but she had a lust for joining battle that won its own rewards. Her long-running engagement with the temporizers on the one hand (especially with the executive staff of the Child Labor Committee) and with the forces of reaction and narrow corporate self-interest on the other would have been enough to discourage a person of less joy in life than she. Irritable she frequently was, and occasionally enraged; but never for long. She possessed a capacity for laughter, for making fun (at herself above all else) that saw her through many a crisis. She could afford to be as demanding of others as she was hard on herself because she knew how dearly she was loved and how deeply admired by her most intimate friends. Thus, she could write with perfect candor to Grace Abbott, in 1927, of her unceasing campaign to get her dearest associate, Lillian Wald (with whom she lived at 265 Henry Street for many years), to force the Child Labor Committee into a more aggressive strategy: ". . . when I revile her she merely smiles and leaves everything as it is." The letter was signed "Yours hopefully, in spite of Satan." [53] Lillian Wald, in turn, could be forgiven so many sins (mostly of omission, as Florence Kelley saw it), because she ever demonstrated the capacity to accept the transgressions of others. When life became too thick to bear longer, off to her Connecticut farm went Miss Wald, more often than not with house guests that might include Florence Kelley, or Jane Addams, or Alice Hamilton, or the Abbott sisters, or Julia Lathrop. Mrs. Kelley had a summer retreat in Maine where she could retire temporarily from the field of battle.

To each his own source of comfort and joy. Owen Lovejoy's was, without doubt, a deep religious conviction in the divine purposefulness of a life lived in conformity with God's will. For thirteen years a minister of the Gospel before he enlisted in the cause of social service, he developed a ministry to the least of God's kingdom. His presidential address in 1920 to the National Conference of Social Work bore witness to his faith. Regardless of formal religious commitment, he said, the social worker and social reformer were in the line of the devoted, the communion of those who did good works. Concern for the youth of the nation must take precedence over all else, for it was through an uplifted and liberated youth that the kingdom of God on earth would be won. The social worker had respect for the rights of all others, even those with whom he differed, because he trusted in "the essential divinity of every man." His philosophy of life he summarized in the peroration ". . . light is stronger than darkness, love is mightier than hate, good can outreach evil, intelligence can overcome ignorance and . . . the race can be led where it cannot be driven." [54] It took more than a few setbacks to discourage a man of such abiding faith and hope.

In perspective, the decade had not been as devoid of fruitful accomplishment in the battle against child labor as some who were caught up in its turmoils must certainly have concluded. Despite the collapse of federal regulation and the failure of the constitutional amendment, and despite the reluctance of the several states to raise standards and tighten up enforcement, there was some progress. By the end of the decade, while agriculture still commanded a large number of young workers, in the textile industry (particularly in New England but in the South as well) the decline which had set in around 1910 continued. Measured in absolute numbers, the 1920's marked a steady decrease in the employment of children, even if many hundreds of thousands of minors were still exploited in field, mill, and mine.

The decade had opened with plans to broaden constructive programs along the lines of education, recreation, and child welfare. This had been the strategy of the Child Labor Committee. This had been the resolve as well of the White House Conference on Child Welfare Standards in the spring of 1919. The first White House Conference, called by Theodore Roosevelt in 1909, had resulted in the creation of the Children's Bureau and in the inauguration of programs of mothers' assistance and had acted as a spur to national and state regulatory legislation; how much better the chances for progress in 1919 seemed to many of the delegates. And so the emphasis was placed not only upon legislative prohibitions of child labor and the establishment of industrial minima, but upon physical and mental health, recreation, education, adequate family income, the care and prevention of dependency and delinquency. The conference called for pioneering action in the fields of nutrition, child guidance, infant and maternal health, hygiene, parent education, juvenile courts and probation. The conservation of childhood was to be the keynote for the coming decade.[55]

From the conference came four specific charges for the new decade: to protect the health of mothers and children; to advance study and research in order that future programs could draw upon sound statistical data; to establish minimum standards for children in industry; to meet the needs of certain children for special care, such as juvenile delinquents. It was only the adverse decision of the Supreme Court in 1922 that temporarily distracted the crusade for children from these goals. By the end of the decade, many reformers, taking defeat of child-labor legislation as for the moment irrevocable, had turned again to positive welfare measures. In doing so they could build upon a record of some substance.

Progress was marked in the field of mothers' assistance or mothers' pensions as they were more often called. Missouri, California, and Illinois had pioneered, back in 1911, in providing special funds for dependent widows and "half-orphans." Other states had picked up the new responsibility until by the end of the teens, all but about ten of the states had some kind of assistance program. These programs were expanded and extended in the 1920's, with such notable success that by 1930 only four states provided no assistance and state financial aid was going to over 200,000 dependent children whose fathers were dead or incapacitated or were absent from the home because of divorce, desertion, or imprisonment. "Motherhood has been lifted out of its long association with pauperism and the stigma of dependency has been removed from children who have lost a father's support," concluded an expert in 1925. The payments, he continued, were a kind of social insurance, the money going "to the mother as her right for service rendered to the community . . . The waste of child life is lessened; aid comes in time and the spread of poverty is prevented." [56] A ten-year study (1914–1924), underwritten by the Rockefeller Foundation and conducted by the New York Association for Improving the Condition of the Poor, had indicated that regular aid programs, at levels above that of minimal subsistence, were able to break "the vicious circle of poverty and ill health, and ill health and poverty" until a succession of "'redemptive forces began to work *of their own accord*." [57] Opposed by many prominent social workers when first proposed, mothers' pensions were viewed by 1930 as a proper assumption of the public's responsibility for those who were dependent through no inherent personal fault. They also afforded a means for providing such financial aid as would permit private social casework agencies to handle more effectively noneconomic sources of family maladjustment. Whereas once relief had been made available only after the mother had been forced to seek employment outside the home and the children had fallen into delinquency, mothers' pensions served as a preventive force by enabling the mother to stay home and attend to her primary task of child care.

The extension of mothers' assistance programs was a measure of the advance of child welfare in the 1920's, but the passage of the Federal Maternity and Infancy Act of 1921 was the first major victory won by women's organizations after ratification of the Nineteenth Amendment. On Julia Lathrop's initiative a program of federal grants-in-aid to states had been proposed, for many studies of her Children's Bureau had shown clear correlations between infant mortality and ill health, on the one hand, and low wages, crowded housing, parental ignorance on the other. Bills to incorporate the principle of federal aid to state health programs had failed in 1919 and 1920, but in 1921, with but seven dissenting votes in the Senate and thirty-nine in the House, the first Sheppard-Towner Act was passed. With limited funds (about a million dollars a year) a great deal was accomplished in the setting up of public health centers, prenatal clinics, and hygiene and child-welfare divisions in all but two states in the Union. Responsibility for its administration was granted to the Division of Child Hygiene and Maternal Health in the Children's Bureau. Biennial squabbles over appropriations required that the reform associations remain eternally vigilant. In 1927 a filibuster of conservative Republicans and southern Democrats threatened to kill the chance for any appropriations at all. In order to win another two years, Grace Abbott, who had succeeded Julia Lathrop as Children's Bureau director, consented to an amendment to the renewal bill calling for the final expiration of the act in 1929. Even the formidable Florence Kelley was persuaded to accept the amendment in the expectation that the decision could be overridden two years hence. "It seems inconceivable that the next Congress should be as bad as this one," she wrote to Grace Abbott. "I don't believe it can." [58]

But it was. The act was scheduled to lapse on June 30, 1929, so a bill was introduced in Congress early in April to extend maternity and child care funds beyond that date. Although the bill had the endorsement of the new President, Herbert Hoover (and he had urged Grace Abbott to stay on as bureau director), the White House did not press aggressively for its passage; the bill languished; the aid program died. And Florence Kelley scribbled off a memorandum for her file: Why are "seals, bears, reindeer, fish, wild game in the national parks, buffalo, migratory birds, all found suitable for federal protection; but not the children of our race and their mothers?" [59] President Hoover, who had taken the lead in 1920 in creating the American Child Health Association and who had served as its president as long as he was secretary of commerce, formally endorsed efforts in 1930 and 1931 to restore funds for federal aid to child-health programs particularly in rural areas, but other issues were more pressing; good intentions alone did not suffice to spur an indifferent Congress to action. Not until 1935, as part of the Social Security Act, was the aid program picked up again.

After eight years of substantial achievement, another setback; but the efforts were not lost. Together with state aids to dependent widows and children, the Sheppard-Towner programs had set precedents for child and maternal health and welfare upon which more effective programs would later be built.

Reformers had put great faith in the improvement of education as a way indirectly but substantially to overcome the evils of child labor. Certainly there was comfort to be got from certain educational reforms achieved during the 1920's. More children, in absolute numbers and relative to the school-age population, stayed in school longer by the end of the decade than at the beginning. The proportional increase in children attending high schools was especially dramatic, one study by the Children's Bureau indicating a fourfold increase in the number of children attending public secondary schools over the two decades 1905 to 1925.[60] Another survey presented data which showed that whereas only 10 per cent of the high school age population was actually in school in 1904, 53 per cent was in attendance in 1928.[61] The Smith-Hughes Act, first passed in 1917, appropriated funds on a dollar-matching basis to states that established vocational and continuation schools (programs which, presumably, most directly offered a constructive alternative to child labor). Although the states that needed the programs most desperately — in New England and in the South — did not generally take advantage of this form of federal aid, over half the states of the Union offered facilities for vocational and continuation schooling by the end of the decade. Throughout the nation, but particularly in the wealthier and more progressive states, other educational reforms were instituted: a tightening up of compulsory school attendance laws; special ungraded schools for the mentally retarded (a reform that the settlements pioneered); technical schools for the training of children in skilled crafts and trades; programs of vocational guidance as well as vocational training; the enrichment of curriculums with courses especially designed for pupils in non-college preparatory courses of study; courses in diet and in hygiene for all students; school-directed programs of supervised athletics and recreation.

The Child Labor Committee's goal of a full and normal childhood, freed from the stresses of premature gainful employment, was more nearly realized in the 1920's than ever before. Under private agency auspices the validity of providing special counseling and guidance services for children in one sort of trouble and another was demonstrated, and public agencies implemented the findings with programs of their own. To these ends the Children's Aid Society of New York City devoted money and thought and time that all children could enjoy equal opportunities — "the child of peculiar personality, the sick child, the under-nourished child, the mentally retarded child, the child with an unhappy psychological makeup, the misunderstood child, the wilful child, and even the wayward child." [62] Working along parallel lines were voluntary associations, many of them founded in the postwar era — the Mental Hygiene Institute, the Child Development Institute, the National Committee for Mental Hygiene, the American Child Health

Association. Through the Child Welfare League of America, organized in 1915 and carried through its early years by assistance from the Department of Child Caring of the Russell Sage Foundation and later by grants from the Commonwealth Fund and the Rockefeller Fund, a large number of affiliate associations were able to coordinate their diverse activities. During these years foundations engaged in child-welfare activities doubled both in number and in expenditures (from six million dollars in 1921 to twelve million in 1936). Facilities for psychiatric counseling of children increased at least ten times during the same decade. Parent education, in the narrowly practical fields of home management and domestic science and in child development and recreation as well, was spurred on by the Federation for Child Study and the Parent-Teachers Association, two organizations that had been active for at least a generation, and also by the National Council of Parent Education and the National Committee on Nursery Schools.

All this activity added up to a substantial, if still preliminary effort to promote what that generation knew as "mental hygiene." Mental illness was to be made subject to scientific diagnosis, treatment, cure, and prevention by competently trained psychiatrists, psychologists, and psychiatric social workers, just as physical illness was attacked by the medical professions. From the pioneering work of Clifford Beers, founder and secretary of the National Committee for Mental Hygiene, and of William Healy, whose assistance to delinquents in Chicago opened up the possibility of constructive remedial and preventive measures, a large number of child-welfare workers took their cue in the postwar decade. They emphasized research, demonstration, education of the public to new attitudes, the establishment of pilot clinics and institutes, and the inauguration of "visiting teacher" services (which sent social workers trained in education and psychology into the homes of problem and disturbed children). The Commonwealth Fund provided money and direction for much of this experimental work, the significance of which was not abundantly evident until the 1940's.

On another level, youth-serving agencies — the Boy and Girl Scouts, the 4-H clubs, the Campfire Girls, the Big Sister program, the YMCA and YWCA — all demonstrated the capacity to grow not only in size but in variety of programs offered and diversity of needs served. Recognizing that Negro children faced special handicaps of both race and class, the Urban League devoted a good deal of attention to the educational and recreational needs of colored children and to problems associated with ghetto, slum housing, dependency, and delinquency. Still other groups worked with a large measure of success toward the strengthening of laws dealing with sexual offenses against children, for codes which would protect the status of illegitimate children, and for social hygiene and the control of venereal disease. Proposals which required no extensive outlay of new funds, need it be pointed out, tended to be received more cheerfully by economy-minded legislators than did measures that carried a price tag.

In juvenile courts and probation for juvenile offenders, research and demonstration ran far ahead of practice. The prewar movement had quickly established the principles upon which juvenile procedures should be based, particularly the legal concept that, in the words of a Children's Bureau publication, "the delinquent child is not to be proceeded against as one who has committed an offense against the State for which the State must mete out punishment, but is a subject of the State's special protection, care, and guardianship in exactly the same degree as the child who is neglected or homeless." Rehabilitation rather than retention was to be the rule. Informal chancery procedures, private hearings, case studies of personal and environmental data by trained officers attached to the courts, were to be the means for shifting the law from penalty to protection.[63] Faced with a great variety of cases — truancy, delinquency, neglect and dependency, offenses against children, nonsupport, placement of the mentally defective — judges of juvenile courts often had more cases than they could handle without many more court officers than they were usually provided. Research into the causes of delinquency was still in a pioneer and even primitive stage; trained social workers could easily find positions more rewarding and better paid with other agencies and were generally and understandably reluctant to pursue a career in corrections or probation, in which fields petty and even corrupt local politics still so often prevailed. Implementation of known principles proved difficult in all but the most enlightened cities, while rural areas relied almost universally on older procedures. The pioneer work of such leaders as Miriam Van Waters would lead, in time, to a wide adoption of new techniques and attitudes; for the 1920's, however, research and demonstration and the growing recognition that treatment and prevention required the study of the whole child in his whole environment were the primary legacies.[64]

This same sense informed the work of the Children's Bureau through-out the 1920's. The welfare of the child was not something to be treated in separate compartments by separate agencies using separate and spe-cial techniques. The child was one, and unless the organic unity of the child was kept constantly in mind, welfare work would surely falter or go astray. The doctor and dentist, the teacher, the recreation super-visor, the judge, the social worker, the psychologist and psychiatrist all had special roles to play; none could perform his special function effec-tively and humanely without an awareness of all areas of the child's life. In this spirit the Children's Bureau, together with many other agencies and associations both public and private, sought in the sev-eral states the compilation of all laws bearing upon the child into single comprehensive codes. Whatever the lapses in practice, the goal of the crusade for children was more the achievement of constructive and positive programs of welfare than prevention and child-saving.

It was this concern that somewhere in government there be a single agency responsible for the total welfare of each child that prompted Grace Abbott to launch an attack on the proposal made during the White House Conference on Child Health and Protection in November of 1930 that the health services of the Children's Bureau be transferred to the United States Public Health Service. The recommendation had been brought forward, innocently enough, by the conference's commit-tee on health with the tacit approval at least of Dr. Ray Lyman Wilbur, Hoover's secretary of the interior and over-all chairman of the confer-ence, and with the knowledge of the President himself. Backed by the American Medical Association and by Surgeon General Cumming, the proposal aroused the ire of Grace Abbott and all the women's organiza-tions who saw any proposal affecting the integrity of the Children's Bureau as a move to undermine its effectiveness. The vehemence which the measure aroused came as a shock to its proponents and before it was set aside the entire conference had been damaged. That the Presi-dent was, as in so many other matters, well-intentioned but inept was not generally appreciated by devotees of the Children's Bureau. So-phonisba P. Breckinridge was moved to record her "horror" at what she took to be the President's "incredible betrayal of all we thought he stood for." "Still," she added quickly, "I have to confess, it was hard for me ever to believe that he really cared." [65]

In other ways, however, the third White House Conference was a suitable climax to the decade's work in child welfare. Sixteen months of elaborate preparation preceded the convening of the delegates in November of 1930. Directed by Dr. Harry E. Barnard, a careerist in public health, and Martha Van Renssalaer, pioneer in home economics education at Cornell University, the planning staff called upon the testimony and research of over twelve hundred experts. If the "Children's Charter" — adopted by the three thousand delegates as its platform — was a document of clumsy length and often ambiguous language, the thirty massive volumes of reports that followed contained comprehensive summaries of the decade's progress and pointed with explicit detail to policies and programs awaiting implementation. Financially underwritten by a half-million-dollar grant from private foundations and taking its cue from the presuppositions of the Hoover administration, the conference favored local over national action, voluntary over governmental initiative. It focused upon serving the thirty-five million children who could be counted as "normal" as well as upon meeting the problems of the ten million children who in some way stood in special need. A recurring note was the recognition that the totality of the child's welfare rested upon the stability of the family in which he was nurtured and that the family's health in turn depended upon the security that society afforded. The nation would soon confront the problem of promoting security in an era of gross economic insecurity and want.

Those who were in the advance guard of child-protection and child-welfare work had been driven, long before 1930, to accept the conclusion that Julia Lathrop had set forth in 1919: "Children are not safe and happy if their parents are miserable, and parents must be miserable if they cannot protect a home against poverty." The implications of this simple conclusion Miss Lathrop had spelled out: "The power to maintain a decent family living standard is a primary essential of child welfare. This means a living wage and wholesome working life for the man, a good and skillful mother at home to keep the house and comfort all within it. Society can afford no less and can afford no exceptions." [66] A hostile male critic, seeking to discredit Miss Lathrop's authority to speak in behalf of the children of the nation, had once inquired if she had ever been a mother; her rejoinder entered the folklore of the reform movement — "No sir, have you?" [67] Such impertinence endeared her to many and sharpened the cutting edge of her attack upon all forms of cant and hypocrisy. When she gave way as chief of the Children's Bureau to another Hull House alumna, Grace Abbott — empirical of mind, compassionate of spirit, candid in manner, direct in action — aggressive national leadership for the total welfare of the child persisted, for the lady from Nebraska was as deeply committed to the notion of society's responsibility through government to enlarge opportunity and enhance security as was her friend and former chief.

Throughout the years of normalcy the Children's Bureau returned to the theme that after all means had been employed to serve the child, his welfare ultimately depended upon the social health of the nation. When the effect on children of the depression of 1920–1921 was measured, the bureau staff discovered that hard times had led to the exhaustion of savings, privation, "debt and discouragement," the loss of homes, illness, "uncertainty and fear." The conclusion was obvious to all who cared: "unemployment, then, because it means lowered family standards, anxiety and dread, the loss of savings, and the mortgaging of the future, has a direct and disastrous effect upon the welfare of children." [68] Time and again Miss Abbott hammered on that simple point. Before congressional committees she defended the efficacy of the child-labor amendment: "Child labor and poverty are inevitably bound together and if you continue to use the labor of children as the treatment for the social disease of poverty, you will have both poverty and child labor to the end of time." [69] Before the Child Labor Committee's conference in December 1929 she persisted: problems of health and recreation related to economic dependency, dependency to child labor; child labor goes "with low wages, with unemployment, with widowhood and orphanage, with schools poorly equipped." [70] To the delegates of the Women's Trade Union League convention the same year she expounded upon the intimate relationship "between infant mortality and low wages, the relationship between delinquency and low wages, the extent of dependency and low wages." The greatest measures for child welfare, therefore, were those that promoted "the proper kind of home surroundings and the proper kind of opportunity for child development, and that comes only with an adequate wage and with a stability of employment." [71]

Upon the same premises Professor Paul Douglas built his argument for family allowances. From the same presuppositions, Francis Tyson proclaimed the need for society to provide minimum, continuous family income through times of unemployment and sickness. Mothers' assistance programs showed the way, he wrote, to provide security of income without the stigma of charity. Old-age assistance was the next proper step and, after that, insurance against the hazards of unemployment, sickness, and disability.[72] So too argued Neva Deardorff — insecurity and insufficiency of income bore on housing, nutrition, health, and morale; war and industrial strife, "defective social organization," were proper objects of social research and legitimate concerns of professional social caseworkers.[73]

The crusade for children was not a single coherent movement. It advanced on many fronts — child labor, mothers' pensions, infant and maternal health, institutional research, child-guidance clinics, education, juvenile courts, recreation. It pursued many strategies — legislative lobbying, political campaigning, research and publicity, casework, psychiatric counseling, service. It called upon doctor, teacher, judge, probation officer, publicist, bureaucrat. In seeking the welfare of children it was finally driven to seek the welfare of women and mothers, family welfare, the general welfare of society.

THE CAMPAIGN FOR
WOMEN'S RIGHTS

"The industrial advance . . . has entailed problems all its own. In the surging, congested masses, notably of unorganized and inarticulate women and children workers, summoned to create wealth in mass production, it is increasingly hard for us to find our neighbours! The Providence which lay in the intimacy of small neighbourhoods is lost in the mazes of the tenement, and charity becomes unintelligent and futile as a mere casual grace between strangers. For such reasons the factory and workshop, as they grew, became more and more impersonal, conditions in them became nobody's business, and their social consequences eluded the knowledge of the consumers of the products until the exhaustion of long hours, the degradation of inadequate wages and the diseases of the sweatshop stood out as evils which not only deprived defenceless women and children of a fair chance in life, but menaced the vitality and morality of the race."

— Foreword by Newton D. Baker in Maud Nathan, *The Story of an Epoch-Making Movement* (Garden City, N.Y.: Doubleday, 1926), pp. xi–xii

THE children of the nation were always the special concern of humanitarian reformers in the 1920's. Especially were the children of the poor the object of programs aimed at liberation from premature and excessive labor, at the enlargement of opportunity through educational, recreational, and welfare measures. If efforts had often been thwarted, the results of reform activity were nevertheless substantial. If the decade had proved uncongenial to statutory regulation, at least the advances in other areas gave cause for authentic satisfaction.

The hope that another disadvantaged group in the population — working women — could win the protection of the state against unreasonable exploitation proved less valid. Two lines of ameliorative action had taken form during the Progressive Era. One pointed toward the organization of women workers into labor unions in order that they might gain, through union, the strength to bargain collectively with employers. It was for this end that the Women's Trade Union League, with the nominal and rhetorical support of the AFL, strove with zeal if not with very large success. The second path led toward legislation, particularly at the state level of government, which would set standards of maximum hours, minimum wages, and decent conditions for women employees. Here notable advances had been won during the culminating years of the Progressive Era just before the nation's entrance into the Great War.

The regulation of hours and conditions had come first, the Supreme Court in the classic *Muller v. Oregon* case in 1908 upholding such legislation as an entirely reasonable exercise of the state's police power to promote the health, morality, and welfare of the community. Minimum-wage legislation came a bit later, but in the five years before America went to war, eleven states invoked the power to set a floor under wages earned by women. The argument that women, as mothers of the race, required the special protection of the community acting through government presumably applied as logically to the one area, minimum wages, as to the other, maximum hours. The Supreme Court did not see the parallel quite as clearly as the reformers did, but in 1917 — as noted earlier — it had sustained by a tie vote an affirmative ruling of the Oregon Supreme Court. Following this *Stettler v. O'Hara* decision, three other states, Puerto Rico, and the federal Congress acting for the District of Columbia had established special commissions with the power to set minimum-wage levels in accordance with subjective criteria of health and morality.

Wartime demands had brought tens of thousands of women into the labor force, where they enjoyed relatively high wages and augmented opportunity, if never equal pay for equal work with men, or equal opportunity to enter certain crafts and trades, restricted to men as often by custom and prejudice as by physical requirements. The Woman in Industry Service had proved competent, however, in winning for women special positions of economic influence not previously enjoyed. Women continued, in the postwar decade, to join the labor force, often to supplement the husband's income when it was insufficient to support the family at a decent level, until by 1929 over ten million women were gainfully employed where but eight million so labored at the end of the war. The ratio of working women to all women of working age in the nation remained roughly constant — approximately one to five.

With a total labor force pushing fifty million by the end of the decade, women constituted approximately one-fifth of all those employed. Millions of girls and married women worked in the service trades, of course, as waitresses or hotel domestics or telephone operators, as stenographers and as retail clerks; millions more were employed in textile mills, in the garment trades, and on the assembly lines of light industries, many of them, like the household appliance industries, new in the 1920's. The proportion of women working in a particular area of the economy changed but slightly within the decade: about a third of all working women were employed in domestic or personal service, a quarter in manufacturing, a fifth in agriculture, and a tenth in trade and transportation.

Motives for entering the labor force remained much as they had been before the war — to earn at least partial financial independence, to escape from household drudgery, to save up a little extra money before marriage, to find companionship and a more satisfying career than housewifery or spinsterhood offered, and above all necessity. Careful studies of the female working force made during the 1920's indicated that most women sought gainful employment outside the home because they had no alternative — they had to find a job or be thrown onto charity. Many working women were widows or victims of desertion; others were wives of chronically sick or unemployed husbands, or were married to men who could not command wages sufficiently high to supply the family's basic needs. The old notion that women worked for "pin money" was dispelled by studies that proved that most working women earned "the whole or a necessary part of the family income." In any case there was no wage differential between those who worked for the "extras" of life and those who drudged from sheer necessity. A very substantial number were not only wives but mothers of young children as well, driven out of the home into the labor market by the pressures of existence. One analysis, made in mid-decade at the very peak of prosperity, concluded that "the mother works because she has to work, and unless some other method of raising the family income is devised she is in industry to stay."[1] Another study of 728 working mothers in Philadelphia, made by Gwendolyn S. Hughes under the auspices of the Seybert Institution and the graduate department of Bryn Mawr College, indicated that 89 per cent worked from economic necessity — some to meet emergencies, sickness, or unemployment; more to meet regular household expenses.[2]

Although the Women's Trade Union League continued to seek better conditions for women workers through unionization and stepped up these organizational efforts toward the end of the decade, many reformers drew the lesson from long and often humiliating experience that only the rigid enforcement of regulative legislation could be counted on to alleviate the grievances which sprang from the excessive exploitation of the labor of women. Women workers for the most part were lacking in skill; they had few resources to fall back upon other than their availability for cheap labor; the organization of women into trade unions was "a slow and arduous process requiring long periods of time."[3] Frances Perkins added the salient observation, derived from hard factual analysis of female labor in the state of New York, that nearly three-quarters of all women factory workers were employed in plants with fewer than fifty workers; in these small plants the unionization of employees, never easy, was particularly difficult; and management in these small factories could rarely afford the luxury of enlightened or "scientific" policies.[4]

Some studies stressed the objective causes of exploitation and proposed specific remedies; other surveys stressed the subjective costs paid by working women and ultimately by society itself. Those who strained, day after day, month after month, on the assembly line or in sweated industries, before the loom or the sewing machine, could best testify as to what the pace of machine labor involved. Asked by the instructor of a course in remedial English, established by the Women's Trade Union League for immigrant working girls, to write compositions on their factory experience, the class responded with essays later compiled and edited for publication. Complaining of constant fatigue and depression, the girls noted that even the machines on which they toiled were rested and oiled; why, then, could not the same concern be shown for the health and vigor of the workers, whose energies were sapped often beyond repair. From experience they had learned the costs in health and character that excessive hours of labor under conditions of the stretchout and speedup exacted. From their evening classes, apparently, they had picked up a bit of basic economics as well. Maximum-hour legislation, they argued, would spread employment; minimum-wage legislation would increase purchasing power; enlarged leisure and purchasing power would promote sound prosperity throughout the entire economy. Rarely was the pragmatic argument for maximum hours, minimum wages, and full employment put more cogently in that decade.[5]

Confident that their cause was just and that their arguments were irrefutable, encouraged by the sense of organic community which the war had fostered, the reformers set out to consolidate their gains and advance into new frontiers of social action. The immediate goals were the achievement for women workers of an eight-hour day and a forty-eight-hour week, one day of rest in seven, and a prohibition on night work in every state in the Union. Massachusetts led the way with the passage of a forty-eight-hour bill in April 1919. Exemptions there were — of chambermaids, stenographers, and domestic servants — but the Consumers' League and the Women's Trade Union League were generally pleased. Their pleasure was short-lived. The pattern in New York soon proved different.

In New York, the Women's Joint Legislative Conference was able to win a nine-hour day and a fifty-four-hour week for a limited number of women workers in 1919, but subsequent attempts to broaden the coverage and to reduce the maxima were blocked by the Republican-dominated State Assembly. Probably in no other state was there quite such a vigorous proponent of protective labor legislation as Governor Alfred E. Smith, but neither his endorsement nor favorable action by the State Senate was ever sufficient to override the negative of the lower house. Up to Albany from New York City the women went to lobby, only to be rebuffed by arguments of the conservative speaker of the Assembly, Thaddeus Sweet, and others that labor legislation would increase costs and drive industry from the state. Florence Kelley might argue that the "orderly processes of the law" were to be preferred to "clumsy, costly, painful" strikes, but few seemed to fear that the alternative of direct action would be resorted to. "More leisure and more money women must have unless the public health and morals are to suffer irreparably," she protested; but the times seemed prosperous, and to the comfortable and complacent an enlargement of government power appeared not only inappropriate, but downright wicked.[6] Moreover, was not the liberty of employer and employee to bargain and make contracts a sacred freedom? Far from winning new gains, the reform groups had to throw all their resources into a struggle to block repeal of the prohibition on night work in some industries. Distraught and giddy from months of frustrating toil, the WTUL solemnly recorded in the minutes of the executive board, toward the end of the session in 1921, a bit of doggerel which labeled their foes as "tools" and "fools," as "bad" and "mad":

> They're overfed,
> And anti-red,
> And rave around like loons.
> They wave the flag,
> And chew the rag,
> But all of them are prunes,
> Prunes, prunes!
> Yes, all of them are prunes![7]

In 1924, Molly Dewson, formerly of the Consumers' League but now civic secretary of the Women's City Club of New York (whose vice president was Eleanor Roosevelt), carried through a survey of women workers to test their attitudes toward maximum-hour regulations. She reported her findings to bureaus of the state government and to the legislature — a substantial majority of working women desired a forty-eight-hour week, even if a cut in weekly income were involved. A bill put forward in 1926 was set aside and a study of the issue proposed in its place. When the special Industrial Survey Commission reported back, its recommendations included not only a forty-eight-hour week, but minimum wages and equal pay for equal work as well. With these recommendations before it, the state legislature reduced the maximum from fifty-four hours to fifty-one and adjourned.[8]

New York, not Massachusetts, set the pace for the nation. Here and there, partial gains were achieved. As often as not the gains were illusory or temporary as in Minnesota, for example, where a fifty-four-hour law was set aside by the State Supreme Court on a technicality; efforts to amend the bill to make it constitutional were unavailing. Over and over legislative committees and governors, ladies' clubs and associations of social workers were told that "Physical debility follows fatigue. Laxity of moral fibre follows physical debility."[9] But the nation's attention was focused on other issues; the nation's energies were consumed by other affairs. From the end of the war to the election of 1932, only two states added maximum-hour legislation where none existed before; substantial improvements of the regulations were won in twelve of the forty states which had statutes on the books by 1918.

At mid-decade, a special subcommittee of the WTUL, charged with re-evaluating the league's entire legislative program, acknowledged broad and increasing "dissatisfaction with legislation for women as a means to the end for which the Women's Trade Union League" was organized. Political action had become a "slow and painful process" of achieving reform. Perhaps it was time to consolidate forces and place emphasis again on the league's alternative line of action — the organization of women into unions. The board, after prolonged and bitter debate, finally accepted the recommendation to close its Chicago office and invest legislative moneys in one central office in the nation's capital, and acted at the same time to reopen the unionization campaign;[10] this activity will be traced in a later chapter.

If the women's reform associations had been able to hold the line on maximum-hour legislation and win a few slight gains from time to time, no such good fortune attended the parallel movement for minimum-wage statutes. The Consumers' League, the Trade Union League, and the American Association for Labor Legislation had seized the initiative during the years preceding America's entrance in World War I in coordinating the drive for state minimum-wage legislation. They had joined to persuade Massachusetts, in 1912, and eight more states the following year to establish minimum-wage commissions, with permissive rather than mandatory authority. By 1918, eleven states plus the District of Columbia and by 1923 fifteen states in all had regulations of some sort. There the matter rested. That moderate but nonetheless significant benefits had derived from this body of legislation the reform groups knew. The procedures of enforcement were often clumsy and rested as frequently upon the sanction of good will and enlightened public opinion as upon the coercive power of the state; but levels of wages for women had generally been raised, and the minima had not become maxima as some trade union spokesmen had feared. Ten years of experience, it was believed, gave ample evidence that higher wages had a clear bearing on health, moral decency, and industrial efficiency. Furthermore, it was argued, the extension of the principle was justified on the premise that employers properly should bear the costs that society otherwise had to assume in the form of charitable relief to those who broke down from ill health, fatigue, and insufficient income. The minimum wage was a means to prevent the delinquency and disease which, if unprevented, society would have to cure. To the employers it was said that regulations lessened labor turnover, increased worker morale and efficiency; no one, save the marginal, unscrupulous, and unfair producer, had anything to lose.

There was, of course, overt opposition to the extension of minimum-wage regulations. A move in Ohio by the Council of Women and Children in Industry (composed of representatives of the Consumers' League, the Women's Trade Union League, the Urban League, the YWCA, and the WCTU) was successfully blocked by the Ohio Manufacturers' Association. More often, however, the drive for minimum wages was diverted or stopped by apathy and unconcern, and by a widespread feeling that such legislation was of doubtful constitutionality. The Supreme Court of the state of Oregon had upheld minimum-wage legislation in two parallel cases, back in 1914, on the ground that the wages of women workers were a legitimate concern of the state in seeking to improve the health, morals, and general welfare of the community. But the tie vote by which the United States Supreme Court in 1917 sustained the Oregon decision certainly was no ringing mandate to encourage other states to act.

Then, in 1921, the constitutionality of the District of Columbia's minimum-wage act was challenged. The Consumers' League rushed to the defense. Molly Dewson was retained to prepare the factual material for the case, while Felix Frankfurter volunteered his services as counsel. Florence Kelley sensed at once that the crucial battle was at hand. Dropping everything else for the moment, she threw herself into the task of finding the money to underwrite the legal and research costs and to publicize the cause. There is "Merry Hell in general," wrote Mrs. Kelley to Adolf Berle, Jr., describing the office of the Consumers' League as the brief was finally being assembled. "Even Felix up in Cambridge is jumping high jumps twice daily," she added in a postscript.[11] In November 1922 the District Court of Appeals, by a vote of two to one, found the law null and void. The *Adkins* case was taken on appeal at once to the Supreme Court. But Florence Kelley was not hopeful. "There is no short road to Justice and Mercy in this Republic," she wrote dejectedly to an old friend.[12]

Mrs. Kelley's forebodings proved accurate. By five to three (Justice Brandeis again abstaining), the highest tribunal knocked down the District's act, sounding the "death knell" (as Felix Frankfurter said later in life) for all kinds of social legislation and inhibiting the launching of new welfare experiments.[13] Frankfurter had argued that the statute Congress had passed, sitting as the "state legislature" for the District of Columbia, fell well within the boundary of what was reasonable; it was not "arbitrary, wanton, or spoilative." That wages for women workers were considered to have a clear bearing upon health and morality was evidenced by many regulations of several states and by the action of nearly every industrial nation.

To George Sutherland, who had been recently added to the Supreme Court by President Harding, it was not all that clear. Drawing upon the ancient and honorable tenets of nineteenth-century individualism, Sutherland announced for the majority its conviction that minimum-wage legislation constituted arbitrary interference of the state in the private affairs of citizens competent to use their inviolable liberties in such ways as to promote the well-being and progress of society. The freedom of employers and employees to make a contract clearly was covered by the due process clause of the Fifth Amendment. As for the unanimous decision of the court in the Oregon case, the premises on which it rested no longer applied, for women, he argued, had gained a kind of equality with men that rendered special legislative protection for women obsolete. He cited the Nineteenth Amendment as proof that differences in civil status between men and women had reached the "vanishing point." The law was, in light of these historic changes, "a naked, arbitrary exercise of power."

To William Howard Taft, new chief justice, Sutherland's logic was deficient. "The Nineteenth Amendment did not change the physical strength or limitations of women upon which the decision in *Muller v. Oregon* rests," he wrote in dissent. Oliver Wendell Holmes, Jr., made a more elaborate attack upon the majority decision. "Freedom of contract" was nowhere to be found in the Constitution. The state had for generations legitimately restricted individual freedom; if legislatures deemed it essential that the government set minimum wages as well as maximum hours, the courts were obliged to accept their judgment as reasonable unless there were overwhelming evidence to the contrary. "It will need more than the Nineteenth Amendment to convince me that there are no differences between men and women or that legislation cannot take those differences into account." Irony and indignation availeth not; Sutherland spoke for the majority of five, and that was that.[14] Mary Dewson, who had labored for months on the case, recalled later in life the bitter conclusion of her legal comrade, Felix Frankfurter: "Molly, you must learn that if the U.S. Supreme Court says a red rose is green, it is green. That's final." [15]

John Kirby, in a cartoon for the *New York World*, depicted a gracious Justice Sutherland handing a scroll to a shabbily-dressed and dejected woman worker and saying: "This decision affirms your constitutional right to starve." Other comments were no more subtle. Even the usually mild-mannered and courtly Mr. Gompers announced that the court had "usurped" authority nowhere granted to it in the Constitution, and concluded that the "brutality of the majority decision can beget nothing but wrath." A more careful critic, Henry R. Seager, noted that five men had overridden three other justices, majorities of two houses of Congress and thirteen state legislatures, thirteen governors, the President of the United States, and many previous courts. It was left to the good gray feminist, Florence Kelley, to comment that not a single woman had participated in the judicial process at any point. Francis Bowes Sayre concluded that the traditional judicial practice of finding in favor of a law in the absence of substantial legal doubt had been violated by the majority. The decision, he said, indicated that the Supreme Court was arrogating to itself a veto power not unlike that exercised by a House of Lords. Governor Louis F. Hart of the state of Washington labeled the decision as infamous as the Dred Scott ruling and stated categorically that any business that could not pay a decent wage was not a desirable business. Governor Walter M. Pierce from Oregon (home of so many pioneer measures of social legislation) was more temperate, but perhaps more to the point: "It is neither humane nor wise socially to allow the untrained to become public charges or worse through lack of a living wage. It is detrimental to the future of individuals as well as the nation to permit child labor under improper conditions. Since the untrained and young cannot hope to stand up under the competition and demands of industry, only government had so far been able to afford them protection." Father John A. Ryan, one of the very first propagandists for the living wage principle, particularly in its application to women workers, blamed the court's ruling upon the persistence of nineteenth-century utilitarianism with its extravagant insistence upon the individual's freedom to do what he wished as long as the freedom of other autonomous individuals was not thereby limited; that such a philosophy was irrelevant in an industrial era, that its capricious application led to inhumane practices, was clear to him as to many others.[16]

Florence Kelley had been through enough battles to know that verbal protest alone was never sufficient to carry the day: the heavier artillery of action would have to be unloosed. Invitations were sent to reform association leaders and to state officials to confer jointly on how best to meet the emergency. On 20 April 1923 — Felix Frankfurter and Florence Kelley taking the lead — the delegates gathered in New York City to deliberate upon strategy. Jesse C. Adkins, chairman of the District of Columbia Minimum Wage Board, was there; so were representatives of law-enforcement agencies in this area of social legislation from Wisconsin, Washington, North Dakota, Minnesota, Massachusetts, and New York. Representatives were sent by all the major reform associations — the Consumers' League, of course, the Women's Trade Union League, the League of Women Voters, the National Catholic Welfare Association and the National Council of Catholic Women, the Child Labor Committee, the American Association for Labor Legislation, and the WCTU. The chief of the Women's Bureau, Mary Anderson, arrived; so too did Mary Van Kleeck, now with the Russell Sage Foundation; and Paul Kellogg of the *Survey*.

Felix Frankfurter led the discussion. There was little hope that the court would reverse itself in the near future, he observed. Justice Brandeis' vote could be counted on, of course, in cases on which he would not feel obliged to abstain; but otherwise the lines were drawn rather sharply for the moment. Sutherland was clearly hopeless; and as for Justice Butler, "He is a farmer, and spent from twenty to thirty years of his life in working up a practice [in law]. This is very confining and limited." His major recommendation, therefore, was to revise state minimum-wage legislation along the permissive lines of Massachusetts' law rather than try to incorporate mandatory provisions. In the meantime, he reminded the conference, the court had acted on the District of Columbia statute and nothing else. The "continued aggressive enforcement" of all state laws was absolutely essential. The court had always recognized local differences and until it specifically rejected state laws, the presumption that they were constitutional stood. The analysis and the conclusions were generally shared by the other delegates. F. A. Duxbury, chairman of Minnesota's Industrial Commission, resented, however, what seemed to him slurs on the integrity of Sutherland and Butler; respect for the law and for the courts was called for, even by those who could not agree with the decision. Father Ryan, who had joined Frankfurter in chiding Sutherland and Butler, replied that he had intended no disrespect, that he had merely wished to point out that the five justices were living in the eighteenth century. If any feelings were hurt, he was sorry but he felt it was hardly appropriate for him, above all others, to concur in any notion of judicial infallibility.

Out of the conference came no formal resolution, but only a general agreement. State laws should be enforced with vigor, as always. The suggestion that New York press for a permissive law, on the Massachusetts model, was endorsed. Further study of the economic and legal aspects of the decision would be made, and at once.[17]

Not satisfied with the inconclusive results of the April meeting, the WTUL called one of its own in mid-May, on the eve of the annual Conference of Social Work. Many of the groups represented at the April gathering sent delegates to this one as well. Mary Anderson set a tone of objective analysis, presenting evidence of the disparity in bargaining power that women workers suffered under, of the sub-standard wages that existed in states and in industries not covered by wage minima, and of the obvious relation between decent wages and community health. The presentation was forceful, if objective, but added little to the conclusions stated so cogently, although with so little practical effect, by Frankfurter and Dewson in the Adkins case. Dean Acheson was present to offer advice similar to Frankfurter's several weeks earlier — the states should continue to enforce their own minimum-wage laws; all interested groups should work unceasingly for a redefinition of due process of law along lines that would permit and encourage a reasonable extension of the state's police power. Other delegates were less patient. To wait for the Supreme Court to change its mind on what constituted reasonable regulations and proper procedures was to postpone indefinitely the enforcement of sound measures. Why not amend the Constitution, asked Molly Dewson, to authorize federal regulation of women's wages? Why so delimited a proposal, replied Maud Swartz for the Trade Union League? Why not work for an amendment which would grant broad powers to regulate conditions of labor, of men workers as of women? Elisabeth Christman and Rose Schneiderman, on the other hand, despairing of both judicial self-reform and the amendment procedure, demanded an energetic campaign to organize women into unions as the only valid course. Still others suggested that perhaps the time had come to limit the powers of the high tribunal to review both state and federal legislation.[18]

Divided counsel merely deepened the sense of demoralization. More than two decades of crusading had taught the reformers how to lobby, how to get around recalcitrant employers, how to by-pass stubborn legislative committees, how to stir up public support, how to argue the rule of reason before reasonable courts. It had not taught them how to react to hostile court decisions from which there was no appeal. For the moment they had lost both momentum and equilibrium. John R. Commons, accepting election as president of the Consumers' League in the autumn of 1923, summed it up exactly: "You find yourselves baffled and your work, at least an essential part of it, brought to a standstill by the recent adverse decisions of the Supreme Court" bearing upon child-labor and minimum-wage legislation.[19] Florence Kelley put it more picturesquely: "Truly we are like a semi-paralyzed centipede with its legs all moving at different rates of speed, if at all, and how few legs moving!"[20] In the middle years of the decade, she fell into the closing salutation when writing to intimate friends "Yours, *still* hopefully." But throughout 1923 and 1924, and on into 1925 when the child-labor amendment failed to win ratification, there was little cause for hopefulness. Reporting to the Board of Directors of the Consumers' League in October 1923, Jeanette Rankin, field secretary for the league in Illinois, reported that the "total legislative harvest" for that year was "a law adopting a state flower!"[21] And two years later, with reform still in eclipse, a Seattle lawyer confessed his discouragement to Mrs. Kelley: "the tide is running out now and all we can do is hold fast to our moorings until the tide turns."[22]

Mrs. Kelley was not about to accept the Supreme Court's negative actions as final and irrevocable. Other obstacles had yielded; the court could be circumvented or brought to its senses. The task was clear — to modernize the eighteenth-century Constitution in such ways as to make it possible to meet the new industrial demands of an urban civilization. Until the Constitution was transformed, and until the "court that interprets the Constitution" was modernized, it was "purely academic" to discuss industrial legislation.[23] The goal was clear enough, but not the means. Some advised an amendment authorizing Congress to re-enact by a two-thirds majority any federal statute found to be unconstitutional by the court. Others would require a two-thirds majority of the court to rule a state or federal legislative enactment null and void. (At various times the ante was raised to seven and eight judges, until finally a unanimous court was suggested.) A more widely favored proposal was to grant to Congress, by the amendment procedure, broad authority to act in the large arena of social legislation. The legalists tended to prefer persuading the courts, by trying one case after another, to adopt a more permissive attitude toward legislative experiments; judicial self-restraint, not coercive action against the court, was the more efficacious path, they insisted. A few hardy souls suggested enlarging the court to fifteen members, or eighteen; but with Harding and then Coolidge in the White House, what a later generation would know as "packing" the court did not win wide support among reformers who were disrespectful enough of the court as then constituted but were not foolhardy. Whatever means were explored, even Florence Kelley knew they were "far easier to name than to draft." [24]

For a while Mrs. Kelley leaned toward an amendment requiring a seven to two majority to find state and federal legislation unconstitutional, but her closest legal adviser, Felix Frankfurter, would have none of it. "The 7 to 2 proposal will not come off," he advised, "and at the rate at which the Sutherlands and the Butlers are being appointed to the Court, it wouldn't do any good if it did." [25] This proposal might have the backing of Senator Borah and Father Ryan, but it was "utterly hopeless" to expect that either a bill or an amendment so providing could ever be passed. It was unwise, in any case, to seek such a deceptively simple "mechanical remedy" for a complex legal dilemma. The point rather, Frankfurter continued, was to improve the quality of the court itself.[26] Roscoe Pound concurred. The amendment procedure was clumsy; "legislative revision of judicial action" was inadvisable. Ultimately the only proper means of securing the court's approval for social and industrial legislation, without jeopardizing other rights, was to persuade the justices to make a broader and more flexible interpretation of the due process of law provision and the police power. He recommended popular agitation for court reform, however, as one way to bring about "a better judicial frame of mind." [27] Zechariah Chafee added one final caveat — reformers should not forget, in their desire to limit property rights, that legislative bodies often limit personal rights; if a seven to two majority were required to set aside a law, a minority of three could block the unconstitutionality of laws subversive of civil rights.[28]

Agreement upon a single viable course of action was not to be had. The inadvisability of restricting the court's powers came to be abundantly evident. To wait for the court to change its mind seemed futile. In the meantime, as Florence Kelley noted, women and children remained exposed to exploitative actions of unscrupulous employers.[29]

A move to win agreement on a strategy of assault upon the court, in July 1924, was abortive.[30] Reformers by that time were focusing their energies upon the child-labor amendment and upon La Follette's crusade for the presidency. The court issue was relevant enough, there was just no way to bring the court to its senses without jeopardizing the equilibrium of government and the security of individual rights. Another battle had been lost, but not before the need for judicial self-restraint had been recognized by this handful of rebels. Almost every legal and political argument of the great court fight in 1937 was anticipated back in 1923 and 1924. Ultimately the issue was resolved as Frankfurter, Pound, Chafee, Freund, and Acheson had recommended — not by statute, not by amendment, but by the addition of new personnel to the court dedicated to a broader interpretation of social welfare and willing to accept legislative action as legitimate unless obviously unconstitutional beyond all reasonable doubt. The frontal assault upon the wisdom — and even, at times, the integrity — of the court may have helped to clarify the issues and thus served to prepare the way for the constitutional revolution that began in 1937.

As for practical and immediate achievements, there were few. The court continued on its path, undeflected by the feeble efforts of the critics. "Don't hurry away from the scene of battle," pleaded Florence Kelley to Molly Dewson in 1924. "So long as there is a *glimmering* chance of usefulness, that's the place to be."[31] Three years later, Mrs. Kelley confided to John R. Commons that their function should be study, research, publicity until the times should change: "Keeping the light on is probably the best contribution that we can make where there is now Stygian darkness."[32]

The candle was kept lit, and was set upon a hill. It was no floodlight or searchlight as long as the mood of normalcy prevailed, but it burned persistently. The motto of the Consumers' League continued to be implemented — "Investigate, Record, Agitate." Throughout the remainder of the decade, the league regularly remained in touch with state officials desirous of enforcing industrial minima. Effective regulation, however, all but collapsed. The voluntary, permissive arrangement in Massachusetts won partial advances for limited numbers of women workers but never more than that. And, at that, Massachusetts led the nation. Arizona's law was struck down by the Supreme Court in 1925, Arkansas' in

1927; local courts followed suit in Kansas and Puerto Rico; in Texas and Nebraska the laws were repealed; in Minnesota the attorney general ruled that its law was no longer enforceable. As late as June 1936, the United States Supreme Court in *Morehead v. Tipaldo* ruled that the *Adkins* decision was still controlling, this in negation of a 1933 New York State fair-wage law. Not until 1937 was the *Adkins* rule explicitly overridden.

Just as the Children's Bureau under Julia Lathrop and Grace Abbott was the coordinating agency of federal government in the field of child welfare, so the Women's Bureau under Mary Anderson played a similar role in parallel fields. Its central commitment was to the national community's obligation through government to protect the women of the land for the general good of society. With no regulatory laws to administer, it relied entirely upon "fact finding and fact furnishing" to achieve its ends. "Every movement making for reform needs a reservoir of reliable data upon which to draw and by which to be guided," an official publication of the Women's Bureau declared.[33] Through research and publication, speeches and reports, and sponsorship of conferences, and through cooperation with state labor bureaus and with voluntary associations, its influence was extended to every section of the nation. When the occasion demanded, it could call out a host of allies: the Women's Trade Union League, the Consumers' League, the League of Women Voters, the WCTU, the YWCA, the PTA, the General Federation of Women's Clubs, the American Association of University Women, church and labor union groups. These associations had been formed into a loose alliance in the Women's Joint Congressional Committee, the clearinghouse and coordinating federation which crusaded for maternal and infant health programs, the regulation of child labor, adequate appropriations for the Children's and Women's bureaus, welfare legislation for the District of Columbia, social hygiene, and public health. Mrs. Maud Wood Park, president of the League of Women Voters from 1920 to 1924 and Belle Sherwin, its president from 1924 to 1934, were among the committee's most effective and loyal leaders, but every other member group could also be counted upon to work with Grace Abbott and Mary Anderson within government for common objectives.

Of the making of committees, of course, there was no end; and committee meetings and resolutions can never be taken for effective action. With the best of intentions, women reformers often assembled determined to strike a blow for welfare only to play out a ritualistic role of protest. One woman reformer, long active in the WTUL, once wrote to a friend about the quality of committee work and rhetoric: "I was trying to *show* a dear old Boston lady how a rich man's *do-nothing* son was a worse tramp than the *other* tramps — 'Oh Mrs. Faxon, I don't believe you mean that.' — 'Yes, I do.' — 'O,' she says, 'I've heard people talk on committees like that!' — Now my family says whenever I *get to* talking — 'Now don't talk like a committee!' "[34]

There was a good deal of committee talk in the 1920's, particularly when the National Woman's party, a stridently feminist group that had fought for the Nineteenth Amendment, proposed still another amendment to the federal Constitution designed to remove all legal discriminations relating to sex. The proposed amendment took several forms during the decade, but the intent of its original phrasing persisted: "Men and women shall have equal rights throughout the United States and every place subject to its jurisdiction." Put forward by ladies drawn primarily from the wealthy and professional classes, the proposed amendment was viewed at once by a vast majority of women reformers as a measure subversive of all protective and welfare legislation. Florence Kelley, herself a suffragette and feminist, would have nothing to do with a measure that proposed to establish complete "legal equality of the sexes," when it was clear, on the face of it, that because of the special sexual functions of women they could not be afforded absolute equality of treatment without placing in jeopardy their hard-won legal right to special protection.[35] It would be "insanity," she wrote to Newton Baker, to follow the lead of Alice Paul and the Woman's party down a path that would utterly destroy maximum hours and minimum wages, mothers' pensions, and maternity insurance.[36] The proposal, moreover, was legally ambiguous: no one was really against "equal rights," Mary Anderson later recalled of the struggle, but what did "equal" mean and what really constituted "rights"?[37] For a generation women had benefited from legislation designed to protect them from "untrammeled exploitation," wrote Dean Acheson to Ethel Smith. "All this, to my mind, is now threatened by this sweeping prohibition of unnamed inequalities and disabilities." The courts were likely to rule, he warned, "that this new-won equality guarantees to women all the intolerable and anti-social conditions which their brothers in industry now enjoy."[38] What of the status of laws of desertion and nonsupport, queried Florence Kelley? What of the rules of illegitimacy, seduction, and rape? What of conscription in time of war? "Will husbands need to continue to support their wives?"[39] A special conference of women's groups, in early December 1921, arranged by Florence Kelley, concluded with Alice Paul's announcement that despite the fears of the reformers that, even if the amendment did not pass Congress, its agitation would imperil the whole movement for social legislation, the Woman's party was determined to press for its enactment and ratification.

From this point forward the dispute became increasingly embittered. Alice Hamilton set down her indignation in a draft letter to one of the "equal rights" proponents: "I could not help comparing you as you sat there, sheltered, safe, beautifully guarded against even the ugliness of life, with the women for whom you demand 'freedom of contract.'" Laundry workers, textile workers, "the great army of waitresses and hotel chambermaids, unorganized, utterly ignorant of ways of making their grievances known, working long hours and living wretchedly" would be left unprotected if the amendment carried. A sweeping amendment was not the proper means for removing the discriminations and legal disabilities of sex.[40] The main business of the Women's Industrial Conference, called by the Women's Bureau in January 1923, was interrupted by altercations over the amendment; the conference in January of 1926 was all but broken up by this hotly disputed issue. Sarah Conboy of the AFL fired a parting shot by publicly expressing her wish that the Woman's party ladies might be afforded the opportunity of working in mine and factory so they could learn first hand the problems of working women. Mabel Leslie reported to the Trade Union League that the Woman's party members were "merely theoretical ultra-feminists who [did] not have to work for a living."[41]

The squabble was of no particular significance — the proposed amendment never had a chance of serious consideration — except that it illustrates the kind of irrelevant wrangle which so often engaged the social reformers during the twenties. Their energies were often dissipated in countering charges of radicalism and subversion, and in this instance charges of antifeminism. The thousands of reform-hours consumed in fruitless and rancorous debate with the Woman's party represented time the reformers would have preferred to invest in other pursuits. Year after year, Mary Anderson recorded bitterly in her reminiscences, reform associations "had to lay aside the work they were doing to improve conditions for women and spend their time combating the equal rights amendment."[42]

Less spectacular but of surpassing significance was the workers' educational movement which was so often linked to the reform activities of women's associations in these years. The WTUL had pioneered during the years before the war in training potential trade union leaders in a program that Margaret Dreier Robins inaugurated in Chicago. Arrangements had been made for young working women to enroll as special students at Northwestern University and in the Chicago School of Civics and Philanthropy. Of the forty working girls from seventeen different trades who enjoyed formal course work from 1913 until the program was discontinued in 1926, nearly three-quarters remained active in trade union leadership, a record which the league took as justification of the time and money it had invested in the enterprise. The difficulty of integrating young working women, who were so often of recent immigrant origin and who so rarely had formal educational training, into university classes (even when conducted by such sympathetic professors as Paul Douglas) tended to vitiate the experiment, however, and this particular form of workers' education was never widely adopted.

Established in April of 1921, the Workers' Educational Bureau set out to stimulate and coordinate educational efforts of all sorts. Chaired by James H. Maurer, a functionary of the Socialist party and president of the Pennsylvania Federation of Labor, the bureau drew as well upon the diverse talents of such typical reform leaders as Fannia M. Cohn, of the International Ladies' Garment Workers' Union and the Trade Union League; John Brophy of the United Mine Workers and Abraham Epstein, then secretary of the labor education committee of the Pennsylvania Federation of Labor. Through the Workers' Educational Bureau and through the Brookwood Labor College which it helped to sponsor, the promotion of the ideas of industrial unionism and of political action by labor was achieved. Generally "leftist" in its leanings, the Brookwood Labor College, directed by A. J. Muste, trained a number of young trade union officials who would later contribute substantially to the formation of the CIO.

The major effort for the education of women workers came at the Bryn Mawr summer school, opened first in 1921 on the instigation of Mary Anderson, Hilda Smith, and Dr. M. Carey Thomas, president of the college. Hilda Smith, who later headed up workers' education in the WPA, was named the summer school's director. Raised in a devout Episcopalian household, Hilda Smith turned very early in her life to a career of social service. A graduate of Bryn Mawr in 1910, she had worked summers in settlement camps and had gone on to do casework with the Girls' Friendly Society and to take courses at the New York School of Philanthropy before returning to her alma mater as dean of the college in 1919. Under Miss Smith's direction from 1921 to 1934, the Bryn Mawr School for Working Women drew its students from the trade union movement, from local units of the WTUL and, in the South where trade unionism was unknown, from the YWCA. Here the students received courses in economics, government, the history of the labor movement, remedial social legislation, the causes and cures of unemployment, trade union procedures, public speaking, and composition. That the sessions offered a lively opportunity for curious young women is attested to by the mixture of ethnic and religious groups that composed the student body and by the excellence of its faculty which included outstanding experts like Paul Douglas, Alice Henry, Broadus Mitchell, Carter Goodrich, Colston Warne, Mark Starr, and Stephen Raushenbush. Dedicated to such objectives as widening the influence of the trade union movement, training the students in "clear thinking," stimulating in them "an active and continued interest in the problems of [the] economic order," and promoting "the coming social reconstruction," the Bryn Mawr school made a major contribution to the elaboration of concepts and leadership in the social reform movement.[43] The school had immediate practical consequences as was evidenced by the successful move on the part of the students to organize college employees and to win for them an eight-hour day not only during the summer session but during the regular academic year as well.[44]

The significance of the Bryn Mawr School for Working Women and similar programs conducted at Barnard (1927–1934), the Vineyard Shore School for Women Workers in Industry (1929–1934), and the Brookwood Labor College is difficult to measure. It is fair to suggest, however, that they kept alive a commitment to trade union activity; they trained many young men and women who were to become union and political leaders of some note during the depression decade; they kindled the aspirations of many young people in times of moral slump; they kept open the path of purposeful social change. Eleanor Roosevelt summed it up at a banquet honoring Dr. M. Carey Thomas, whose initiative had been crucial in the establishment of the Bryn Mawr school: If the New Deal were to win through to higher levels of life, the people must participate intelligently and constructively in social affairs. It was to this end that worker education had been directed, she said, toward giving "people the tools so that they [could] work out their own salvation wisely and well."[45] In so doing the workers' education movement contributed to the larger movement for reform.

Together, proponents of industrial minima, particularly for women and children, enlarged the rationale for legislative action, until by the end of the decade the philosophy of New Deal action in this arena had been elaborated in nearly every detail. Research notes of John R. Commons, made sometime in the mid-1920's, included an observation of Lord Northington's: "Necessitous men are not, truly speaking, free men, but, to answer to present exigency, will submit to any terms that the crafty may impose upon them."[46] The idea could hardly claim originality, but in the United States it did not, until the interwar era, receive much notice or elaboration. It came to be basic to every consideration by liberals whose central commitment was still to the enlargement of individual opportunity and freedom. Necessitous men, insecure men, men made anxious by low wages, uncertain employment, long hours at labor, and arbitrary industrial discipline were truly not free men. The establishment of industrial minima, of measures of social security broadly conceived, it followed, was essential to human liberty.

On the heels of this simple conclusion came another axiom — society, through government, had an obligation to force industry to bear its just burden of responsibility for community welfare. If industry paid substandard wages, argued Ethel M. Johnson in 1927, society would somehow in some way have to make up the difference. It might be through "hospitals and dispensaries to care for women who are broken down in health because they did not earn enough to permit them sufficient wholesome food and suitable living arrangements." Or it might be through charitable relief. A minimum wage assessed the burden upon industry where it belonged.[47] If floors under wages could be set by law or administrative ruling as a proper charge against industry, then it could be left to collective bargaining by unions to win living wages above that level.[48] Unless workers, particularly women workers, enjoyed these minimum guarantees, they could not build up reserves for sickness or unemployment. A woman employed at "oppressive" levels, below the minimum, thereby became a "liability rather than an asset to the community," and a burden upon society.[49]

Over and over the point was hammered home — industrial minima were required not alone as humanitarian considerations or as charity but as measures essential to the over-all long-run efficiency of industry, to community health and welfare, and to social stability and orderly progress. The New York Consumers' League offered as its slogan for 1927 "Social Justice Is the Best Safeguard against Social Disorder"; while Florence Kelley, commenting on the violent textile strikes of 1929, insisted that the only alternative to industrial disorder and social strife was "peaceful progress" through legislation.[50]

It was perhaps Newton Baker who best summarized the need for social action to remedy the grievances associated with intense industrialization. Given the growing impersonality of all society, the sanctions of civilization were not as easily applied as once they were. The role of voluntary associations, such as the Consumers' League, was to "investigate, record, agitate" in order that men of good will might act with the knowledge of the consequences of their behavior, while the law coerced the "recalcitrants." The league and its allies could show the way for society to accomplish "on a large and collective scale, in a collective way, that which we so delighted to do as individuals under simpler conditions."[51]

The New Deal drew heavily and specifically upon these concepts, which had grown out of progressivism and had been tempered in the 1920's. The depression afforded the occasion for their implementation, because economic crisis overrode most other considerations in 1933. The

National Recovery Administration prohibited child labor, and encouraged codes of labor standards governing hours, wages, and conditions for both women and men workers. When the NRA was broken, the industrial minima were rewritten in the Fair Labor Standards Act of 1938; and this time the Supreme Court concurred. The contribution of liberal reform in the 1920's had been to keep alive the progressive objectives, and then to modify them, extend them, and elaborate a rationale which, under the pressure of emergency, was incorporated as part of the New Deal consensus and program.

4

THE "CAUSE" AND "FUNCTION"
OF SOCIAL WORK IN
THE 1920's

"Whether we emphasize the elimination of evil or the establishment of a positive good as the objective of the cause, it seems to be true that once the elimination of evil is accomplished, once the new positive good is established, interest in it is likely to slacken. The momentum of the cause will never carry over adequately to the subsequent task of making its fruits permanent. The slow methodical organized effort needed to make enduring the achievement of the cause calls for different motives, different skill, different machinery. At the moment of its success, the cause tends to transfer its interest and its responsibility to an administrative unit whose responsibility becomes a function of well-organized community life.

". . . Zeal is perhaps the most conspicuous trait in adherents to the cause, while intelligence is perhaps most essential in those who administer a function. The emblazoned banner and the shibboleth for the cause, the program and the manual for the function; devoted sacrifice and the flaming spirit for the cause, fidelity, standards, and methods for the function; an embattled host for the cause, an efficient personnel for the function."

— Porter R. Lee, "Social Work: Cause and Function," Presidential
Address, National Conference of Social Work, 1929

"I have said that positive good is our goal. For the past dozen years the vital dominating thought in our social program, which even the destructive confusion of the Great War never blurred, but rather sharpened, has been this raising of life to its highest value. A more abundant life — the individual to become the best he can be — the community to become the finest and fullest expression of social life that it can be, with no one left behind: such is the goal that grows more clear before us. . . . The positive good, including as it does the earlier efforts mercifully to relieve and righteously to prevent evil, is our goal."

— Gertrude Vaile, "Some Significant Trends since Cleveland,
1912," Presidential Address, National Conference
of Social Work, 1926

VOLUNTARY associations, most of them born during the Progressive Era, had remained faithful to the cause of reform throughout the 1920's. Often buffeted and disappointed, they continued to play out their prophetic role, proclaiming the need for remedy and alleviation, for prevention and for cure. While seeking to consolidate old gains and extend them, they pioneered new experimental lines of social action. Some of these "social engineers," as they often thought of themselves, died or turned to other interests and careers; but most of them stayed on the job. Florence Kelley, Lillian Wald, Margaret Dreier Robins, John B. Andrews, Owen R. Lovejoy, Paul U. Kellogg, John R. Commons, Frances Perkins, Felix Frankfurter — these were substantial middle-class and professional men and women, many of them of independent means, who continued to seek all the old humanitarian goals. If the means they proposed in the postwar era were sometimes novel, the postulates from which they proceeded and the forces which moved them were in the main stream of the social reform tradition.

Of long-standing experience as well were diverse groups of welfare agents who gradually came to conceive of themselves as social workers rather than reformers and to prefer "social service" to "social reconstruction." They constituted the paid staffs of all manner of charitable and remedial welfare organizations (some of them national associations with local units and affiliates, some purely local groups): the Children's Aid Society, the Society for the Prevention of Cruelty to Children, the Child Welfare League of America, the Association for Improving the Condition of the Poor, the Institute of Public Service, the American Association for Organizing Family Social Work, the Charity Organization Society, the Legal Aid Society, the YMCA and the YWCA, the Urban League, the Juvenile Protective Association, the Associated Jewish Charities, the

Red Cross, the settlement and neighborhood houses, to cite representative illustrations from a list of hundreds of such welfare organizations.
On many occasions, these workers had formed common cause with the
reformers. Indeed in the years before World War I the difference between reformers on the one hand and social workers on the other was
often difficult to discern, for their functions had not yet become as dis-
tinctly separate as they were to be in the next generation. The original
labors of social workers, in the nineteenth century, could be summarized
under the headings of the association they had formed back in 1874, the
National Conference of Charities and Correction, but early in the twentieth century they turned increasingly to prevention rather than alleviation or cure and exposed conditions that made organized charity
necessary. Porter R. Lee recalled in 1926 that progressivism had inspired
men and women to social reform as well as to social service. These welfare workers constituted a cadre "with a clear perception of the cost
of human misery, abiding faith in the possibility of reducing it and the
prophet's power to tell the story in a way which fired the imagination
and enlisted the support of the rank and file of men." Out of social service
came the broad acceptance of social responsibility on the part of the
public, whether that sense of obligation was implemented through private agencies or through governmental bureaus.[1]

In 1912, social reformers joined with social workers, through the Committee on Standards of Living and Labor of the National Conference of
Charities and Correction, to propose a platform of "Social Standards
for Industry," which in turn strongly influenced Roosevelt's Confession
of Faith and the platform his Progressive party endorsed. (Paul Kellogg
had been named the committee's chairman in 1909, Florence Kelley had
taken charge in 1911, and in 1912 Owen Lovejoy served as chairman and
Margaret Dreier Robins as vice chairman.) The platform called for a
living wage, reasonable hours of labor, government regulation of industrial conditions, the prohibition of child labor, and systems of social insurance to cover the hazards of industrial accidents and occupational
disease, sickness, old age, and unemployment. Adopted by the conference delegates in June, the platform was carried to Theodore Roosevelt
by Paul Kellogg, Henry Moskowitz, and John Kingsbury. When Roosevelt embraced its essential planks, distinguished reformers and social
service workers rallied, in turn, to his cause. Settlement leaders led all

others in their devotion to the progressive crusade — Jane Addams, Mary Simkhovitch, Harriet Vittum, Graham Taylor, Mary McDowell, and Robert Woods, most notably. The social reformers were well represented by Mary Dreier and Margaret Dreier Robins, Raymond Robins, Owen Lovejoy, Samuel McCune Lindsay, and Paul Kellogg. The social service agencies were represented by Homer Folks, then president of the New York State Probation Commission and for many years a leader in State Charities Aid work; Frances Kellor, secretary of the New York State Bureau of Industries and Immigration; Frederic Almy, secretary of the Buffalo Charity Organization Society; and John Kingsbury, director of the New York Association for Improving the Condition of the Poor. The alliance of social reformer and social servant in this period was an intimate one, cemented by common cause and by long friendship. Set back by Roosevelt's failure to recapture the presidency in 1912, it nevertheless continued to function in the Wilson administration, seeking enactment and extension of the 1912 program. But American participation in the Great War carried its members into diverse fields of activity and service; when the guns were silenced and the return to family and career was effected, it proved difficult to re-establish the informal cooperation that had marked the prewar era.

The climate of the 1920's was just not hospitable to the extension of reform measures, as we have seen, or to the initiation of new programs. Twice the Supreme Court knocked down congressional statutes prohibiting child labor while the child-labor amendment went begging for support. The courts whittled away at the labor sections of the Clayton Act until union labor enjoyed fewer rights than perhaps ever before in its modern history. With a few exceptions, legislative proposals for social welfare were met with indifference, disinterest, or hostility, whether in national or state government. To social reformers the strategy was perfectly clear — keep on the firing line, study and agitate and propagandize, beat tactical retreats when necessary, engage in flank attacks, never for a moment surrender the initiative, and wait for the breaks. The line of action was less clear to the social workers, but most of them returned to careers of professional welfare service, leaving for odd moments the task of reconstruction.

Some few leaders tried to combine, in even balance, the tasks of reform and service, of cause and function. Frank J. Bruno — like so many of his generation of social workers a minister of the Gospel before he became a minister to human needs — was one such leader. Trained at Yale Divinity School, he served as pastor of several Congregational churches in Connecticut and Colorado, stepping over into social welfare in 1907 when he became executive secretary of the Associated Charities in Colorado Springs. Before he moved on into the field of social work education, in 1925, he served for ten years as general secretary of the Associated Charities of Minneapolis and, during his last year in the Twin Cities, as chairman of the Minnesota Committee on Social Legislation. He summarized for his committee that year the crisis they faced together. The one overriding feature of contemporary politics, he said, was "the terrific reaction against all attempts to say by law what people shall do or shall not do." Every attempt to better social conditions was met by the rejoinder "You cannot make people moral by legislation." The reactionary mood he attributed to several sources, most importantly the postwar letdown. The "let-down from idealism and from the sacrifices stimulated by war psychology, but especially the facing of the cold facts of social results so different from what was promised in the heat of conflict, deadens the sensibilities and discourages the generous impulses of most men." Added to this slump in morale was the hysteria which marked the immediate postwar years. The shortcomings of prohibition tended to deepen the disappointment of Americans who sought reform through legislation. Everywhere — from business, from politics, even from the churches — there was opposition to welfare measures of all sorts, but the need for social legislation had in no way lessened. Social workers knew better than any other group the enormous "cost of unsocial behavior." The costs would accumulate and the needs would persist because the forces making for "the breakdown of our simple communities," and the substitution of "huge, incoherent, badly stratified ones" would proceed apace unless blocked by programs for social reconstruction. Professional social workers, then, Bruno insisted, had obligations beyond service to a particular agency or bureau; they had the obligation to study the causes of poverty and exploitation, to measure their costs, to engage in "propaganda" (or "interpretation" if that phrase was less objectionable), to assist in the drawing of technically sound bills, and to lobby for their enactment.[2]

Frank Bruno by no means stood alone. In many states conferences of social workers regularly devoted time and energy to the tasks of social reconstruction which transcended the routine duties of welfare agency employees. The role of the social worker remained ambiguous, nevertheless, throughout the decade of normalcy. The public itself was not quite certain what its response to the social workers should be. The story was told, toward the end of the decade, of a social worker who, having heard complaints from her club girls of being pestered in a neighboring park and guessing that they may have been "meeting the boys half-way," set out on a field experiment to test her hypothesis. Dressing herself in the style of her club girls, she stationed herself on a park bench to await results. Nothing happened at all until she was approached by a man who addressed her: "Say lady, if you want to pick up anybody around here, you'll have to leave off them ground-gripper shoes."[3] The story was undoubtedly apocryphal, but truthful if not true, and spoke to the problem of identification that social workers suffered in the twenties when it was not clear either to the public, to the clients, or to the welfare workers themselves whether they were "officious and · ground-grippered, or . . . saintly and sacrificing, or . . . repressed and revolutionary," as one agency official complained in 1930.[4]

From the many diverse specialties that made up social work (as distinguished from social reform groups) in the 1920's, we may safely conclude that it was then (as always) in a period of transition. Composed of tens of thousands of practitioners, both amateur and professional, in hundreds of different fields of activity, employing many varied techniques, social work did not present a united front. Admitting that social work cannot be treated as a single entity, recognizing that variety and diversity were its most distinguishing features, the student of the 1920's can nevertheless see certain main lines of development in that postwar era.

One important development was the new and widespread concern with winning professional status. It was in 1917, long after the philosophical base of welfare work had shifted in emphasis from amelioration to cure and from cure to prevention, that the National Conference of Charities and Correction changed its name to the National Conference of Social Work. (A second shift in designation to the National Conference on Social Welfare was made in 1956. That title had been proposed in 1917 and voted down by a narrow margin.[5]) In the same year, 1917, a National Social Workers' Exchange was created which, four years later, was transformed into the American Association of Social Workers (AASW), a group whose primary objective was to define and secure professional standards for social work. Accompanying these movements was the creation of professional social work schools: whereas in 1915 there were but five, by 1930 at least forty were going concerns. Consistent with these developments the New York School of Philanthropy was renamed the New York School of Social Work in 1919, and in 1920 the Chicago School of Civics and Philanthropy became the Graduate School of Social Service Administration.

Dr. Abraham Flexner, at the 1915 Conference of Charities and Correction, had suggested criteria by which the progress of an occupational group toward professional status might be measured: the existence of formal educational training, both theoretical and applied; the development of a specialized body of knowledge and of special techniques and methods of procedure; the establishment of standards under the supervision of state governments; the creation of professional associations; and the elaboration of codes of ethics and practice.[6] Toward each of these goals social workers strained in the 1920's. The American Association of Social Workers, for example, concerned itself with the task of defining the various specialized areas of social work, with recruiting able young men and women into social work careers, with improving salaries and status, with drawing up codes of ethical practices, with inaugurating special schools and short courses for workers already in the field. It maintained an exchange for job placement. It attempted to define both the responsibilities and the rights of agency workers, whether private or public, and insisted on the right of social workers to participate in policy making as well as in policy execution. It sought to establish objective standards for the accreditation of professional schools and the certification of trained personnel. The tasks were not easy. Everyone working for a service agency was clearly not a qualified social worker, but who was to determine the training required or the competence for professional certification? Thousands of workers had grown up in their jobs; were they to be denied membership in the American Association of Social Workers because they could not meet abstract and often arbitrary standards? The files of at least one social worker engaged in organizing and running a local chapter of the AASW — Catheryne Cooke

Gilman of the Northeast Neighborhood House in Minneapolis — were jammed with correspondence, minutes, memoranda bearing on all these problems, but particularly concerned with the single issue of defining eligibility for membership.[7]

The desire for professional status was assuredly legitimate. The raising of standards in training and performance undoubtedly took place. The costs of this professional preoccupation are not so easily assessed; but in retrospect certain conclusions can be drawn. In so far as social workers focused upon new methods and techniques, especially in casework and in the new and exciting field of psychiatry, their attention was concentrated on procedure and the adjustment of the individual to his environment, rather than on the transformation of the social environment within which the individual lived. Where professionalization demanded specialization, the field of vision was invariably narrowed for all but the most discerning and most broadly concerned workers. Specialization required objective and scientific attitudes toward both the problem area and the client himself. Enthusiasm for reform was not high among the qualities making for success in research, theoretical or applied. For many social workers the new path toward "social betterment" had become "scientific, constructive, rather than emotional and 'charitable.'"[8] A kind of professional myopia, then, was often the consequence of specialization.

Writing in 1928 about these trends, Abraham Epstein bemoaned what he saw as the loss of missionary zeal in reform and welfare work. Social workers had come to concern themselves with means rather than ends; the recurring concept, in casework and in counseling, was "adjustment"; agency workers had given but halfhearted support, if that, to the mothers' pension movement (many, indeed, had been downright opposed) and but casual support to the child-labor amendment crusade. The only spirited enthusiasm they evidenced, Epstein complained, was during the annual "zip-zip" community chest drives for funds.[9]

Porter R. Lee, a prominent social work educator, saw these trends in a different light. In his presidential address before the National Conference of Social Work in 1929, Lee took note of the movements for the prevention of social evil and need and commented that when the reforms had been won and consolidated they were then institutionalized — cause became function. The winning of reform had called for enthusiasm, sacrifice, and the exercise of prophetic virtues; but the administration of reform, in the twenties, called for other qualities — intelligence, prudence, efficiency, accountability. The loss of reform zeal was not, by implication, to be decried; the day of the zealots had been fulfilled, now the need was for administration and organization.[10]

Other forces within social work distracted the profession from a concern for social action. The growing size of institutional operations, for example, often meant that the individual worker was caught up in a bureaucratic routine that afforded little opportunity for observing more than a thin segment of a problem. In her presidential address to the National Conference of Social Work in 1926, Gertrude Vaile attributed the decline of crusading leadership to the emergence of a new kind of institutional leader, more an administrator and an organizer than a person likely to be distinguished by penetrating insight or broad social vision.[11] Agency executives and board leaders had always played the dominant role in policy matters of course, but many individual social workers nevertheless felt a diminution of their own influence because of the increasing bureaucratization of welfare work. Further, as Karl de Schweinitz observed, looking back upon these trends that set in about the time of World War I, the social worker came to be sheltered from criticism and the requirement that he justify his policies and articulate his programs to a broad audience of his peers; and there followed a loss of "independence and invigoration inherent in debate and the urging of our cause."[12] The trend toward institutional bigness was evidenced everywhere in society — in government, in business, in labor, in welfare. Everywhere the organization was taking over. In time, it was possible to meet in part the problems posed by bureaucracy, to work out procedures through which the main echelon of workers could participate in helping to formulate the policies which they executed; but to many leaders in the 1920's the prospect was discouraging. Dr. Richard C. Cabot, who had introduced professional social work into the outpatient service of Massachusetts General Hospital before the Great War and was later to lecture at Harvard University in the field of social ethics, wrote to Gertrude Vaile, after reading her address in which the perils of organization had been suggested, to support her major thesis. If bigness is inevitable, he said, then surely we are "doomed." Personality and leadership developed "only in solitude and in small groups." There was an inverse ratio between size of operation and its spirit or morale. "Christ had twelve not twelve hundred. . . . *Things have got to get smaller*, not bigger," he concluded, "or evolution will mean degeneration."[13]

Of all the forces making for professional parochialism during the 1920's, perhaps none was more significant than the new developments in psychology. Looking back across the decade from the vantage point of 1930, Paul Kellogg, editor of the *Survey*, observed that in "recoil" from progressivism and war, in the years of "postwar sag," social workers had turned to "individual readjustment" rather than to social reform. "The drama of people's insides rather than the pageantry of their group contacts and common needs were foremost."[14] Psychology and psychiatry opened a new frontier. The new psychology forced an awareness of the complexity and the inwardness of many problems; it portrayed man as moved less by rational considerations than earlier generations had believed; it seemed to deny the existence of will and consciousness, reason, and moral values.

That the new psychology had positive and constructive contributions to make, particularly in child and family welfare, is now abundantly clear. If social psychiatry offered no panacea, neither did it endanger the client's integrity as some critics had claimed. It did, however, force a concern with the individual and his total well-being and, by so doing, de-emphasized the older concern with all those social arrangements that deprived the person of opportunity and liberty. As a casework device it had great virtues when properly applied; it provided tools for what was known as "supportive listening" and nonauthoritarian direction, and thus often helped the individual client to find his own way to a solution of his problems. At the same time — and that generation of social workers trained in an older tradition could never accept this — it focused on problems other than those of economic dependency, and this at a time when social environmental problems persisted as a primary source of the difficulties toward the eradication of which social work was presumably dedicated. Isaac M. Rubinow, pioneer in the field of social security, writing in 1929 of those social workers who had accepted the findings of the new psychology and psychiatry, concluded: "To a very large extent they have substituted the concept of personal inadequacy and individual maladjustment for the theory of the responsibility of the

environment." Poverty and economic and social need had not disappeared, even in prosperity, he argued; and he chided his colleagues
who held forth "readjustment" when what the client more often required was release from economic dependency.[15] As the nation plummeted into panic and depression, an old-line reformer, John A.
Fitch, reminded his associates how inadequate the craze of psychological adjustment had been to the solution of welfare problems. It is true, he
said before the National Conference of Social Work in 1930, that "insufficient income" was not alone the source of personal maladjustment,
but such maladjustment could be understood only in the broad context
of the individual's total environment and "far the most important element in the social environment is the degree of mastery or lack of it
possessed by the individual . . . over those aspects of life that are
economic in character."[16]

It is probably incorrect to conclude — as a labor educator did in 1930
before a social welfare gathering — that social work had "gone psychiatric in a world which has gone industrial."[17] But this movement
away from reform toward adjustment, together with the growing specialization within social work, the increasing bureaucratization of its
functions, and its passion for professional stature, undoubtedly contributed greatly to the quieting of enthusiasm for broad social action.
For better or worse, the interests of social work were different in the
1920's from what they had been a generation earlier or would become
a decade later.

Those social reformers who had stood with Theodore Roosevelt at
Armageddon and battled for the Lord felt uneasy with what they believed to be the impersonality and blandness of the twenties. At annual social work conferences, sessions on professional standards, on
special phases of social work, on mental health and social psychology,
on public relations and administration began to predominate. In 1921,
Allen T. Burns called for the organization of social forces as well as the
organization of social work, but his plea was received with only mild
politeness. By 1923, it was reported that the old alms and charity delegates had all but disappeared, and in their place were younger delegates, trained workers, intensely empirical and pragmatic in outlook.
Julia Lathrop, grand old lady of social work and social reform, brought
before the conference that year a series of resolutions on peace, prohibition enforcement, child-labor and minimum-wage legislation, and

amnesty for political prisoners. They were received with applause and with the respect and devotion which Miss Lathrop had won through years of leadership to these causes, but a rule against consideration of social policy resolutions was upheld by the chair, and the conference turned to other issues. To a disconsolate reporter of the 1926 conference, it seemed that all the old enthusiasm had departed forever. The delegates, he wrote, were seeking "to build up, by organizing and rationalizing, a sense of professional separateness, identity, coherence. But in the end they are 1926-model Americans. And as such they share the spiritual lethargy of 1926 America, which is itself a sign of spiritual confusion and conflict." Not even Jane Addams, who gently chided her fellows for playing it safe, could arouse much excitement. At the plenary sessions the delegates "sang as decorously as suburban Presbyterians." Technique and method, procedure over substance, seemed to be the themes that year. The conference demonstrated "too little deep feeling"; there was, he concluded, a general feeling of unease and insecurity.[18] Surface complacency was far more the sign of internal conflict than of disinterest.

What remained largely unrecognized then as now, however, was that a new understanding was arising out of new circumstances and out of the confrontation of new problems and new ideas. Particularly was this evident in casework, a phase of social work that rapidly matured in the 1920's owing largely to the surpassing influence of a frail little pioneer in that field, Mary E. Richmond, who throughout her life had to overcome chronic invalidism in order to help others. Rarely is it that to a single person or a single monograph can be attributed a major advance in any field as complex as casework; but for Mary Richmond such claims can be made. As a young woman she had found what would later be designated as family casework in the hands of volunteers, charitable "friendly visitors." Within a generation, by printed word, by word of mouth, and by her remarkable personal influence, Miss Richmond brought to the field professional standards, a new expertise, and a new philosophy, all soundly based in painfully detailed research, practical experimentation, and broad reading in allied social and psychological studies. Among her contributions, many of which were widely adopted in the years following publication of *Social Diagnosis* in 1917, must be counted the synthesis of diverse and sometimes apparently contradictory themes.

In the process of working out professional and scientific standards for casework practice, where amateurish philanthropic programs had prevailed, there had sometimes crept in cold formality and dehumanization. Miss Richmond, working together with other leaders, was able to restore a human perspective while, at the same time, adding insights from sociology and psychology. Consideration of immeasurable subjective factors, she insisted, was vital to an understanding of the client's problems. The older paternalistic relationship she rejected on grounds that it rendered the client dependent upon the caseworker; self-reliance and self-dependence were the proper goals, and these were achieved by working with the client so that he could be led toward self-understanding and toward self-help. Respect for the integrity and potential dignity of the individual, together with acknowledgment of the infinite variety of persons and the infinite complexity of each problem, was central to her thought. As for the division between social reform and social work, Miss Richmond saw it as false. The enthusiasm for a transformation of society, which had been so marked among many of her associates in the prewar years, she confessed she had not been able to share. Social reformers, she wrote in 1925, had been sure "that legislation and propaganda, between them, would render social work with and for individuals quite unnecessary." Prevention of social dependency had been their proper objective to be sure, but poverty and human need could not be repealed. Legitimate and necessary as social reform was, there would always persist the need for individual treatment.[19] As an associate put it, social action dealt in wholesale, casework in retail reform. Both were essential.[20]

The momentum of Miss Richmond's influence, which had been gathering force since the turn of the century, carried over into the postwar era. But as social work turned toward psychological factors and tools it swerved away from the kind of sociologically oriented casework techniques that Miss Richmond had pioneered. Ignominiously defeated for the presidency of the national conference in 1922, she lived on for several years to see many of her devices of analysis and treatment severely challenged. But however passé the specifics of her case procedures may have seemed to many of the younger generation, her balanced approach toward service and action continued to inform social work generally. Following her lead, caseworkers in the 1920's could concentrate with equal facility on helping the individual client to find his own way to self-dependence and on working for protective legislation which would uplift family life generally, especially for those millions of families who lived along the margin of decent existence, by rooting out the causes of dependency, exploitation, and social insecurity. Gertrude Vaile put it in religious terms: as God loves each person, with full knowledge of his limitations and potentialities, so must the caseworker take people "where they are, with deep knowledge and constant remembrance of their difficulties and weaknesses," and strive to open up opportunities and enable the individual and his family to do the best they can.[21]

In the general field of social work, a new philosophy was being worked out, less out of study and research than out of the day-by-day, month-by-month application of old programs and the elaboration of new. Once amelioration of grievance and the correction of those who had fallen away from what society expected of them had been the chief objectives of charitable and philanthropic work; emphasis on the cure of personal failings and social evils had followed; and from cure, social work had moved into prevention through measures designed to enlarge social justice. In the process of moving from "humane care, the correction of abuses and neglect" to preventive measures, Homer Folks noted in 1923, the profession had advanced from charity to service.[22] During the Progressive Era, in response to those developments, the state began to assume an ever larger responsibility for meeting the minimal needs, at least, of all members of society. Informed by new attitudes toward society, and moved by religious and secular forces of humanitarianism, progressives found the source of human troubles in the environment and sought to eradicate evil and injustice through social reform. The point was to prevent trouble by overcoming its causes. Moving from palliation to prevention, voluntary welfare agencies "saw at first hand the effects of bad housing, lack of recreation, the blight of tuberculosis, the adverse effects of child labor," wrote one social work educator, Leonard Mayo, at mid-century, "and they gave voice to the resulting needs and became articulate concerning the causes of such disorders and defects in society."[23]

The 1920's were marked by a subtle advance from the prevention of social ills to more constructive measures which sought the positive creation of a freer, fuller, more secure, and "more abundant life." This insight Gertrude Vaile had expressed in her presidential address before the national conference in 1926. The profession's aim now was to extend the opportunity to all members of the community to share in enlarged virtues and participate actively in the building of a fully just society and a fully radiant life. If earlier steps forward had called for inspiring crusaders (she named Jane Addams, Graham Taylor, Robert Woods, and Florence Kelley among others), the present need was for "a widely diffused decentralized leadership." By way of illustration Miss Vaile cited recent developments in the field of health. Earlier generations had labored first to care for the sick and to cure illness, then to control and prevent epidemics, and to eradicate the sources of public infection. The new trend was toward well-baby clinics, health education, instruction in cleanliness and diet, periodic examinations, and even health insurance.[24] She might have illustrated with equal force from developments in child welfare, in which reformers had moved from negative regulation (the prevention of exploitation) to programs of enriched education, recreation, vocational training, child guidance, special treatment of juvenile delinquents, and to programs (especially in the settlements, and in the scouting and 4-H movements) in the arts, music, theater, sports, and camping.

The shift in emphasis from preventive to constructive measures was not immediately or widely recognized; the two phases of social welfare were, after all, mutually interdependent and overlapping, and many social workers were still legitimately engaged in care and cure. The concept, moreover, if not its broad acceptance, antedated the 1920's. Jane Addams, always a lively jump ahead of most of her contemporaries, had suggested the point in her presidential address before the national conference in 1910: "The negative policy of relieving destitution, or even the more generous one of preventing it, is giving way to the positive idea of raising life to its highest value."[25] To this goal Miss Addams and many of her associates had dedicated their careers, but it was not until the postwar era that her vision came to be widely shared by social work practitioners in settlement work and in other fields as well. In the National Playground Association, for example, and in the National Society for the Promotion of Industrial Education as in the Child Welfare League and its forerunners, social welfare leaders sought nothing less than the democratization of the opportunity for a full and rich life, what would come to be called the enfranchisement of personality. In the 1920's workers engaged in the often routine business of welfare were everywhere becoming more aware that the mere prevention of social ills was not in itself enough; beyond amelioration and beyond prevention lay the need to build a finer community. The forces of social disorder and community disintegration had somehow to be overcome, not by regulation, but by seeking what William James had called a "moral equivalent," whether to war or to injustice. Just as all the community forces had been mobilized for war and military victory, so should society mobilize for the arts of peace. The need was to overcome the divisive forces of class and race and religion, to restore the community to wholeness, to relieve urban congestion, to organize industry along democratic lines so that those who labored could participate in all the decisions that vitally affected their lives. Was progressive technology in industry attended by job dislocation, unemployment, and a loss of a feeling of creativity on the part of the assembly-line worker? Then society had an obligation to provide subsistence during times of unemployment, to ease the worker's transition to other industries or jobs, and to find means to fill the vacuum of his life.

"Social work has its roots in the Christian doctrine — in the democratic doctrine — that all men are brothers and equal in the sight of their Creator," wrote Robert W. Bruère in 1923. There were no limits, therefore, he concluded, to the concern that the profession must feel for all aspects of individual well-being and community welfare. It must act to relieve individual need and assist in personal self-realization; it must seek remedial and regulative legislation; it must collaborate with those who felt the "irrepressible urge" toward "industrial government." [26] Mary Van Kleeck, who after establishing the Woman in Industry Service during the war had moved on to do industrial social research for the Russell Sage Foundation, urged the same breadth of vision and action. The social worker, she wrote to Lillian Wald, must advance "better community organization" while at the same time working to restore to usefulness the individual member of society who had "failed to measure up to his social responsibilities" whatever the cause.[27] John A. Lapp of the National Catholic Welfare Conference felt the same compulsion: "It would be a travesty on modern social work to make of social workers merely the salvage corps of a savage and unrestricted industrialism." Social action was required all along the line to ameliorate social ills and promote community betterment.[28]

Homer Folks, who stood substantially to the political right of Lapp,

Van Kleeck, and Bruère all of whom had reputations as "social radicals" in the 1920's, concurred in their belief in the constructive mobilization of the total resources of society for community welfare. Addressing the Council of Social Agencies in Ithaca, New York, in 1928, he took as his theme the conservation of human resources. Social policy, he argued, should never presume to tell an individual what he should do or what he should become; it should provide, however, through constructive measures a "fair and even chance" for every individual. If through group action the individual could be made more secure against social hazards over which, acting alone, he had no control, his opportunity for self-realization and for success was, to that degree, enhanced. The community should seek not only to restrict unsocial behavior but to open up new avenues of opportunity.[29] On other occasions he hammered at the same points. Those who thought of family aid in terms of relief alone had little concept of the constructive possibilities involved in aid to dependent mothers and children, in the visiting nurse and visiting teacher service. Assistance, properly given, offered care and helped to forestall ill health and prevent educational deficiency; it also strengthened the family as the basic unit of society and opened up new avenues of opportunity. The legitimate end of social work assistance was "releasing the best energies of individuals by giving them an assurance of security and opportunity." From such programs society as well as the individual benefited. "Human happiness *per se*" was a proper concern of the social worker, whose function it was to guarantee that every man, woman, and child had the chance to live "happy and useful lives" free from the burden of social deprivation.[30]

In nearly every phase of social work there were spokesmen for this new point of view. In child welfare, perhaps most notably, the belief was widely expressed that while child-saving, restrictive laws were essential, they merely provided the opportunity for constructive growth. In the field of public welfare, similarly, horizons were broadened to include constructive as well as remedial and preventive programs — the fullest possible development of human resources. Howard W. Odum proclaimed that public welfare could accomplish over the next generation what public education had earlier won, "the technique and means for making democracy effective in unequal places."[31]

Eduard C. Lindeman, whose primary contribution was to educational and recreational work with rural youth in the 1920's, made significant contributions as well to broadening the philosophical bases of social work as a professor at the New York School of Social Work and to community understanding and reform as a member of the Commission on Race Relations of the National Conference on the Christian Way of Life (better known as the "Inquiry"), sponsored by the Federal Council of Churches. To the influence of Lindeman and others can be traced the insistence that in an era devoted to the discovery of new techniques of analysis, understanding, and treatment of individual and social problems, traditional values of social philosophy had to be maintained. Committed to group process and democratic planning, Lindeman, long-time friend of Harry Hopkins, later had the opportunity as consulting director of the Division of Recreation in the Works Progress Administration to put into practice many of his ideals. Throughout the 1920's Lindeman, while seeking new techniques, particularly in the as yet unnamed field of group work, constantly called on his colleagues for qualities of statesmanship above and beyond skilled technical assistance to individual clients. The mobilization of community forces for the constructive promotion of social progress was, to him as to many others, a legitimate program for social work to promote; and social progress required both the adjustment of the individual to his environment and the reconstruction of the environment itself, primarily through the activities of voluntary associations of citizens working in a pluralistic society.[32]

This new line of social work theory, "good will in action," according to the distinguished philosopher William Ernest Hocking, demanded "a sort of engineering, a constructive task." Its proper goal was the liberation of the individual from all forms of dependency so that his latent power to give could be released, for the ultimate joy arose out of a sense of participation and a sense of contribution.[33] Socially and psychologically, as well as spiritually, it was more blessed to give than to receive; social workers, it followed, must give in such ways that the powers of the recipient to give in return would be enlarged rather than impaired.

Many social workers themselves employed the concept of social engineering. Miriam Van Waters, pioneer penologist and teacher, began her academic course in social work with the observation that whereas an earlier generation had assumed that assistance was "needed only when something was wrong with society," contemporary social work proceeded from the premise that constructive "social engineers" were needed on the job all the time.[34] One of the recurring themes of the annual Conference of Social Work in 1924 was the belief that social workers were no longer to be considered as "salvagers and repairmen," but as "social engineers," professional experts with a major obligation "for social invention, for shaping public policy into freshly creative channels."[35] Social workers, said Homer Folks, must articulate their belief in humanized social science, "wholly empirical and pragmatic, trying all things and holding fast to that which works, unfettered by a preconceived theory." Social work clings to no dogma, claims no school. The social worker "looks only to results; he is not afraid of any device or plan which, to the satisfaction of all reasonable tests, contributes to human well-being."[36]

Pragmatism might do as a method, but when dogmatically applied it could distort the humane impulse. The literature of social work in the 1920's was filled with exhortations, therefore, not only to be objective and scientific and experimental, but also to be humane, compassionate, subjective; to practice the art as well as the science of social service. Lovejoy, Folks, Vaile, Lindeman, Lathrop, Abbott, Addams were rooted in a tradition of humanitarianism both democratic and religious. Others, in all probability, required the admonition.

Few sensed the dangers in objectivism and scientism with greater intuition than Bruno Lasker, secretary, from 1923, of the "Inquiry." Born of Jewish parents in Germany, Lasker had emigrated to America before the war and had moved into the Henry Street Settlement where he became a lifelong intimate of and adviser to Lillian Wald. Broadly educated and widely traveled, Lasker possessed a cosmopolitan and catholic spirit which encouraged in him a kind of intellectual detachment toward whatever project engaged his talents. Not a practicing Jew, he retained a certain prophetic vision of a just society. A pragmatist by inclination, he abhorred formally scientific dogma to which some of his associates had elevated the system of James, and Dewey, and Mary Follett. Social workers, he felt, had come in the postwar years to dwell too often and too much on material conditions and objective facts, to stress analysis and techniques to the detriment of substantive matters. The insistence upon professional training and competence represented, in itself, a salutary development; but only if social work remained attached to broadly humane considerations could it serve the individual and society with full efficacy. It was not sufficient to be skilled at some specialized application of techniques; loyalty to some larger cause was necessary. Intellectual freedom, human rights, the practice of "neighborly kindness" were as deserving of the attention of the specialist as substandard housing, delinquency, and dependency. If social agencies were necessarily engaged in creating for their clients "a little more happiness here and there," they had also ultimately to strive for "the creation of new foundations for a social life of security and freedom where each may find his happiness in his own way." In this sense, social workers were not merely patchers or mediators but conservators of human values through constructive reforms.[37]

The social worker must concern himself with the objective facts of life, Lasker believed; he must deal with "motives and desires and interests and needs," as well. The social worker must recognize that in the elaboration of policies and the implementation of programs there should be a survey of objective needs and of the commitments of client, agency, and community in a climate of "complete mutual trust." Having given to social work a scientific base, he concluded in 1927, "we shall in the coming decades probably endeavor to make it more of an art and also more of a consecrated call. That does not mean a going back to sentimental good-natured incompetency, but it does mean a new and more correct understanding of scientific efficiency. For, without a deep spiritual concern, or without esthetic joy in the doing of the task, even the most intelligently planned social work will be lacking in vitality." [38]

Professionalization there was in the 1920's, the rapid growth of new specialities and new techniques, a consequent narrowing of vision, a consequent introspection, and a turning in some places from reform to welfare. Counterforces, however, worked to lead social work from care to cure, from cure to prevention, and from prevention to sweeping constructive measures for personal and community betterment. Many welfare agents turned to the "ologies" of social science for guidance, but as many were informed by a broad humanitarianism and were moved by highly subjective and compassionate considerations.

Social work was not of one mind in the 1920's; the image of role was blurred; the main lines were diverse and ambiguous, and sometimes contradictory. The alliance between social work and social reform persisted if it no longer prevailed; new lines of constructive community action, pioneered by prewar progressives, were propagandized and made more elaborate in the decade of normalcy. Speaking in 1923, Robert W. Kelso, executive secretary of the Boston Council of Social Agencies, wrote: "In our doubt of existing institutions, and our fear of chaos, we cast about for instruments with which to repair the breach in our social order." He went on to predict that "the principles which shall guide the splendid thirties of the present century are being hammered in the forge of these nervous days." [39]

This prescient view is one that the passing of time has justified to a remarkable degree. By standing firm in the old progressive faith, by exploring new lines of theory and practice, the partnership of social reformer and social worker anticipated in broad concept and often in intimate detail the New Deal welfare programs and their rationale. Confused and contradictory as social forces were in the years between armistice and panic, there was a larger element of constructive creativity and a broader continuity between progressivism and the New Deal than has been generally credited.

5

THE SETTLEMENTS IN SERVICE
TO THEIR NEIGHBORS

"It seems that we have a tremendous vacuum in American life today [1926], and under the present control of government today we are not getting the spirit we had 15 years ago in the educational field, and there is a strong tendency toward research and specialization rather than toward common action. The Foundations are avoiding controversial issues as if they were polecats. The Community Chests are rather nervous when any organization takes up a thing with teeth in it. It seems to me that we have in the Settlement one of the few organic institutions or groups in America that can exercise leadership."

— Paul U. Kellogg, address before the Fifteenth Conference
of the National Federation of Settlements, 24 May
1926 (typescript in NFS files)

"May I warn you against doing good to people, and trying to make others good by law? One does good, if at all, *with* people, not *to* people. . . . Democracy is perhaps not an attainment, but a process — the process according to which we do not force law upon others, but make it for ourselves, and morally binding on ourselves therefore as its makers."

— Jane Addams, Address at Rockford College, 1931, quoted in
James W. Linn, *Jane Addams* (New York: Appleton-
Century, 1935), p. 387

"[Greenwich] House is not an institution, but a center for stimulating an interest in the full life of humanity, the life of a strong body, a free mind, humane tastes, and the unplumbed possibilities of group action."

— Annual Report of Greenwich House, 1921, p. 14

O F A L L the welfare agencies, none perhaps were more creative, more flexible and imaginative, quicker to elaborate new programs in response to changed conditions than the social settlements and neighborhood centers. Indeed in the prewar era, from the establishment of the very first settlements down to America's entry into the Great War, many notable social-welfare or social-reform leaders lived in or worked through a settlement house; and however brief the residence — sometimes no longer than a summer — the settlement experience had a profound impact on hundreds of workers, both professional and volunteer. For the indomitable Florence Kelley, home was either with Jane Addams at Hull House or with Lillian Wald on Henry Street. The Abbott sisters, Grace and Edith, who enjoyed such long and influential careers in public administration and social-service education, were alumnae of Hull House. Alice Hamilton and Julia Lathrop too were among the legion of those who were moved by their experience.

To go and live among the disinherited, to dwell with those who were alien to the main centers of American life — whether because of their immigrant origin or because they were members of the submerged classes — demanded an investment of self that only those Americans of remarkable sensitivity and imagination could afford. The idea may have been originally English; Canon Samuel A. Barnett's settlement at St. Jude's in Whitechapel, London, was the immediate source of inspiration for many American pioneers including Stanton Coit, Jane Addams, Charles Zueblin, Graham Taylor, Jane E. Robbins, Jean Fine, and others. However it originated, the times were ripe for such a social tactic as evidenced by the host of settlements that sprang up in America, almost spontaneously, during the last decade of the nineteenth century. Coit's Neighborhood Guild, founded in 1886 in the teeming Lower East Side was the first true American settlement; Jean Fine's College Settlement nearby on Rivington Street, and Jane Addams' and Ellen Gates Starr's Hull House followed in 1889. In 1891 Everett P. Wheeler located his East Side House, Charles Zueblin the Northwestern University Settlement in Chicago, and Robert A. Woods Andover House (soon renamed South End House) in Boston. To those six frontier settlements were added over fifty more in the depths of the desperate depression that followed the Panic of 1893; by the turn of the century the number had increased to a hundred. By 1911, when the National Federation of Settlements was formed to coordinate their programs, more than four hundred settlements, scattered from Boston to San Francisco and from St. Paul to New Orleans, joined together their common efforts.[1]

Each new settlement was a bit different from others, and all received the impress of strong personalities. Some, such as the House on Henry Street, grew out of the desire to provide visiting nurse service for poor immigrant families, ridden by ill-health and disease. Others, Hudson Guild on the West Side for example, stressed arts and crafts as means to redeem an otherwise drab and culture-bare environment. Still others specialized in adult education, in Americanization (classes in English and in civics), or in day-nursery care for the children of working mothers. Yet for all their differences in emphasis, the early settlements were undoubtedly moved by similar motives and as much by the "subjective" need of the privileged classes to be of service as by the "objective" need of the deprived and dispossessed to be served.[2]

Often the impulse was an explicitly religious one, or at least a spiritual one — to bear witness to a transcendent concern for the disinherited; to comfort the lowly, clothe the naked, heal the sick; to bridge the gulf that separated class from class, race from race, man from man; to establish that kingdom of God which was not some ethereal Utopian state but a potential condition to be released in the eternal now. Certainly these were the words and the concepts which informed those centers that were church-sponsored; but the nonsectarian settlements, and they were always far more numerous and influential, were often inspired by motives of equally unashamed spiritual concern. Thus, in almost every case, young men and women set up housekeeping in slum areas not (at first at least) to offer a specific program and service but merely to live by their neighbors and share with them their common lot. To share was the declared objective, not to uplift. As an early pamphlet, "What It Means to Be a Member of the College Settlements

Association," put it: "That you have a vision of brotherhood wherein no man lives unto himself; of a neighborhood wherein no man lives unto himself; of a neighborhood where no man may fall among thieves; of a house wherein are many mansions and no dark rooms, of a freedom that is perfect service." [3]

Class guilt and class anxiety were certainly evident. Vida Scudder, child of privilege, recalled in later life the "intolerable stabbing pain" and then the "dull chronic ache" that had insinuated themselves into her soul when first she looked on the grimy face of poverty. She came to feel imprisoned by the customs and assumptions of her class, enclosed by "gracious manners, regular meals, comfort, security, good taste." She hungered for fellowship with the poor, for were they not "nearer perhaps than we to the reality I was always seeking?" And so Vida Scudder (and she spoke for many of her contemporaries) was driven not so much by the urge to serve as to share. It was a desire not without its romantic and sentimental aspects, as she well knew; it was an effort impossible, in an ultimate sense, to realize fully. Yet always the gnawing doubt was there. "Shame had awakened, and an uneasy sense of responsibility; privilege unshared was a fret that would not heal." [4]

Perhaps it was, as Professor Kenneth E. Boulding has suggested, that pioneer settlement leaders were moved to seek out those who were alienated from the main centers of American life by their poverty or their immigrant origin exactly because they themselves, members of the comfortable middle and professional classes, suffered a profound sense of psychological alienation from a society which increasingly deferred to new centers of financial power and from a culture which denied to women the right to participate fully in the life of the community (many of the early settlement leaders were feminists as well). [5]

To accept these views as valid is not, however, to assign to class guilt and status anxiety the whole explanation of settlement motives and designs. Concern about a lost sense of community, about relationships broken by arrangements more exploitative than neighborly, about an environment more restrictive than liberating, about a society which denied the opportunity that had always been the hope and the ideal of the egalitarian spirit — these too were their anxieties and their cares. Was the civilization molded by the factory, the machine, and the city a hard world, impersonal, drab, devoid of grace and compassion? Then there was a need for some few to bear witness to their concern, and to seek "to rescue, purify and liberate" all that was worth preserving from the past. Social disorganization was the symptom and the cause. Millions of Americans, wrote Jane Addams in 1893, "live for the moment side by side, many of them without knowledge of each other, without fellowship, without local tradition or public spirit, without social organization of any kind." Somehow a sense of organic human relationship had to be restored. A "simple acceptance of Christ's message" was in order, and the acting out of the belief that neighbors "should live with opposition to no man, with recognition of the good in every man, even the meanest." The residents, she urged, "must be emptied of all conceit of opinion and all self-assertion . . . [and] must be content to live quietly side by side with their neighbors until they grow into a sense of relationship and mutual interests." [6]

Living with their neighbors, the settlement leaders were soon moved to action, to programs which related organically to the felt needs of the immediate community rather than to preconceived notions on the part of the residents of what might be good for the neighborhood. Programs successful in one settlement, however, were often quickly taken up elsewhere, particularly after the turn of the century when the settlement technique was rapidly adopted throughout the nation, except in the South where there was a lag in this area as in so many other progressive efforts. To visiting nurse services, kindergartens and day nurseries for children of working mothers, classes in the English language and in civics were added other activities: clubs for boys and girls, sports, dances and parties, expeditions to museums and parks, summer camps to which the children could escape from the oppressive heat and squalor and enervating idleness of city slums; youth courses in arts and applied crafts, woodwork, pottery, fabric weaving, needlecraft, typesetting, printing, sewing, domestic sciences; folk dancing, singing, theatricals, and folk festivals; evening programs for mothers in public health, personal hygiene, and infant care, well-baby clinics, demonstrations in proper diet and in dental hygiene.

The settlements often offered the lead to a job, a chance for immigrants to escape from conditions of intolerable exploitation, advice to those who had run afoul of the law, protection of mothers or children from drunken and abusive husbands and fathers, a basket of food or a bundle of clothing in time of family crisis, comfort and a helping hand in time of bereavement. Indeed the settlement often competed with the political machine, whatever its party label, in providing these kinds of informal care and assistance, and participating as neighbors at special moments of family history — the birth of a child, a christening, a marriage, a funeral.[7]

The settlements were conceived, by those leaders who thought of themselves as "pioneers," as "outposts" in the city wilderness from which sociological observations and surveys could be made. Settlements maintained the closest relations with universities and colleges. Social scientists and humanists came to teach and to learn. Graduate students and scholars used the settlements as bases for research into housing, delinquency, health, education, and recreation. The opportunity they afforded for firsthand observation and experience was the one great advantage that the settlements enjoyed over other reform associations or welfare agencies. Many years later, Helen Hall, whose career spanned nearly a half century of settlement history, stressed the informal, direct understanding that settlement work at its best provided: "You are more likely to be stirred to social action," she said, "if something is happening to people you know."[8] Jane Addams expressed the same sentiment a half century earlier when she wrote: "The only way to learn about conditions isn't to go to work in a factory for a few months and write a book; but to have genuine sympathy and continued relations with those who work, day after day, year after year; do our part to help them to express themselves and make articulate their desires."[9]

Others, with Jane Addams, daily observed the problems of municipal housekeeping which cried for solution if modern society were to survive. The settlements forthwith turned to the often humdrum pursuit of ameliorative measures. They propagandized for closed sewers and for adequate garbage collection; they were on hand to help organize their neighbors in campaigns for public baths and drinking fountains, parks and supervised playgrounds, and adequate police and fire protection. They set in motion neighborhood self-improvement crusades, clean-up and paint-up campaigns; they encouraged the planting of flower and vegetable gardens on whatever plots were available. They argued, often successfully, for nurses in the public schools and for visiting teachers (in place of truant officers), for school lunches, for use of school facilities after hours, for the establishment of special classes for physically and mentally handicapped children. To protect juvenile offenders they helped to establish separate courts in which private hearings provided a security that public trials denied.

These efforts represented unspectacular, piecemeal measures, significant enough to those who daily enjoyed their benefits but not designed to set the soul aflame. Many settlement leaders, therefore, demanded action more forthright, more bold, to overcome the evils of a distorting environment. To most of them, the greatest social evils derived from the gross exploitation of the labor of children and of women, both defenseless and vulnerable to the fatigue, ill health, loss of morale, and degeneration that accompanied premature and excessive labor. Childhood, wifehood, and motherhood were sacred and inviolable. Supervised recreation, day nurseries, arts and music, and sewing circles were clearly insufficient. Direct political action, the enactment of protective legislation and its rigorous enforcement were in order.

The fact that the settlements were established in the midst of the ugly depression of the 1890's served to purge them of "any lurking element of sentimentality, of superficiality, of mere palliation," two settlement pioneers recalled. Those were "cruel years," Robert Woods and Albert Kennedy recorded, in which the settlements learned that the causes of human suffering were broadly social, not narrowly personal.[10] They learned that involuntary unemployment was demoralizing to the worker and to his family, that charitable alms robbed the needy of their self-respect. Anticipating a conviction that came to be widely accepted only during the years of the Great Depression in the 1930's, settlement leaders (to use the words of Woods and Kennedy again) saw clearly that among the consequences of unemployment had to be counted the breakdown of "habits of work and of the instinct for economic self-sufficiency. The degradation of poverty, however temporary," they concluded, "affects moral vitality so deeply that recovery is often difficult."[11]

Many leaders, moreover, not only participated in movements for municipal and legislative reform, they also occasionally supported organized labor in its sporadic efforts to wrest more decent conditions from unwilling employers. Thus Mary McDowell, who began her career in Hull House's kindergarten, as head resident of the University of Chicago Settlement behind the stockyards, swung her support to Michael Donnelly in his efforts to unionize the packers. In her settlement, during the great strike of 1904, the workers and their leaders found

financial and moral support. So, a decade later, in the hopelessly disorganized garment industry, the union that became the Amalgamated
Clothing Workers of America received strike funds and supplies through
Hull House while Jane Addams worked to win public support for their
cause, and Ellen Gates Starr walked the picket line in symbolic protest.
If settlement leaders more often preferred political to direct social action, mediation to alliance, such proponents of unionization as the
Women's Trade Union League were nevertheless assured of loyal support from their settlement allies.[12]

The dedication was to service, to research and understanding, and
to reform. Beyond program and political action, the settlements aimed —
through immediate and practical means — at ultimate justifications. They
combined poetry and pragmatism, said Albert Kennedy, and were committed to the notion that an idea is what it does. As leaders drawn from
a Bible-reading native American middle class, comfortable and well
educated if not affluent, the settlement workers envisioned a nation organized for righteousness.[13] It seemed to Vida Scudder, a profoundly
religious woman, that they offered a twentieth-century Franciscanism.
They sought to overcome the centrifugal forces of urban disintegration,
to restore order to a society that had lost coherence, to maintain face-
to-face friendship in a society increasingly impersonal and anonymous.
They labored to foster better understanding between classes, generations, religious communities, and peoples; and the difficulty of that task
was not appreciated, said Lea Taylor of Chicago Commons, until one
faced the crisis when "the washline of an Irish family broke and fell
down on the tomato paste spread out on boards to dry by an Italian
family."[14] To these ends the settlements maintained open forums at
which every view could find expression, every speaker a rostrum.

By seeking to re-establish what Graham Taylor called the "instinctive
relationship" where "artificial relations" had become dominant, the
settlement movement aimed at providing a home for the uprooted, the
detached, the alienated, a haven for all those who felt "utterly lost and
alone."[15] The metaphor of family and home was a natural one; to Mary
Simkhovitch, the settlement was "a family living its life with its neighbors." Beyond the family lay the neighborhood, the community, the nation. The need was to "form a more coherent and closely-knit nation,"
to foster "a political coherence which will unite the nation from top
to bottom, and the right method is to work from bottom to top." The

settlement had a national and a religious purpose — "to hold up a common life and through a common life a common faith." [16] Jane Addams agreed and, borrowing from William James, held forth the prospect of a "moral equivalent" to war, a "new heroism" tied to a "universal determination to abolish poverty and disease." [17]

But then came the war and a unification of thought and action imposed by widely shared patriotic passions and by military exigencies. Robert Woods, who had envisioned "the neighborhood as the vehicle of secular good will, and as the unit of civic and national reconstruction," joined the Wilsonian crusade with a good deal of enthusiasm. A nation totally organized for victory on the field of battle must carry on its "vast organism of service, of fellowship, of creative power" for reconstruction and welfare, he said.[18]

Settlement workers, whether committed to the war (as most of them were) or not went about their daily round, adding new programs to well-established routines. They stepped up educational and recreational work for youth, particularly for the children of mothers employed in war industries. The settlements became centers for classes in first aid and nutrition, and campaigns for war relief, food and fuel conservation, liberty loans, and draft registration. They helped aliens to accommodate to new government regulations. Social action was focused on prohibition of liquor, prostitution control, and the winning of woman suffrage.

Settlement leaders were among the first reformers to recognize, however, that reform was not necessarily or easily to be resumed after months of violence. Others, in the immediate postwar years, rushed to get on record with reconstruction platforms often in the full expectation that the transformation of society could now be finally realized. Back in Minneapolis the Northeast Neighborhood House planned a glorious reception for its returning heroes; the settlement's band was down at the depot along with the boys' and girls' and mothers' clubs carrying banners and flags. But when the veterans got off, a "straggling line of limping, weary, unkempt soldiers, there was chagrin and silent grief." So Catheryne Cooke Gilman remembered that awful moment. "Even the gladness in the eyes faded and the joy in the hearts of waiting relatives was stilled by the sight. . . . [And] the most remarkable and disturbing thing about it was the silent acceptance of it by the men and their families." [19]

To some, the tone of postwar life came as tragic confirmation of wartime fears that social coercion would close down on the openness of American life. "The end of the convulsion," prophesied Vida Scudder in 1917, "must inevitably be a fearful restlessness, a fever will shake society for many a long year." [20] So it had seemed, looking forward. Looking backward from the perspective of 1936, she set down her despair. "The Great War had not made the world safe for democracy; intelligent reformers had never expected it to do so, yet it was not easy to watch the surging flood of disillusion which threatened to submerge the idealism and drown the hopes of the world, nor to see the reforms on which hope and effort had centered, hardly with exception halted or destroyed." [21]

The Red Scare and the decade of attacks upon civil liberties that followed undoubtedly hurt the settlements more than other reform associations or welfare agencies because they had been so long associated with an open-forum policy hospitable to the expression of all kinds of economic and political theories by all sorts and conditions of social dissenters. Enthusiasm for social reform was squelched by the "paralyzing fear" that the Bolshevik Revolution had created throughout the Western world, just as the specter of the French Revolution had quieted liberalism in England and elsewhere a century earlier, recorded Jane Addams. "Any proposed change was suspect, even those efforts that had been considered praiseworthy before the war," she continued and went on to conclude that even "social workers exhibited many symptoms of this panic and with a protective instinct carefully avoided any identification with the phraseology of social reform." [22] The indictment was a bit harsh and a bit extravagant, but that the climate of conformity influenced settlement activity is abundantly clear. In New York, Chicago, Boston, many settlements found their fund-raising activities jeopardized by the tag of "radicalism." With few exceptions the most notable settlement leaders stood firm, refusing to modify the public expression of their unpopular views. Many of them, moreover, counterattacked as best they could through the American Civil Liberties Union, which they had helped to form and to which they continued to lend their support in order to protect the right of every citizen to speak freely without fear of legal or extralegal retaliation against the expression of embarrassing and unwanted ideas.

But here and there the war and the postwar reaction took their toll — in caution, in moderation. When Charles Cooper, director of Kingsley Association in Pittsburgh, suggested that the settlements state their opposition to capital punishment (the year was 1927, the year marked in red by Sacco and Vanzetti), other settlement leaders warned against committing the entire movement to such a controversial and potentially divisive issue; to which advice Cooper replied with a bitter remark that he had always thought the settlements were centrally committed to the sanctity of human life.[23] Graham Taylor, no longer as directly active as once he had been in settlement affairs and never a social radical, also hedged. His advice to Cooper (ever impatient with shilly-shallying) on settlement strategy in the face of postwar reaction was to stand fast, "to retreat as little and advance as much as we can, while facing the worst and doing our best. . . . But it behooves us to hold our own without imperiling it by going too fast and too far afield," he quickly added, "to dig in where we are sure to hold the ground and not provoke attacks on frontier points, the defense of which, at present at least, is not worth the waste of ammunition."[24] Although a good number of settlement leaders and their allies were involved in the defense of Sacco and Vanzetti, it was not until 1931, after the crisis had passed, that the National Federation of Settlements recorded its opposition to capital punishment on the grounds "that in the creation of conditions which lead to crime, the whole community is to some measure responsible, and that this responsibility cannot be wiped out by the death of the offender."[25]

The relationship of the settlements to the labor movement in the 1920's was less intimate and sympathetic than it had been in the prewar generation. Trade unionism had enjoyed substantial gains during the war years and its aims and procedures no longer required interpretation by settlement leaders for the general public. The postwar trend toward welfare capitalism and company unions and the growing caution of craft-minded labor leaders themselves, constantly on the defensive throughout the 1920's, significantly retarded the actions of both settlement and labor leaders. In joining local community chests, moreover — a tactic to which many of the weaker neighborhood centers found it expedient to resort — local settlement leaders often felt obliged to stress their service functions and to restrict their social-action programs. "Labor has become less and less cooperative with the settlement," Graham Taylor reported in 1920, "whereas within the last year or two the employers are more open to settlement suggestion. Can the settlement afford to forfeit the loyalty of conservatives?"[26] By 1926, the lack of contact and understanding between labor and the settlements had proceeded so far that a young resident at Chicago Commons was moved to propose that the National Federation of Settlements establish a committee to promote "Education in Social Relations" which would give special attention to the whole field of industrial relations and to the obligation of settlements to "interpret the labor movement, its need and its results to our working people and also to help the employers to understand the workingmen's viewpoint and organization." In candid explanation of his motives he noted that the older generation had known "sympathetically, interpreted effectively and aided wisely the labor movement." But he confessed that his generation, the new generation of young residents, did not have the same experience and knowledge. There is no evidence that the NFS ever acted upon his proposal, but it may be taken as a symptom of the widening gap between labor and settlement leaders in the 1920's; if residents had to be taught about labor, rather than learning firsthand, a marked change had surely come upon the movement.[27]

The postwar reaction was not the only problem the settlements had to confront in the 1920's. Ironically, new problems accompanied the prosperity that brought economic opportunity, often for the first time, to old neighbors and caused their mass exodus from the Lower East Side up to the Bronx, over to Brooklyn, or across the river to New Jersey. Settlement leaders could not but rejoice at the good fortune of their friends: "Fewer families are afraid to meet their landlords, furniture no longer fills the sidewalk. . . . Gone are the shawls from the heads, the breakfastless children." So recorded Mary Simkhovitch in 1927.[28] New neighbors pressed in — southern Negroes, Latin Americans, other minority groups — but programs tailored for and personnel trained to deal with eastern Europeans were not always easily accommodated to these new neighbors. The dedication had always been to racial equality, and it still was, but increasingly in the 1920's the tension was not between the native and the immigrant but between different groups of newcomers. Henry Street experimented with separate colored clubs, but that didn't work; neither did the attempt to maintain no distinction or discrimination at all, for "while the Jewish adults accepted the Colored without prejudice, on account of the cultural differences between them, the former were inclined to be patronizing in their attitude." [29] At Hull House a group of Italian-Americans threatened to withdraw if Mexican-Americans were permitted to use its facilities, for people of "color" would lower its prestige. Moreover it was not always as easy to raise funds for Negro Americans as it had been for the European immigrants.

Some settlements — it was particularly true of many Jewish community centers — tried to move into the new neighborhoods to which their constituents fled from the slums. One such center, in Cleveland, moved four times in the single decade of the twenties before its directors finally gave up the chase. Not only had its friends moved farther and faster than the center itself could manage, but the need for ethnic identification had become less intense, at least for the moment; trained to leadership by the center, many of those formerly dependent on the settlement were now using their skills through more regularly accepted channels. The center had become merely a place where one could rent rooms for weddings and receptions.[30] Increased mobility made it difficult to maintain a coherent program and to instill a sense of community cohesion in a neighborhood.

Not unrelated was the problem of raising money and recruiting board directors. The easy prosperity which marked the years of the twenties caused a relaxation of concern among some donors for the plight of what many still conceived to be the dangerous classes. Wasn't poverty on its way toward oblivion? Wasn't American ingenuity reaching toward a rapid solution of all those ancient human problems? And weren't mass production and mass distribution a more American way than social action? Those who were interested in philanthropy often found more congenial outlets — community chests and specialized service agencies. Increasingly the research functions of the settlement were taken over by professional social scientists; the settlements might still depend upon the universities, particularly for the recruitment of trained personnel, but the universities now had other listening and observation posts than the settlements. Many of the most prominent settlement leaders turned to causes more pressing — world peace for example, which consumed the energies of Jane Addams and so many others during the interwar era. The settlements' endorsement of prohibition, moreover, tended often to cut them off from their neighbors who were less prim and fussy on that particular social issue.

The settlements had always prized their identification as the "general practitioners" within the social work profession. Mary Simkhovitch employed this metaphor in her annual report in 1921 — just as the general medical practitioner used the medical specialist, so the settlement could employ the services of the social work specialist, she wrote. But "at the core of the neighorhood house," she insisted, "must be a small group who know the whole life of the neighborhood . . . the habits, tastes, pleasures, passions, struggles and aspiration" which moved the neighbors. Only then could all the needs of the whole community be served.[31] But a half generation later, a serious and astute student of the settlement movement reported that the trend toward specialization, toward the institutionalizing of activities, toward the formal bureaucratization of structure which characterized other aspects of social work, had encroached upon the settlements as well. "Anyway, the settlement's attempt to consider with sympathy and not too much specialized skill the total personalities of its clients," he concluded in 1937, "has become almost as much outmoded as the old family doctor who is surrounded by an ever increasing crowd of buzzing young specialists."[32]

Where once they received a constant flow of young men and women, eager for adventure, longing more to experience than to serve, the settlements now depended increasingly on paid professional specialists to staff the programs. If there was a consequent gain in expertise, there was a corresponding loss in spontaneity and enthusiasm. Head residents particularly were drawn increasingly from persons holding the master's degree; but even at the departmental level, the settlements preferred to hire specialists with proper credentials in physical education, hygiene, arts and crafts, recreation, casework. Neighborly informality declined as settlements became institutions and had departments; settlement workers tended to be known no longer as "neighbor" but as "boys' workers," and the children of the neighborhood came to know all residents as "teacher."[33] To the older generation of pioneers, the trend toward specialization was a source both of amusement and of disappointment. Maryal Knox, who devoted fifty years to settlement work in New York, commented, only partly in jest, just before her death in 1955 that "no settlement would hire me today"; she wouldn't be able to communicate in the language of abnormal psychology. Perhaps there had been too much fuss about psychology and the other ologies: "If you give children a good time and make them feel secure and happy, they come out all right. You have to be fond of them — whether you know the names of all the complexes they might have or not." [34]

If the movement was away from amateur friendliness toward professional services, the institution of residency, so crucial to the pioneer settlements, was also under attack. It had been assumed without question, before the war, that the residents would live in the settlement or at least in the neighborhood, and that volunteers would come into the neighborhood regularly to assist with club work and other activities. To Catheryne Cooke Gilman the three "R's" of settlement work were "residency, research, and reform." The principle of residency, that workers make a commitment to live with their neighbors, was neither a "convenience, nor an obsession," it grew not out of "self-glorification, nor to satisfy morbid curiosity." Residency was a principle solely because it offered the only means by which the settlement worker could learn "to know intimately" the neighborhood so that he could work with the neighbors to overcome "unemployment, bad housing, unsanitary conditions, ill health, civic neglect, vice, delinquency, and crime." Residency was essential to valid research and the means to reform, to "reclamation and rehabilitation." [35]

So it seemed to Robbins Gilman as well: "The living among people, the maintenance of a home in the midst of the neighborhood . . . gives the settlement that strategic hold on the affections and confidence of its neighbors, that no other community organization has secured." [36] At the Gilmans' Northeast Neighborhood House in Minneapolis the residency principle was maintained down into the war years of the 1940's. The head resident and his family, together with most others on the professional staff, continued to live at the House; they were joined by students from the University of Minnesota, particularly during the summer months, and by young men employed in industry or government who provided evening or weekend volunteer labor in return for room and board. Lea Taylor, who took over as head resident from her father at Chicago Commons in 1922, continued the practice there, and as long as Graham Taylor was on hand evening vespers in the parlor for the residents was the rule. In numberless other settlements, scattered throughout the country, residency, at least for the head resident, continued to be the practice.

In many places, however, the principle was difficult to maintain in the face of changing conditions. At least as early as 1922 some settlement work leaders recognized the challenge to familiar techniques. Mary Simkhovitch raised the question that year of "how the goodwill of young people who wanted to be engaged in the settlement scheme, but who didn't care to live in the settlement, could be salvaged." Albert Kennedy, in reply, urged that there be no break with the residency principle although, he added, the stage of "amateurish" service, whose accomplishments had been so often truly miraculous, was passing.[37] By 1933, Mr. Kennedy had been forced to recognize that "The antagonism which certain young staff workers feel to residence is based partly on their thinking of themselves as professional men and women, rendering a specific service desired by the neighborhood, however paid for, rather than as 'neighbors' or 'social explorers,' and partly because they feel they can be more completely themselves if their leisure time is spent elsewhere than in the atmosphere of their work. At bottom the revolt is against that grain of sentimentalism, about the people worked with and the task in itself, which the older generation still cherishes and finds serviceable."[38] The fact was, hard as the settlement pioneers took it, that many of the younger generation just did not wish to live in the slums with their families. Indeed many of the second-generation workers were themselves children of the very slums which now they sought both to serve and to escape. Here and there, slowly at first, a new relationship began to creep in: less that of friend and neighbor than that of social worker and client. The 1930's saw a reversal of the trend as young men and women came to the settlements both as a cheap place to live and as a base from which the force of social reconstruction could operate; not until the years of World War II and after was the residency principle finally abandoned.

This subtle shift had begun to take its toll early in the settlements' history. Vida Scudder set down her disillusionment with the settlements as they moved toward social service: "As settlements like the rest of social effort became professionalized," she wrote, "my interest, though not my loyalty, waned a little." The difference between the professional workers and the amateur pioneers was the difference "between a salaried clergy and the mendicant orders who had become fools for Christ." [39]

Problems, external and internal, there were, disappointment and disenchantment, but the determination to posit new goals and to implement old objectives with new means was present as well. If the settlements were facing another era of crisis, that was nothing new; a goodly number of leaders in the 1920's could easily recall that some had written off the movement as early as the turn of the century.

Some accommodations came easily. The settlements had, from the beginning, deliberately experimented with new techniques and services, hoping that if some of them worked, regular welfare agencies, public and private, would be willing and eager to take them over. In this process, they had happily turned over a number of programs to the schools, to museum and park boards, to the Boy and Girl Scouts, to family and child welfare associations. The settlements had worked themselves out of a number of jobs before; well and good, they would do so again. But they would continue to think of themselves as general practitioners in an age increasingly specialized. Moreover, they clung to their determination to work with what was "right" with people, to set loose the potential that lay locked within persons and within groups. They would share rather than give and work with the whole person, the whole family, the whole neighborhood, leaving to the specialized agencies the segmented and particularized tasks. [40]

When nearly fifty settlement leaders were asked by Albert Kennedy, in mid-decade, to evaluate settlement programs and goals, about half of the replies reflected habit and tradition. These stressed the need for neighborship, interpretation of class to class, reformation of industrial conditions, brotherhood, "the coming of the kingdom of good will." Others, however, were more specific in their recommendations — a crusade for more adequate housing, acceptance of the Negro into urban life in the North, the building of a better and richer life above the level of poverty through creative cultural activities and through social education, the eradication of dependency and delinquency. [41] On other occasions, settlement leaders spoke for the need to work intensely with individuals to affect the lives of a small group deeply rather than a large group superficially; to stand against the social trend toward institutionalization, regimentation, the pressures to conform and to adhere to a common standard.

These trends and their own self-examination suggested new paths to the younger generation of workers, but they could not easily strike out upon them. The pattern was too firmly established, the old saints still dominated the scene — they were "paralyzed by their reverence for the pioneers," observed Isabel Taylor at the end of the decade. "The founders of the settlement had higher hopes than we, who have lived through the war, can have. . . . Today we are confused and overwhelmed by the complexity and size of our task." There was no use pretending to be heroic, she continued, we cannot "deceive ourselves into thinking we shall save civilization by our efforts." Still there was joy in the task even if a new order was not about to be established, the joy of living with others "richly as well as self-forgetfully." The world's work was not yet done.[42]

So the familiar round of activities continued. The children of working mothers were left off for day-nursery care; after school hours came supervised recreation, arts and crafts, music, dancing, and drama; evening brought together the mothers to gossip and to sew, or to study nutrition and child care. Well-baby clinics and health demonstrations, often under the auspices of field representatives of the Children's Bureau working with Sheppard-Towner funds, were regular features. So, too, were dental clinics, prenatal clinics, mental hygiene institutes, and child guidance clinics. Public health officials came in to implement programs for inoculation, vaccination, and immunization. Milk stations were provided for undernourished children. Some settlements maintained informal employment bureaus for counseling, training, and placement, particularly of young people just entering the labor market. The settlements offered a place for parole officers and juvenile offenders to meet in a friendly and informal environment. Other youth workers sought to transform street gangs into boys' clubs through sports and, in the summer months, through camping. Assistance to prohibition enforcement and to prostitution control consumed a good deal of effort; so too did neighborhood improvement projects. Some settlements offered short-term small loans, without interest, out of revolving funds. Many welfare agencies worked out of the settlements, using both casework and group-work techniques to assist families in need. And always there were the family emergencies to be met — illness, accident, truancy, unemployment; drunken fathers, deserted mothers, incorrigible children. A typical day might involve first aid to a boy beaten by his father or a young wife beaten by her husband; assistance in finding a new job for an unemployed person and a home for an illegitimate child; and help in filing a complaint against a landlord. On the Lower East Side the day might require supervision of a children's argument as "to whether God was a Jew or an Italian." [43]

All these were services long part of the familiar settlement routine. There were, however, certain not insignificant shifts in emphasis during the 1920's. Because of advancing prosperity (even if the neighborhoods in which settlements were located did not share fully in good times), and because the public schools had taken over so many of the special programs which they had earlier pioneered, the settlements consciously shifted into educational and recreational work of a different sort. If once the arts and crafts had been conceived as means to bring a bit of "color" into lives otherwise "drab," the objectives in the 1920's were far more elaborate: "to develop a desire for better use of leisure time, a clearer understanding of relative values, opportunities for social contact, and appreciation of mutual contributions to the common welfare of the community." [44]

Hudson Guild, Greenwich House, Hull House had pioneered in arts programs before the war; these activities were widely expanded and everywhere emulated in the postwar era, with Christodora House, New York, and the Irene Kaufman Settlement in Pittsburgh becoming renowned for their music schools. By mid-decade settlements were directing over eighty music centers in twenty cities and nineteen states. Hull House sponsored exhibits of settlement art throughout the 1920's, thus launching many careers for persons in the visual arts; in 1925 the National Federation of Settlements gathered an exhibit of settlement craft and art work that was shown in ten major cities. As with music and the visual arts, so with settlement theater — the pioneering went back to the turn of the century (the Hull House Players were organized in 1901, the Henry Street Players in 1907), but it was not until the 1920's that drama became a lively concern of centers throughout the nation. The Neighborhood Playhouse on Grand Street in New York City under the exciting and brilliant direction of Irene and Alice Lewisohn brought distinction to the House on Henry Street, with which it was affiliated from 1915 to 1927; but Greenwich House, New York, and Peabody House in Boston won local acclaim as did many other centers. Shaw, Bennett, O'Neill, Galsworthy, Chekhov, Shakespeare,

Ibsen, Barrie, Wilde were all part of the repertory. The settlement theater was probably never more vital a force than in the 1920's.

Albert Kennedy, of all settlement leaders the one most explicitly concerned with the arts, declared their ultimate intent "to enrich impoverished personalities, to open the doors of self-expression to thwarted and repressed people of all classes. . . ."[45] Robbins Gilman echoed Kennedy's belief that beyond a regard for the neighborhood lay a concern for the individual, crowded upon by a confining environment. The arts could instill a spirit of adventure, establish pride in craftsmanship, set standards of beauty, sharpen the intuition for dignity in all areas of life. They could provide a "very essential antidote to the mechanical, passive, conforming habits of industrialized communities."[46]

Where earlier they had emphasized the arts as a way to uplift neighborhood standards and to relieve the sordid grimness of slum poverty, the settlements shifted in the postwar years to transcendent goals, "not merely a less hungry, harassed and unhappy society," Kennedy recalled, "but a genuinely more interesting and delightful social order."[47] Helen Hart, of Kingsley House in Pittsburgh, noted that modern techniques of mass production and high-pressure salesmanship had made it possible for Judy O'Grady to model the "outer trappings of her life, however shoddily" on those of the Colonel's lady. The settlements had earlier aimed at helping people discover the common humanity that underlay external differences; now the task was quite the opposite — "to show them that in spite of appalling external resemblances they are really individuals underneath." Through the arts the settlements could rescue individual personality from the oppressive forces of materialism and standardization; "nonmaterial values of life" were to be promoted.[48]

To some settlement leaders and critics, however, the stress on the arts seemed to have diverted the movement away from its proper focus on social justice and social reform. The excitement of cultural activities that had marked the early years of the decade had begun to pall. From the perspective of 1929, it seemed to Jane Addams that the pioneer commitment to social experimentation and amelioration had, since the war, been pushed aside; the settlements no longer won the emotional response to social effort that they once had evoked. But lately she had observed signs of "great doubt" and that, she said, was the settlements' "salvation," that they were "continually filled with a holy discontent."[49]

Paul Kellogg, who as editor of the *Survey* reacted to every new tremor among social workers, publicly praised the settlements in 1928 for their contributions to the revival of the arts in the 1920's: "the plasticity of the settlement movement in pushing out this salient during our ten years of sag in the political and economic fields, is prime evidence of its vitality."[50] Privately, however, he had written to persuade Albert Kennedy, executive secretary of the national federation since 1923, that the time was overdue for social action again. To Kennedy he expressed appreciation for the work he had done "in developing standards of vision in the cultural activities of the settlements — in art, music, drama, and the like"; but without an equal and parallel stress upon their "civic functions" the settlements were "likely to become more like abbeys and monasteries than like missionary posts." Setbacks there had been but, he concluded, "the trend of the times is not any more adverse to social adventure and espousal today than it was when the settlements loosed their dynamic in the Nineties." He ended with a plea that the settlements develop new leadership to explore new problems. Albert Kennedy wistfully agreed. It was true that his influence, and the national federation's under his direction, had been primarily in the arts, he hoped not to the exclusion of other programs. When new officers could be installed, he would happily resign in order that the will of the majority of settlement workers could become effective.[51]

In 1930 Lea Taylor, whose capacity for practical social action had always been her sustaining quality, entered on a term of office as president of the federation that extended until 1934. Her first act was to lead the Executive Committee in a reorganization of its main divisions to include Unemployment, Prohibition, Housing, Race Relations, Old Age Pensions, Work with Little Children, and Visual Arts. At the same time Lillie Peck, who had practiced settlement work for years in Boston, was named as assistant to Kennedy, who lingered on as executive secretary until 1934 at which time Miss Peck stepped up into his position.[52]

Miss Taylor and Miss Peck together quickly directed the federation's primary attention to social issues again. Changing conditions had called forth new programs and modified social theories, but the two strands of service and vision had never parted company. By the end of the decade the settlements had returned to the original principles of the settlement founders and were engaged in seeking paths toward the inauguration of new programs.

THE SETTLEMENTS' DRIVE FOR
SOCIAL ACTION

"Hundreds of millions of dollars ought to be devoted to this purpose [of housing reform], by means of which fine, well-planned communities could be developed, similar perhaps to English Garden Cities and with features that would conserve to the community all increments of land value and would provide houses at the lowest possible cost affording the finest environment for the development of a physically, mentally and morally sound citizenship."

— Statement of the National Federation of
Settlements, 8 September 1922

"Poverty becomes the more poignant in the shadow of great wealth; idleness the more demoralizing beside the feverish activity of great competition. And America can show greater contrasts on these pictures than any other country I know on earth."

— Karl Borders, of Chicago Commons, quoted in
Survey, 62:1 (1 April 1929), p. 4

THE service aspects of settlement work took precedence over its commitment to social action throughout most of the postwar decade. For the moment the exploration of the liberating potential of the arts seemed more exciting and more significant than seeking release from deprivation through political crusading. But the social-reform impulse had not died or even become dormant in these years of reaction; it persisted, and by the end of the decade it represented again the dominant tone of the whole settlement movement.

As in the prewar years, much of the social action in which settlement leaders participated was unspectacular and not always clearly visible to the general citizenry. Thus, for example, there was always the persisting task of organizing neighborhood committees to petition for the removal of a railroad track, for the strict enforcement of smoke control or red-light abatement ordinances, for the more effective implementation of compulsory school attendance laws, or for the building of a new primary school.

Beyond these efforts the settlements, in the 1920's, enlarged their concern with child-welfare programs of all sorts. The settlements were among the more insistent partisans of the federal child-labor amendment. In Chicago, the Federation of Settlements initiated action that led to a conference on the prevention of crime. Constructive community action as well as police control to prevent juvenile delinquency was, the settlements stressed, an unceasing public obligation, as was the search for ways to restore rather than punish.

Related to the settlements' anxiety for child welfare was their concern for the acceptance of all peoples and races, and their hope that every child would enjoy equal opportunity to realize his own potential whatever it might be. Having failed in their attempts to block or to modify the restrictive immigration laws of 1921 and 1924, settlement leaders did the best they could to ease application of the laws to relatives of their neighbors living outside the United States.

More difficult in the postwar years, as was noted briefly in the previous chapter, was the task of promoting neighborship among native and immigrant groups on the one hand and men and women of color on the other. Here were tens of thousands of Negro Americans — unwilling immigrants of generations earlier, dragged in chains across the dreaded middle passage into slavery — now migrating out of the rural South into the urban North. Wartime labor shortages had opened opportunities for colored Americans in industry for the first time on a large scale. Once set in motion, the surge northward continued only slightly abated even after peace brought lessened economic opportunity. The last to be hired, and the first to be fired, the Negro nevertheless had got a taste of industrial employment and urban living; there was now a social alternative to second-class citizenship, rural poverty, economic dependency, Jim Crow, disfranchisement, and violence. As the newer immigrant groups began to move up and out, southern Negroes moved into the neighborhoods served by settlements. In some places the settlements sought to soften racial tension in times of rapid transition. In many neighborhoods, centers were soon serving an entirely colored clientele. That these migrants were Americans and that they were (for the most part) Protestant in religion did little to overcome the handicap of color; their reception proved to be less cordial than that accorded to immigrants from abroad, and the passing of time did not bring the mobility that every other migrant group had enjoyed.

For the time, then, those settlements located in neighborhoods that became rapidly colored had to endure tensions created by race prejudice, just as they were confronting frustrations of their other programs as well. Understandably, settlements were among the first welfare agencies pressing for fair employment practices in the 1930's and 1940's. In the meantime, settlement facilities and leaders were often drafted for Urban League activities while settlement-rooted reformers gave support to the National Association for the Advancement of Colored People. Jane Addams, Lillian Wald, Mary McDowell, Florence Kelley, Catheryne Cooke Gilman, Grace Abbott, Helen Morton, Helen B. Pendleton, and Paul Kellogg were numbered among those who gave more than their good names to either or both of these associations, one oriented toward direct action, the other toward welfare and amelioration. In any case the reliance was less on preaching than on practicing that equality which was their hope for society.

In New York City, Bruno Lasker, long associated with the House on Henry Street, was close to the race problem in his capacity as secretary of the Commission on Race Relations of the National Conference on the Christian Way of Life, the "Inquiry." His first formal report, in 1924, laid down the premises on which his commission intended to operate, none of them easily optimistic in tone: that the race problem was not simply a sectional but a national problem; that "mere good will" would not suffice, that the evolution of solutions would involve "mastery of a technique of social living"; that the complexity of the problems forced recognition that no solution would be found in "a single line of action"; and that solutions "must be approached experimentally without fear of possible initial failure."[1]

The Inquiry published two tracts — *And Who Is My Neighbor? A Case Book and Study Outline on Race Relations* and *All Colors: A Study Outline on Woman's Stake in Race Relations* — both of which were designed to stimulate discussion among study and action groups throughout the nation. All during the 1920's Lasker and his colleagues sought to apply the same techniques to the race issue that social workers had used in the prewar years to discover the roots of poverty, dependency, delinquency, and unemployment; appeals to moral principles, exhortations to set prejudices aside would never work; the need was, by analysis and by education, "to deal with the specific causes of maladjustment between racial groups."[2] Through the Inquiry and through his many friends in the settlement movement, Lasker was able to make a contribution to the growing awareness among social workers and social reformers of the pressing problem of race. The point remains, however, that the result rarely went beyond study and concern. Both the NAACP and the Urban League were the products of prewar progressive ferment; not till the 1930's and thereafter were clear advances won. Later generations would deal with America's great dilemma in a more forthright manner. It is not without its significance, however, that the settlements and their alumni, allies, and friends did as much as any group to keep alive a concern with the problem when most Americans had put it out of their minds.

Of larger importance, undoubtedly, both for the 1920's and for the New Deal years that followed was the settlements' commitment to housing reform. Living in the slums, observing daily the human consequences of bad housing — disease, delinquency, immorality, and crime — settlement leaders were naturally driven to action in this field. The Hull House group had been influential in the establishment in 1900 of the Chicago Homes Association, whose chairman was Robert Hunter. In 1907, Florence Kelley, living then at Henry Street, initiated the formation of a special citizens' committee on congestion, whose chairman was Mary Simkhovitch and secretary Benjamin Marsh. Marsh and John Fox put together an exhibit on slum conditions that was on display in 1908 and moved Governor Charles Evans Hughes to appoint a State Commission on Congestion and led as well to the formation of the National City Planning Commission in 1910. Part of the wartime mobilization of the home front involved the building of government housing near munitions plants. With the return of peace and the opportunity for reconstruction, the settlements inquired: "If such enterprise could be undertaken during the emergencies of war, why not now?"[3]

The East Aurora conference of the National Federation of Settlements in 1920 therefore devoted more attention to the problem of housing than to any other single issue. Despairing of the possibility of private philanthropy in this field, knowing that regulatory ordinances did nothing constructively to create better housing (and not much negatively to eliminate unsanitary, unsafe, and overcrowded conditions), the delegates declared the need for the assumption of public responsibility. Just how the goal of decent housing, particularly for low-income groups, was to be implemented wasn't at all clear. Such questions as these were raised: Under whose auspices should the initiative be seized, city or state government? What measures would be required to stimulate cooperatives or "limited dividend companies" to take action? What agencies would be required to relocate families displaced by slum clearance projects? Should the flight to the suburbs from the inner city be promoted? What of the need for city-wide zoning and condemning powers? And what of the moral problem; might not public housing subsidize exploitative conditions of labor employment? These were questions not to be answered casually, and they required technical knowledge as well as good intentions. But while the search for answers was under way, at least the settlements could call attention to the problems created by substandard housing — lack of privacy, sickness, inadequate recreation space. To the ends of study and preparation for action the federation conference established a committee of which the chairman was Lillian Wald.[4]

Her committee quickly established certain premises and priorities: the right to conscript property, the necessity to focus on the destruction of central city tenement areas and the construction, presumably under municipal authority, of large, multiple-dwelling units with surrounding parks and playgrounds. But the first task was the formation of citizens' committees to explore the problem, to broaden the base of public acceptance, and to "get out and moan in common."[5] The federation's committee, drawn primarily from New York workers, served as the center of concern for that city. In Minneapolis, the Gilmans' Northeast Neighborhood House kept up a regular agitation. Mary McDowell's University of Chicago Settlement explored the need for housing action, particularly in "frontier" areas on the advancing edge of the sprawling city. In Chicago, also, the settlements played a primary part in establishing a Public Committee of Fifty on Housing with Walter F. Dodd as chairman and including among its membership Jane Addams, Mrs. Harold Ickes, Mary McDowell, Graham Taylor, and Harriet Vittum.[6] Housing reform represented one area, at least, in which the old crusading spirit was kept alive; a dunning letter from Jane Addams to Anita McCormick Blaine ended on a nostalgic note: "We had a fine Housing Conference last week, almost like the good old days of 1900."[7]

Two years of intensive study made it possible for the federation's 1922 conference to answer some of the questions raised in 1920. First came the statement of priority — improper housing was responsible for so many of the social ills which the settlements were seeking to alleviate and cure that housing reform was deserving of first attention. Next came the premise — the wages of low-income families were insufficient to cover the costs of minimally decent housing; private capital could not, therefore, earn a high enough return on decent, low-cost housing to justify the investment of capital. And finally the major conclusion: "the housing problem should be recognized as a community problem — one which cannot be solved without community aid."

What then of program? As a first step the NFS called for the establishment of coordinating housing commissions at every level of government. Out of these, it was hoped, could be created a model minimum housing code which could be adapted to local circumstances. Government aid could be afforded in several ways. Low-interest loans could be made for housing projects "with preference to limited dividend companies, co-operative societies and building loan associations." The government might also purchase tracts of suburban land to be held off the market until plans could be made for their socially efficient use. Tax exemption for slum clearance and housing projects might be granted under some circumstances. Finally came the statement of ultimate purpose: "Hundreds of millions of dollars ought to be devoted to this purpose, by means of which fine, well-planned communities could be developed . . . with features that would conserve to the community all increments of land value and would provide houses at the lowest possible cost affording the finest environment for the development of a physically, mentally and morally sound citizenship."[8] (The tone of the statement suggested the persisting influence of Henry George, whose picture hung with Lincoln's and her father's in Jane Addams' office.)

Minutes of the Executive Committee meetings after the stand of 1922 reveal a continuing and recurring concern for housing; they suggest as well, however, that the resolution of 1922 was not fully accepted in every detail by settlement leaders in all parts of the nation. Some clearly preferred drastic slum clearance action by direct government subvention; others had more modest aims, preferring indirect encouragement of private housing projects for middle-income groups so that lower-income families could move up into housing vacated by the former groups.

Study and agitation on the part of settlement leaders continued throughout the placid years of prosperity; but only in New York, on Governor Smith's initiative, was there any constructive accomplishment. There, in 1926, the state provided support for cooperative and limited dividend housing. Under the terms of this act, private, state-chartered corporations were granted powers of condemnation and relief from state tax burdens. Limited as it was, the New York statute stood conspicuously alone in the nation; and even in the Empire State an attempt to tighten the housing code, as late as February 1929, failed of enactment although it proposed merely the goal of a separate toilet for each family in tenement housing, the removal of all outside toilets, and the prohibition of cellar dwellings by 1935 — hardly to be considered "revolutionary demands," complained Lillian Wald to "Dear Friend and Lieutenant Governor" Herbert Lehman.[9]

The settlements' program for housing accomplished practically nothing as long as prosperity was sustained. Housing reform failed to catch on with other reform and welfare associations — the settlements' active concern for decent housing was all the more remarkable for the silence and apathy of other organizations. Worthy of note as well was the detail with which the settlements anticipated the major outline of New Deal housing measures in the 1930's.

Not at all surprising was the leadership that the settlements gave to housing reform in the depression era. From Washington at the end of 1933 wrote an old friend of Lillian Wald's, Katharine Faville, rejoicing at the "zest" which infected everyone in Harold Ickes' PWA housing division. "It is no wonder the housing people are bubbling over — think of the magnificent chance to give people the decent homes they have never had!"[10] Ickes' own concern undoubtedly was influenced by his long alliance with Jane Addams, whose proxy on the Progressive National Committee he had voted, 1913–1914, and by the activities of his wife who was the daughter of Mary Wilmarth, for years one of Hull House's most generous benefactors.

It wasn't all that easy, as housing reformers learned before depression passed into war again. Starting from scratch, housing reformers had to form public opinion and lobby in Congress before partial measures could be won. The year 1931 saw the formation of the Public Housing Conference, Mary Simkhovitch president and Helen Alfred (a settlement associate of Mrs. Simkhovitch's, much of whose career had been spent at Madison House, New York) secretary, and including Harry Laidler, Charles Poletti, L. D. Lasker (of the *Survey*), Irving Brant (of the *St. Louis Star Times*), Father John O'Grady (secretary of the National Conference of Catholic Charities), Bishop McConnell, and Rabbi Israel, and Ira Robbins and Louis Pink (legal advisers to the New York State Board of Housing) among its members. This group was influential in getting a housing division added to the PWA and in having the Federal Housing Administration established in 1934; but its major accomplishment was in working through Leon Keyserling in Senator Robert Wagner's office to do all the detailed legislative work that finally culminated in 1937 in the establishment of the United States Housing Administration. By that time the National Public Housing Conference had won allies among organized labor and among other municipal reform committees, and support from the housing committee of the National Conference of Social Work (Abraham Goldfeld was chairman) and from the Urban League. Responsibility for its passage must be credited to many associations and persons; ultimately the maneuvering by Wagner and the support given to the measure within the administration by Harold Ickes, Harry Hopkins, Frances Perkins, and Mrs. Roosevelt proved crucial; but it is instructive to compare the measure with the National Federation of Settlements' elaborate resolution of 1922, and to note the continuity of leadership provided by settlement leaders, especially by Miss Alfred and Mrs. Simkhovitch.

Housing reform was a unifying force for the settlements during the 1920's; another great social issue — prohibition — was nothing but divisive. From the beginning, some social workers had endorsed national prohibition as a measure aimed at eliminating the poverty, dependency, and family troubles which derived from alcoholism and the corruption and depravity which flowed from the saloon. But they were embarrassed by the strange bedfellows they were forced to embrace. Their normal allies had always been urban reformers, organized labor, new immigrants, Catholics and Jews; everywhere they had run up against the rabid enmity of employer associations, rural legislators, conservative, evangelical Protestant sects, white supremacists in the South. Prohibition shifted the alliance pattern. Prohibition, moreover, cut them off from friends, neighbors, and clients — the poorer folk, particularly the new immigrant slum-dwellers. To these latter groups prohibition seemed to be nothing less than class legislation, aimed at the workingman's saloon not at the rich man's salon. Had not the birth of a child always been celebrated with a toast, weddings enlivened with the cup of cheer, grief softened by the friendly sharing of spirits? Now the Yankee custodial powers were to deny them these traditions. But social workers and settlement residents who had seen the destructive poverty and violence that use of hard liquor so often brought, welcomed the elimination of the saloon. To them, prohibition promised relief for their neighbors from drunkenness, absenteeism, domestic quarrels, graft, prostitution, and general social misery. The National Federation of Settlements rejoiced at the ratification of the Eighteenth Amendment in 1919 and as late as 1924 went on record endorsing its strict enforcement, "practically feasible in every community," as "vital to the safety and well-being of the nation."[11]

Enforcement, at first rather effective, began to falter and to slip into wholesale corruption and evasion after several years. Even Graham Taylor, at first an advocate of prohibition, was forced by events to recognize that defiance of the amendment, "especially by wealthier consumers, and the failure or refusal of local authorities to enforce the law, [had] set an example of lawlessness, which the youth [had] been quick to follow."[12] A cynical disregard for law, racketeering, class and ethnic bitterness, increased drinking among youth and women were among the consequences. Clearly the time had come, by 1926, to reassess the experiment; and re-evaluation demanded sober research into prevailing conditions. The national federation turned naturally to the device of the survey, naming Lillian Wald as chairman of a study committee, and Martha Bensley Bruère, a frequent contributor to the *Survey*, as its director.[13]

Mrs. Bruère quickly drew together a staff — composed of a "wet," a "dry," and a "doubter" — gathered detailed reports from 193 informants (most of them settlement or other welfare agents), and then set out across the country on a protracted field trip to check on regional differences. Her report, *Does Prohibition Work?*, published in 1927 was more a gathering of human-interest stories than statistical analysis. Her findings offered solace to neither proponents nor opponents of prohibition. She reported that wherever there were large settlements of foreign-born or first-generation citizens prohibition was least observed, but it was exactly with the interests of these groups primarily in mind that social workers had endorsed prohibition. She reported that "all through the American Belt . . . wherever the Americans of the earlier immigrations are still in control, our reports show that prohibition works." Working-class, recent immigrant groups somehow found access to their traditional drink, so much was clear; but the grosser violations, and the more dangerous to civic righteousness, were among the richer classes. "No rum-runner operates to supply the thirst of the man who earns four dollars a day." Official graft was the inevitable concomitant of illicit traffic. Other evidence, however, suggested that the drunkenness of misery had declined, that community health standards had improved, that absenteeism from work had declined.[14]

Prohibition was but one issue that spilled over into the arena of partisan politics during the 1920's as far as settlement and other social workers were concerned, but it may have been one of the most crucial; certainly it did more to fragment political effort among welfare workers than any other single issue. Particularly was this the case in the election of 1928 when social service workers were forced to choose between Governor Smith, a reform liberal but "wet," and Mr. Hoover, whose reputation as the Great Engineer and the Great Humanitarian and as a "dry" was as yet untarnished. Settlement leaders, of course, had rarely been intensely partisan in their loyalties, preferring to achieve their political ends by independent action. A large number of social workers had gone over to Roosevelt and progressivism in 1912; a large share of these, in turn, had swung to Wilson, reform, and peace, in 1916. No real choice had been offered in 1920. The confusion was merely compounded in 1924; some leading social workers endorsed La Follette, and assuredly neither Coolidge nor Davis could make the heart beat faster, but it is probably safe to conclude that there was no substantial outpouring of enthusiastic support for "Fighting Bob."

The election of 1928 seems to have aroused more passion and dispute than that in any year since 1916. Mary Van Kleeck, a professional social worker and research scholar generally thought of as among the more "radical" in the profession, formed a nationwide committee of social workers for Alfred Smith. Lillian Wald and John L. Elliott, both of them professed prohibitionists, joined at once, soliciting the support of welfare workers throughout the nation. Governor Smith, they wrote in a circular to hundreds of colleagues, will end "hypocrisy and evasion" on the prohibition issue. In public health, labor relations, crime prevention, and public power he had proved himself a "vital humanitarian" second only to Lincoln. "He is a realist and a hard worker," they concluded. "He has a genius for comprehending what social work is and he sees straight through unhindered by abstraction and academic proposals."[15]

The response to the Wald-Elliott letter suggests how profoundly social workers were divided by the prohibition issue. One can imagine that hundreds of busy social workers filed the letter among the wastepaper and went about their business. Sixty-six of them, however, were moved to reply at some length. Of these, forty-five declared for Hoover (including Jane Addams, Sophonisba Breckinridge, Lucile Eaves, H. H. Hart, Robert Kelso, and Mary McDowell), seventeen for Smith (Frederic Almy, Joanna Colcord, Edward T. Devine, Paul Kellogg, Lucy R. Mason, and J. Prentice Murphy), two confessed to being undecided, and only two respondents (one of them Helen Alfred, the settlement-based housing reformer) declared for Thomas. Jane Addams' terse reply to her old friend was both the briefest and the best-hearted — "Voting for Hoover but send good wishes for Smith campaign." At the other extreme were letters such as one which bitterly declared: "By broadcasting your views in this unsolicited fashion you have alienated many of us who feel it is rather cheap to trade on your otherwise fine reputation to influence votes for the man who publicly stands for disregard and disobedience of established law." A social agency official wrote from Columbia, South Carolina, in much the same vein: "I have the same contempt for social workers dabbling in politics that I do for ministers who do the same." Don't forget that Smith is a Roman Catholic, he wrote, and "wherever the Catholic Church rules, there is darkness, superstition, and deterioration."

These were extravagant statements, reflecting nativist, dry, and Protestant prejudices, but even the more considered replies fell back on the prohibition issue and on Smith's lack of formal education and his identification with corrupt machine politics. The director of the Tulsa Community Fund found Smith to be "a rather cheap politician" and Hoover "a constructive statesman." A former admirer wrote that she was disappointed that Miss Wald would "prostitute" her talents by endorsing a wet and an "arch politician" when the Republican candidate was "an efficient, cultured, competent, experienced, tolerant Quaker." Evident also were feelings of regional resentment toward the domination of politics and of social work by New Yorkers. The director of the Omaha Welfare Federation, for example, wrote that Miss Wald's letter would come more "appropriately from someone not a member of the community of greater New York — a city alien to the country as a whole and its ideals and opinions." Another social worker, from Detroit, complained about Miss Wald's "endeavor to capitalize the national standing which social workers on Manhattan may have in political communications to the supposed benighted residents who are social workers in the provinces."

Those who replied to Lillian Wald in support of her candidate either felt it superfluous to explain their position or wrote in guarded terms that they intended to stand with the cause of liberal reform despite Smith's presumed commitment to repeal. Many who declared they might otherwise support Smith protested they could not vote against a man who promised the honest and efficient administration of the Eighteenth Amendment.[16]

To a Yankee social reformer in Boston, Elizabeth H. Tilton, 1928 loomed as the greatest crisis in her life. A lifelong Republican, Mrs. Tilton had worked for such diverse causes as the prohibition of child labor, federal aid to education, penal reform, international peace and disarmament, the protection of women in industry, the Sheppard-Towner program. In local and state politics her influence had always been thrown on the side of what she defined as the "back-bone" of the Republican party, "the middle class respectable people" and "progressive moral-leadership," and against the "obstinate and near-sighted . . . Special Interest" faction. When the Republicans turned to Hoover and the Democrats to Smith, she saw the contest as "between two levels of civilization — the Evangelical, middle-class America and the Big City Tammany masses." In mid-July of the campaign year she set down her thoughts again: "It is the old American, Puritan-based ideals against the new Latin ideals. . . . It is old stock agin the loose, fluctuating masses of the Big Cities. It is dry agin wet. It is Protestant against Catholic."

By election day Mrs. Tilton's anxieties proved almost unbearable. "My America against Tammany's. Prairie, Plantation and Everlasting Hills against the side-walks of New York!" she recorded in her journal on election eve. "Women meeting on the street clasping my hand to cry, 'We can not live if Hoover is not elected!' . . . Women say, 'We feel like night before our wedding!' — Life held in terrifying suspension!" But then, late election night, came the reassuring news by radio that Hoover had carried the day. "We are saved! . . . I feel this great Country, its presence, lying out there in the vast darkness, like a soft thing enveloped in sweet, misty night, immense but one in purpose for the Clean Man, the Free Man." [17]

Mrs. Tilton was a typical New England Republican, feminist reformer — a bit more nervous and unstable, sentimental and poetic than many, perhaps, but nevertheless representative of a large body of middle-class, Protestant, native American crusaders for good causes. Family circumstances may have inclined her toward greater personal fanaticism on the prohibition issue than many other reformers, but her response to the issues of 1928 — or perhaps one should say to the symbolic quality of the contest — was not untypical. Although Governor Smith's record as a welfare liberal was unassailable, Hoover's legitimate appeal as a humane administrator made him as attractive as Smith to many reform-minded welfare leaders. The division within reform ranks related, on a national basis, to prohibition, on other grounds to religious and ethnic considerations. Settlement leaders were as torn as others.

However important the issues of prohibition, religion, and machine politics may have been, prosperity was probably the Republican's most valuable asset. The promise of a chicken in every pot undoubtedly over-weighed the fear of a Catholic in the White House in making possible the Hoover landslide of 1928. But there were some few critics in America who recognized that good times unevenly shared made prosperity precarious.

At Chicago Commons, in the winter of 1928, residents began to report growing unemployment in the neighborhood; boys were coming to club meetings in threadbare clothing, and sometimes hungry. When Graham Taylor and his daughter Lea took their evidence of unemployment to the Chicago Federation they discovered that other settlements were similarly disturbed. For the national federation meeting in April, a session was arranged on the problem of unemployment. Dr. Harlow S. Person, director of the Taylor Society, spoke; so did Dr. Isaac M. Rubinow, director of the Jewish Welfare Society, Philadelphia; but it was Lea Taylor's stirring, if matter-of-fact, account of the consequences of unemployment that drew fire. The settlement was the "listening post" of society, she said, and what she was hearing, like others, was of widening unemployment in the midst of hectic prosperity. And what were the human consequences; to what did unemployment, occasional and protracted, lead? "[T]o the overburdening of women already under heavy strain, to prospective family discord, to illicit money getting, to humiliation, to loss of neighborhood standing, to under-nourishment, disease, disorder and dissension, to the undermining of the will to work." In the neighborhood of Chicago Commons, one out of every four able-bodied men had no work.[18]

Miss Taylor's remarks ignited the tinder. Some delegates, perhaps, remembered the Panic of 1893 and the soul-searing experience the infant settlements had suffered in those formative years when the residents had been forced to carry vicariously the physical suffering, psychological demoralization, and social bitterness that hard times had entailed. When the Executive Committee met to discuss its business for the year, there were comments at once that routine matters of settlement program were consuming entirely too much time of boards and committees.

The delegates insisted that the national federation's Executive Committee free itself from administrative minutiae and take up more pressing matters. Is any group in America "closer to the wreckage of unemployment than we are?" asked John Elliott, "its resulting sickness, moral degeneration, filling up of jails?" His suggestion that the committee take up the challenge was quickly seconded by Paul Kellogg, who commented on the "sense of insecurity, the moral despair in unemployment periods." George Bellamy of Hiram House, Cleveland, made the expected resolution to appoint a committee of study to gather the facts and to search for solutions. The precedent of the prohibition study was cited, and a committee was chosen with Helen Hall as its chairman and Mrs. Irene Hickok Nelson, of Union Settlement, New York, as its secretary.[19]

The selection of Helen Hall to head up the study proved a shrewd move. A member of the generation that stood between the older settlement pioneers and the younger professionals, she had been trained at the New York School of Social Work (when it was still known as the School of Philanthropy) and entered settlement work directly, in Westchester County. During the Great War she served overseas in the Red Cross and spent the immediate postwar years with the YWCA in Alsace and later as education and recreation director for enlisted men in China and the Philippines. From 1922 to 1933 she was director of University Settlement in Philadelphia, moving to Henry Street as head resident when Lillian Wald's illness made necessary the appointment of a successor. If settlement work for Miss Hall was more a career than a mission, she was deeply committed to the social-action role of welfare work; she believed in the necessity of social research; she was as relentlessly insistent upon social justice as ever the pioneering generation had been.[20]

Miss Hall and her committee proposed not to make a statistical study of unemployment but rather to select representative cases from settlement neighborhoods throughout the nation, to analyze the factors making for loss of work which lay beyond the control of the individual, and to describe and evaluate its social and psychological consequences. By June of 1929 a preliminary report had been submitted to the national federation, and the Executive Committee, shocked by evidence of "serious family and individual deterioration under involuntary unemployment," made arrangements for its immediate publication and urged

that a copy be given to the President so that he might "institute measures for the elimination of this inhuman and economic waste." [21]

Probably in response to Mary Simkhovitch's hope that a little "ginger" could be put into the study, the federation decided to push ahead
quickly with the publication of a popularization of the report; it appeared in 1930 under the ironic title *Some Folks Won't Work*.[22] Mrs.
Charles Marquis Merrell of Philadelphia, writing under the pen name
of Clinch Calkins, set forth in this book the evidence to dispel three
prevailing illusions: that unemployment came only with hard times,
that only those who were thriftless and lazy suffered unemployment in
good times, and that "if a man really wants to find work, he can find
it." The settlements knew not a one of these assumptions to be in accord
with the objective facts. As for the alleviation of unemployment in
normal times, she suggested (speaking for the federation) that employers seek means to regularize employment, that a coordinating federal employment service be established, that governments budget ahead
for public works to be initiated in slack times, and that security against
unpreventable unemployment be provided through a social insurance
system.[23]

By the time Miss Hall's more serious and elaborate *Case Studies of
Unemployment* was published, in 1931, the national concern with the
causes and consequences of unemployment was a bit more urgent. Using
the cases collected in months of flushed prosperity back in 1928–1929,
she traced the ways in which families accommodated to loss of wage
income. Savings were the "first cushion, cash savings first of all." The
lapse of insurance, the loss of furniture (when installments could not be
covered), the surrender of a house (for failure to meet the mortgage
payments) were the next steps. The piling up of unpaid debts soon followed, until the family owed everyone in sight — the landlord, the
grocer, the milkman, the fuelman. "When other resources have been
exhausted, and in most instances only then, the family asks for charity."
But private assistance was not easy to win and many families could
"never reconcile themselves to accepting help from strangers. . . . They
lose something, as they see it, when they take help, even if the cause for
asking for it lies outside their own control. It means a serious break in
family pride and self-confidence, a self-confidence which seldom blos-
soms again with the same sturdiness." Other makeshifts follow quickly.
The family budget is pared down; expenditures for clothing and food

are all reduced. The family moves to cheaper quarters. Somewhere along the downward slide, the wife and mother throws herself on the labor market, often having more luck finding a makeshift job than her husband. The human consequences of prolonged unemployment were unhappily easy to summarize: malnutrition, sickness, comfortless homes, crowded housing, family discord, desertion, lowered morale and loss of self-respect, humiliation and pervading anxiety, hopes abandoned for talented young children, bitterness and resentment for the parents. "Losing faith and confidence in some one you have leaned upon and trusted is about the worst thing that can come to a human being." Time and again the unemployed neighbors had reported: "It's not the going without we mind: it's the insecurity." Above all else, concluded Miss Hall, what "unemployment does to people is to take the spring out of them."

Possible lines of social action were barely hinted at in the report — the stabilization of employment, "long-term planning for public works," the coordination of employment services, and (citing the precedent of workmen's compensation) some form of insurance against "unprevented or unpreventable unemployment." But the significance of the report lay less in these vague suggestions than in the presentation of evidence of the existence of widespread unemployment, its impact on family life, its social costs. Once again the settlements had pioneered in the initiation of a dialogue on a crucial community issue, whose description and dimensions so few Americans knew.[24] From the beginning of the project, Helen Hall had seen her role as that of creating public opinion and stimulating public action. John Elliott's views along these lines were taken down by the Executive Committee's recording secretary in rough, handwritten notes: "Up to Setts to take cognizance of any big troubles in neigh. Unemp one of chronic troubles. Gotten used to it. Fine chance to get facts — speak up loud. Then Gov and big orgs got to handle it."[25]

By exploring housing reform during the 1920's, by launching their studies of prohibition and of unemployment, the settlements were reasserting their long-established role as pioneers. By continuing to testify to the felt needs of their neighbors, settlement leaders continued to act implicitly on the premise of spiritual witness. No metaphors appeared more often, in the interwar years as in the prewar years, than those of the "pioneer" and the "witness," and if the latter concept arose explicitly out of the Christian experience and heritage, those whose religious commitment stood upon the Old Testament alone were not untouched by the belief that there were times when the best one could do was to stand and testify to a transcendent concern. If the parable of the Good Samaritan was often cited on formal occasions in answer to that ancient question — Who, then, is my neighbor? — the answer to that older protest — Am I my brother's keeper? — was habitually given: Man is not his brother's keeper but his brother's brother.[26]

Many of the settlement leaders who continued to inform the movement and its ideology in the 1920's were consciously working out their religious faith. Mary McDowell, Mary Simkhovitch, Paul Kellogg, Graham Taylor, Robbins and Catheryne Cooke Gilman invariably fell back on Christian concepts and metaphors when explaining what they were about. From Graham Taylor, an ordained minister, one could expect affirmations of the faith that the settlement found "expression not in creed but in deed; not in ritual but in the sacraments of daily life . . ." and that where the divine ideals could not be "preached out and prayed in" the settlements could "live them out and love them in by reverential ministries to the commonest human needs."[27] Throughout the 1920's, in public statement and in intimate letter alike, he poured out his faith and his religious hope "that right is might and must prevail, that truth will outlive error, that love abides and cannot fail."[28]

So too did other settlement workers choose religious expression of motives and goals. Mary McDowell traced her career and commitments to many sources — from a childhood carpenter friend the dignity of labor, from mingling with many peoples and from her abolitionist family tradition a sense of racial equality, from the efforts of labor to organize in the stockyards the recognition of brotherhood principle in industry, from all her settlement experience "a reverence for human beings, and a humility in the presence of their struggles. . . ." But it was from going among her neighbors that she learned to comprehend "that Power not myself working for righteousness, revealing the 'contemporary Christ' in the midst of the city of many nations, races, and faiths."[29] On another occasion, to the delegates of the first international conference of settlements in 1922, Miss McDowell defined the settlement not as a "colony of well-intentioned middle class people that has thrust itself into a poor district" but as a center of common social action where people could "enter into the joy of life" together, thus demonstrating "that we are all members of one body." [30]

Mary Simkhovitch, an Episcopalian churchwoman, regularly confessed the religious motive of the settlement: whether they were explicitly Christian or "non-religious or irreligious," settlement leaders were disciples of Jesus who, she wrote, cherish "followers rather than worshippers who fear to walk in His way of love and self-surrender." [31] Lesser known settlement leaders echoed these sentiments and used these root metaphors. Catheryne Cooke Gilman thought of the settlements as the "leaven" in the loaf, and as "applied Christianity . . . deeply religious, but not sectarian." [32]

Although a very substantial number of settlements continued to be church-affiliated — exactly half of New York's settlement centers were church-connected in 1927 — and although the official and private statements alike of settlement leaders continued to proclaim spiritual motives and goals, the religiosity of the pioneer generation began to pale in the 1920's and the younger generation tended to build other, though often related, rationales. The younger generation, entering settlement work during the interwar years, tended to be embarrassed at and sometimes impatient with the unashamed piety of their elders. Helen Phelan, of Merrick House in Cleveland, came before her colleagues in the national federation in 1930 with an apology: "I am old-fashioned enough to have a religious motive for doing the thing I am doing. It is old-fashioned in these days, isn't it, to mention religion." Still, there it was, she confessed, the old Franciscan idea of doing things for "the love of God, and we hope to help man to become, perhaps, a little Godlike." [33]

During the interwar years the secular democratic philosophy of the movement, from 1886 a central ingredient, received new emphasis as the religious impulse began to fade. The settlements offered the means to strengthen individual self-development and procedures for working out group decisions and group programs. Robbins Gilman came to see in the postwar years that new factors of "collective living" were forcing persons everywhere in society "to live and move in a labyrinth of group adjustments." The neighborhood center, "individually developing and socially useful," could — by practicing voluntary, democratic relationships — help to lead the group toward constructive programs and to train the best to cooperative leadership. [34] The point was to broaden participation, to strengthen self-determination, to lead away from dependence upon authority and toward self-determination. Particularly in an age increasingly characterized by massive organizations, wherein vast, impersonal, environmental forces molded and directed the course of history, it was essential that the chances for individual autonomy and group self-direction be given vigor. It was not enough alone to release the poor from material poverty, George Bellamy exhorted his colleagues in mid-decade. "It is possible for one to be well housed, well fed, well clothed, well educated, well organized and well rotted." [35]

The urban environment provided so little open space for creative and spontaneous activities. Men and women and children were crushed not only by sordid and overcrowded surroundings but by mechanized, routine, monotonous employment and recreation; the individual was ground down, and democracy ceased to function vitally. Man must be saved from the massiveness of society. These words echo through the settlement papers: self-development, self-respect, self-support, self-motivation, self-sufficiency, self-dependence. Only in a self-directed, noncoercive, spontaneous community could the principle of mutual interdependence through the voluntary participation of all its members make possible the full realization of each person's potential and the implementation of true democracy in the nation.

When it came to social reform, the settlement could act both to channel neighborhood understanding and action and to inform society at large of the special problems associated with life in disadvantaged neighborhoods. The settlement must serve, said Graham Taylor, as the community's "eye, ear, and touch, in order to report what is seen that is out of sight, what is heard that is unheeded, what is felt that otherwise fails to touch the community's great heart." [36] Between class and mass the settlements reached out to reconcile and to restore communication, to interpret the ways of one to the ways of the other. They were, said Paul Kellogg, "centers of contact, understanding, impulse" where "connection springs warm from personal contact." [37]

Other social-work agencies might establish artificial and mechanical routines, and fail to respond quickly and deeply to changed conditions, but the strength of the settlement was nourished by daily contact with the intimate details of human life. The quick concern of settlement leaders for housing reform and social security when most other agencies were blind or dumb, their ready response to social problems that accompanied panic and depression were quite in accord with long experience and tradition. Because sentimentality had been burned out of the movement back in the desperate nineties, it was all the more ready to recognize need and to initiate ameliorative action when hard times came again. The motto of the settlements, Catheryne Cooke Gilman suggested, might be "Keep your fingers on the near things and eyes on the far things." [38]

THE SEARCH FOR SECURITY

"[T]here can be no peaceful advance as long as the pressing problems of human destitution remain unsolved, and nothing short of a comprehensive national system of social insurance against all the factors of poverty, such as death, sickness, accident, invalidity, old age, or unemployment, offers even a semblance of an immediate solution."

— Isaac M. Rubinow, *Social Insurance* (New York: Holt, 1913), p. 501

"Not only are the relative numbers of the aged increasing . . . but they are also finding it more difficult to obtain gainful employment. . . . if the older worker once loses his position because of illness, a reduction in the size of the working force, etc., he finds it far more difficult than would a younger man to obtain employment elsewhere. . . .

"When to insufficient earnings are added the disasters which so frequently sweep upon families in the shape of serious accidents, prolonged unemployment, protracted illnesses, and death, it becomes apparent that a large section of our population finds it virtually impossible to build up a stake for old age."

— Paul Douglas, "Introductory Note" to *The Care of the Aged:*
Proceedings of the Deutsch Foundation Conference, 1930
(Chicago: University of Chicago Press, 1931), pp. vii–viii

"Ever since Adam and Eve were driven from the sheltered Garden of Eden, insecurity has been the bane of mankind. The struggle for human progress has been a battle for security.

"The challenge confronting us in the twentieth century is that of economic insecurity, which weighs down our lives, subverts our liberty, and frustrates our pursuit of happiness. The establishment of economic security has become a paramount issue because our modern system of industrial production has rendered our lives insecure to the point of despair.

"The sinister specter of insecurity not only undermines the physical and moral welfare of the individual worker, but is to-day the outstanding obstacle to national well-being and prosperity. It is both the cause and effect of depression."

— Abraham Epstein, *Insecurity: A Challenge to America* (New York:
H. Smith and R. Haas, 1933), pp. 1, 17–18

T H E year was 1911. Theodore Roosevelt would soon be proclaiming the need for a Gideon's army to rise up and establish a decent, just, and mighty nation. Within the year Woodrow Wilson would put forward a program which would assure to every citizen a new birth of freedom. Louis Brandeis, soon to be named chief adviser on domestic legislation to the Democratic President, proclaimed before the National Conference of Charities and Correction his thesis of economic rights: Modern democracy, he said, professed a fundamental belief in the free citizen; but "can any man be really free who is constantly in danger of becoming dependent?" And to what conditions could dependency be traced? To "sickness, accident, invalidity, superannuation or unemployment, or to premature death of the breadwinner of the family." These were root causes of dependency over which individual workmen, with their painfully limited capacity, had little or no control. Nothing less than a comprehensive insurance system would suffice to cover the social risks of modern industrial life. A national insurance system could both ameliorate the human suffering attendant upon sickness, accident, dependent old age, and unemployment and help to reduce their incidence. On another occasion he put forward similar principles in words still more eloquent: "For every employee who is 'steady in his work,' there shall be steady work. The right to regularity in employment is co-equal with the right to regularity in the payment of rent, in the payment of interest on bonds, in the delivery to customers of the high quality of product contracted for. . . . Each of these obligations is equally a fixed charge. . . . The reserve to ensure regularity of employment is as imperative as the reserve for depreciation; and it is equally a part of the fixed charge to make the annual contributions to that reserve. No business is socially solvent which cannot do so." [1]

The year following, 1912, delegates to the national conference endorsed a reform platform which included the insurance principle to promote security in the face of unemployment, old age, industrial accidents, and disease. A generation earlier Bismarck's Germany had set a precedent for social insurance as a means to take the sting out of socialist criticism: compulsory sickness insurance had been inaugurated in 1883, industrial accident insurance in 1884, old-age and invalidism insurance in 1889. It was this comprehensive system that had won attention in the United States with the publication in 1893 by the federal commissioner of labor of a report written by John Graham Brooks. England was not far behind: workmen's compensation had been instituted in 1897, old-age pensions in 1908, and in 1911 comprehensive health and unemployment insurance, the latter system made general for all industries in 1920. The British example was thus fresher in mind as the Wilson era began — and after war broke out in the heart of the West, it was taken as entirely a more reliable democratic precedent.

Although the Progressive party in 1912 had endorsed "the protection of home life against the hazards of sickness, irregular employment and old age through the adoption of a system of social insurance adapted to American use," American reform movements had not generally advanced that far in the prewar era. Some few pioneers had discussed the issue seriously — Henry R. Seager in a series of lectures at the New York School of Philanthropy in 1910 and Isaac M. Rubinow before the same audience two years later. Seager had been among the first to encourage at length the growing recognition on the part of that generation of welfare reformers that a collective answer to social hazards through insurance was the only sound way to save the individual citizen from economic dependency. Regularization of employment and a coordinated system of employment agencies together with industrial training and guidance could go far to eliminate the problems of unemployment; old age, he insisted, was clearly an insurable risk; for the moment, at least, insurance against unemployment was probably feasible only in the well-organized trades.[2]

Isaac M. Rubinow went a bit further. The successful experiments in comprehensive insurance schemes on the continent of Europe and more recently in England, together with America's happy experience with workmen's compensation, made it imperative that the United States explore the social necessity and practical feasibility of all kinds of social insurance, he insisted. Without some provision for security of person and income against the hazards of an industrial civilization, human freedom was placed in jeopardy. Against the argument that high wage levels eliminated the need for insurance in the United States, he paraded statistical evidence that 80 to 90 per cent of all wage workers earned less than enough to cover the costs of maintaining a normal family standard of health and efficiency, and at least half of them earned substantially less. The alternative to insurance was charitable relief; relief was degrading to the recipient and in no way acted as a preventive. The obvious superiority of a comprehensive, national, compulsory insurance system was that it promoted steady economic advance by distributing national income more equitably, strengthened security, and provided the best means to "orderly social progress."[3] Three years later, in 1916, noting an upsurge of interest in sickness insurance — or what he and others preferred to call health insurance, stressing its preventive aspects and drawing from the British precedent — Rubinow published a pioneer study that was to remain the standard work for a generation. The rationale was simple and well-buttressed with relevant facts: illness was an insurable risk whose cost could be borne only if distributed over a large number of wage earners; wage levels in America did not provide income sufficient to permit the worker himself to save for a time of need; if properly drawn, enabling legislation was fully constitutional under the police power of the state.[4]

Some few other reformers also spoke out. To the 1915 conference of the National Federation of Settlements, John L. Elliott spoke of the inevitability of some scheme of unemployment insurance which, together with public labor exchanges, vocational counseling, and the planning of public works, could do much to eliminate the human waste of industrial disorganization.[5] So too did Mary K. Simkhovitch, writing on the eve of America's entry into World War I; she placed job security high on her list of society's obligations to help remedy the imprisonment of life by poverty. Charitable assistance, whether offered by private or public agencies, required supplantment by positive welfare measures, for friendship between unequals, patron and patronized, was impossible.[6]

It was in Greenwich Village that one of the earliest case studies of dependency in old age was carried through under the direction of Mabel Louise Nassau. Intensive research into one hundred cases demonstrated that "economic fear" was the prevailing sentiment of the aging — fear of unemployment, want, dependency upon others, illness, institutional care. Where the aged were thrown on the resources of children an intolerable strain was placed upon the family; grandchildren were often forced on the labor market; bitterness and loss of pride were the fruits of these arrangements. The conclusions were clear from the evidence: private pension schemes were not feasible; private charity was inadequate and carried the taint of paternal benevolence; institutional care was invariably destructive of morale; some form of insurance, to which the ultimate recipient would contribute and from which he would receive pension aid as of right, provided the only effective and humane solution.[7]

In the years preceding America's entrance into the war, however, this modest agitation won but little public attention. Other issues took precedence on the progressives' agenda. Furthermore, a series of crises in American-Mexican relations was followed by the more clamorous events that led, in two and a half years, from neutrality to intervention in the European conflict. Suddenly it became "pro-German" to propose social insurance, even as the government moved to provide for the needs of servicemen and their families through government insurance and disability programs. The latter measures — which included medical care, vocational rehabilitation, and graded compensation for disabled veterans — continued to expand during the interwar era; but government life insurance policies, taken out during the emergency, were allowed to lapse by millions of veterans until by 1926 only approximately a half million policies out of an original four and a half million still remained in force. Further, the precedent of wartime government insurance made slight impact on the postwar era; for while other nations were expanding or initiating insurance schemes, in America little if anything was accomplished.[8]

Undismayed, social reformers attempted to drive ahead toward the goal as part of their crusade to reconstruct American society, now that the nation — and presumably the course of democracy and humanity — had triumphed over the forces of autocracy and inhumanity. Health insurance, many reformers believed, should have first priority in any program for reconstruction. In this crusade the American Association for Labor Legislation, under whose auspices the first American conference on social insurance had been held in 1913, led the way. Its model bill incorporated the principle of compulsory health insurance with benefit costs to be shared by employers and employees and with costs of administration to be borne by the governments of the several states; the bill had been set aside during the national emergency, but was revived in the closing months of war. Gompers and the AFL were adamantly opposed, but a significant if small segment of the medical profession had expressed its interest if not yet wholehearted support. Other associations had demonstrated their enthusiasm — the National Consumers' League, the Women's Trade Union League, the YWCA, various state federations of women's clubs and state suffrage associations — and even the American Hospital Association had come to consider it as inevitable social policy.

The assignment of first priority to health insurance was justified on several grounds: the movement could build upon the precedent of workmen's compensation; sickness appeared to be the primary source of poverty and dependency among wage earners; the rejection of young men under military conscription for reasons of substandard physical condition dramatized the need for preventive and positive health measures. John R. Commons and others were particularly hopeful that insurance would prove an incentive for preventive medicine. Furthermore, argued John Lapp, the social costs of ill health were being carried in some fashion already by those least able to do so; health insurance in no way increased the cost, it merely redistributed the burden more equitably; and when combined with prenatal and infant-care programs, with protective labor legislation, and with public health measures it wculd go far toward helping to build a strong and secure nation. Rose Schneiderman of the WTUL proclaimed health insurance to be one way of assisting industry to reduce excessive labor turnover, increase efficiency, and improve relations between management and labor.[9]

Of the several states willing to consider the issue, only New York advanced beyond a casual display of interest. There, Ogden Mills had introduced the AALL's model bill in 1916 and again in 1917; it was considered still again in 1918; and in 1919 — with Governor Smith's support and the endorsement of the Women's Joint Legislative Conference — it passed the Senate only to be killed in the Assembly's Rules Committee. The year 1919 proved not to be as fruitful as reformers had hoped. The legislature soon demonstrated that it preferred coercion over prevention as a way to quiet social grievances. Labels of "made in Germany" or "made by Bolshevism" were slapped on insurance schemes; the medical profession and private insurance companies launched a counteroffensive; workers were told by their employers that the cost of insurance would necessarily come out of their paychecks and that they would feel the pinch every time "some dago's wife . . . had a baby." [10] When New York faltered, the rest of the nation fell back.

Retreat became rout; by 1920 health insurance was dead, and subsequent discussions did nothing to revive it. John B. Andrews, Isaac Rubinow, John Lapp, Michael M. Davis were among the tiny band of those who continued to raise the prickly issue during the years of slump, but their occasional remarks served no more than to embarrass their associates with painful reminders of high hopes dashed or deferred. Even professional social workers, who daily witnessed the ravages of illness, could not be brought to recognize that health insurance would help to keep family beneficiaries, when overwhelmed by sickness, from becoming mere recipients of charitable handouts. So complained Isaac Rubinow at the end of the decade. Proponents had erred, he concluded, in their "over-confidence, based upon implicit faith in the justice and social value of the measure" and in their failure to consider the class and group interests united against the effort.[11]

Throughout the mid-twenties other aspects of social insurance fared but little better. The depression of 1920–1921 revived talk of unemployment insurance (and of centralized employment services and public works); but the nation's recovery from the brief setback was rapid, even though coal miners, textile workers, and farmers did not share in the general advance. State programs of aid to dependent mothers and their children continued to expand, but the elaboration of new devices for welfare was rarely to be found. Paul Douglas' pioneer study on family allowances, published in 1925, drew upon European experience, but there were few who found his suggestions applicable in the American environment. As for the National Conference of Social Work it concerned itself more regularly with the perfection of casework techniques than it did with wholesale reforms designed to lessen the need for individual care. William J. Norton, in his presidential address in 1925, renewed the plea for guaranteed minimum economic standards that would enable the worker "to support himself and his family in reasonable comfort, in health and in sickness, in youth and in old age, through all the vicissitudes of life." [12] But his address, stirring enough in rhetoric, was lacking in specific suggestions and fell, for the most part, upon deaf ears. John Lapp's presidential address before the same conference, two years later, was a bit more explicit, perhaps because as director of the Department of Social Action of the National Catholic Welfare Conference he had to confront these issues in season and out. The great causes of poverty, he said, were quite beyond individual control — "war, floods, and tornadoes, sickness, unemployment, under-employment, mental deficiency, death or desertion, inadequate wages, business failures and dependent old age." Social action, including social insurance, could alone provide security, equity, and true Christian justice.[13]

It was understandable enough that those who profited mightily from postwar prosperity were indifferent to the needs of those not quite so fortunate; the apathy and even the hostility of many social workers and labor leaders were less easy to accept. How could any person of intelligence and good will, unblinkered by class interest, fail to be moved by evidence of poverty and gross insecurity of life, even in the midst of plenty? Assuredly the nation was enjoying unprecedented prosperity, observed Dr. Rubinow in 1926; real wages were going up but so was the social service case load, so too were industrial accidents increasing, while there was no startling reduction in ill health or in unemployment. Efforts at private relief of socially derived need he described as "puny"; "one cannot sweep away the ocean of human misery with a charitable broom." Let professional social workers turn from their present preoccupation with "bad physical heredity, inadequate personality, lack of initiative, psychoses and neuroses, constitutional inferiority . . ." he pleaded, and take up the cause of social insurance.[14] The response must have been disappointing, for later Rubinow recorded that between 1920 and 1930 his 1913 preface to social insurance had been forgotten, and the very meaning of the concept lost. The time to repair the roof was when the sun shone. Well, he wrote, it stopped raining in the 1920's but "Did we grasp the opportunity? We did not. But as compensation we developed the new scientific theory, 'It ain't gonna rain no more, no more.'"[15]

Other reformers were hardly less bitter. John B. Andrews traced the failure of social security to win a hearing in the twenties to "post-war hysteria," "political indifference," and "commercial stupidity." Paul Douglas cited the traditional individualism of America, labor's reliance on economic action, rising prosperity, constitutional scruples, and the lack of a reform political party. Abraham Epstein was less charitable. He charged business leaders with "blind greed and stupidity" and assailed their "campaign of deliberate misrepresentation . . . carried on during the Hoover-Mellon era." "Whoever doubted their invincibility was condemned as a crank or characterized as un-American." Solomon F. Bloom put it more bluntly — how could a nation consider social security when it believed in the dogma of eternal prosperity? "Utopia needed no social insurance." [16]

Few Americans were in a better position to judge the degree of concern for social security than Andrews, Douglas, Epstein, and Rubinow, men who did more than any others to keep alive the movement. They were engaged in a lonely battle against seemingly prohibitive odds. But they were in a larger and more goodly company than sometimes they knew.

There was, for example, an increasing agitation for old-age-security measures throughout the decade, particularly on the part of dedicated social workers who saw about them the economic devastation and psychological demoralization that accompanied dependency in old age. Here and there labor leaders, benevolent organizations (the Fraternal Order of Eagles most notably), government officials, and university professors added their support. The American Association for Labor Legislation regularly carried studies on old-age security in its *Review*, and more than passing interest was evidenced by the Consumers' League, the Women's Trade Union League, and the League of Women Voters both on their national levels of organization and in some of their local and state units.

First came the exploration of need and the elaboration of a rationale for state pension action. The facts were simple enough; at least they seemed obvious to some. American wage rates, high enough when compared with wage levels in earlier generations or with rates prevailing in other countries, were not sufficient to permit a worker to set aside savings for old age. The segregation of the needy aged in old people's homes was both expensive and inhumane. How cruel it was, said John B. Andrews before a conference on problems of the aged in 1924, to "tear a veteran of industry away from wife or children or cronies after a lifetime of honest toil and commit him to the uncertain care of strangers in a strange place." The aged did not wish to be set apart; they wished to live in their own neighborhood, among familiar landmarks, with old friends and family. "A continuation of established habits, occupations and adjustments," Homer Folks observed, "may in a great majority of cases mean a much greater probability of health and of a comfortable and agreeable old age than a sharp break with the habits of a lifetime." The same principle that dictated caring for children in the home rather than in an orphanage applied with equal force to people at the other end of life's cycle.[17]

The need clearly was for the establishment of old-age pension systems to be financed out of regular tax reserves of the state. A detailed study done by the Research Department of the Women's Educational and Industrial Union of Boston under the direction of Lucile Eaves indicated that dependency in old age was the normal expectancy not only of the poor but also of families that lived at a level permitting decent standards of health but that could not save against the emergencies of life — ill health, business failure, unemployment, death of the breadwinner. How was the need to be met, justly and humanely, asked others, if not by the government's taking the responsibility? Charitable funds were always insufficient in amount and debasing to the recipient; private insurance schemes were too expensive for the greatest number of the citizenry; to require children to support their parents was to pass the burden of poverty along from generation to generation until a virtual caste system would be developed.[18]

In a simpler age, it might have been logical to expect the children to care for their parents in old age, so the argument ran; but the extended family system no longer prevailed in an urban and industrial society in which the children were fewer in number and often scattered throughout the nation. The ability of children to offer assistance did not always equate with their cheerful willingness to do so; handouts grudgingly given did little to bolster family morale or deepen affection. Was not the responsibility of a couple more properly toward their children than toward their parents? And was it not, as one proponent put it, a "hideous . . . distortion of natural affection" to force the aged to live upon the hospitality of their children and grandchildren when a modest pension might enable them "to pay board, and make them self-respecting and welcome guests in the home, instead of scarcely-tolerated burdens"?[19]

Whose was the responsibility for dependency, whose the obligation to provide a remedy? Again the answers seemed obvious to pioneers in the pension movement. Society in an industrial era was responsible. The pace of urban industry tended prematurely to age the worker so that by age forty or fifty he could often no longer maintain the required speed and efficiency; at this point, with no job security, he was thrown out in favor of younger, quicker, stronger men. Men and women, thanks to improved conditions of health, were living longer; the proportion of the aged in society was increasing steadily. Nothing was more certainly a responsibility of society, therefore, than to provide a regular allowance through a government system to all citizens "in consideration of past services," proclaimed a pamphlet of the Fraternal Order of Eagles. "Those who through years of humble toil have helped to create the wealth by which taxation is borne, are just as much entitled to honor and independence in their old age through pensions as the teacher, the judge, and the fireman." The obligation, finally, had been assumed by every civilized nation in Christendom; why should the greatest of democracies hesitate where lesser nations had forged ahead? [20]

As long as prosperity held, most proponents of government assistance to the dependent aged preferred the principle of granting pensions out of the general revenues of the state to the newer concept of contributory insurance. But whatever the procedures endorsed, the ultimate goal was acceptance by the community of the responsibility to "care for its aged men and women, not as an act of charity, but as an act of simple justice." [21] Where once Americans had accepted the almshouse as the logical place to care for the dependent, just as they had supported orphanages before the concept of foster home care became widely accepted, now they were beginning gradually to recognize (wrote an associate editor of the *Survey* in 1927) that "old people, like the rest of the human race, want not a Home but a home." [22] Addressing a Chicago conference on the aged in the spring of 1930, Isaac Rubinow rang the changes on all these themes in words more sharp than moderate reformers habitually employed. Incarceration of the able-bodied aged in institutions — "these concentration camps for the aged" — was "frequently unnecessarily cruel, and not infrequently unnecessarily expensive." [23] As for those who opposed social insurance, he said on another occasion, why did they never state candidly the real reasons for their obduracy? "Old age pensions are not fought because indirectly they might cut into profits or large incomes," he observed. "They are fought because they would be destructive of filial affection, because they would break down the spirit of family solidarity or the entire spirit of independence so characteristic of American manhood." [24]

Well might Rubinow and his associates have been bitter. By 1930, after many years of agitation, so pitifully little had been accomplished. Yet the American conscience had been pricked, studies of need had been made, the theory of government obligation had been elaborated, and in certain states preliminary if often faulty steps had been taken toward the inauguration of pension systems.

Arizona and Alaska had experimented in the years just before the war, but Arizona's law had quickly been struck down as unconstitutional. Commissions of study had functioned in Connecticut, Ohio, Pennsylvania, and Wisconsin, with major support for the investigations coming from the American Association for Labor Legislation and the Fraternal Order of Eagles, both of which groups had also played a key role in the winning of workmen's compensation and mothers' pensions.

The report of the Massachusetts Bureau of Statistics of Labor, written in 1905 by its chief, Charles F. Pidgin, traced the European precedents for old-age assistance, set forth his own state's need, and forecast many of the arguments that pension proponents would employ over the next generation, especially the conviction that pensions constituted the only humane alternative to charity or institutional care. In the flurry of interest and controversy which followed a special state investigatory commission was established in 1907. Its report of 1910, which recommended strongly against the inauguration of a pension system, received wide publicity and quashed further serious consideration of old-age pensions in the Commonwealth of Massachusetts and in many other states as well. [25]

Although the Massachusetts study had a disheartening effect upon the movement, other states in the postwar years began to investigate this problem which became more serious with every passing year as the percentage of the aged in the total population slowly increased, as life expectancy increased, and as the superannuation of many workers in industry became a larger concern. Montana, Nevada, and Pennsylvania acted in 1923; Wisconsin followed suit in 1925; Kentucky in

1926; Colorado and Maryland in 1927. The terms varied from state to state, but the broad outline of these acts was drawn primarily from the model bill put forward by the Fraternal Order of Eagles: eligibility at age seventy; fifteen years' residency in the state; possession of no more than three thousand dollars in property; a maximum payment of one dollar per day; exclusion of clients with children or other close relatives with the means to assist. Without exception, morever, the states merely authorized the counties to establish systems at their own option; no state moneys were provided. Not many counties proved eager to take up the option when to do so meant an increase in the already burdensome local property tax rate. Public ignorance and apathy, the climate of prosperity and normalcy, the weakness of union labor, the failure of pension proponents to stir up the aged themselves to political action all conspired to minimize the efforts of those few associations actively committed to this issue.[26]

Out of these conditions came the organization of a group whose dedication was first (in 1927) to promoting security among the aged and later to the adoption of comprehensive social insurance: the American Association for Old Age Security (AAOAS). Abraham Epstein, research director of the Pennsylvania Old Age Pension Commission since 1918, was the moving force in its formation. A graduate of the University of Pittsburgh, Epstein had gone directly from school into government research, in which capacity he had published, in 1922, a study entitled *Facing Old Age*. Here he declared that to throw the burden of support upon the younger generation was to serve the past at the expense of a hopeful future. All other civilized nations had some mode of meeting the problems of poverty in old age; for the United States he recommended the British example of a noncontributory pension system rather than the French or German system of compulsory old-age insurance.[27] His efforts had led to the enactment of the Pennsylvania act of 1923, but when attempts to have it rewritten after the State Supreme Court had nullified its provisions came to naught, he resigned and organized the AAOAS. Epstein moved in as executive secretary, Bishop Ethelbert Talbot of Pennsylvania as president (succeeded at his death within the year by Bishop Francis J. McConnell). Operating on a budget of less than five thousand dollars in the first year, Epstein built up the dues-paying membership to four hundred in 1928, thirteen hundred in 1929, twenty-six hundred in 1930, and over four thousand

in 1931. By this year, well into the depression, the association had a
working budget of around forty thousand dollars; but still expenses
tended to outrun receipts as publications and extensive travel consumed
all available funds.

The strategy of the AAOAS was much like that of other reform
groups — research and publicity, drawing up model bills and lobbying
for their enactment. Epstein found ready if small audiences on university campuses, before religious societies, fraternal associations, civic
groups, social service agencies, and labor unions. It is clear that Epstein
often received his most vocal support from local leaders of the Socialist
party and the League for Industrial Democracy. James Maurer, vice
presidential candidate with Norman Thomas in 1928 and again in 1932,
and president of the Pennsylvania Federation of Labor, was an old
associate of Epstein's on the state's Old Age Pension Commission and
one of his most vigorous allies during the first years of the depression.
Early files of the association contain letters from local Socialist leaders —
Robert Hoffman of Buffalo, New York, for example — boasting of their
influence in old-age conferences and deriding the more cautious professional social workers: "I told you in the final showdown your group
will have to DEPEND on a few Socialists like myself," Hoffman wrote to
Helen Alfred, field worker for the AAOAS in New Jersey, in 1929.
"These social workers are frauds — they talk big but really at heart don't
want any legislation passed and enforced which will in time abolish
the necessity for their kind of work." In response to this evaluation
Miss Alfred, herself a settlement worker, was forced to admit that
social workers generally weren't, for the moment, inclined "to push
this matter very dynamically." [28] As the movement gained momentum,
and when prosperity was broken by panic and the economy slumped
into depression, the old reform alliance began to roll again — professional reformer, social worker, labor leader, legal expert, professor and
scholar, philanthropist, minister, priest, and rabbi. Whose was the
largest influence and whose the least was not always easy to determine.

The arguments pressed upon an apathetic public in the twenties
proved more plausible when hard times followed good. It was altogether
easier to persuade the public that men could be in need through no
fault of their own when widespread unemployment demonstrated the
individual's impotency than when relatively full employment and rising
real wages marked the economic climate. Where once it had been

difficult to get a broad hearing, Epstein found he had more invitations to speak than he could possibly fill after 1929. In 1928, *Harper's* magazine had rejected a manuscript he had submitted to them with the explanation: "There is a lot of hard truth in this article which you have been so good as to let us see, but it is rather too hot in its presentation, so that it has what might be called a 'Bolshevik' air about it." [29] By 1929, Epstein could write to George Soule that "at this time there is more revolt and more energy among the worthwhile elements in attempting a real alignment and a re-vitalization of the progressive movement than perhaps have occurred in the last ten years. Personally, I have never been as inspired and thrilled with the possibilities of a new day as I have been the last few weeks." [30] Others pointed to the upward surge of old-age pensions throughout the Western world — in the twenty-four years from 1890 to 1914 fourteen countries had provided assistance; in the fourteen years from 1914 to 1928 fourteen more had joined the crusade. In the United States it could be reported that there was "keen interest" in the movement throughout the country. A few years earlier he had addressed assemblies of thirty or forty interested citizens, Epstein reported in 1931; now his audiences ran to two hundred and three hundred.[31]

In this context of upsurging interest, Minnesota and Utah had joined the states authorizing county-option systems, during the months just before the panic, while California and Wyoming provided programs mandatory upon the counties with statewide control and contributions from state government. The pension movement was catching fire, but nothing moved as fast as its champions would have liked. A partial victory in New York State, however, gave hope to the movement's leaders that in time their cause might triumph.

The original bill for New York had been drawn up in 1927 by Joseph Chamberlain of Columbia University for the AALL, which arranged to have set up a sponsoring committee representing the International Ladies' Garment Workers' Union, the Amalgamated Clothing Workers, the Electrical Workers Union, the Teachers' Union, the New York Consumers' League, the New York Women's Trade Union League, and the Fraternal Order of Eagles. The AAOAS and individual social workers and religious leaders joined the combined effort in 1928. Efforts to discharge the bill mustered but thirteen votes in the State Assembly in 1927, forty-nine in 1928, and sixty-one (still fifteen short of a majority) in 1929. The new governor, Franklin D. Roosevelt, appointed a committee of study in that latter year, and when the legislature met in 1930 he pushed for a true contributory pension system, but reluctantly consented to an old-age assistance measure. The terms, especially those providing for a means test, were as unsatisfactory to the governor, to Lieutenant Governor Herbert S. Lehman, and to F. D. R.'s advisers, Henry Bruère and Frances Perkins, as they were to most of the proponents of old-age security. Eleanor Roosevelt expressed these sentiments when she wrote: "Many of us do not feel that it is a very satisfactory bill but these things come slowly and a little at a time." [32] Nevertheless, the New York experience was significant: It educated F. D. R. to the principle of old-age insurance, which he soon came to connect with unemployment compensation, and for the national old-age security movement it represented a major break, inadequate as were its terms.

In Massachusetts, the bill that finally became effective was even more primitive. Financial assistance to men and women over seventy was to be paid according to need and only to those who were deemed to be "deserving" citizens; recipients were permitted to have no more than three hundred dollars in cash savings and no more than fifteen hundred dollars equity in real estate; children and grandchildren were required to file financial statements; aid could be denied or withdrawn if it were determined that the elderly were not living "in a decent way." [33]

Other states proved to be more generous. Colorado, Delaware, Idaho, New Jersey, and New Hampshire were added to the list of states providing old-age assistance in 1931, while other states liberalized their programs; two years later, the first year of the New Deal found nine new states inaugurating old-age assistance of some sort.

After a slow beginning, the leap forward came in the early years of the depression. Whereas by the end of 1929 state assistance was being paid to slightly more than a thousand pensioners throughout the nation, over ten thousand were on the lists in 1930, seventy-five thousand in 1931, and well over one hundred thousand in 1933, by which date the total cost had increased from approximately a million dollars in 1930 to around twenty-five million. To Epstein and his associates the laws seemed barely satisfactory: benefit payments, although more substantial than public relief normally provided, did not begin to match need; however liberally administered, the means test was universally applied because the systems were noncontributory and financed, therefore, out of general revenues; in most states meager payments were doled out by casework administrators habituated to close supervision of their clients' budgets. By 1933, moreover, the states, hard-pressed by demands for mass relief and many of them near bankruptcy, began desperately to plead for federal action. As Roosevelt moved from Albany to Washington, the focus of the battle shifted from the states to the nation.

To achieve even these ends had required the kind of long-suffering patience and arduous labors with which reformers had become familiar since the Great War. Legislative debates — with labor, fraternal, and religious groups on one side, industrial and agricultural associations usually on the other — were frequently prolonged and sharp. At times there seemed to be no just correlation between the energy invested and the scanty achievement. Knowing that a pension, awarded as of right, was the only satisfactory way to support the dependent in old age, reformers had frequently to accept old-age-assistance rules that smacked of charity and means-test clauses whose operation could not but undermine the self-respect of the applicants. At times Epstein spent as much effort privately reassuring his associates of the expediency of consenting to distasteful compromises as he did fighting publicly for measures more fully in accord with the principles of security he held dear.

There were critics to be mollified, pamphlets to be written, speeches to be delivered, local associations to be founded, bills to be written, legislators to be inveigled and cajoled, money to be raised. And always there stretched ahead the business of research, publicity, and lobbying. Appeals were both to "social value" and "political expediency" — "sincere sympathy with the needs of our aged dependents" and "incidentally" the political advantage which would accrue to that party initiating "a good old age assistance plan." [34] The association worked on legislators directly and indirectly through their constituents, where the tactic was to present both hard, statistical analyses of need and emotional human-interest stories of particular cases.

Events, however, were fast outrunning effective political responses. The association had to measure success in imperfect little driblets while hundreds of thousands of aging citizens were plunged into utter despair — their labor no longer needed, their savings quickly exhausted, their children thrown on the scrapheap by mass unemployment. The association had originally sought implementation of the pension principle — regular monthly payments to elderly citizens as of right, whether out of funds to which the recipients had themselves contributed or out of general tax revenues of the state. Its conferences in 1928, 1929, and 1930, moreover, had devoted sessions to the exploration of the whole field of social insurance. The practical week-to-week battle to get some form of old-age assistance legislation on the books, however, had tended to divert the association from its ultimate goal of old-age security. Spokesmen for the association, appearing before state legislative committees, soon learned that the one factor above all others which blocked serious consideration of even the most niggardly old-age assistance proposals was reluctance or inability to raise taxes in the face of a rapidly shrinking tax resource base. Delegates to the association's conference in 1931 queried Epstein: What do we reply when legislators ask us how old-age pensions are to be financed? This was the sticking point, Epstein confessed; use of the inheritance tax was perhaps the most equitable means, but any discussion of raising taxes from whatever source usually aroused bitter opposition, particularly from industry. The more expedient tactic was to evade the question and urge that the problem of raising funds be shifted to legislative finance committees. "First get the bill passed and let them worry about the money," he concluded. "It is not a very admirable stand to take, I admit, but it is the safe stand for success." [35]

Others saw, as Epstein often did himself, that success achieved on these terms did little to advance the ultimate cause of old-age security. Rabbi Stephen Wise called the association back to the central issue at the 1931 conference: "I want security for the aged, not charity. Let's have an end of the notion that we are seeking just some miserable little dole of pittance with which to make life livable for the aged." [36] Benjamin Glassberg, executive director of the Federated Jewish Charities in Milwaukee, hammered at the same point: "It is high time that some effort be made in the direction of the development of a system of contributory social insurance to include old age." [37] In 1933, Nicholas Kelley announced that the AAOAS had changed its name to the American Association for Social Security (AASS), explaining that although it had been urged since 1927 to expand its program the association had determined to focus on the winning of old-age security as its first priority of business; now that progress had been achieved toward that end, and now that dependency in old age could no longer be treated as an isolated phenomenon, the crusade would be for old-age, health, and unemployment insurance.

The association's renewed concern for the whole field of social security reflected a national trend; provision against the hazards of unemployment was surely more urgent in 1933 than it had been in 1929, but even during the prosperous twenties the interest had been kept alive by social reformers of many convictions, particularly by those affiliated with the American Association for Labor Legislation. Its interest in the promotion of industrial stability, in turn, went back to the prewar years when the ups and downs of the business cycle wreaked havoc with all attempts of workers to provide for their own welfare in good times as in bad. When in 1914 the economy showed every sign of slipping into depression, the AALL made a quick but careful study of the consequences of hard times in over one hundred American cities and a survey of what measures had been taken to relieve and cure the slump. From these analyses, the association drew up a series of recommendations for action when business should decline again. First, it suggested the creation of citizens' committees that would regularly survey needs and programs, seek out the facts, and publicize them, for it hoped that communities would not be caught ill-informed and unprepared again. It urged discrimination in treatment between employable and unemployable workers and the avoidance of indiscriminate relief to able-bodied men. It advised employers to explore means for regularizing employment and for spreading the work when cuts in production were unavoidable. The AALL recommended that central labor exchanges be established on a permanent basis and that local governments plan ahead for public works in slack seasons and years. Finally, the association recommended careful consideration of study and action which would lead toward compulsory unemployment insurance with the costs being shared by employers, employees, and the government.

Events of the immediate postwar years suggest that these analyses and suggestions had gone little noticed. Congress cut appropriations for the United States Employment Service in the spring of 1919, despite its substantial contributions to wartime labor mobilization in recruitment, placement, and conservation of manpower. By fall its funds were exhausted and its offices closed. It was replaced by no other agency; and no means existed, therefore, to direct an orderly transition to peacetime production.

With government controls relaxed or withdrawn, with labor and capital fighting it out again not at the bargaining table but on the picket lines and in the courts, the nation's economy lurched awkwardly into the postwar era. Demobilization had proceeded without plan or design; nature was allowed to take its course of spiraling inflation, unemployment, a break in farm prices, and then collapse. When prodigal wartime spending was finally curtailed, and government price supports for farm commodities were withdrawn, the day of reckoning quickly came. Drawing perhaps on the precedents for government initiative in time of national emergency established during the war, President Harding called a Conference on Unemployment in August 1921, with Secretary of Commerce Herbert Hoover serving as chairman. Hoover set a tone of urgency for the conference by expressing his conviction that no economic failure was so terrible as that of a nation that possessed a surplus being unable to provide employment for "willing and anxious" workers. A way out had to be provided if America's "moral and economic system" were to survive.[38] What his secretary of commerce set forth, the President withdrew: ". . . you are not asked to solve the long controverted problems of the social system," he announced to the delegates. "We have built the America of today on the fundamentals of economic, industrial and political life which made us what we are, and the temple requires no remaking now." In conclusion he made known the lack of enthusiasm with which he would greet any proposals that sought "either palliation or tonic from the public treasury."[39] There should have been no cause for surprise when the preliminary recommendations were set forth. The responsibility for providing relief belonged to the local community. Public construction was to be encouraged, and federal projects already authorized were to be moved along quickly. The conference urged business and industry to spread the work and to invest in repairs and upkeep during the slack winter months ahead. In any case reliance was to be placed on voluntary actions of business, labor, private agencies, and public officials.

The depression, which began in early 1920 and had begun to break by the summer of 1921, stirred up a temporary congressional interest in providing for the collection of more abundant and accurate economic statistics and for the planning of public works, but the aberration soon passed. Labor preferred restriction on immigration as a way to protect wage standards and reduce unemployment; business fancied higher tariffs, trade associational activity, and tax cuts to shake loose investment capital; agriculture turned to various schemes, most notably the proposals known as McNary-Haugenism, to uplift the farm segment of the economy.

The reformers, of course, were disappointed with the failure of the conference to come to grips with the fundamentals of the crisis as they saw them. William L. Chenery, reporting on the conference in the *Survey*, attacked Harding and the delegates for neglecting to consider unemployment insurance. "Unemployment is a risk of industry," he insisted, "as measurable and as recurrent as fire loss or work accidents. The most important device which society has developed for protection against risk is insurance." [40] Otto T. Mallery, secretary of the conference's subcommittee on public works, replied, in direct rebuttal, that for the conference to have considered unemployment insurance — an untried measure with no public support whatsoever — would have been to jeopardize serious discussion of other relevant issues. [41]

Mallery's rejoinder undoubtedly accorded with the temper of the conference and with current public attitudes; insurance against unemployment appeared to most Americans, if they thought of it at all, as an exotic, foreign, and wholly inapplicable and inappropriate device. Still, Chenery's reservations were not entirely exceptional. The National Child Labor Committee, for example, in a statement released to the press coincidental with the opening of the President's conference, proclaimed that involuntary unemployment was always a "humiliating" experience that led invariably to a loss of "self-respect," particularly for men who were out of work when women and children found ready employment. The unemployed were not only unfortunate citizens, they were "victims of a social crime." [42] The WTUL, shocked by society's failure to rise to the emergency, accepted in 1922 the report of its committee on unemployment which charged industry and finance with deliberately shutting down production as "a means of profit to themselves," and called for the re-establishment of a federal employment service, for public works, and for the study of unemployment compensation. The latter expedient was based on the notion that the burden of providing compensation should fall upon employers, whose failure to regularize employment was the primary source of depression. An insurance system, whose funds were raised from a tax on employers, would place upon industry "a continuous economic incentive to prevent unemployment." The delegates clearly had in mind the precedent of workmen's compensation.[43]

Florence Kelley, of the Consumers' League, was thinking along the same lines when she urged upon Allen R. Forsberg, of the University of Chicago, and Wisconsin's John R. Commons the publication of a pamphlet which would set forth the principles of unemployment compensation and their implementation. To an officer of the Amalgamated Clothing Workers, Mrs. Kelley wrote of her conviction that, following workmen's compensation, unemployment insurance was the next necessary step toward eliminating the industrial causes of poverty. In the long run, she predicted, a compulsory national system of insurance would be in order but that was "still in the future"; for the moment it was better to seek unemployment reserves through voluntary agreement of unions and management.[44]

This had been the line of the AALL, its officers and directors, ever since their hope for a comprehensive system to cover health and old age as well as unemployment collapsed in the hectic months immediately following the armistice. By December 1920, when it assembled in national conference, the postwar slump was well along. Upon the need for action all the speakers agreed. Unemployment together with the fear of unemployment had a disastrous impact on worker morale and on industrial efficiency; its sources lay far beyond the control of the individual worker; nevertheless there was nothing inherent or inevitable in recurring unemployment, it could not be considered or tolerated "as part of the natural order of things." [45] But what system of unemployment compensation could America inaugurate? John B. Andrews, for the moment, clung to his hope that together with a federal employment service and a coordinated program of public works a system of unemployment insurance — with the burden falling upon employers, employees, and the general public — could be initiated. Responsibility for leadership, he added, lay primarily with managers of American industry.[46] Other spokesmen preferred the expediency of starting with industry-wide systems, perhaps guided and supported by state government, but with industrial management itself taking the initiative.

Although there were dissenters within the AALL, its prevailing view in the mid-years of the 1920's stressed the creation of unemployment reserve funds, the moneys to be raised by industrial taxation and drawn upon during "temporary periods of involuntary idleness," the tax burden in turn to serve as an incentive to management to regularize employment and to deter unsound, speculative overexpansion. In 1929, this tactic still had the official support of the AALL; it also recommended the limitation of benefits to a maximum of ten dollars a week for thirteen weeks; eligibility through a work test administered by state employment bureaus; and the denial of compensation during strikes.[47]

John R. Commons, whose student and collaborator John B. Andrews had been, became the most important American academic economist working in the field of unemployment insurance in the 1920's. An adviser to La Follette on progressive legislation before the war, Commons was an advocate of effective collective bargaining, industrial regulation, government-established minima, and workmen's compensation, and a proponent of constructive, step-by-step advance of reform. When the health insurance movement collapsed from 1919 to 1920, he turned to unemployment reserves as the next logical advance.[48] As to many others the parallel of workmen's compensation pressed itself upon Commons. Because the primary purpose of workmen's compensation was not to pay out benefits but to prevent accidents, the overriding purpose of unemployment compensation was to forestall unemployment. Like the AALL he believed that employers should be required to establish reserve funds through mutual insurance companies under the general control of state government. The higher the unemployment rate in industry, the higher its insurance payments; employers, moved by the desire to minimize costs, would have every incentive to regularize employment. To forestall the possibility of labor's malingering, the benefit payments should be limited to a dollar a day for a maximum of thirteen weeks, and no worker would be eligible if he were not honestly prepared to accept employment at prevailing wage rates.

On Commons' advice, and with the assistance of Edwin E. Witte, chief of Wisconsin's Legislative Reference Library during the 1920's, and Arthur J. Altmeyer, secretary of the State Industrial Commission, a series of bills incorporating these principles were introduced and debated in the Wisconsin legislature. Commons' arguments were hard and pragmatic: the system had proved its workability elsewhere; it was "business-like and self-respecting" and in no way paternalistic or socialistic; while it provided benefits to those in need, its central motive was prevention not amelioration; by spreading the risk over many employers it made feasible the bearing of the cost; it promoted steady income, prevented worker demoralization, spurred efficiency; its benefits extended to the consumer and therefore to the general public, for "Increased efficiency and stabilized production, resulting in lower overhead costs for each unit of output, will decrease the costs of production, thereby making lower prices possible." [49] These bills won the support of the Wisconsin Federation of Labor, the Wisconsin Consumers' League, and the Women in Industry Department of the state League of Women Voters and were widely debated in Wisconsin and before select groups and legislative committees in other states.

Not until the depression had made the pressure of mass unemployment unbearable, however, did Wisconsin in January 1932 finally pass a bill. At that the original proposal for industrial reserves had had to be substantially watered down before it could be passed — employers had until 1 June 1933 to provide company reserves for unemployment compensation; if by that time firms with a cumulative figure of 175,000 employees had not voluntarily created reserve funds, a compulsory system would be imposed by the state. Reluctant to have Wisconsin go it alone and hopeful that national action in the field would be forthcoming, the legislature, in 1933, moved the day of reckoning forward to 1 July 1934 and added other modifying amendments. By that date plans covering but ten thousand workers met the standards, so the compulsory features of the act automatically went into effect. By then, however, the New Deal had turned to a serious consideration of unemployment insurance as part of a coordinated social security system and had called Edwin Witte to be executive director of the Committee on Economic Security, while Arthur Altmeyer, who was already an assistant secretary of labor, became chairman of the committee's technical board. If the Wisconsin experience did no more than train Witte and Altmeyer to an understanding of complex and highly technical issues in the field of social security it had a profound impact upon one of the most crucial welfare measures of the New Deal.

Wisconsin had set the pace but she had not run alone; New York,

California, Massachusetts, Oregon had all explored the feasibility of unemployment compensation before 1929, and with the growing burden of unemployment in the early depression years other states began seriously to explore unemployment insurance as an alternative to public relief. Conditions of mass unemployment, moreover, tended to discredit the Wisconsin belief that industrial reserves could act as an incentive to employers to stabilize production and employment. The catastrophe that followed 1929 proved clearly beyond the capacity of any single firm, or industry, or state to correct. In the midst of depression, therefore, Ohio's proposal for compulsory unemployment insurance (which owed so much to the influence of Isaac Rubinow and William M. Leiserson) won wider appeal than Wisconsin's program for employer reserves.[50]

Pending state or federal action, a certain number of industries had, on their own initiative or when prodded by labor, set up experimental unemployment reserve funds. In the highly irregular and seasonal clothing industry, near-anarchy had led to strikes in 1910 in Chicago and New York out of which came agreements between the Amalgamated Clothing Workers and certain corporations — most notably Hart, Schaffner, and Marx in Chicago — providing for boards of arbitration and boards of control. Margaret Dreier Robins had played a major role in persuading industry to accept these arrangements in Chicago while in New York Louis Brandeis, Abraham Cahan, Henry Moskowitz, Lillian Wald, and William J. Schieffelin had helped to mediate between labor and the employers. In 1923, prodded by Sidney Hillman of the Amalgamated Clothing Workers, the Chicago clothing industry inaugurated an Unemployment Insurance Fund, to which employers and employees made equal contributions; John R. Commons was accepted by both sides as impartial chairman of the Joint Board of Trustees. The arrangement was extended to New York the following year by which time over forty thousand workers were covered.

Following these precedents, the International Ladies' Garment Workers' Union demanded and won a similar unemployment insurance pact the same year, with a special mediation commission appointed by Governor Smith helping to implement the details. By the end of the decade the clothing and garment industries, in New York and Chicago and in such centers as Cleveland and Rochester, had been covered by such agreements. In every case the benefit payments were low, but high enough to provide partially for need and to encourage management and unions together to regularize production in an industry notoriously speculative, competitive, and seasonal. Beyond the clothing industry a few other firms — the Dennison Manufacturing Company, Procter and Gamble, and General Electric among the most publicized of them — established unemployment benefit plans, some through insurance funds, some through guaranteed employment arrangements; but Paul Douglas estimated that in 1929, after thirteen years of experience (the Dennison Company had pioneered its first efforts in 1916) only eleven firms in all industries throughout the entire United States had established programs. At a maximum no more than a hundred thousand workers had ever been covered by voluntary unemployment compensation programs of all varieties and many of these proved unable to withstand the demands made upon them by mass unemployment.

The experience was there to be utilized for educational purposes, but as practical measures to meet the problems of mass unemployment these programs were pathetically inadequate. Panic and depression brought most of them tumbling down. Not everyone, moreover, agreed with the AALL or with Professor Commons when they said that recurring unemployment in modern industrial society was "solely the responsibility of the employers and can and will be controlled by them." [51]

Leo Wolman, director of research for the Amalgamated Clothing Workers and a member of the New School of Social Research, had sensed from the beginning of the decade that voluntary, industry-wide programs would never suffice. The American experience had clearly indicated, he noted, "the narrow limits of persuasion and understanding as effective motive power in the accomplishment of social reforms." The risks were so great, the incidence of unemployment so unpredictable that only a general, compulsory, comprehensive insurance program had any chance of success. Toward the end of the decade he would point to the irony that in poorer nations, where the costs were presumably proportionally higher, governments had experimented with systems that had proved largely valid; only in the United States, which could safely afford a substantial program, had the "social conscience" been so "dulled" that nothing had been tried.[52] Within the AALL, as the decade drew to its close, the tone became more insistent. Four million workers were unemployed, John Andrews estimated in 1928; why, then, was nothing being done? Because the official political spokesmen could afford to see nothing but prosperity, because employers blindly asked only to be let alone. Now is the time to move, wrote Margaret D. Meyer in 1928 in the AALL's official journal, when the nation's energies and resources were "not of necessity consumed in temporary relief measures." [53]

A. J. Muste, disciple of a revitalized social gospel, reviewed for a social work audience in 1927 the evils of modern industrial society and exhorted them to press forward toward social reform. It was not only that exploitative forces denied decent men and their families a decent income, herded them into unsanitary and immoral neighborhoods, and rewarded "luck, cleverness, and the speculators' nerve and reckless-ness" over the traditionally professed economic virtues of "sobriety and industry." Beyond its specific evils, modern capitalism had created a society of "landless, houseless, tool-less, skill-less, religion-less, root-less, get-rich-quick-if-possible" citizenry; the course of life was directed by "vast, impersonal, relentless, erratic forces" before which man's in-dividual powers were "puny." But it need not be so. Men had it within their power to build a better society through regulation and planning, through trade unions and industrial democracy, through social insur-ance against "accident, sickness, occupational disease, unemployment, resourceless old age." By these means social self-determination and the integrity of family life could be advanced. [54]

By 1928 an increasing number of social analysts and critics were becoming aware of the ever increasing numbers of unemployed and the paradox of poverty in the midst of potential plenty. Evidence abounded of depression in coal and textiles and agriculture, but hard times extended beyond these sick industries. How could one account for the estimated four million unemployed in a booming economy? How could one tolerate it? If four million unemployed could be traced neither to seasonal nor cyclical oscillations the conclusion was clear that the condition had become chronic. Family welfare agencies re-ported that the burden of private relief was increasing annually; 1928 proved to be the heaviest time of need since the winter of 1920–1921. A disgruntled social worker from San Diego, Daisy Lee Worthington Worcester, was irked by the apparent apathy of the public and even of her associates; she cited Federal Trade Commission figures on the ownership of wealth to goad them into an awareness of economic mal-adjustment and social injustice. One per cent of the nation, at the top of the pyramid, controlled 59 per cent of the nation's wealth; the 87 per cent at the bottom controlled but 10 per cent. A majority of American families lived below a level of minimum health and decency. The consequences for social service were daily before her eyes: living along the line of chronic want, a family struck down by any of the normal hazards of life — unemployment, sickness, or death — was driven at once to seek public or private assistance.[55] Karl de Schweinitz, a continent removed from Mrs. Worcester, wrote from Philadelphia of the insidious influence upon the human spirit of prolonged poverty in the face of abounding prosperity. A society dedicated to the realization of each individual's inherent potential, a society given over to the proliferation of material goods — and families were forced by poverty to live in crowded and squalid surroundings. "Think what our most prevalent evil, overcrowding, means: Never from childhood to have a place of one's own. Never to have a room to oneself. To sleep three in a bed . . . Never to be alone, to have a chance to think apart."[56] In bulletins of the Women's Trade Union League, in New York, Philadelphia, and Chicago was carried news, throughout 1928, of precarious conditions of employment, for women and for all workers. At the National Conference of Social Work, assembling in Memphis in May, sessions were given over to the problems of poverty and unemployment, and ways of alleviation were discussed: a living wage, employment exchanges, public works, social insurance. In July of that year the United States Senate authorized a special study of unemployment, which was to investigate both cure and prevention.

There was even greater cause for alarm in 1929. Senator James Couzens' special committee on unemployment filed a report in March which proceeded from the explicit premise that all men possessed a fundamental right to work and that society must either provide the constructive opportunity to exercise that right, or in its denial afford financial compensation. At the National Conference of Social Work in June, Edward Lynde, general secretary of the Associated Charities in Cleveland, speaking for casework agencies, cited the corroding effect of charity upon a worker's self-reliance and a family's self-respect. Unemployment insurance could act as a "stopgap" income supplement, but a job was more important than assistance.[57]

It was, however, left to Paul Kellogg, who had participated in the agitation leading to the settlements' unemployment survey, to keynote the need for study and action at the 1929 conference. Unemployment, he observed, was a major social cost of technological advance, yet industry had rarely considered the setting aside of reserves as it did for depreciation and dividends. Admitting that unemployment insurance, on the English and European pattern, might not fit the American temper, he predicted that the task of social security was "going to be the great social cause of the next ten years." Professional social workers must accept and act upon the "profound conviction that no nation is economically healthy and solvent which does not set a fair bottom level below which it shall not let the hazards and vicissitudes of modern organized production press down the individual and the family." [58]

Even before Black Thursday on the Stock Market Exchange, social reformers, economic analysts, labor leaders, social-service workers were busy compiling evidence of maladjustment, publicizing their findings, proposing remedies. On the cloistered campus of Bryn Mawr College, in 1928, the Labor College of Philadelphia sponsored a conference which endorsed insurance against sickness, old age, and unemployment. Before the national convention of the Women's Trade Union League, Frank Morrison, secretary of the AFL, called for old-age pensions and regularization of employment at a wage level to assure "reasonable comfort." Even the League of Women Voters had been led by that time to launch a study of the social insurance principle. Perhaps the time had come, cried William Leiserson, who had helped to carry through the earlier drive for accident prevention and workmen's compensation, to take off from the campaign of "Safety First" and launch a drive for "Security Next." [59]

Not many Americans, however, were listening. Deaf and blind to evidence that did not fit the prevailing mood of speculative optimism, most Americans and most public leaders remained inattentive to the shrill demands of social critics; or when they were forced to listen they laughed off what they heard with a scorn and derision for the malcontents who — like Thorstein Veblen — suffered a constitutional incapacity to say yes.

Then came the panic. As panic deepened into depression the nation, slowly and painfully, was forced to confront the specter of want and pain, insecurity, and anxiety for the morrow. Crying babies, children kept from school for want of shoes or a warm coat were not easily blotted from the consciousness. To Solomon F. Bloom, long a proponent of social insurance, speaking from the perspective of 1934, it seemed that instead of hostility, the mood of the twenties had been one of callous indifference: "It was not until America became aware, at long last and slowly, and painfully, of the dreadful amount of suffering, the amazing lack of security for savings, and the utter absence of any provision against nationwide want, that the first cries were raised for social protection."[60]

His feelings cannot casually be disputed. But if a broad revival of interest had to await hard times, the issues had been kept alive during the twenties by old-line progressives who would not say die and by a new generation of liberals who would find their home in the New Deal. Reforms that broke through in the depression decade grew from progressive agitation before the war or were pioneered during the years of normalcy. Hesitantly by 1929, in full measure by 1933, hundreds of reform and welfare leaders had come to share with Abraham Epstein the conviction that personal security and individual liberty far from being antagonistic principles were interdependent and mutually supportive aspects of the general welfare. Without security, no man was truly free; without liberty, security implied tyranny.

The concept was hardly novel. "Liberty can be neither exercised nor enjoyed by those who are in poverty," Samuel Gompers had observed in 1905. "Can any man be really free who is constantly in danger of becoming dependent?" Louis Brandeis asked in 1911. That insecurity subverted liberty was the distillation of Abraham Epstein's experience. Accepting renomination on the Democratic ticket in 1936, Franklin D. Roosevelt recalled that by 1929, "A small group had concentrated into their own hands an almost complete control over other people's property, other people's money, other people's labor — other people's lives. For too many of us life was no longer free; liberty no longer real; men could no longer follow the pursuit of happiness." And as the foreign crises deepened, the President traced the rise of dictatorship abroad to the failure of government to provide employment and security until "in desperation" the people "chose to sacrifice liberty in the hope of getting something to eat." This was a point to which he would return, again and again, in proclaiming the Four Freedoms, in declaring an Economic Bill of Rights. "We have come to a clear realization of the fact that true individual freedom cannot exist without economic security and inde-

individual freedom cannot exist without economic security and independence. 'Necessitous men are not free men.' People who are hungry and out of a job are the stuff of which dictatorships are made." [61]

Of all the New Deal measures aimed at this end, the Social Security Act of 1935 stood first in importance. In this, as in so many other regards, the program and the philosophy upon which it rested were accepted as part of a new consensus in life because they constituted the common sense of the matter. Without the spur of hard times, social security would never have come as soon as it did; without popular pressure for old-age and unemployment insurance, presidential leadership would have pushed as on a string. Without the persistent crusading of a relative handful of effective community leaders when the times were inhospitable to social experimentation, without their research and their propaganda, the search for security could not so quickly have reached its culmination.

8

THE UNEMPLOYMENT CRISIS

"As early as last May, we began to notice the great influx of unemployed girls . . . I feel that our greatest constructive contribution in the present situation has been our effort in keeping the spirit of play in the lives of our girls. . . . We have urged our girls to join and attend social clubs, come to dances, play bridge and use our swimming pool and gymnasium. We have instituted Sunday afternoon teas with elaborate programs of interesting and entertaining variety. . . . And yet, despite the fact that these activities and opportunities for recreation [cost] them nothing, it has taken salesmanship of a persistent and forceful kind to make the girls respond."
— Mrs. Jerome J. Hanauer, Young Women's Hebrew Association, radio address, early 1931, quoted in E. P. Hayes, *Activities of the President's Emergency Committee for Employment*, 1930–1931 (Concord, N.H.: Rumford Press, 1936) pp. 127–128

"Mr. Gordon had a good wife, one daughter of seventeen, another of fifteen, and three other young children. He was an intelligent, hard-working man and had never before been in straits. . . . Then came the depression, no work, tension. . . . When their resources were exhausted the public welfare department allowed the family $5 a week of relief and the man got one day's public work at $3. . . . Finally one night Evelyn disappeared. She had gone to work in a 'closed dance hall' . . . She earned about $4.85 a week from the dancing and what she could get from the sale of her tired body after three. . . . Meanwhile her family had lost its place in the community."
— Family case study from a city in upstate New York, quoted in James Mickel Williams, *Human Aspects of Unemployment and Relief* (Chapel Hill: University of North Carolina Press, 1933), pp. 104–105

"[O]ne of the most loyally followed of our laws is that 'a Girl Scout's duty is to be useful and to help other people at all times.' Girl Scouts try, always, to find out what is the greatest need around them, and then to take their full share of responsibility in overcoming that difficulty or improving those adverse conditions."
— Mrs. Herbert Hoover, radio address, 23 March 1931, quoted in E. P. Hayes, *Activities of the President's Emergency Committee*, p. 129

"I think this is a good time for social workers; the only people who seem to be employed, — alas!"
— Lillian Wald to Rosa Fried Caiton, 12 January 1932, in Wald Papers, File 1, Drawer 2

IT'S the worst winter I have had," complained Lillian Wald in November 1931, adding quickly the reminder, "and I began, you know, in the terrible times of '93." The settlements were being purified of romantic notions again in the days and months of suffering that followed 1929. "I am almost swamped with the unemployment situation," she wrote to "Uncle Henry" Morgenthau. "Every minute seems to be taken, and I come back toward the end of the day unfit for intelligent discussion." Her own utter fatigue was the least suffering she witnessed. The nurses from Henry Street were visiting fifteen hundred homes a day; they reported former breadwinners slumping dejectedly in the home, undernourishment and malnutrition in every dwelling, starvation in many; babies lay naked in filthy beds in the same chilly, drafty rooms in which adults were coughing away their lives. At day's end Miss Wald returned home to piles of pathetic letters, many of them from out of the city and even from beyond the state, pleading for assistance, a loan, a lead to a job. With these burdening her heart, she had to compose begging solicitation letters of her own. As the case load went up, her funds went down. In 1932–1933, she was forced to cut back her nursing staff from 245 to 200, while her home patients increased from 60,000 to 100,000. Her own health beginning to break under the strain, Miss Wald bore the suffering of neighbors with mounting pain. "I can't endure the thought of the loss of dignity to the people who are beggars for a job," she confessed. "One of the tragic elements is that those who have not been dismissed are scared, expecting reductions in their wages, and trying to look the other way."[1]

As month followed terrible month not many Americans found it expedient or even possible to look the other way, for wherever the glance fell there were scenes of mounting misery. The descriptions of need became steadily more explicit, more frantic. "Have you ever heard a hungry child cry?" Miss Wald asked rhetorically in 1932. "Have you seen the uncontrollable trembling of parents who have gone half starved for weeks so that the children may have food? Do you know what it means to try to minister to the sick or the dying or the newly born in an overcrowded home where there is no heat, no food, no clean clothing or bedding, gas and electricity turned off, no furniture worth pawning or selling, an eviction notice tacked on the door?"[2]

From all corners of the country came echoes of Henry Street's bad news of humans in need through no apparent fault of their own — news whose constant repetition failed to dull the conscience. Everywhere settlement workers sought to meet the deepening problem. At Chicago Commons there had been the impulse to study the sources and consequences of unemployment as early as 1928; now from the Taylors, father and daughter (Graham and Lea), came reports and programs for action. They gathered special emergency funds to be invested in families who could not qualify for regular charity or who could not wait for the unwinding of agency red tape — back rent was paid to forestall or postpone eviction, milk and free nursery care was provided for infants, carfare and lunch money was awarded so that children might go to school, in some cases small scholarships were granted to promising high school students who might otherwise have been forced to throw themselves on a market already glutted with cheap labor. The Taylors strove to make it possible for young people, "discouraged and disheartened" at the prospect of being forced to drop out of school, to continue their education and thus keep alive their "prospects of self support which is what they of course want[ed] more than anything else."[3] Wherever possible they paid out their meager funds for needs that other agencies could not or would not meet. Finally as important as emergency work was the maintenance of character- and health-building programs — infant and maternity clinics, supervised recreation, arts and crafts, social activities — all of these designed to support the morale of "bewildered neighbors" and to prevent that "loss of poise through fear" that menaced both "the family and the social order."[4]

Just as pioneer settlement leaders had attempted to interpret class to class, now that emergency had struck again the Taylors carried firsthand impressions of their neighbors' suffering to well-meaning citizens who happened to live in better communities than the West Side. Most significant of all, however, were the efforts to encourage combined social action by the unemployed workers and neighbors, on the one hand, and professional social workers on the other. Where once, brief months or years earlier, separate ethnic groups had used the halls of Chicago Commons for educational or recreational activities — citizenship classes, folk celebrations, dances — Italians, Poles, Greeks, and Mexicans began to assemble together in 1930 and 1931 to study the depression, to establish action committees. Discussion and debate ranged over many topics: the need for work relief through public works, the need for state and federal assistance to cash relief funds, the need to develop security through old-age pensions and unemployment insurance. Out of this agitation was formed, in 1932, a city-wide Workers' Committee on Unemployment composed of fifty-seven local units, twenty-two of which were settlement based and led, with a mass membership of over twenty thousand. Of the work of this committee, Lea Taylor reported to the National Federation of Settlements at the end of the year: "The men are developing initiative and responsibility through serving on committees and delegate bodies. They have organized self-help projects and have sought direct contact with legislators interested in relief measures." When relief food budgets were cut 25 per cent in October because of lack of funds, the Workers' Committee locals joined with more radical elements among the unemployed in a joint march of protest. "This direct experience with methods used by Communist elements," she concluded, "has proved to the Workers Committees that further cooperation or joint effort is impossible."[5]

Henry Street and Chicago Commons set an example that many other neighborhood centers sought to emulate. Since an increasing proportion of the community's charitable funds had to be funneled into direct relief for family maintenance, the service agencies — including the social settlements — had to make do and carry on as best they could. One beneficial by-product of hard times for many settlements was the return to the residency principle, which as we have already seen came less from moral commitment than from the desire of young men and women, unemployed and homeless, to find decent but cheap rooms and to be occupied at constructive tasks. For a brief time, at least, the settlements welcomed the amateur back into the fold; and whatever their lack of training and skill, these nonprofessionals injected imagination, vigor, and dedication into programs too often routinized during the prosperous twenties.

Facing daily emergencies — eviction, starvation, desertion, acts of aimless violence — the settlements did their best to carry on familiar programs to fill the hours of enforced leisure for the idle poor. Although other agencies bore the primary burden of providing food and clothing, the settlements found themselves being forced into the distribution of relief in kind, so often against their better judgment. But when neighbors knocked on the door, asking for food, clothing, and fuel, they could not cheerfully be turned away or always easily referred to other sources of aid.

Just as in Chicago the settlements had seized the initiative to stimulate and indirectly to guide social protest, so elsewhere settlement leaders, alone or in cooperation with other agencies or with their neighbors, moved toward direct political action. By 1932 the issues of social policy which had been explored during the twenties and made more explicit in the early years of the depression constituted new points of agreement: federal aid to local and state government for relief was essential; constructive work relief was superior to the cash dole and assistance in cash was preferred to relief in kind; the extension of mothers' pensions was vital to family welfare; public works and the investment of government funds in slum clearance and public housing provided means for stimulating recovery while bolstering the general welfare; social security, old-age pensions, and unemployment insurance were vital to sustaining both life and morale. The settlements, at least, were ready for a New Deal.

They were not alone. Social workers generally, engaged in whatever kind of specialized service, could not avoid the evidence of widespread want or evade the questions it posed. The averted glance, the easy reassurance of prosperity just around the corner were not for those who daily confronted the plight of the needy. Economists close to the felt facts — Leo Wolman, for example — doubted that traditional approaches, however modified, would any longer suffice and doubted that recovery was likely without more heroic efforts.[6] The latter view prevailed among articulate social-work spokesmen. Homer Folks, dean of the profession who had witnessed many bad times and good, contrasted the emergency of war with the crisis of depression that came quietly in the night. The hidden pain and humiliation of the ten or eleven million workers who had "laid aside their working clothes simply because there was no work for them" would never be known. Unlike the soldier, the army of the unemployed "received no orders, except to quit. They are under no direction. None of them know where to go. They have no voice, no appointed spokesman, no means of expression."[7]

The first task, then, was to set forth the evidence and articulate the needs. The *Survey* magazine, which had carried stories on marginal groups in society throughout the golden years of prosperity, was among the first to cover in depth the story of hard times. Here the readers learned that unemployment, this time, was not a temporary phenomenon but a stubbornly persistent and ugly fact of modern industrial life. The casualties were to be measured in "disheartened men outside the factory gates, over-worked relief agencies, harassed merchants and landlords, homes where children were cold and hungry, where living standards were debased, self-respect broken, family relations wrecked." But the "unpardonable crime of disorganized industry" was more accurately deemed to be the uncertainty of life; that was the worst, that "men and women and children should endure unending strain and insecurity, not knowing today whether tomorrow will yield the day's work and the day's wage on which depends the life of the body and of the spirit." The old familiar cycle of "emergent need; public concern; reports, programs; business recovery; dust covered reports; forgotten programs" was not to be repeated this time around.[8] Something other, something more, something better was required.

Along with settlement workers, family caseworkers were among the first to recognize the flaws in prosperity, for there was an increase in relief demands upon their agencies well before 1929. During the winter of 1927–1928, the Family Welfare Association of America began to carry news and articles in its official journal, *The Family*, about the increased casework load that unemployment created, and it urged that family agencies join with other groups to develop community committees which would coordinate efforts for remedial and preventive action. When mass unemployment descended upon them in 1930 family welfare leaders and professional workers from many other of social work's diverse specialties began to agitate and to express their professional fear that social service was breaking down under the impact of mass need, and their growing conviction that aggressive social reform was in order again. At meetings of community chest boards the debates went on long into the night; before municipal and state conferences, caseworkers arose to protest the conditions under which their clients lived; at the annual national conference they delivered their papers and exchanged ideas and insights; with committees and councils of labor unions, chambers of commerce, and reform associations they explored alternative paths of alleviation and prevention. They insisted that it was improper for the community to expect that private agencies could absorb the burden of bulk relief without placing in jeopardy their other, more important programs of care and prevention, and their constructive services. They sought ways to make it clear that philanthropy was no substitute for wages, made-work no proper alternative to jobs. They stated their obligation to study the means of prevention, including public employment exchanges, public works, and social insurance.[9]

When hard times became desperate times, the tempo of protest picked up. At the national conference in 1931 Jacob Billikopf's paper stressing the inadequacy of traditional charity and pleading for unemployment insurance and planned production and distribution was followed by an overflow meeting of the conference's Division on Industrial and Economic Problems. Here the reassuring remarks of Fred C. Croxton, speaking for the President's Emergency Committee for Employment were coolly received, while John Ryan's attack on Hoover's theories and programs provoked a "storm of applause." John Lapp, James Mullen and others put forward demands for public assumption of responsibility for relief, for the initiation of public works, for the maintenance of wage rates, and for the continuation without curtailment of character-building aspects of social service by private agencies.[10] A half year later, in January of 1932, with the downward plunge still unretarded, the American Association of Social Workers announced that the situation had become catastrophic, that the costs of national disaster were being carried by those least able to do so; social workers, who knew the importance of work as a means of livelihood and "as a form of self-expression," demanded an immediate program of public relief and constructive measures to distribute purchasing power.[11]

The presidential address to the national conference that year, delivered just on the eve of the nominating conventions of the political parties by C. M. Bookman, executive director of the Cincinnati community chest, proclaimed the nation's utter failure to come to terms with the emergency. After listing again, as myraids of social workers had been doing for months, the human consequences of unemployment, he asked the President of the United States to call leaders from every area of American life to consider and seek solutions — solutions which should include the immediate extension of direct public relief by the states with financial backing from the federal government, the acceleration of public works, community planning, and the establishment of unemployment reserve funds (insurance, not the dole). Before the conference broke up, several hundred of its delegates attending a meeting sponsored by the Joint Committee on Unemployment at which resolutions were enthusiastically endorsed demanding immediate appropriation of five billion dollars for public works and a half billion dollars for federal aid to state systems of unemployment insurance, and calling for a reduction in the workweek, the prohibition of child labor, old-age pensions, and progressively graded taxation on personal and corporate income and on estates.[12]

It became increasingly clear with every passing month, as millions more fell into the ragged ranks of the unemployed, that the awarding of relief had to take precedence over other social measures. Once professional social workers had prided themselves on having moved beyond amelioration to cure and prevention, to the rooting out of the causes of dependency; they had now to swallow their pride and take up the nasty, elemental task of human salvage again. In so turning to amelioration they quickly discovered the inadequacy of old ideas dearly held. Private aid had usually been preferred to the granting of public assistance. Government relief had always been niggardly in quantity, grudging in spirit, haphazard and indifferent in administration not infrequently riddled with petty graft. The Protestant ethic of work and thrift and the traditional American faith in individualism — "rugged individualism" as the popular designation had it — tended to promote these attitudes and policies. The charity organization movement, in the late nineteenth and early twentieth century, had elaborated casework procedures that would permanently liberate the needy from their dependency and, in some cases, would suppress those social evils that ground the worthy down into dependency; but the more usual practice of public assistance had been to grant relief "in such a way as to carry with it a measure of discipline, a measure of warning, and a measure of reform."[13]

The first winter of despair, 1929–1930, brought dismal evidence that reliance on private relief associations would not suffice if the depression became prolonged. Accustomed to dealing with chronic dependents, often with those who were for one reason or another unemployable, charity directors now came face to face with those whom some called the "new poor" — good, experienced, reliable workers forced for the first time in their lives to seek charity.[14] As 1930 gave way to 1931, traditional casework concepts of family assistance began to break down before mass need. Concepts tailored for retail assistance proved irrelevant to wholesale procedures; the need was no longer for family counseling or for vocational guidance, the need was for employment or, in default of constructive work, for cash relief. Not all social workers were eager or even willing to surrender the traditional responsibility of private agencies in this field; jealous of their prerogatives and fearful of the "political" administration of assistance, many of them resisted the advance of public welfare measures. Linton B. Swift, executive secretary of the Family Welfare Association, spoke the view of most others, however, when he urged in 1930 that the public would have to provide an increasing share of relief money. But to meet the depression needs by the extension of relief alone was to demoralize government and pauperize the community; social action which would strike at the roots of need, he concluded, was clearly in order.[15]

The wonder is, looking back from the perspective of a more affluent age, that voluntary charity and local relief were able to expand as substantially as they did before the resources of the federal government were tapped. One reasonably reliable estimate indicates that in 1929 the total national cost of direct cash assistance to dependent persons was approximately $43,000,000 ($10,000,000 from private funds, $33,000,000 from public sources). For 1930 the cost had jumped to approximately $71,000,000 ($17,000,000 private and $54,000,000 public); by 1932 the figure for the nation was $307,000,000 ($56,000,000 private and $251,000,000 public). After 1933 the public outlay increased spectacularly while the voluntary contributions shrank; but the more than fivefold increase in private charity over the first four years of the depression — in dollars of appreciating value — at a time when national income was being cut in half remains a tribute to the persistence of a spirit of self-help deeply ingrained in the American character.[16]

Throughout 1930 the pressures accumulated. The St. Louis Provident Association reported that its relief budget had been two-thirds consumed by mid-year and that five hundred new applicants had to be turned away every month beginning in July in order that funds would still be available for the harsh winter that lay ahead. The Charity Organization Society of New York City reported a threefold increase in families seeking assistance in June 1930 over June 1929. At the end of the year, Professor Sumner Slichter of Harvard University lashed out against the double standard in public policy that denied relief to the unemployed while indirect "dole for employers" was offered. Labor, by sharing the work and accepting lower standards, and the public, by contributing to private charitable drives, were carrying industry's cost of labor overhead while industry itself continued to pay out dividends not from current earnings but out of accumulated capital reserves.[17]

In the fall of 1930, recognizing that official reassurances alone would not suffice to see the nation through its second winter of depression, the President established an Emergency Committee for Employment and named Colonel Arthur Woods, who had worked with Hoover on the 1921 Conference on Unemployment, as its director. A commanding figure, Woods brought to the effort his experience in business, in the army, and on philanthropic boards and foundations. The membership of the committee, however, was drawn essentially from business, public administration, industrial research, and academic administration circles; professional social work was represented by Porter R. Lee, director of the New York School of Social Work; the closest labor came to representation was in the figure of Leo Wolman, Columbia University professor and sometime research expert for the Amalgamated Clothing Workers. Few of its members dissented from the President's conviction that the committee should confine itself to study, the collection of data, the coordination of local relief efforts, the stimulation of sound community public works projects, and the acceleration of projects already authorized.

The committee's appeal was to the enlightened self-interest of business to spread the work, hold the line on wages, and establish rational priorities in the release of employees; to the enlightened self-interest of communities to repair and improve public facilities and buildings while prices were relatively low; and to the enlightened self-interest of individual citizens to repair, modernize, and "spruce up" the home. As during the great emergency of war, the resort was first to written and oral exhortations: the committee distributed hundreds of advisory pamphlets; it also sponsored unnumbered radio addresses by businessmen, religious leaders, public welfare administrators, engineers, teachers, club women, Girl Scout directors, and even the President's wife.

The reliance on voluntary efforts and on rhetoric did little, unhappily, to relieve the plight of the unemployed. Colonel Woods and Porter R. Lee, at least, were eager to launch a more forthright attack and recommended that the President seek inauguration of a coordinated employment service, enlargement of the public works program (especially highway construction), and initiation of relief assistance in some areas. Hoover would have none of it, for to him (as still to most other Americans) the overriding need was to balance the budget and thereby restore the confidence of the business community and stimulate private investment while maintaining the American traditions of voluntary action and local responsibility. The failure of the federal government to respond with vigor and imagination to the crises of human need associated with the all but total collapse of the southern Appalachian coal industry and the drought of 1930, together with Hoover's veto of the Wagner Federal Employment Service Act in March 1931, persuaded Woods to resign.[18]

The experience of 1931 was even more terrifying to those who cared and daily had to work with the desperate. At the University of Chicago Settlement, which had been forced into part-time and informal relief work for neighbors who could not qualify elsewhere, the relief office was moved to another building in order that "hungry waiting applicants" would not have to "see the residents going to meals or smell the food, a situation last year almost unbearable for all concerned."[19] From every agency and from every city came complaints of the utter inadequacy of relief. The executive director of Cincinnati's community chest related again the immeasurable social costs of continued unemployment, and noted that the city's Negro community, composing but 10 per cent of the population, contributed half of its relief clients.[20] In New York, Homer Folks, secretary of the State Charities Aid Association, began to argue the "practicality and desirability" of work relief as a form of assistance preferable to the cash dole.[21]

In New York City, the Association for Improving the Condition of the Poor was already engaging in experimental work relief projects under private auspices through its newly created Emergency Work Bureau. The bureau, established in October 1930, received its operating funds from voluntary contributions and expended them on quasi-public work projects and on programs of nonprofit agencies. It attempted, wherever possible, to put a worker on a job in which his particular training could be utilized in the hope that this would lead to constructive achievements for the community and help to maintain the worker's skill in his craft at the same time. The bureau applied no test of an applicant's "worthiness"; it steered clear of "politics"; it provided no follow-up supervision on how the wage income was spent by the worker's family; it carried, thereby, a minimum taint of relief. Unemployed men and women were used for maintenance and custodial work on parks, playgrounds, hospitals; they were employed by churches, schools, settlements, orphanages, libraries and museums, recreation centers. Here was an alternative to the dole, concluded William H. Matthews, its director, justified by the "heads up" bearing of the men and women when they reported for their paycheck — "the absence of shame . . . the sense of not being licked — all so different from the beaten, crushed, weary-looking people I have seen so often in relief stations — waiting for food tickets." [22]

By the end of the year, the clamor for work-relief programs and for the assumption of federal responsibility could no longer be ignored. It was the open letter addressed to President Hoover by William Hodson, executive director of the Welfare Council of New York City, on 13 October 1931 that won the widest notice. Mr. Hodson was an experienced and respected national figure, noted for his practical and moderate views as for his sound administrative practices. Praising the President for his past record, Hodson judiciously suggested that the emergency now required that the federal government do more than merely "stimulate and coordinate local effort." Private funds together with the resources of local government would not suffice to meet the winter's needs, he advised. Federal grants-in-aid of relief to the states would open up new resources while preserving the principle of local administration.[23] Although this open letter won wide publicity and support, and gave added impetus to the proposals of Senators Costigan and La Follette for just such action, the administration remained adamant in its insistence that the time had not yet come for the nation to turn its back upon the voluntary principle and the primary obligation of local units of government.

Declaration of high principle, unhappily, did not make the need disappear. Ugly evidence of unmet needs piled up throughout 1932.

In New York, the creation of the Temporary Emergency Relief Administration, whose activities were underwritten by state bonds, did something to take up the slack, but the private agencies continued to bear a heavy responsibility even in New York. William Matthews reported that the Emergency Work and Relief Bureau had spent over fifteen million dollars in the ten months beginning in October 1931 and had provided part-time jobs for over forty thousand of the city's unemployed.[24] Gifford Pinchot, who had fought a largely unsuccessful campaign as governor to get the state of Pennsylvania to provide for its unemployed, publicly called for federal aid to the states as "our clear duty and our best hope of prompt and permanent recovery." If one major cause of the depression had been the failure of purchasing power to keep pace with the power to produce, then the expenditure of federal funds in the states — raised by taxation on higher income families — would become a way to help the needy and a way to stimulate recovery.[25]

The administration was unmoved. To mounting criticism, Walter S. Gifford, chairman of the President's Organization on Unemployment Relief (which had taken over from the abortive Woods Committee in August 1931), replied that voluntary agencies together with local government were still able to meet the need for mass relief efficiently and humanely. Federal aid, he insisted, would dry up voluntary efforts and encourage local units of government to slough off their responsibility. Moreover, an unbalanced federal budget would seriously undermine the nation's credit. If the government's credit were to be questioned, he concluded in a statement aimed at the social-work profession, "the real cure for unemployment which is obviously the restoration of normal business would be retarded." [26] The *Chicago Tribune* put the case bluntly: "The recipients of unemployment relief are objects of charity. . . . Money has been given to them not because the victims have a right to it but because the community has a heart. . . . The assumption . . . that they are entitled to support by right . . . if it is allowed to go unchallenged will place a premium on incompetence, laziness and shiftlessness . . ." [27]

Professional social workers dissented. At a special Conference on the Maintenance of Welfare Standards, held in Chicago 18–20 November 1932 under the auspices of the American Public Welfare Association and the School of Social Service Administration of the University of Chicago, delegates from private and public agencies assembled, debated, and hammered out an agreement of general principles. The nation must take on the obligation to act in time of national emergency. "The United States government is responsible for seeing to it that those who are out of work through forces over which they have no control must be provided for according to decent standards." These standards of adequate relief must include provision for recreation and education and "the maintenance of wholesome normal life, including health and morale." Direct federal grants (not loans) to be administered by the several states through trained personnel were now in order and, in fact, long overdue.[28]

In the meantime, professional social workers talked to themselves and to agency boards, to friends and allies; they testified as well before legislative commissions, most significantly before committees of Congress. A handful of progressive senators — Wagner of New York, Costigan of Colorado, La Follette of Wisconsin, Couzens of Michigan — moved to consider unemployment, its extent, causes, and consequences. To those who sat through the hearings that began in March 1930 there could be no doubt that the nation was in for a prolonged siege. Frances Perkins — onetime secretary of the New York Consumers' League, for many years a member of state industrial boards and now Governor Roosevelt's industrial commissioner — testified to the chronic and acute problem that plagued the nation's largest state: the six months of winter in 1929–1930 had seen a doubling of relief applicants; conditions were worse than at any time since 1920–1921. Helen Hall, whose *Case Studies in Unemployment* was in the process of publication, stressed her findings that unemployed workers used every expediency before turning to charity or relief and that prolonged unemployment forced steady and skilled workers into the ranks of the unemployable; the need for action was already urgent.[29]

The next round of hearings, in December 1931 and January 1932, was more extensive. William Hodson appeared to present his personal estimate that the nine hundred private agencies whose services he coordinated lacked the resources to carry through the winter. Agencies that usually served only chronic dependents had taken on marginal dependents and were now helping to support normally independent persons. Unemployment and its attendant problems, he concluded, constituted the most serious crisis "that this country has probably ever faced throughout its entire history." Samuel A. Goldsmith, executive director of Jewish Charities of Chicago, submitted evidence that the Windy City was worse off than New York. Even though relief standards had already been cut far below adequate rates, the city of Chicago and all its private agencies would fall far short of covering anticipated needs in 1932. Recalling that a "little rent riot on the South Side, in the negro district" had helped the drive for charitable funds in the year just passed, he was certain that no amount of pressure was likely to result in the raising of the ten million dollars needed in 1932. J. Prentice Murphy, executive director of the Children's Bureau in Philadelphia, related the same sad tale. The City of Brotherly Love took seriously its welfare obligations but even at inadequate levels of care, voluntary and local governmental assistance could not provide subsistence to say nothing of satisfying men's needs for security, recognition, and opportunity, and for a "spiritual and cultural life." Other Philadelphians were present to offer their views. Their conclusions were blunt: relief standards were inadequate, indeed far below an "irreducible minimum"; normal, constructive social work was being sacrificed to the demands for cash assistance; federal aid was essential.[30]

The testimony was grim — of, for example, a family of ten who had recently moved in with a family of five in their three-room apartment — but there were moments of ironic humor. "In your examination of the text of Isaiah," Senator Costigan inquired of Jacob Billikopf, "have you found any references to 'rugged individualism'?" When laughter had subsided Billikopf replied with a brief commentary on the trials of Job, who had borne with patience the assurances of his false comforters that his prosperity would return. His concluding remarks were from Job: "Sorry and hypocritical comforters are you all. When will your windy words have an end?"[31]

Corroboration for these views came from other national social worker leaders who presented the same evidence of overwhelming need and the same demands for federal action. Walter West, executive secretary of the American Association of Social Workers; Paul Kellogg, editor of the *Survey*; Linton B. Swift, executive secretary of the Family Welfare Association of America; Allen T. Burns, executive director of the Association of Community Chests and Councils; Joanna C. Colcord, director of the Charities Organization Department of the Russell Sage Foundation — all chipped away insistently at the myth that voluntary charitable

giving could meet human need without the help of government contributions. The word "dole" was being used as a catchword to confuse
the public and to hold the federal government back from playing its
proper role of protection in the midst of an emergency more pressing
than the crisis of war. Edward L. Ryerson, Chicago industrialist who
had been educated to the needs of the submerged classes by the Taylors
of Chicago Commons, testified in his capacity as chairman of the Governor's Unemployment Commission in Illinois that 20 per cent of all
available private relief funds in the state for the entire year had been
paid out in a single month, and this at the niggardly rate of twenty
dollars per family per month. With over six hundred thousand unemployed in Chicago and over a million in the state, Illinois could not
possibly meet its minimum obligations throughout 1932. Gifford Pinchot, old Bull Mooser and now governor of Pennsylvania for the second
time, laid it on the line even more bluntly. Republican members of
the state legislature had authorized but nineteen million dollars for
direct relief when the state's need was closer to one hundred and twenty
million, and then had failed to provide the means of raising even that
paltry sum. President Hoover's policies he labeled "vicious," and warned
that national indifference and continued inaction would lead to widespread bitterness against the government.[32]

When toward the end of the hearings, on 8 January 1932, Walter S
Gifford appeared to outline the administration's official position, members of the special Senate committee had already suffered through two
weeks of heartbreaking accounts. Gifford had been appointed director
of the President's special Organization on Unemployment Relief after
a distinguished career as president of American Telephone and Tele-
graph and as president of the Charity Organization Society of New
York. He was not unfamiliar with the principles and methods of social
service but his indelible commitment (like Mr. Hoover's) was to voluntary giving. His testimony opened with a matter-of-fact recital of the
methods of the President's organization which he directed — they were
to coordinate the raising and spending of private and public relief funds
throughout the country, to mobilize, to advise, to cooperate with local
associations. As for the extent of need he predicted that each state
would "care for its own who must have help this winter." Local and
state control of public relief meant "discriminating and effective expenditures," whereas federal aid "would doubtless" lessen local efforts

and encourage thereby the evasion of local responsibility. The only constructive solution to the problem of unemployment was, after all, the revival of business. When pressed for specific evidence in support of these views he begged off with the repeated confession, "I do not know." What was the extent of unemployment? He had no reliable figures. What standards of relief prevailed, how many families were currently receiving assistance? He could not guess; and although he doubted William Hodson's estimates, and challenged Governor Pinchot's, he had none better to offer. When requested to file whatever reports he had from local units of his organization, from governors, from local relief associations and councils, he replied, "I have none, Senator." [33]

The hearings did nothing to swerve the President's Organization on Unemployment Relief. Gifford proved to be both more cautious and less well-informed than Colonel Woods before him. His will to believe the most hopeful reassurances that voluntary efforts and local action were still equal to the task was surpassed only by the President's. Ignorant of mounting evidence that voluntary and local efforts were, by the winter of 1931–1932, utterly and woefully insufficient, Gifford and his committee — and the President — stood pat. When Congress failed to appropriate sums for its continuance, it folded up its prudent policies and quietly stole away.

When unemployment hearings were renewed a year later, January 1933, during the interregnum, the evidence was more of the same only desperately worse. Jacob Billikopf returned to relate what had happened in Philadelphia during 1932. One out of five families seeking relief had to be rejected not because they failed to qualify but because there were no funds. The five million dollars allocated to the city's Unemployment Relief Committee by the united fund campaign had been consumed in four months; the state legislature appropriated a supplement of two and a half million dollars and that had melted away by June; the average weekly family allowance when relief was cut off in June had been $4.35. What happened until relief was resumed in late September? Bills went unpaid, no clothes were purchased, neighbors helped out when all else failed. "The primitive communism existing among these people," he reported, "was a constant surprise to the visitors." As for the united charities drive in the fall of 1932 it had been able to raise only half of what it had accumulated in 1931. The conclusions to be drawn were obvious and quickly to the point: it was preposterous to consider federal loans to bankrupt cities and states; outright federal grants were required; public works and unemployment insurance should also be on the agenda.[34]

Other welfare leaders were back before the committee again, as well — Linton B. Swift, Helen Hall, and J. Prentice Murphy. In England, reported Helen Hall who had visited there in the summer of 1932, the security afforded by social insurance had helped to sustain morale; in America many citizens were down to a diet of gravy soup — flour and water. The cry of "local responsibility" for relief, she charged, was a device to evade federal obligation. The experience of unemployment, particularly if extended, caused irreparable injury. "I think most people will never be as employable or as good citizens again, nor the kind of citizens we like to feel that Americans are, with a sense of independence and self-reliance." Swift emphasized again his conviction that the offer of federal loans for relief did little practical good, for governments could not borrow when they knew they could not repay. Harry Lurie, director of the Bureau of Jewish Social Research in New York City, concurred and added a warning of "resentment, disaffection and threats" unless something positive were done, and that quickly. Harry Hopkins, chairman of New York's Temporary Emergency Relief Administration, came armed with statistics to prove the same point — New York under Roosevelt had gone far to meet the needs; now only federal aid would suffice. So, too, testified Grace Abbott; as chief of the Children's Bureau she put in a special plea for youthful transients who had hit the rails after the events of late 1929 and succeeding years closed down the chances for a constructive career or even a decent job.[35]

It remained for Isaac Rubinow, member of the Ohio Unemployment Insurance Commission, to present the most sharply critical testimony. The unemployment rate in Ohio had doubled in the two years from December 1930 to December 1932, he said, rising from 17 per cent to between 35 and 40 per cent. Ohio's power to tax or to borrow was at an end; it was federal aid now or nothing. Public works and unemployment insurance were better means than relief; jobs, of course, were even better, but there weren't any. The commission on which he served had concluded that charity was, by its nature and in practice, "inadequate, inappropriate, and undesirable." Yet the cry that the dole was destructive of morale, valid as it was, was but a partial truth, for "what really produces demoralization is not so much the dole as the inadequate amount of the dole." [36]

Time was running out for the United States. Never had there been a winter more cruel than the months between Roosevelt's election and his inauguration. By March 4, nearly four years, four bitter years of failure and frustration, had passed, years during which the investigations, experience, and testimony of social workers had contributed immeasurably toward the formation of a new relief policy.

That so little was accomplished toward the implementation of these views until after the inauguration of a new president can be attributed to the dogged opposition of President Hoover to all proposals for relief that would unbalance the budget or invade states' rights, to the deadlock (after the elections of November 1930) between the White House and Capitol Hill, and to the inability of proponents of federal action to agree among themselves upon procedures. The Wagner Federal Employment Service Act had been vetoed by Hoover in 1931. The 1932 La Follette-Costigan bill, providing for federal relief, failed because of Republican anxieties about sound fiscal policy and because many conservative Democrats were equally reluctant to embark upon an untried course that carried an implied threat to local initiative. As the stalemate persisted into the summer of 1932 with signs only of deepening despair and social unrest, congressional and administration scruples were finally set aside with the passage of the Emergency Relief and Construction Act, 21 July 1932, which authorized loans totaling $300,000,000 to state and local governments to be made under the auspices of the Reconstruction Finance Corporation. (An earlier version of the bill, which had provided for an ambitious public works program as well as loan funds substantially larger than finally authorized, had been vetoed.) The federal government had finally — if ever so reluctantly and partially — assumed an obligation for unemployment relief. But it was a matter of too little, too late; before many months more had passed the expedient of loans gave way to outright federal grants.[37]

The old American ideal of voluntary charity and local responsibility — an ideal that both Hoover and Roosevelt had shared in the sunny climate of 1929 — had been shattered beyond repair by 1933. Put to the test, it just hadn't worked. Hopkins and Perkins and company knew it; Gifford and company did not.

Social workers were not alone in recognizing the consequences of unemployment and the problems of its amelioration. The Child Labor Committee's concern, however, was unique — rising unemployment among adult workers had been accompanied by both an actual and a relative increase in the employment of minors. At its silver anniversary conference in December 1929, delegates were told that with two million men unemployed two million children were still at work. In the years that followed the absolute number of children employed, particularly in the fourteen to sixteen age category, increased slightly. Depression forced the committee and its allies to renew the crusade for more severe regulatory legislation, and to pick up the campaign to win ratification of the still pending Twentieth Amendment.

Stunned by the catastrophe of 1929, little aware of alternative proposals for amelioration and cure, the voting public and state legislators responded sluggishly to these pleas for action. The legislative year of 1931 passed with practically no constructive action — only eight states seriously considered ratification of the amendment and of these only Colorado acted affirmatively; only three states tightened up their regulations, and these in minor ways. Fourteen additional states joined the ratification ranks in 1933, but the total number still fell far short of the required three-quarters. By that time, however, the focus had shifted to national legislative and executive action, a shift that the blanket codes of the NRA, including the prohibition of child labor (except in those exempted industries in which the employment of children was most persistent), seemed to justify. Although the New Deal continued to urge ratification of the amendment, the reliance came to be upon federal statutory action and more permissive judicial rulings. When — essentially on the urging of Grace Abbott and her successor as director of the Children's Bureau, Katharine Lenroot — prohibitions on the employment of children in interstate commerce were written into the Fair Labor Standards Act of 1938, and when the courts upheld the constitutionality of the act, the cause was finally won. Unceasing agitation in this, as in other regards, was the price of ultimate achievement.

The Women's Trade Union League was another association facing special problems and it proved to be quicker in understanding their nature and solution than the general union movement with which it was so loosely allied. Like the settlements, the Association for Labor Legislation, and other groups, the WTUL had concerned itself with unemployment even before the great crash. During prosperity the league had been forced to recognize that its traditional reliance upon minimum wages had been rendered largely ineffective by hostile judicial rulings and by irregularity of employment. Rose Schneiderman sparked a discussion on inadequate income related to insecurity of employment at the league's national convention in May 1929. "You may have a leisure wage or a cultural wage this week and next week apply to the charity organization to pay your rent," she observed. "It is terrible to live on the brink of something all the time in a condition where you don't know whether you can continue your child at school or whether you can buy him the clothes he needs or any of the other necessities that mean life today." [38]

Depression rendered all these problems more acute as wage standards were cut and as increasing numbers of wives and mothers were forced onto the labor market seeking some way to maintain family income when their husbands, the fathers of their children, were thrown onto the streets. Like other witnesses who were close to the human impact of hard times, spokesmen for the league were quick to testify to its psychological consequences. The pace of modern production contributed to fatigue and emotional unbalance, wrote one correspondent in the league's official bulletin; but worse were the distractions of depression. "Worry and fear develop physical symptoms, invalid attitudes, and feelings of inadequacy and inferiority." [39]

The league's response became increasingly combative as the nation fell deeper and deeper into the slough of depression. Individual leaders of the league and the league committees and conventions protested against the insufficiency of relief; they joined in the move to make more strict state regulations of the conditions under which women and children were employed; they endorsed the creation of a coordinated employment service and public works; they fought for welfare measures of all sorts and for the creation of agencies for economic planning; against the advice of the AFL, whose leaders they regularly consulted on national policy, they sternly protested President Hoover's eviction of the bonus marchers from Anacostia flats. By 1933, they were so bold (given the constitutional scruples of the federal courts) as to stand with other reform associations in favor of federal legislation setting maximum hours and minimum wages not only for women but for all workers.

The American Association for Labor Legislation — like other all-purpose reform groups — had many arrows in its quiver. In 1915 and again in 1921 it had sponsored comprehensive, if conservative, programs calling for coordinated employment services and unemployment reserve funds set up so as to provide a maximum incentive to individual firms and industries to regularize production; but its primary interest lay in the long-range planning of public works which would, it was hoped, take up the slack in times of seasonal or cyclical unemployment and stimulate the construction and allied industries — iron and steel, lumber, brick and stone, gravel, cement, and asphalt. Wages paid out for construction work would increase gross purchasing power and brace up business generally all along the line. Without careful planning, purely in response to the need for hard-surfaced roads and without thought for its broad economic impact, billions of dollars were poured into roads and bridges throughout the prosperity decade when the automobile was reshaping the American landscape. In light of the universal acceptance of the principle that public funds had to be expended for vital public works, it seemed a logical next step to manipulate expenditures for essential projects in ways designed to promote maximum economic stability.

This was the stated intent of the bill put forward by Senator Wesley Jones of Washington, submitted first in 1924 but not seriously debated until 1928. By its provisions, a "Prosperity Reserve" of federal funds would be accumulated to be spent on roads, river and harbors, flood control, and public buildings when employment in the construction industries fell below a certain level. The principle was known to have Herbert Hoover's blessing, although his endorsement remained vague enough concerning specific details as to raise a serious question within the AALL in regard to the enthusiasm with which he might be expected to implement theory in actual practice. Adequate safeguards would have to be provided, of course — the careful coordination of local, state, and federal measures; the concentration on useful and permanent contributions to community wealth; the employment of workers already displaced at reasonable wage rates over a regular season. William Trufant Foster and Waddill Catchings published brilliant studies in support of the contention that public works projects — highways, flood control, and slum clearance, for example — if carefully planned and combined with progressive tax policies could, in times of industrial lag, give a boost to recovery forces. Professor Paul Douglas concurred and stressed particularly the possibilities of public housing in providing a stimulus to the construction industry, jobs for the unemployed, and decent housing for lower income groups.[40]

Others, most notably Leo Wolman in his meticulous study of 1930, warned that public works were better conceived as means to stabilize certain segments of the economy than as means for emergency employment during times of depression; construction projects could not be expanded rapidly enough to absorb significant numbers of the unemployed efficiently; construction work, moreover, did not often utilize labor at those skills that the unemployed often possessed; at the most, coordinated works programs offered a means of stabilization which, when taken together with other measures, might afford some antideflationary pressure. This had been the point, as well, of Philip Klein's definitive and intensive study of the depression of 1921–1922. The coordination of employment services and of relief measures had been more constructive and effective than public works and work relief projects which all too often, under the exigencies of emergency, took on the haphazard quality of made-work. Public works were effective economic stabilizers only if they were carefully planned and coordinated well in advance of crisis.[41]

The panic of 1929, however, caught the nation and its leaders unprepared in this as in other ways. Agitation for careful long-range planning had been unceasing but for the most part to little avail. After 1930, when the Democrats returned to control of the House of Representatives, federal politics became deadlocked between President Hoover's stubborn insistence that federal moneys be appropriated only for self-liquidating projects and the equally intransigent insistence of Wagner, La Follette, Costigan, and Cutting that priority be given to measures that would get men to work regardless of other considerations. Gross federal expenditures on all public works were increased steadily throughout the four years of the Hoover administration but this increase was barely enough to offset the steady decline in private, local, and state projects. The President remained skeptical, not without good cause, that public works even if expanded far beyond the limits of fiscal prudence could absorb more than a small fraction of the unemployed. In the meantime annual budgetary deficits, the product of falling tax revenues not of design, piled up. Government policy, no more coherent in the legislative than in the executive branch, continued to drift; not until after 1933 did public works become a major weapon in overcoming hard times, and not even then was the extravagant expediency of deficit financing embraced.

The experience of 1929 to 1933 dampened whatever hopes there may once have been for easy solutions to difficult problems. Before many months had passed it was clear that there was to be no simple way out of hard times. From setbacks and suffering had come certain conclusions. A regular job was better than relief or made-work; direct cash relief was preferable to relief in kind; work relief was better for morale than a cash handout; when local resources were exhausted there was no alternative to direct federal assistance. A coordinated system of public works could help take up the slack of unemployment, stimulate construction industries, and enlarge purchasing power. The maintenance of decent standards of relief and of reasonable conditions of labor (maximum hours and minimum wages and the prohibition of child labor) was essential to the preservation of a humane civilization and to the creation of a socially efficient nation as well.

Finally, it became increasingly clear, as Senator Robert Wagner phrased it in December 1930, that the "right to work" had become "synonymous with the inalienable right to live." Millions of honest workmen were on the streets through no fault of their own because of the operation of "forces beyond their control," he declared. No law, he continued, "economic or otherwise, ever validly ordained that millions of people willing to work shall be condemned to want and privation in the midst of national plenty." Upon the nation rested the responsibility not of creating a "new economic order" but of bringing "greater precision and better organization in the existing order." [42] In specific terms, it became clear that the right to a livelihood must perforce include security against the hazards of modern life — dependency in old age, accident, unemployment. Social insurance was a necessary and integral part of the new consensus.

9

DEMANDS FOR FEDERAL ACTION

"Let us put ourselves on record as unwilling to participate in a civilization, to say nothing of profiting by one, which does not work ceaselessly and fruitfully towards the achievement of economic security. That hundreds, thousands, millions of human beings, despite their integrity, earnestness, and willingness to work, should live for days, weeks, and years with no assurance from day to day that either food or shelter or the wherewithal to secure them can be made available is abhorrent not only to an exalted sense of justice but to a sense of common decency."

> — Porter R. Lee, "Social Workers: Pioneers Again," Address before the Association of the New York School of Social Work, 1933, in *Social Work as Cause and Function, and Other Papers* (New York: Columbia University Press, 1937), p. 189

". . . Fear and worry based on unknown danger contribute to social unrest and economic demoralization. If, as our Constitution tells us, our Federal Government was established among other things 'to promote the general welfare,' it is our plain duty to provide for that security upon which welfare depends.

"These three great objectives — the security of the home, the security of livelihood, and the security of social insurance — are, it seems to me, a minimum of the promise that we can offer to the American people. They constitute a right which belongs to every individual and every family willing to work. They are the essential fulfillment of measures already taken toward relief, recovery and reconstruction."

> — Franklin D. Roosevelt, Message to Congress, 8 June 1934, *Public Papers and Addresses*, Volume III, pp. 291, 292

JUST as the move to provide for old-age pension systems at the state level took precedence over schemes for unemployment compensation, so at the national level did old-age security assume priority over unemployment insurance. The federal government had established a system of compulsory, contributory old-age and invalidism insurance, financed by a 2½ per cent salary deduction, for its own employees in 1920. It had been hoped, then, that federal action, covering nearly a half million civil servants, would encourage state governments to follow suit, a hope that was not immediately realized. The drive for general old-age legislation in the states, which began to pick up momentum toward the end of the decade, carried over into national politics as well with the proposal, first put forward by Congressman William I. Sirovich (Democrat, New York) in 1927 that federal aid be extended to state old-age assistance programs on a dollar-matching basis, one dollar of federal funds supporting every two dollars provided locally by the several states. This formula, which in 1932 became known as the Dill-Connery bill after Senator Clarence C. Dill (Democrat, Washington) and Congressman William P. Connery, Jr. (Democrat, Massachusetts), received scant but increasing support with every session of Congress.

To Epstein's American Association for Old Age Security the move for federal action appeared opportunely as a way to overcome the limitations of local action, for the desire to get some legislation on the books, any legislation it seemed at times, had led the association to make one distasteful compromise after another. The association and its allies had consented to long residency and high age qualifications, to the application of degrading means tests, to niggardly schedules of payment, to the principle of noncontributory general assistance programs rather than the principle of contributory insurance or pension arrangements. Not one of these compromises was agreed to cheerfully.

But federal grants-in-aid would open the way to the imposition of federal standards and, it was hoped, in time to the inauguration of a contributory or insurance principle uniformly throughout the nation.

As the drive for action on old-age security moved from the states to the arena of national politics, its proponents unlimbered all the arguments they had elaborated over years of agitation. Time and again the reformers proclaimed the country's scandal and shame, that of all the civilized nations of the world the United States alone had made no provision for the welfare of its aged dependents. They argued the primacy of human rights above property rights, social justice before charity. At times, particularly after 1929, they argued that old-age insurance payments and pensions paid out of general revenues would help to sustain purchasing power in time of deflation and would thus provide an incentive to recovery. To the opposition's claim that federal aid represented an unconstitutional invasion of states' rights, the reformers replied that if the national government, working through the dollar-matching device, could supplement funds for road building, rural education, and maternal and infant health, and promote control of the Mediterranean fruit fly, the corn borer, and hog cholera, surely the federal government could enter more vigorously into the promotion of measures for human security against the ravages of time.

In 1932 the field representative of the AAOAS, Mrs. Richard Hogue, reported growing support for the Dill-Connery bill, with the congressional concern for government economy in an election year constituting the one significant negative influence. "The idea of old age security has come into its time, ripe and ready for legislative fulfillment, because of the scientific research and the mature study that have gone into the movement from its beginning," she reported to the association's annual convention that year. Epstein and others had testified before the appropriate committees and had met individually with each of Connery's committee members. Epstein's tactical advice had been followed: "Spend most of your time rallying your friends — very little of it in trying to convert your enemies." The depression, Epstein reported, had greatly accelerated the interest in social welfare measures; the progressive forces, without regard to party affiliation, were daily growing in strength.[1]

The time for accomplishment was closer at hand, in fact, than even the most optimistic dared hope in 1932. In that year of deadlock when both parties were jockeying for favorable electoral position and when bitter partisanship stalemated serious consideration of federal unemployment relief, public works, and payment of a veterans' bonus, the Dill-Connery grant-in-aid of state old-age-assistance programs won a favorable report from the House Committee on Labor only to be tied up in the Rules Committee. Two years later it passed the House and fell short of a majority in the Senate primarily because Roosevelt preferred to tie old-age assistance to a comprehensive insurance program. When presidential support was thrown on the side of the Committee on Economic Security's recommendations in 1935, and when the Townsend movement threatened a fiscally unsound alternative, Congress responded enthusiastically and without major dissent to the inauguration of old-age security as a major part of the Social Security Act of 1935. The President's committee, from the beginning of its deliberations to the filing of its final report, considered the need both for general assistance programs for the dependent aged and for a contributory insurance program through which workers could accumulate benefit claims against retirement. Generally in accord with these commitments, Congress did provide both for an old-age-assistance program and for old-age insurance (which became old-age and survivors insurance by amendment in 1939).[2]

The response to the movement for old-age security was relatively hearty and generous when compared with the hostility and misunderstanding that greeted the companion crusade for unemployment insurance in the years following the great crash. Hard times were a spur to interest, however. "We see hopes of unemployment insurance," wrote Lillian Wald in December 1930, "and find some comfort in the fact that a hearing is given to the arguments for it, which would not have been possible five years ago, perhaps not three years ago."[3] The interest in unemployment insurance grew in direct ratio to the ever increasing number of men out of work and to the ever broadening recognition that it offered the means most likely to sustain worker morale and purchasing power during hard times.

From the ranks of professional social workers and social reformers came the initiative. Jewish social agencies in particular quickly accorded vigorous support, for among the leading pioneer proponents of unemployment insurance and social security one must include not only Abraham Epstein and Isaac Rubinow, but also Soloman Lowenstein (director of the Federation of Jewish Philanthropy, New York City), Harry Greenstein (director, Associated Charities, Baltimore), Harry Lurie (of the Bureau of Jewish Social Research, New York), Jacob Billikopf (head of the Philadelphia Federation of Jewish Charities), Dorothy Kahn (long-time associate of the Jewish Welfare Society and from September 1932 executive director, Philadelphia County Relief Board), and Frances Taussig (head of the Jewish Social Service Association of New York and onetime president of the American Association of Social Workers). The support of the Jewish community for welfare measures, and the dedicated and brilliant leadership which it provided, may have derived from the tradition of social justice so deeply rooted in the protests of the Old Testament prophets, as some students have suggested; or it may have derived from the religious practice of *tzdakah*, provision for the human needs of the entire community, a tradition of giving that combined the concepts of both charity and justice; or it may have come out of the ancient ethnic instinct for survival that placed the value of the whole community above the value of particular classes or individuals. Used to caring for its own, the ethnic-cultural-religious Jewish community could easily and logically embrace a social security system that provided sustenance in time of need not out of the charitable impulse to assist the less fortunate but as of right in answer to the claims of all men for due justice. Through Jewish mutual aid and benevolent societies, through the order of B'nai B'rith, these principles had been implemented in action over several generations of Jewish experience in America. They had been worked out by Jewish family welfare agency programs, as well, which very early rejected institutional care for widows and orphans. Sensitive to all forms of discrimination, admiring the philanthropist and reformer, through their ties with an international intellectual community far less parochial than other ethnic groups, convinced of man's capacity to achieve a larger measure of justice through social action, leaders of the Jewish community (especially in New York City, of course) were in the advance guard of those who pioneered urban reform measures, particularly social insurance. That the Jewish community was heavily new immigrant in origin, that it had come over to the Democratic party with Al Smith in 1928, were factors helping to make it one of the most loyal segments of the New Deal coalition that Franklin Roosevelt assembled in the 1930's.[4]

Jewish social reformers and welfare leaders shared their position in the vanguard with many other professional social workers. The pioneer role of the settlement movement in promoting social security was notable. Settlement leaders in Chicago sparked the formation of the Illinois Committee on Economic Security which fought for a national system of unemployment insurance and helped to secure state legislation implementing the federal Social Security Act following 1935. Outside of New York and Chicago less enthusiasm was evidenced. Maynard Krueger, University of Pennsylvania economist, complained to the annual conference of the National Federation of Settlements in 1931 that in his state agitation for social insurance derived to a much greater extent from trade unionists and socialists than from settlement and social workers. "Social workers, with honorable exceptions, have constituted a profession cursed by the overwhelming necessity of maintaining their gentility in the face of adverse criticism by board members," he explained. Full-scale national planning was, for the moment at least, inexpedient and the only path to economic security other than socialism, he concluded, was the creation of a comprehensive insurance system against "unemployment, old age, ill health, and accident." Throughout 1931 and 1932, Helen Hall and other settlement leaders testified in favor of unemployment insurance measures in Wisconsin and Ohio, but it was not until June 1933 that the National Federation of Settlements officially stated its support for old-age pensions or insurance as necessary to secure the "benefits of modern medical skill to the masses of the country," and reaffirmed its belief in the necessity of unemployment insurance.[5]

Many other social work leaders joined the parade. Joanna C. Colcord had included unemployment insurance as a positive alternative to charitable relief in her study of *Community Planning*, published in 1930.[6] In the pages of the *Survey*, Paul Kellogg made certain that news and analyses on unemployment insurance were regularly featured. The indefatigable Jacob Billikopf seized every occasion to speak out for unemployment insurance and to spur his colleagues to action. From his experience as impartial chairman of the unemployment reserve program of the men's clothing industry in New York he drew the lesson that whereas insurance against unemployment was an absolutely essential requirement of simple justice and a practical means for maintaining purchasing power, attempts to establish security within a single industry were doomed to failure; because the causes of unemployment, except for seasonal variations within the clothing industry for example, lay far beyond the control of a single firm or even a single industry, the creation of a universal, nationwide system of compulsory, contributory insurance through federal action was imperative. "The worker wants a job in preference to insurance," he announced in 1931 before a congressional committee, "and he prefers insurance to charity." [7]

In 1933, Porter R. Lee proclaimed that social workers were now "pioneers again." In his presidential address to the National Conference of Social Work four years earlier, when he had drawn a careful distinction between social work as "cause" and as "function," he had observed that with the passing of time crusades for social reform came to call for the bureaucratic talents of the judicious administrator more than the fiery enthusiasm of the zealot. Apparently the day of the zealot had arrived again, for Lee spoke in terms less measured and objective than he had employed in 1929. The profession must investigate and contribute to the elaboration of programs of hours and wages, economic planning, and social insurance; in support of the latter measures, social workers must demonstrate the human costs of insecurity and must work for the establishment of efficient and adequate standards of compensation. Clearly "function" was giving way to "cause" again. [8]

The early 1930's saw the publication of three major works on unemployment and social security, studies that received wide notice and stimulated national attention. The first, Paul Douglas' *The Problem of Unemployment*, was the product of a decade's research into the subject by the energetic and incisive economist from the University of Chicago. Combining a commitment to social reform that grew naturally from his religious experience with a hard pragmatic sense of social reality and with the scholar's tenacity in the search for the meaning of facts, Douglas made many studies of wages and living standards and conditions of employment. An advocate in the 1920's of the living wage principle and its implementation through a family allowance system of state aid, Douglas was invited to direct a special investigation of unemployment at Swarthmore College in 1930. From this project, carried out in cooperation with Aaron Director, came his report of 1931. Under prevailing circumstances, said Douglas, the unemployed worker, once he had exhausted his meager savings, was necessarily driven to seek charitable relief which was "humiliating, inadequate, and uncer-

tain." If industry found it legitimate and expedient to accumulate reserves out of which dividends could be paid, why was it not proper and
wise to require reserve funds out of which workers could receive compensation in times of unemployment? If an unemployment insurance
system, even one which permitted the levying of differential rates upon
different industries, was unlikely to act as a major incentive to industrial regularization, at least the provisions for compensation would
regularize workers' income to a certain degree and thus help to maintain purchasing power as a brake against depression. To avoid the
stigma of the "dole," Douglas favored a system of compulsory, joint
contributions by employers and employees. He foresaw that the initiative would have to come from the states, but hoped that federal grants-
in-aid would provide both incentive and some degree of national
control.[9]

The burden of Abraham Epstein's massive *Insecurity*, published in
1933, was simply that unemployment was inevitable in an industrial
society, and that the costs of unemployment were measurable in the
loss of purchasing power and in the loss of homes and health and self-
respect. Reliance upon what he called on another occasion "private
charity through organized ballyhoo" was no substitute for a comprehensive, compulsory system of insurance to which employers, employees, and the public itself (through tax revenues) would contribute.
Because the incidence of unemployment was rarely directly the fault
of management, and because the hazards of sickness and accident and
dependency in old age were inherent in life and in modern industrial
society, the whole community, he believed, must take up the full responsibility of providing security. The first objective of social insurance
was the maintenance of income and purchasing power, but just as significant was the promotion of public health, industrial efficiency, and
social stability. Before a Senate Committee on Unemployment, Epstein
made explicit his belief that progressive income and inheritance taxes
were the best means by which society at large could assume its rightful
obligation. "Such taxes are socially just," he testified, "provide the best
guarantee for the stability of the social order, and, by making possible
increased purchasing power through the alleviation of poverty, also
make possible greater and more steady profits." [10]

Isaac Rubinow's *Quest for Security*, published in 1934, represented
the culmination of a long one-man crusade that had been launched in

1913 with the publication of *Social Insurance*, one of the first attempts in the United States to set forth a comprehensive analysis and rationale of the subject. During his lengthy career not a single phase of social insurance escaped his scrutiny — workmen's compensation, health and invalidism, old age and unemployment. With the panic and depression, the Russian-born statistician stepped up the tempo of his research and propaganda. "It is not so much the wisdom of social science but the brutal pressure of economic development which has brought the movement to life again in 1930," he reported at the end of the year.[11] Named to the Ohio Commission on Unemployment Insurance, whose research committee he chaired from 1931 to 1933, he appeared before legislative committees, civic groups, fraternal organizations, professional associations, and hammered at what was to him the common sense of the matter. Broad social planning and the prevention of unemployment were not alternatives to social insurance, he said; they were not competitive and exclusive ways to meet the problems of unemployment, but mutually supporting programs. To insist, as did William Green of the AFL down to 1932, that the American worker wanted a job, not the dole, was beside the point. How were jobs to be provided and how were the families of the unemployed to be supported awaiting the day of recovery? Of course, reformers sought prevention not alleviation, but unemployment compensation was a way to provide minimally for human needs and one way, among others, actively to advance recovery by stabilizing purchasing power.

In his *Quest for Security*, Rubinow summarized what he had learned from a lifetime of study. He offered no quick and easy cure for society's ills. Unemployment insurance in and of itself could never eliminate unemployment, although it might act indirectly as an incentive to industry to stabilize its activities; high wages and trade unionism even when combined with economic planning, industrial regulation, and social case work could not completely solve the problems of insecurity. Yet action was essential, for insecurity was destructive of the American ideal: "A father who works. A mother who tends house. Children who look to mother for care and to father for support." A comprehensive system of health insurance, old-age pensions to be followed by old-age insurance, and compulsory, contributory unemployment insurance provided no ultimate panacea but together they offered the possibilities of a more stable, a more humane, a more just and equitable society.[12]

The American Association for Labor Legislation pursued quite a different line of reasoning from that of Douglas, Epstein, Rubinow, and the bulk of the social-work leaders. Drawing on its experience in workmen's compensation, in which taxation imposed upon the employers to finance reserve funds had acted as an incentive for inauguration of accident-prevention programs, the AALL throughout the 1920's and on into the 1930's continued to argue for unemployment insurance primarily as a direct means to encourage industries and firms to regularize employment. The value of such insurance as a preventive force was most often and persuasively argued, although its proponents also insisted that when depression did occur it would place a reserve of purchasing power in the hands of the consumers and thus would act as a stimulus to recovery. Under the influence of John R. Commons it was this version of unemployment insurance — which threw the burden of taxation upon the employers alone — that was introduced in a series of bills that the state of Wisconsin considered from 1921 to 1932, and it was to this concept, therefore, that many other reformers had to offer their grudging support, there being none other or better beyond the talking stage. Returning to New York after testifying for the Wisconsin Unemployment Insurance Bill, Helen Hall felt obliged to apologize to her colleagues in the National Federation of Settlements for its conservative and restrictive nature; it was not a model bill, she sighed, "indeed its chief virtue is that it could be passed." [13]

Other reform associations joined the campaign for social insurance, none of them with the unrestrained enthusiasm and wholehearted concentration of effort that marked the interest of Epstein's and Andrews' groups. The National Consumers' League and its New York and Ohio affiliates had long demonstrated a casual concern for the principle of social security but had never studied with care the various specific proposals for its implementation. Molly Dewson had discussed the viability of social insurance with her good friends Eleanor Roosevelt and Frances Perkins while F. D. R. was governor of New York. In 1931 the national Executive Board had assigned one of its staff to work with the AALL in drawing up model unemployment reserve fund bills, and in Wisconsin the league's efforts were aligned on the side of the Commons-Andrews proposals. In Ohio, on the other hand, where Isaac Rubinow and William Leiserson were the guiding force in the campaign for social insurance the Consumers' League, ably led by Amy Maher and Elisabeth S. Magee, aided in writing an insurance bill which provided for contributions from both employees and employers, for the accumulation of a statewide fund without regard for differential rates for different industries, and for control of the system by a government commission.

The League of Women Voters formally endorsed the principle of unemployment compensation in 1932; and in the same presidential election year the national convention of the YWCA endorsed a forward-looking platform which included unemployment insurance. In 1933, after two years of study, the National Federation of Business and Professional Women's Clubs followed suit. These formal endorsements, however, can better be taken as tokens of a growing concern and a widening acceptance of the need for broad programs of social security than as signs of a commitment to work vigorously for such measures. Their support was not unimportant, but the initiative clearly lay elsewhere.

The Women's Trade Union League — like the labor movement to which it was so loosely attached and with which it so often spat — was divided. Readers of the league's *Life and Labor Bulletin* were asked to ponder the question "Just why it should be considered bad to hand out meagre doles to unemployed workers and good to distribute great amounts of money to stockholders whose factories are not working." [14] Other articles discussed more often the unemployment reserves proposal than contributory insurance plans and it was the former that the league's Executive Board debated throughout 1931 without being able to arrive at a position acceptable to all its members. Other issues were more easily resolved, but it put off a decision on unemployment insurance by throwing this issue back to the local affiliate leagues for study and debate.

In accord with this decision Elisabeth Christman, the league's secretary, circularized all the local leagues in December 1931, explaining to them the nature of various proposals before the states. Their precedent, she advised, was workmen's compensation and their purpose was to prevent unemployment by giving "the employer a direct incentive to keep his workers steadily employed. These bills," she continued, "are based on the principle that industry is as responsible for the prevention of unemployment as it is for the prevention of industrial accidents, and that irregularity of employment is part of the real cost of doing business." [15] The response from the local leagues was disappointing, but when the national board was polled in January of 1932 on this principle only one negative vote, Agnes Nestor's, was recorded. Still it seemed unwise publicly to commit the league to a stand on an issue that was, apparently, relatively little understood, especially since hard times had forced the league to postpone the national convention which had been scheduled for that year. At this juncture the debate was stilled by Matilda Lindsay's discovery that the league had endorsed the principle of unemployment compensation in its 1924 convention; no further action was therefore required, she advised the Executive Board.[16] The league's resolutions in 1924 had indeed included one favorable to unemployment compensation (also endorsed in it were a federal employment service, public works, minimum-wage and maximum-hour regulations, and ratification of the child-labor amendment); but the statement was no more clear as to specific details in the earlier year than the later. To the league members, some form of compensation for the unemployed remained, then, a good but nebulous idea; other planks in the organization's program took precedence by far.

The reluctance of the WTUL to declare itself forthrightly may have arisen, in part, from the traditional opposition of the AFL to any measures that might, if only remotely, jeopardize the main battle for union recognition and its preference for economic action, unionization, and collective bargaining. Just as Gompers had opposed unemployment insurance as a "socialistic" scheme subversive of the principle of voluntarism, so William Green and many of his associates argued against it down into the early years of depression on the grounds that it threatened to establish paternalistic controls over a free labor movement. The responsibility rested upon the employers, they said, to regularize production and employment and, in slack seasons and years, to spread the work through the adoption of a five-day, thirty-hour week. Because a federal insurance system was regarded as unconstitutional, the AFL's effective majority leaned toward state legislation which would establish company reserves with a built-in incentive for individual firms and industries to stabilize production.

As early as 1930, however, dissenting voices were raised and in 1931 proponents of state action precipitated a sharp debate at the federation's annual convention. In January 1932, the United Mine Workers embraced the principle of unemployment insurance; in February the powerful New York Federation of Labor added its endorsement. When William Green began to hedge it was clear that local pressures could not be resisted much longer. The Executive Council authorized Green to explore various proposals in the field with an eye on ways which would afford maximum security for the union movement, and his report — which recommended federal coverage of workers engaged in interstate commerce, state systems of insurance for all others with the full burden of cost falling upon the employers alone, and protection of the union movement — was accepted first by the Executive Council in October and then by the general convention in November. In such states as New York, Pennsylvania, Wisconsin, and California the state federations demonstrated substantially greater enthusiasm for social insurance than did the national council and convention, and by 1935 when unemployment insurance was made an integral part of the Social Security Act, organized labor's support was not insignificant; but the major drive never came from the ranks of organized labor.[17]

Elsewhere in the nation social security was ever more widely being discussed and more favorably. The *New Republic* had found by the end of 1930 that unemployment insurance, while no substitute for jobs, was a better way than the charitable dole to maintain health, morale, and purchasing power. Labor leaders more radical than the AFL supplied, labor educators, economic and legal scholars affiliated in one way or another with the labor movement were together beginning to feel their way toward the insurance principle. In 1931, the Conference for Progressive Labor Action, an *ad hoc* group pressing for more forthright action than the AFL would permit, drew up a model unemployment insurance bill. A. J. Muste, onetime preacher turned labor reformer, professional committee-maker and conference-goer, chaired its deliberations. Joining him were John A. Fitch of the New York School of Social Work, Harry W. Laidler of the League for Industrial Democracy, Alfred L. Bernheim of Labor Bureau Inc., Murray W. Latimer of Industrial Relations Counselors, and Nathan Fine of the Research Department of the Rand School. Bills were offered and received some notice at least not only in Wisconsin and Ohio but in Connecticut, Maryland, Michigan, Missouri, Pennsylvania, and New York; this in the 1931 legislative year.[18]

In Congress Senator Wagner, whose thinking as late as 1931 was closer to the AALL program for wage reserves with incentives to industry to stabilize employment than along the line of contributory insurance, was joined by other senators and congressmen in a public airing of the issue. A Wagner resolution calling for exploration of unemployment insurance was adopted by the Senate in February 1931, and led to a series of hearings in the fall chaired not by the blunt New York senator, as senatorial custom made appropriate, but by Senator Felix Hebert, who was skeptical about all social insurance proposals. The committee's majority report — signed by Hebert and by Senator Otis F. Glenn of Illinois — submitted in June 1932 declared that a federal program would be unconstitutional and "impracticable," federal aid to the states inexpedient, and state systems unwise. Their endorsement of company reserves voluntarily established was rejected by Wagner, the third member of the committee, who preferred at that time compulsory statewide programs.[19]

In 1931 a People's Lobby — another *ad hoc* reform coalition — had been thrown together, with John Dewey as its chairman and Benjamin Marsh its executive secretary, and with support from many old reformers, socialists, civil libertarians, and social workers such as Roger Baldwin, Harry Elmer Barnes, Morris Ernst, John A. Fitch, Charles Howard, Edward L. Israel, Freda Kirchwey, Harry W. Laidler, Eduard C. Lindeman, Broadus Mitchell, Frank Murphy, A. J. Muste, John A. Ryan, Rexford Tugwell, Oswald Garrison Villard, Edmund Wilson. On the eve of the presidential nominating conventions in 1932, the People's Lobby stated its case: direct action by federal government for relief, public works, and unemployment insurance were vital to the restoration of a feeling of security. The American Academy for Political and Social Science devoted articles to the subject; debaters' handbooks were published providing summaries of arguments pro and con. Organized labor, the one reliable source of strength for social security movements in England and Europe, hung back in the United States or offered merely nominal and verbal support, but the slack was taken up by social reformers working through voluntary associations.[20]

Insurance against unemployment undoubtedly received its biggest boost when Franklin D. Roosevelt proposed its consideration at the Governors' Conference in June of 1930. The depression was but nine months old when F. D. R., with the advice of Frances Perkins, spelled out the terms of what he felt would be a viable program: self-supporting insurance programs in the several states to which employees as well as employers would contribute, benefit payments as of right from funds administered on a sound actuarial basis. Roosevelt's speech may have marked a turning point — at least many reformers so declared, although the wish may have been father to the thought. In November 1930, the New York Committee for the Stabilization of Industry provided a reasoned argument for state unemployment insurance. When, on F. D. R.'s request, Frances Perkins visited England in 1931, she reported back that unemployment insurance there had blocked "desperation and disorder" and had helped to maintain purchasing power and thus cushion the shock of depression. The Democratic platform of 1932 endorsed the principle of state unemployment insurance systems.[21]

Constant agitation had led by 1933 to a widely shared sentiment that if unemployment insurance was no quick cure-all for unemployment at least it offered a way to bolster purchasing power and a way to maintain family income at some minimum standard without the destruction of morale that relief involved. Unemployment insurance, particularly if established on the principle of employee contributions, did not give something for nothing; such a system did not constitute a "dole," as social-insurance opponents always cried, but the only constructive alternative to the true "dole," which was charitable relief.

By 1933, however, there was a mounting impatience with talk, growing anxiety with the drift of affairs, a longing for action. The irrepressible Fiorello La Guardia gave the word before the 1933 convention of the American Association for Social Security: "I have been listening to arguments always proved by charts, and I have seen the same charts used to show the prosperity of the United States, the honesty of our banking system, and the consumption of lipstick in the Polish Corridor. But if you go up into my district and talk to Mrs. Rabinowitz, or Mrs. Esposito, or Mrs. O'Flaherty, they will tell you they can't feed their children on charts." The promotion of interest in state social security might be all right for educational or propaganda purposes, he said, but only national action could meet the challenge of national catastrophe. Industry itself had some responsibility to do what it could to regularize employment — workers and their families had to eat 365 days in the year; but local and uncoordinated efforts would never suffice. "We are either going to have child labor laws, old age pensions, and unemployment insurance in this country, or we are going to have chaos and disorder, and something worse," he concluded. "There is something peculiar about human beings. They just simply refuse to go hungry. And you can't preach loyalty on an empty stomach." [22]

It was in that year of excitement, 1933, when measures dear to the reformers since the lapse of progressivism were being hurried through a Congress eager to cooperate with a President set upon doing something, many things, to lift the nation up from despair, that the American Association for Old Age Security changed its name to the American Association for Social Security. Pensions for the dependent aged may have been as far as reformers dared step toward social justice in 1927, but 1933 gave new hope; 1933 permitted a more rapid breakthrough of reconstruction than they had envisioned a mere year earlier. State pension systems had been a necessary first step, said Warren Jay Vinton, research director of the AASS, reporting on the association's work in 1933. But noncontributory pensions had provided "fragmentary relief," nothing more or better. The association was now dedicated to a new goal: "Instead of pensioning off a small portion of our aged workers, we must insure all of them." Compulsory, contributory insurance schemes under federal direction must take first priority, with benefits paid as of right not according to "abject need" with indigence the test. For workers already in the older age brackets, who would be unable to accumulate credit through their own contributions, security would have to be provided out of funds raised from income and inheritance taxes. [23]

In 1933 a bill modeled on the Commons-Andrews unemployment reserves principle had been sponsored in New York by the AFL and the New York Conference for Unemployment Insurance. The United Neighborhood Houses of New York City immediately began a campaign against it and for the substitution of the Ohio state model of unemployment insurance. The American Association for Social Security came out on the side of the settlement workers, warning that company or industry-wide reserves would lead to company welfare and company unions. In 1934 it was the insurance principle — backed now by the social workers and the AASS, and by the League of Women Voters and the State Federation of Labor as well — that received serious attention. Only John B. Andrews and the AALL persisted in proposing company reserves against unemployment. The social insurance principle had triumphed in New York and throughout the entire nation. [24]

The calendar of events may be recorded briefly: The 8th of June 1934: In a special message to Congress, the President — privately dedicated to security for all Americans "from the cradle to the grave," impelled now by a rising popular demand for action (of which the Townsend movement was most vociferous), confronted with congressional initiative (the Dill-Connery old-age bill, the Wagner-Lewis unemployment insurance bill) — called for a broad program of security, "the security of the home, the security of livelihood, and the security of social insurance." The 29th of June 1934: By Executive Order the Committee on Economic Security was called into existence. The 26th of July 1934: Edwin E. Witte, chief of the Wisconsin Legislative Reference Library since 1922, arrived in Washington to take up his post as executive director of the committee. The 21st of January 1935: The committee's omnibus draft bill went to Congress for committee hearings. The 14th of August 1935: congressional redrafting and passage of the bill having been accomplished, the President signed that act which Frances Perkins later reported gave him greater satisfaction than any other domestic accomplishment. It provided a federal-state system of unemployment insurance; a federal program of old-age insurance; federal grants to the states for old-age assistance, aid to the blind, aid to dependent children, aid to maternal and child-health services, aid to child-welfare services, and aid to public health programs. Before the bill was finally enacted, limitations and exemptions had been added, but only health and invalidism insurance was totally excluded, this against the wishes of Miss Perkins and Harry Hopkins but in accord with the dictates of political expediency, the fear that its inclusion would have placed the entire program in jeopardy.

What was true for social security was true for other reform measures as well. Provision of direct federal aid for unemployment relief; an expressed preference for work relief whenever possible with payment in cash and without casework supervision of family budgets; support of public works; guarantees of the right of labor to organize and bargain collectively; the prohibition of child labor; statutory provision for maximum hours and minimum wages — these were the fruits of crisis politics and the leadership of a President eager to act in an emergency greater than war; they were the fruits of tireless study and propaganda by reformers and reform associations who had hotly contested the issues of social justice while the nation kept cool with Coolidge.

10

TOWARD THE NEW DEAL

"What a sordid decade is passing! . . . The spirit of our democracy has turned away from the things of the spirit . . . What a joy it would be to get out and raise the flaming banner of righteousness! Instead of which we sit in our offices and do unimportant things and go home at night and think humdrum thoughts, with the gorge in us kicking like a mule all the time."

— William Allen White, quoted in Halford E. Luccock, American Mirror (New York: Macmillan, 1940), p. 49

"In short, Roosevelt took advantage of long years of study, research and experimentation in labor legislation; and utilized those responsible for it. He brought to realization many goals striven for for over twenty years. No goals are final, for the desire for better things is inherent in man, but Roosevelt lifted our efforts in this field out of a quagmire of frustration and achieved memorable advances."

— Mary R. Dewson, "An Aid to the End" (typescript autobiography in Franklin D. Roosevelt Library), Volume I, p. 17

SCHOLARS have often engaged in a search for significant turning points in American history. Two such dramatic moments were clearly 1776 and 1861. Some have argued that the 1890's constituted a great watershed between an older America — rural, agricultural, provincial — and a newer America — urban, industrial, internationalist. Certain days have been singled out as historic focal points: 6 April 1917, American entrance into World War I; 7 December 1941, the United States catapulted into World War II; 6 August 1945, the atomic age inaugurated at Hiroshima. The stock-market crash of October 1929 was, it has been persuasively argued, another such turning point.

Before looking further into the course of social reform and social service in the early years of depression following that crash, it would seem useful to pause and review again, however briefly, the diverse lines of force which molded the history of social action during the decade 1919–1929; for against an understanding of some of the complexities of those years major developments of the 1930's can better be fathomed.

Social reformers themselves, who had struggled against odds in the twenties, were acutely aware of the crucial significance of the changed climate of opinion that came with hard times. Many measures which had seemed outrageously radical when first suggested had become part of a new concordance by 1933. Comprehensive social insurance, an impractical ideal when Brandeis and Rubinow proposed it before World War I and a "pro-German" or "Bolshevik" plot in the easy twenties, was not so wild a dream when Governor Roosevelt sidled up to it in 1930 and it became an accomplished (if incomplete) reality in the act of 1935. As Paul Kellogg commented in 1932 to his old associate Graham Taylor of Chicago Commons: "Socially and politically things which were not given a look-in during prosperity are coming into their own. People are thinking. If we can keep a stiff upper lip, serve the situation and strike fire in people's imagination, it seems to me *The Survey* has a better chance than ever before in the next five years."[1] The time for hard analysis and bedrock reform had arrived.

In the months following the armistice all things had seemed possible. The great potential of American productivity had been unleashed; labor and business in partnership with government had worked miracles. The nation, unified for war, could now be mobilized for social justice. Then came the letdown: a vindictive peace, a resurgence of fanatical nationalism, and, at home, helter-skelter demobilization, a Red Scare, labor-capital violence, and before many years had passed hanky-panky in high places, corruption such as the nation's capital had not seen since the days of Grant. Grown men paraded about in white sheets, burned crosses (and not a few Negroes). La Follette went down in 1924; the child-labor amendment had no chance after Massachusetts rejected it and New York evaded it. In some places hope survived down to the *Adkins* decision, 1923, or down to the Massachusetts referendum, 1924. Elsewhere the reaction had set in earlier.

Hopes dashed led some few to bitterness, disenchantment, withdrawal. Generally, however, the men and women intimately involved in the crusade for social justice were not turned aside. What Alice Hamilton wrote of Jane Addams may have been true, partially at least, of that beloved lady and perhaps of some others: ". . . having no illusions to start with, she could never be disillusioned or disappointed. She never shrank from painful facts."[2] Not many of the old reformers joined the battle with quite the robust sense of enlisting in a just and eventually triumphant cause that Florence Kelley displayed. Somewhere between Jane Addams' acceptance (if not accommodation) and Florence Kelley's glorious stubbornness lay the attitudes of the bulk of social reformers who went about their business sometimes with heavy heart, more often in good humor, doing what was expected of them (or more often what they expected from themselves, for most of them were quite old-fashioned in their self-discipline).

The "new era" in economics, a new era presumably of benefits voluntarily granted by efficient and responsible corporate capitalism, a new era of controlled and engineered progress, held forth the promise of material plenty, widely distributed, without resort to social tinkering or bureaucratic regulation. Enlightened business statesmanship seemed to offer stabilization, orderly advance, and welfare for labor and the consumer alike without the disrupting force of labor unionization. Scientific management, the open shop, partnership with government (business, implicitly, the senior partner) represented to most Americans the most viable means to a balanced, progressive, and affluent society. Those who objected, those who pointed to the maldistribution of benefits, whether measured in material terms or in status and morale, were admonished not to rock the boat. Reform and welfare, moreover, were expensive; they required expenditures from the common treasury when the longing was for government economy and lowered taxes (and for hard-surfaced roads, of course). Poverty was not something to be cured by social action when individual industry and a rising national income could do it better. City councils, state legislatures, the Congress of the United States deferred easily to business leaders in a business civilization. "Until recently," complained Abraham Epstein before the Connecticut Federation of Labor in 1934, "Connecticut legislators generally looked with contempt on those of us who appeared in behalf of the aged, although they sat up with profound respect whenever a manufacturer appeared against the adoption of such a law."[3]

Prosperity, the politics of business, and the business of politics were not the only dampeners on reform. The overrepresentation of rural areas in state and national legislatures, and the neglect of states to reapportion in accordance with the accelerating shift in population from countryside and village to city, acted as a drag upon political accommodation to new issues. The national parties, reflecting the complacency of the general public, offered few constructive alternative policies or programs; the distance between Calvin Coolidge and John W. Davis was not great. The Democratic party was traditionally and habitually divided, of course, but never more sharply and evenly than in the mid-1920's when the contest was not only between the provinces of Bryan and the sidewalks of New York, but between village America and the big city, old-stock native American versus the new immigrant, evangelical Protestantism against Roman Catholicism and Judaism, dry against wet, old-style Populist protest now turned socially and morally conservative against new-style welfare liberalism. Social reformers could join in the La Follette crusade in 1924, but not with much enthusiasm, for most of them were astute enough to recognize it as a losing cause.

The cause of reform could expect little assistance from organized labor except in certain states — Pennsylvania, New York, Illinois, California, Wisconsin, most notably — where the state federations of labor worked, if rarely with success, for general reform measures. Other reformers might not have felt as bitter as Florence Kelley who regularly railed at the "stupid folly of that aged Dodo," Samuel Gompers, but the president of the AFL was certainly not a militant ally save on such issues as the prohibition of child labor.[4] Gompers' commitment was to voluntarism, to craft unionism, to the "pork chop" issues; he preferred the bargaining table to the legislative lobby as a way to win labor's rights, piece by piece, step by step. What government gave, government could take away; better to rely on trade unionism than to depend upon the favors of a paternalistic government. The AFL endorsed a reconstruction program in 1919 whose final declared goal was "industrial democracy" and whose specific planks included a living wage, an eight-hour day, equal pay for equal work, civil liberties, recognition of the legal right of labor to organize and bargain collectively, and government ownership of public utilities; it had favored the Plumb plan for nationalization of the railroads at the war's end; it endorsed the candidacy of old "Fighting Bob" La Follette in 1924; but neither Gompers nor William Green, who succeeded him, really had his heart in political action. Organized labor, fighting for survival against the open-shop crusade, had little energy to spare for other matters. For the time it focused upon self-interest, just like the farm bloc and the veterans' lobby.

The war had made a difference, too; nothing would be the same again after those searing years. If social injustice at home had consumed the attention of reformers at the turn of the century, war and postwar international tension seemed the greater evil for reformers, many of whom began to invest their money, time, and energy in the cause of disarmament, international cooperation, and world peace. Jane Addams still called Hull House home, and she did not cease from seeking amelioration of the lot of her neighbors, but her heart was in the highlands of the crusade for world amity and her talents were turned to the work of the Women's International League for Peace and Freedom. Gentle Julia Lathrop returned to Illinois after her retirement as chief of the Children's Bureau in 1922, and picked up her campaign for child welfare and protective labor legislation, working through the state League of Women Voters and through the Child Welfare Committee of the national league, but much of her declining energy she invested in the cause of world peace. Alice Hamilton continued her investigations and exposés of industrial poisons and other health hazards; Lillian Wald too maintained her interest in health and welfare; but their letters and their writings returned often to a concern for good will among the nations.

Margaret Dreier Robins slowly withdrew from direction of the Women's Trade Union League and turned to the labors of the International Federation of Working Women. But even those representatives of working women whom she left in control of the league were swept up in antiwar agitation; the league established a standing committee on national disarmament and affiliated itself with such pacifist federations as the Conference on the Cause and Cure of War and the National Council for Reduction of Arms. The national secretary's reports to local leagues throughout the postwar years regularly stressed Miss Christman's conviction that war was the world's most pressing problem. In 1924 league affiliates were urged to join the campaign for peace with the exhortation that "If We Can't Stop War, Nothing Else Matters . . . Airbombs, poison gas and hate will destroy our civilization if the next war breaks." In 1931, the league's official stationery bore the stamp of a peace group which depicted a lion and a lamb lying together upon a platform that read "Peace is the art of living together." If the good women identified with the lamb, they must have felt an eternal unease of spirit as the precarious settlement of 1919 began to crumble.[5]

Carrie Chapman Catt took with her out of the woman-suffrage crusade into pacifism in the interwar era a large number of women, able and substantial contributors to whatever cause they embraced. Almost every woman's group, regardless of the specific domestic programs it espoused, was married to the cause of peace — the American Association of University Women, the Council of Women for Home Missions, the General Federation of Women's Clubs, the YWCA, the National Council of Jewish Women, the WCTU, and the League of Women Voters (to cite but a fraction of the total number who had signed up for the duration).

The peace crusade diverted energies; those who participated in it laid themselves open to charges of mollycoddle idealism, silly-headed internationalism, and even disloyalty. That peace and progress were so often linked confirmed the suspicions of practical Americans that reform was not only wrongheaded, it was probably downright subversive as well. Isaac Rubinow had to defend his mother's poor judgment in having conceived and delivered him in Russia; Florence Kelley's detractors pretended to find a foreign plot in her marriage, long since dissolved, to a Polish citizen.[6] Some were spared by death from the disillusion that accompanied the breakdown of peace in the tortured thirties, but even before Manchuria, Spain, and Poland, the search for peace was not often rewarded.

The great Red Scare, which shook American society in the immediate postwar years, carried over into the rest of the decade. Architects of the child-labor amendment spent futile hours refuting the ridiculous charge that it had been composed in Moscow to Sovietize American children. Many a proposal went down before loose but effective charges of radicalism and disloyalty.

Then there was the Eighteenth Amendment, and its failure. Surely prohibition was an unambiguous victory for personal health and public morals. Even those who worried more about the human consequences of excessive drinking among poor slum-dwellers than about the abstract immorality of intoxication celebrated the arrival of prohibition though not with the same fervent, Puritan passion. But village teetotalers and urban social workers alike had reason to doubt the efficacy of prohibition by the end of the decade. Margaret Dreier Robins, who stayed loyal to the Grand Old Party even in 1932, might complain at the Democrats' nomination of a vice presidential candidate in that year who happened to be a regular imbiber, but for most reformers, the failure of enforcement together with the coming of the depression rendered the prohibition issue obsolete. Mary Anderson, a young protégé of Mrs. Robins' in the early years of the WTUL, wrote in reassurance to her old friend in 1930 that the people were not "looking for something to drink" but that they were "looking for something to eat."[7] It was apparently worse to go hungry in a society of potential plenty than thirsty in a dry era. But while it lasted, prohibition was a divisive issue, particularly for professional settlement workers and caseworkers who were increasingly torn between their sure knowledge that alcohol so often meant unhappiness for their neighbors and clients, and their commitment to personal liberty. The angry division in 1928 ran along lines of nationality, religion, and class and also along the fissure between wet and dry; and Al Smith's attraction as a man committed to social welfare was obscured by his identification with repeal. Try as she might, not even Lillian Wald, who could charm with impartial success a potential donor or a slum child, was able to persuade very many of her colleagues that Smith promised more practical and constructive welfare programs than Hoover. That prohibition restrained many reformers from forming a tight coalition with their potential allies among new immigrant groups from southern and eastern Europe is abundantly clear.

The 1920's were not conducive to reform. But "normalcy and reaction" were not the only characteristics of that remarkably complex decade. The 1920's were many things to many people. Darrow and Bryan represented contradictory strands in American life and they saw their times from radically different perspectives. Al Smith and William Gibbs McAdoo had little in common save that each bore the label "Democratic." Harry Emerson Fosdick, the liberal preacher, had little in common with Bruce Barton, who made of Christ a modern huckster, or with Pastor William Riley, unordained Protestant pope of the Fundamentalists, except that each was a professed Christian. An understanding of the 1920's must somehow encompass Edgar Guest and T. S. Eliot; Harry Dougherty and Burton K. Wheeler; Kid Ory, Paul Whiteman, Eugene Ormandy, and Rudy Vallee; Clara Bow and Ethel Barrymore; and these folk heroes (among many others) — Babe Ruth, Al Capone, Charles A. Lindbergh, Henry Ford, and Big Red, Man o' War.

The 1920's prized democracy and social mobility, rugged individualism and a classless middle-class society, but the Lynds could write that the division between working class and business class constituted Middletown's chief characteristic. It was an age of welfare capitalism and an era of factory tyranny, at River Rouge, for example, where the discipline was not so much harsh as capricious. It was an age of abounding plenty, but an age that would put two obscure places on the map — Gastonia, North Carolina, where low wages and the stretchout led to a spontaneous, violent explosion, and Harlan County, Kentucky, where want and violence became endemic. It was a Jazz Age and an age of sobriety; a Golden Decade when two-thirds of the families of the land lived below a margin of health and decency. It was an age of disenchantment and of faith, many faiths. It was an age in which some despaired of establishing mastery over the drift of life (Walter Lippmann for one), while others (John Dewey, Eduard Lindeman, Mary Follett) held forth the promise of social engineering. It was a decade of moral revolution in which "everything went"; and a decade that bore "strange fruit" — "black bodies swaying from the poplar trees."

It was an age of normalcy and reaction, and an era in which old welfare programs persisted and were steadily expanded, while the exploration of new reforms and programs proceeded apace. The agitation for McNary-Haugenism, voted down or vetoed as long as prosperity held, broke through in the Agricultural Marketing Act of 1929 and in the price-support and production-control measures of the New Deal. The 1920's saw more than one version of George Norris' Muscle Shoals bill, with an expanded version vetoed by President Hoover; the legislative program of the First Hundred Days included the Tennessee Valley Authority, a multiple-purpose project for the reconstruction of an entire region. In the Agriculture Department and in Interior, the 1920's were years of quiet preparation during which the rationale for comprehensive, co-ordinated planning for natural-resource development was elaborated, and programs of wilderness preservation, soil conservation, and flood control were pioneered.[8] The attempt at federal regulation of child labor may have faltered, but in education, child welfare, and urban reform substantial advances were measured.

Then, of course, came the panic and swiftly following, as night the day, a dark season of depression. For the Women's Trade Union League, which had busied itself throughout the 1920's with holding its own in those northern industries and trades in which it had a foothold, with legislative affairs both state and national, with workers' education, and with the peace crusade, hard times — and they had arrived for millions of marginal workers, male and female, well before October 1929 — came as a shock and a prod to direct action. The league had never been com-pletely diverted from its primary task of union organization, of course; but the rebuffs and disappointments had been so numerous that the thought of launching a drive was more than the resources of the league, human and financial, could bear. The league's Fannia Cohn and Rose Schneiderman, both of the ILGWU, were, however, aggressive trade unionists, and their point of view always had an able spokesman at league headquarters in the person of Elisabeth Christman of the Chicago Gloveworkers, who concealed beneath a gracious manner a stubborn determination that only her flashing eyes sometimes revealed. Fannia Cohn made it clear that trade unionism was required to win higher wages, shorter hours, and better conditions and to salvage the workers' "dignity, self-confidence, and self-respect as citizens and as human beings." Modern industry, she said, subordinated man to the machine: "In our highly organized industrial society, the personality of the in-dividual is reduced almost to insignificance."[9]

The organization of women workers proved difficult, however: the AFL had little desire to invest its limited energies in what appeared to it the futile task of shepherding women into unions. But conditions in the unorganized southern textile industry cried out for action. Living conditions in the miserable little company towns of Tennessee and North Carolina might have been a bit better than in the isolated hill shacks from which the working families were drawn, but measured by any other standards the workers were pauperized and demoralized by low wages, the stretchout, irregular employment, family labor, and company discipline. The industry itself was highly speculative and unstable, given to wild fluctuations in price, production, and profit. However hard labor was squeezed, the profit rates of the southern textile industry were generally low and unreliable. Labor turnover was high and the resentment of the displaced mountain folk was profound and abiding. An eleven-hour day was not untypical and weekly wages ran not much better than twelve dollars; protective labor legislation was nonexistent or weakly enforced; organization was unknown, as the full membership of the United Textile Workers, a weak union even for the 1920's, lay entirely in the North.[10]

In the fall of 1926, Margaret Dreier Robins wrote to Elisabeth Christman from Birmingham, Alabama, after a leisurely trip through the South, of the need for the Women's Trade Union League to do something for oppressed southern women workers.[11] The league established a Committee on Southern Work that year and, in anticipation of fierce opposition, sent Matilda Lindsay, a southerner by birth, down to Virginia and North Carolina to survey the land, seek out allies, and slowly prepare the way. Miss Lindsay reported back, throughout 1927, nothing but discouraging news of indifference of the workers, rivalry among the unions, hostility from the community, resentment of outside assistance. The league authorized Miss Lindsay to establish a field office in Richmond, Virginia, and in 1927 the organizational drive began, very modestly to be sure, with the distribution of sentimental leaflets on the plight of the textile workers, aimed no doubt at potential middle-class allies as well as the workers themselves, who hardly needed to be advised of their lot.

Although the southern drive had first claim on whatever resources the national league could spare, the league found the South to be "another country," the workers inarticulate and suspicious. The trade union women from New York, most of them of new immigrant stock, were bewildered by the anti-Catholic and anti-Semitic response of the southern community. Working out of their Richmond office, Miss Lindsay and Miss Corabel Stillman sought ways to address the workers and community leaders, but in neither effort were they particularly successful. They appeared before union meetings, at YWCA luncheons, at church socials, but to little avail. Even the most concerned of southern women, Miss Lindsay reported, were "proceeding with caution in allying themselves definitely with our campaign."[12]

The spontaneous explosion at Elizabethton, Tennessee, in March 1929, caught the league and the AFL's United Textile Workers unprepared. The strike in the rayon mills erupted when the mill owners refused to discuss labor conditions with representatives of the mill workers; tired of factory tyranny, oppressed by substandard wages, the girls walked out in pure desperation. The companies secured an injunction against picketing and other strike activities, but then decided upon quiet negotiation with representatives of the United Textile Workers. The prospect of compromise with the union movement proved more than the local business leaders wished to contemplate; in April armed mobs resorted to vigilante action; the violence soon got out of hand, with deputy sheriffs and state police finally being called in to restore an order favorable to the companies. By summer the strike had been broken, union members blacklisted, and peace restored, the uneasy peace of unconditional victory.

Gastonia, North Carolina, was the next scene of violence, with the Communist-dominated National Textile Workers Union providing leadership to desperate workers. This was class warfare, however nonideologically the workers themselves viewed the struggle. Violence led to a reign of terror. The strike was broken, the union crushed. But the chain reaction of explosions could not be halted by suppression. At Marion, North Carolina, the story of unpremeditated walkout and violence was repeated.[13]

The experiences of 1929 left both the WTUL and the AFL shaken and determined to be better prepared for the next round. Elisabeth Christman, Agnes Nestor, Rose Schneiderman, and all the others had been through some hard strikes in their day, but employer intransigence at its worst in Chicago and New York before the war had never been like the Piedmont South in 1929. They had pounded the pavements in picket lines and had been hauled into court, they had been intimidated and blacklisted, but the fear of being murdered had never been a part of their anxiety. The AFL stepped up its southern drive throughout 1930; even William Green himself swung through the South in an attempt to sell the industrial stability that orderly trade union procedures offered. But the AFL lacked the funds, the manpower, and the will to carry through the kind of all-out effort that southern conditions demanded.

The Danville, Virginia, strike which broke loose in September 1930 was the only one in this series in which the league played any role. It had been on hand throughout the spring and summer of the year, assisting Francis Gorman and the United Textile Workers. The league threw its influence on the side of moderation, not wishing to get involved in major strike activity until the strength of the union could be built up; it particularly wished to avoid a head-on clash when hard times, depressed prices, and unemployment were rapidly rendering a difficult situation impossible. Matilda Lindsay reported from the field, in midsummer, that it had been "an almost impossible task to hold the workers to a safe and sane policy, but so far we have been successful and are laying our plans for the time when the industry itself is in a better position." The growing strength of the union persuaded the harried millowners that they had better apply pressure before it was too late; they began to dismiss union workers in September, and the union was forced prematurely into retaliatory action. "We have argued and worked for eight months with the workers of Danville to keep them from striking," Francis Gorman advised the league's Executive Board in late September 1930, "but because of the wholesale discharge of our union members we are being forced into it." Elisabeth Christman, who had gone down to Danville to join Matilda Lindsay, wrote of efforts to bring about a peaceful settlement. "We have information that the mill owners have been preparing for a fight. It makes us panicky to think what may happen." On September 29, the workers walked out; the union was now in the midst of action it could not control, a strike it had wished to avoid, with no prospects of victory whatsoever. But it had to see the crisis through.[14]

The league confined its work largely to the collection of relief funds among friends and allies in the North and their distribution to union families in Danville. Clothing was shipped off to strike headquarters, grocery boxes and coal were delivered. The league arranged for union girls to speak before sympathetic meetings in the North. Appeals for funds went out over the signature of Mary Dreier and Rose Schneiderman for the league. The Society of Friends gave generous support; but the Red Cross could not be persuaded to provide relief until the strike was over. The AFL collected over $28,000 in relief funds; the league raised about $5800 in kind and in cash; the major burden, however, fell upon the UTW and upon the workers themselves.

Violence had flared in late November when the mills were reopened with a nonunion labor force. But the mass relief effort kept the strikers out until hunger and cold drove many of them back as winter closed in. On January 29 the union gave up; the workers drifted back without a single demand having been met.

That, for the moment, was that. The drive to organize southern workers had been ill-timed, weakly supported by the AFL, overcome by violent southern opposition. The league followed up its efforts to persuade the mill owners not to discriminate against union workers but where stronger measures had failed, entreaties availed little. Elisabeth Christman confessed, at the end of 1931, that with "so many still out of work and with those who are working afraid to take an active part because of the fear of losing their jobs," there was little interest upon which a vital movement could be built.[15]

These events, together with mounting unemployment and widespread want, broke the placidity of the 1920's. Those who had remained loyal to the causes they knew to be just through the discouraging years of disinterest and drift leaped at once into the fray, with more new friends and allies at their side with every passing month. As month followed month with no sign of recovery, despite reassurances that prosperity was on its way, the demand for action mounted. Public works, old-age assistance, unemployment insurance won ever wider endorsement, from church groups, welfare associations, committees and leagues and conferences and clubs and fraternal orders of all sorts. Even in the field of relief, where traditional beliefs in the virtue of voluntary aid and local responsibility persisted, community leaders slowly came to recognize that cash relief was better than relief in kind, that work relief was better than the dole, that work on constructive programs contributed more to morale than employment on made-work projects, that finally only the federal government had the revenue resources to carry through an effective relief effort.

In communities scattered across the nation, concerned citizens united in action committees to agitate for ameliorative measures and to promote recovery programs. Disaffected labor leaders, dissatisfied with the sluggish reactions of the AFL, answered A. J. Muste's call for the establishment of the Conference for Progressive Labor Action (CPLA) in 1929. Drawing, at first, more enthusiasm from socialists and other reformers than from trade union leaders, it campaigned for organization of the unorganized into industrial unions, a five-day week and better wages, the founding of true cooperatives, and social insurance. A coalition of factions drawn from the non-Communist left, it had no thought, for the moment, of dual unionism. Before it disbanded in 1933, the Conference for Progressive Labor Action had advanced the cause of unemployment insurance and had set forth the need for union organization along industry-wide lines that the CIO would meet following 1935.[16]

September 1929 saw the organization of the League for Independent Political Action (LIPA) — chairman, John Dewey. Its vice chairman was that old stalwart of every independent, radical cause, James Maurer, president of the Pennsylvania Federation of Labor. Other familiar names showed up on the masthead — Paul Douglas, Oswald Garrison Villard, Harry Laidler, Reinhold Niebuhr, Stuart Chase, Paul Blanchard, W. E. B. Du Bois. Both national parties were politically bankrupt, so the LIPA declared; the need was for a new party, a third party, dedicated to social control and planning through the federal government, to a redistribution of national income, to comprehensive social insurance, to guarantees of the right of labor to organize and bargain collectively; congressional reapportionment, civil liberties, and world peace were also among its goals. Finding no grass-roots support for third-party action in 1932, it restricted itself to the composition of a comprehensive platform whose planks prophesied with greater accuracy the New Deal program than did the more moderate and ambiguous Democratic platform that same year.[17]

The organization of the People's Lobby, John Dewey again at the head, and A. J. Muste, Charles Howard, Roger Baldwin, Oswald Garrison Villard, Morris Ernst, Harry Elmer Barnes, Broadus Mitchell, Eduard C. Lindeman, and Rexford G. Tugwell among the ranks, represented still another informal reform association whose directorate was interlocked with others, and whose programs for relief, public works, and social security harped upon familiar themes. The National Unemployment League, Darwin J. Meserole, president, drew the support of Mary Simkhovitch, Harry Emerson Fosdick, John A. Ryan, Ernest Johnson, Harry Laidler, and Agnes Warbasse. The Joint Committee on Unemployment, on whose letterhead John Dewey's name led all the rest, asked for social insurance, maximum-hour legislation, direct federal relief, and all the rest.

As for the churches, if the Social Gospel had relied too heavily during the 1920's upon preaching its good news without elaborating a means either for converting those who possessed power or for touching those who existed largely without it, if its methods were more rhetorical and ceremonial than actionist, as Professor Donald B. Meyer has shown, these were failings common to many other middle-class, well-intentioned groups in the years of normalcy. The Federal Council of Churches of Christ in America had never swerved from its advanced position set forth in the social creed of 1912, but, after 1919, had been able neither to broaden or sharpen the platform nor to secure its adoption in practice. The revised statement, adopted at the quadrennial conference in 1932, was more explicit and incorporated new planks, especially in regard to social insurance and the rights of labor, which developed out of the social agitation of the late 1920's and the early depression years. The hierarchy of the Roman Catholic Church renewed in 1931 its pledge of reconstruction, enunciated first in the bishops' program in 1919, and stressed social insurance, the living wage, and the right of labor not only to bargain but to participate generally in industrial affairs. The promulgation that same year of *Quadragessimo Anno*, which renewed and brought up to date the encyclical *Rerum Novarum*, gave added authority to the reform impulse within the Roman Catholic community. In 1932 the Federal Council, the Department of Social Action of the Catholic Welfare Conference, and the Social Justice Commission of the Central Conference of American Rabbis agreed upon the need for public works, a reduction of hours of labor with no cut in wages, old-age and unemployment insurance, a more equitable distribution of national wealth, and over-all social and economic planning by the government.[18]

Everywhere in the nation pressures for action accumulated force. Franklin Roosevelt's brain-storming sessions in Albany went on long into the night, while delegations waited on city councils, legislative committees, congressmen and senators. Even the AFL was slowly being driven to mass protest; in February 1932, it staged a march of a hundred

leaders to the White House and on to the capitol where they pleaded
for the right to work, for a decent job at a decent standard, for direct
aid to the unemployed (had not Congress subsidized business?), for an
end to the labor injunction, for job security and national economic planning, for public works, for federal aid to states for old-age pensions, for
the imposition of higher taxes upon income and inheritances. In November, unemployment insurance was added to the list. The National Federation of Settlements agreed that all these measures were essential and
added slum clearance and public housing. Debating controversial and
partisan issues, as it had not since the conference of 1912, delegates to
the National Conference of Social Work in 1933 received a platform, assembled by its Committee on Federal Action on Unemployment (whose
chairman was Harry Lurie of the Bureau of Jewish Social Research),
which prophesied a planned society with a "minimum standard of living
for all": government control of hours and wages; public guarantees of the
right to collective bargaining; federal relief, with special provision of
aid for transient and homeless persons; public works, conservation of
natural resources, government development of water power, flood control, slum clearance, public housing, schools; federal grants-in-aid to
states for unemployment insurance, contributory insurance for health
and old age; public employment exchanges; dependence upon income
and inheritance taxes.[19]

Beyond all these specific proposals lay the movement, gradually gain-
ing adherents, for comprehensive social planning, for action by the federal government not only to ameliorate and repair, to regulate and
control, but by constructive and positive measures to promote the general welfare. From such diverse sources as Rexford Tugwell, Mary Van
Kleeck, J. Russell Smith, Stuart Chase, George Soule, Charles A. Beard,
and Gerard Swope came proposals for over-all economic and social planning. The particulars differed, of course; Mary Van Kleeck leaned
toward democratic socialism, government ownership of national resources and the means of production; Gerard Swope, president of the
General Electric Corporation, proposed that trade associations initiate
the planning with government playing a general coordinating role.
Critics said the former path led to socialism, the latter to fascism.

Whatever the details, whatever the ideologies, the President's Research Committee on Social Trends, a group charged by President
Hoover in 1929 with examining social trends over the first third of

the twentieth century, reported in 1933 what appeared to be irreversible trends toward ever increasing complexity and interrelatedness in every aspect of society, trends that required not economic and political planning alone, but planning in science, education, and government as well. Chaired by Wesley C. Mitchell (whose practical experience in Wilson's wartime administration complemented his career as a scholar), the committee drew upon the experience of Charles E. Merriam (another scholar with a deep commitment to community affairs and public actions), Shelby M. Harrison, Alice Hamilton, Howard F. Odum, William F. Ogburn, and Edward Eyre Hunt (a long-time intimate of Herbert Hoover, who served as executive secretary of the project). In every area of life, "generation by generation the right of a man to do what he will with his own has been curbed by the American people acting through legislators and administrators of their own election," the committee observed. "It is conceivable that without any surrender of our belief in the merits of private property, individual enterprise and self-help, the American people will press toward a larger measure of public control to promote the common welfare."

The committee had no desire to predict what would come to pass or to lay down rules of social action, but it could not avoid the conclusion "that the varied economic interests of the country will find themselves invoking more and more the help of government to meet emergencies, to safeguard them against threatened dangers, to establish standards and to aid them in extending or defending markets." Not a single area of life escaped the committee's survey of facts and forces; population, production, labor, education, recreation, religion, family life, the arts, leisure, medicine, and morals — all were scrutinized, described, their tendencies plotted and projected. Each area of life, and all of them together, required the application of social intelligence, a self-conscious effort that would lead to knowledge, understanding, and the establishment of direction. To accommodate "astonishing contrasts in organization and disorganization" progressive national growth now required "a higher degree of coordination" if "unequal rates of change" in different sectors of American life were to be synchronized. Means of "social invention" would have to be devised and institutionalized if potentially dangerous discrepancies and cultural lags were to be overcome.[20]

The committee exercised extreme care, at every point of its findings, to survey trends and not to promulgate specific programs of amelioration and prevention, but it could not escape a statement of the possible feasibility of social insurance, for example, and constructive economic planning to meet the crucial problems related to economic unbalance and social disequilibrium. Perhaps the mobilization of the nation for war and victory in 1917 and 1918 provided a precedent for coordinated national action. How rapidly, and with what unity of will and imagination had the American people risen to the emergencies of war! "No similar revolution could be effected in times of peace, unless a similar agreement on purpose, supplying an equally definite criterion of social values, could be attained. But is it beyond the range of men's capacity some day to take the enhancement of social welfare as seriously as our generation took the winning of a war?" As for the persisting human problems of poverty, disease, and crime: "The amelioration of these conditions is a major objective involving the techniques of modern social science and public welfare. The larger but longer task is prevention and the building of a more effective social structure." Without offering a blueprint for planned reconstruction, the committee clearly preferred the procedures of social intelligence, of social engineering.[21]

No more compelling summary of the complex, sweeping new agreement in American life is available. In the four years of its labors, the committee drew upon the resources of hundreds of leaders in business, government, philanthropy, education, labor, public service, research. Its massive two-volume report, together with separate monographs, constituted a thorough and profoundly critical self-analysis of the quality of contemporary civilization in the United States. The committee's findings furnished masses of information and guide lines of social policy for the events of the next decade.

A grand concept of the potentiality of American society for orderly progress and the growth of the general welfare had been evolved. Glimpses of the possibilities had been caught by hundreds of thoughtful citizens. But men, in fact, seemed helpless before the drift of life. Americans had always been able to accomplish whatever they set their hearts upon — independence, self-governance, the subduing of a wilderness, the settlement of a continent, victory over every obstacle, natural or social, as uncontested as victory on the fields of battle. Why should not the American people rise to the new challenge? But to Anne O'Hare McCormick of the *New York Times* staff, America's mood in the sum-

mer of 1931 was one of lull and suspense. "Un-American as it sounds
we are all waiting, waiting for something to turn up." She reported the
accumulating surpluses of America's productive power that weighed
down the soul. "There are whole regions whose populations go hungry
and sullen in the shadow of immovable mountains of anthracite." Part
of the nation's "aimless motion" consisted of "uneasy loafing and the
ranging hunt for work. With un-American patience skilled workmen
hang around or mill around day after day hoping for odd jobs." No
one seemed to know "which way to turn." From political leaders came
only "timidity and poverty of idea." In her travels about the country
that summer she found but one issue gradually drawing support — the
demand for social security. "This measure of defence against industrial
insecurity neither political party will be able to dodge," she predicted.[22]

In one quarter and another the conviction grew that drift need no
longer be the tendency of life. But whence would direction come? Certainly not from Congress as then constituted; certainly not from the
White House. "You see our President is silent and lets everyone else
be his spokesman and this is very bad for the country," wrote Margaret
Dreier Robins, who had been his enthusiastic supporter in 1928. "We
need Theodore Roosevelt. Do you remember how he took the people
into his confidence, worked out a program, explained it to us and then
told us to go to, knowing it meant victory?" Where was the nation to
find another such Roosevelt? Not in Albany, Mrs. Robins feared.[23] Paul
Kellogg, who had also once enlisted with the Progressives, was even
more disappointed with a President whose first act in domestic politics
had been to support the New Nationalist crusade in 1912. What Hoover
"missed in all those years he was off in China, Africa and elsewhere,
dealing with corporations on the one hand and coolies on the other,"
Kellogg confided to Lillian Wald, "was that very give and take
among the rank and file of folk in a democratic society which is such
a handicap to him now in acting as its chief . . . [he] has surrounded
himself with political advisers who insulate, inhibit and short-circuit
him." The times called for leadership and action.[24]

The list of grievances, both real and imagined, against the President
for whom so many had entertained such hopes in 1928 grew longer
with every passing month. The campaign to have Grace Abbott named
secretary of labor had got nowhere; it was the President's prerogative,
to be sure, to name whom he wished, but William N. Doak pleased

neither labor nor social reformers nor social workers nor very many others, for that matter. Welfare workers had hoped that the President, whose reputation for constructive humanitarian efforts particularly in behalf of child welfare was indisputable, would find ways to restore federal aid to maternal and infant health; but formal requests, which Congress promptly ignored, were all they got. The President's Committee on Employment had won support from welfare leaders, but when it drifted along without that vigorous action they knew to be essential disappointment quickly followed. The President's Committee on Unemployment Relief proved to be even less satisfactory. "I do not know why there isn't more revolutionary spirit developing," Lillian Wald observed and then went on to answer the implied question. "People are so glad to be kept above the starving line that the fear of losing that may be at the bottom." [25]

Congress seemed to know little better than the President what needed to be done. A bipartisan bloc of liberal Democrats and progressive Republicans offered alternative policies — employment exchanges, public works, direct federal grants for relief, social security, maximum hours — but Wagner, La Follette, Black, Cutting, Costigan, Norris, La Guardia, and company could rarely muster a legislative majority and when they did they were often overridden by executive veto. Hoover's plan for control of the waters of the Colorado River, a great self-liquidating project, carried; but the Norris Bill for the multiple-purpose development of the Tennessee River Valley was struck down as a "socialistic" scheme. The Norris-La Guardia anti-injunction measure was passed; a Reconstruction Finance Corporation was created; but Wagner's bill for large-scale public works and relief was vetoed and the mere authorization of three hundred million dollars in loans to the states through the RFC was the best that could be done for relief. An emergency conference on relief was called, in 1932, by the National Council of Community Chests, but according to Aubrey Williams' account the conference leaders "were far more concerned about not embarrassing Mr. Hoover than in doing something for the unemployed." [26]

The search for a leader proceeded. Hoover was destined for renomination; it was up to the Democrats. "How enthusiastic are you about Roosevelt?" Grace Abbott asked Lillian Wald late in 1931. "I think she is splendid and he seems the best on the horizon." [27] The implication that the Roosevelt family could offer a package deal, both Eleanor and Franklin, undoubtedly appealed to other feminine reformers who knew Mrs. Roosevelt's long-standing concern for welfare measures. A committee of settlement and social workers had gone down the line for Roosevelt's re-election in 1930, citing his support of old-age assistance and state unemployment insurance, protective labor legislation, prison reform, and public power. The work of Frances Perkins and Harry Hopkins was widely appreciated, although the former was more widely acclaimed than the latter; F. D. R.'s lieutenant governor, Herbert Lehman, could always be relied upon to support every reform measure, indeed he had always been far more one of their own than the gentleman from Hyde Park. Maud Swartz of the Women's Trade Union League had secured a government appointment through the good offices of Eleanor Roosevelt and Frances Perkins. Mary Dewson, onetime research assistant for the National Consumers' League and president of the New York League, moved over into partisan politics and throughout 1931 and 1932 was on the road drumming up support for Roosevelt's nomination and election.[28]

For all their support of Roosevelt in 1932, many of the New York reformers were happier with Lehman's gubernatorial candidacy than with Roosevelt's presidential drive. F. D. R.'s record as governor seemed substantially better than his campaign, which was often lacking in explicit affirmations of reform issues. At times it seemed that he was outdoing Hoover in his appeals for government economy and a balanced budget, items not of high priority in welfare circles. Jane Addams, who had voted for Hoover in 1928, could not choose either candidate in 1932. Paul Kellogg remained quiet until the very end of the campaign when he came out for Norman Thomas, Lehman and Wagner, and Hillquit for mayor of New York. Some notable leaders privately confided to their friends that, as Alice Hamilton wrote, their "vote is really less for Roosevelt than against Hoover *and* Doak *and* Wilbur. Just to get rid of them would make me sing hymns of praise." [29] Lillian Wald concurred. She proposed to vote for Lehman and Hillquit and against Hoover. "Even Arthur Garfield Hays, a Civil Liberties man and an extreme radical, says he'd rather drink beer with Roosevelt than protest with Thomas. Poor Hoover, he does everything on Friday and with his left hand." [30]

More typical of the support thrown on Roosevelt's side was the reasoned appeal of Sophonisba Breckinridge. Experience indicated, she declared, that "sound social service" required expert professional staff work, constructive legislation, and generous appropriations from public funds. Measured by these criteria, Roosevelt's actions promised effective and enlightened welfare policies. He had sought laws to protect women workers; as governor he had sought to meet the needs of the unemployed; he had drawn upon skilled professional experts for social-welfare administration; he had maintained New York's program of maternal and infant health after federal support had lapsed; he had, moreover, recognized the role of women in public life and what they might contribute.[31]

The campaign may not have made clear what Roosevelt intended to do when elected, but at least he promised to do something, and that was enough for millions of voters. Then came the long wait, from November 8 to March 4. From Washington, deadlock and drift, and the spectacle of a lame-duck President and a lame-duck Congress somehow trying to muddle through until new lines of action could be launched. To Mary Anderson, who had fought so many battles for labor and for welfare, from the perspective of the Women's Bureau in Washington, there seemed so little cause for rejoicing. The Old Guard had been defeated, so much was clear; but what the future held "no one knows. I don't see much hope that the Democrats will be able to do many more things than the Republicans did," she wrote, "and if the depression continues and conditions do not become any better, I doubt very much that either of the two major parties will have a chance in 1936."[32]

After the lull came the storm that cleared the air. First came emergency banking legislation, to salvage the crucial institutions of a capitalistic society; and then, in quick succession, the inauguration of a New Deal — public works, direct emergency relief, economic planning, support for the right of labor to organize and bargain collectively, conservation measures, river valley development, farm price support and production control. Rose Schneiderman, newly appointed to the Labor Advisory Board but still writing as president of the New York Women's Trade Union League, rejoiced: "Yes, it is a marvelous day we are living in . . . Only two years ago we discussed the possibility of National Economic Planning and here we are actually engaged in the very job of setting conditions of employment in basic industries."[33]

To Grace Abbott, who had devoted her life to securing for the children of the disinherited that opportunity and freedom she herself had enjoyed as a child on the prairies of Nebraska, it seemed that the day of fulfillment had come. As a young woman she had drifted to the University of Chicago, there to be attracted into the exciting whirl at Hull House. For a time she had acted as director of the Immigrants' Protective League; but Julia Lathrop had called her to Washington to direct the child-labor division of the Children's Bureau. As chief of the bureau herself, after Miss Lathrop's retirement in 1922, she had stood up for all those welfare measures so dear to her New England conscience — child-labor regulation, maternity and infant health, mothers' pensions, juvenile courts. Of Puritan and Quaker ancestry, "she had a right," said her sister Edith, "to be a little tenacious and uncompromising when she believed in a cause." [34] Stubborn she was, but tolerant and rarely bitter; informal in manner, frank with friend and enemy alike, she survived the disappointments of the years of Republican ascendancy with the conviction that what was right could not forever be postponed. Her humane instincts were kept from slipping into sentimentality by her habit of dispassionate empirical research. "Grace Abbott was more interested in people than in causes," wrote one friendly critic, "because what legitimate end could a cause have other than that of benefiting people?" [35]

Now, in the spring of 1933, Miss Abbott felt that a lifetime of patient labor was paying off. The Children's Bureau had just celebrated its coming of age birthday, its twenty-first, and Mrs. Brandeis had presented a fine picture of Julia Lathrop which was hung in the director's office. Frances Perkins, Miss Abbott reported, had moved in and taken control of the Labor Department in wonderful style; the department was "really beginning to function" as she had "always hoped it might." The credit went as much to F. D. R. as to Miss Perkins, for he was using her in all his "larger plans"; his message on Muscle Shoals, moreover, "said the right thing in the right way." The inauguration of the New Deal promised to cap all her expectations. "I am beginning to feel quite unnecessary," she said with relief. "During the past years one felt that the few liberals in the federal government who were ready to speak up when necessary could not be spared. Now I have the comfortable feeling that my job will be taken care of if I leave." [36]

For Grace Abbott, at least, the crest of the long, steep hill seemed near.

11

"UPHILL ALL THE WAY"

"These voluntary organizations — constantly collecting information, persistently seeking out and adapting for local use the best practical experience anywhere in legislation and administration — render an important public service. . . . In fact, it is no secret that many of the most carefully considered beneficial laws enacted during the past twenty years had their inception in, and in fact were actually drafted by, these social service agencies.

"Where such organizations combine resources of technical training for constructive work with a freedom of public expression which does not falter in making hidden truths known in the interest of the general welfare, they are among our most valuable national assets.

". . . they serve as vigilant sentinels ready not only to challenge anti-social practices but to arouse the social conscience of the time. In a period when leading public officials look to commercial interests to solve our social problems, the persistent wakefulness of social welfare organizations is all the more needed."

— John B. Andrews, "A Social Adventure Invites Your Cooperation," *American Labor Legislation Review*, 18:4 (December 1928), p. 331

"What made the great leaders of the past so influential was their commitment to a cause. They cared desperately about people, they had a vision of the good life, they were morally indignant about one or more social evils. Thus armed, they had the courage never to accept defeat and to bear with frustration, disappointment, and the realization that the job is never done."

— Eveline M. Burns, "Social Welfare Is Our Commitment," *Public Welfare*, 16:3 (July 1958), p. 153

THE day of harvest was at hand. Before the forward surge of reform ran into domestic opposition, 1937–1938, and dwindled away as the nation passed from peace to war again, many bits of unfinished business left over from the Progressive Era and many items on the reform agenda during the postwar years had been taken care of. Child labor was outlawed in the blanket codes of the National Recovery Administration, and when the NRA was found to be unconstitutional, Grace Abbott, Katharine Lenroot, and the National Child Labor Committee's lobby saw to the inclusion of its prohibition in the Fair Labor Standards Act of 1938. The hours and wages of all workers engaged in interstate commerce came under regulation in 1938; and if the standards were modest and the exemptions broad, millions received wage increases and in time, as amendments were added, the standards were raised and the exemptions narrowed. The federal government initiated programs of slum clearance and public housing which, if they never fully realized the hopes of Helen Alfred and Mary Simkhovitch and other agitators for housing reform, did represent first steps at least. Except for the omission of health insurance the federal social security program enacted in 1935 realized just about all the reformers' hopes, even though Abraham Epstein and some others were disappointed that the act did not go far enough or invariably provide the best administrative procedures. To unemployment and old-age insurance were added federal assistance for the dependent aged, for dependent children, for the blind, for maternal and infant health programs. The Federal Emergency Relief Administration, the Civil Works Administration, the Civilian Conservation Corps, and the Works Progress Administration together provided direct cash relief for the unemployed and wherever possible work relief on constructive projects. The Public Works Administration implemented the design for the long-range planning of major construction projects. The Tennessee Valley Authority provided coordinated plans for the manufacture of electric power and fertilizer, flood control, navigation improvement, soil conservation and reforestation, and recreational facilities. To all these programs reform associations and leaders made immeasurable contributions.

The roll call of prominent New Dealers (and of equal significance, hundreds of lesser public servants who packed New Deal administrations) includes the names of many who were either actively engaged in reform and welfare associations or directly moved by their agitation. Frances Perkins and Harry Hopkins lead the list, of course. Not far behind is Mary (Molly) Dewson, whose career carried straight through from progressivism to the New Deal without interruption. Educated at Wellesley College, Miss Dewson went directly from the classroom to investigations of the working conditions of women workers in factories and shops for the Women's Education and Industrial Union in Boston. In 1900 she became superintendent of the Parole Department for Girls of the Massachusetts Industrial School at Lancaster. Before enlisting in the woman-suffrage crusade, in 1911, she served briefly as secretary of the Massachusetts Commission on Minimum Wage Legislation. After a tour of duty with the Red Cross in France she became a research director for the National Consumers' League in which capacity she amassed the factual evidence that Felix Frankfurter employed in the *Adkins* case, after which she moved to New York where she served first as civic secretary of the New York Women's City Club and then as president of the New York Consumers' League, from 1927 to 1932.

With Eleanor Roosevelt she campaigned for Al Smith in 1928, headed the Women's Division of the Democratic party in 1932, organized the quietly effective campaign to put across Frances Perkins as secretary of labor, served on the Advisory Council to the President's Committee on Social Security, and became a member of the Social Security Board in 1937. During Roosevelt's first administration she saw that women received at least some share in patronage. She concentrated her efforts on the use of political procedures for the winning of substantive results. From long association with Florence Kelley she had learned the value in bringing to bear upon one issue at a time all the energy one could muster, and the necessity for sound research and broad publicity before moving into action.[1]

The Consumers' League claimed Mary Dewson as one of its own.

It claimed also Frances Perkins; Clara M. Beyer, who served in the Division of Labor Standards of the Department of Labor; Josephine Roche, who moved to Washington as assistant secretary of the Treasury in 1933; Elinore M. Herrick, a regional director of the NLRB; Amy G. Maher and Rachel Gallagher, both active members of the Ohio League, who served on the staff of the Unemployment Insurance Division of the Social Security Administration, and Marie Wing who went to its legal department. Elizabeth Johnson of the New York League joined the Children's Bureau. Beatrice McConnell of the Pennsylvania league became assistant director of the United States Division of Labor Standards; Metcalfe Walling of the Rhode Island league became secretary of the Fair Wages and Hours Commission; John Winant, president of the National Consumers' League, was named first chairman of the Social Security Board; while in New York, Emily S. Marconnier and Nelle Swartz (also active in the Women's Trade Union League) served, respectively, as director of the Division of Women in Industry and on the State Workmen's Compensation Board. Rose Schneiderman, a charter organizer for the United Cloth Hat and Cap Makers in 1903, becoming an organizer for the Women's Trade Union League and the president of the New York League in 1917, was made a member of the Labor Advisory Board of the NRA and from 1937 to 1944 was an official of the New York Department of Labor. Agnes Nestor, glove worker, and member of the Executive Board of the National WTUL from 1907 to 1948, acted as adviser to government commissions both in the nation and in her home state of Illinois.[2]

The settlements claimed that their leaders had fought in the advance guard of every major reform in the twentieth century; they claimed credit for the public service careers of Julia Lathrop, the Abbott sisters, Alice Hamilton, Florence Kelley, Felix Warburg, George W. Alger Alumni of Henry Street included Henry Morgenthau, Jr., A. A. Berle, Jr., Sidney Hillman, and Herbert Lehman. Frances Perkins was a resident of both Hull House and Chicago Commons; Harry Hopkins once lived at Christadora House, New York; Joseph Eastman, coordinator of transportation during the New Deal years, had lived at South End House, Boston, with Robert A. Woods. The residence was often brief, the relationship was sometimes casual, but many have testified to the profound influence the settlement experience had in opening the way to new insights and new understandings. To attempt to weigh the relative influence of the many complex factors and events of a person's life can be a futile enterprise; but Bruno Lasker, sometime resident at Henry Street, once observed that "even a short residence at a social settlement affects people's character in a most remarkable way. A man like [William] Chenery with his endowment usually goes through life without any pronounced social sympathies at all. But the period he spent at Hull House made him *see* social injustices, made him *see* the worries and difficulties of the poor as nothing else could have done, so that all through his life he has remained a supporter of social causes." [3] Louis Pink, housing reformer and social insurance proponent, looking back upon his own career, recalled the marked impact Lillian Wald, Mary Simkhovitch, and John Elliott had had on his life: "These dynamic people were a ferment, a yeast in the community — trying to make people realize the necessity for a different world, a better community — with parks, playgrounds, education, and all cultural attainments which flavor human life." He went on to record that Eleanor Roosevelt, as well, attributed "her interest in social work and in helping people largely to the two years she spent as a club worker at the University Settlement." [4]

Many others were in government long before 1933, and had labored on board and commission for welfare programs that won more generous backing beginning with the New Deal years. Julia Lathrop, Grace Abbott, Katharine Lenroot of the Children's Bureau, Mary Van Kleeck, Mary N. Winslow, and Mary Anderson in the Women's Bureau maintained the closest working relationships with the Consumers' League, the Women's Trade Union League, and the League of Women Voters, and with friends in settlement and social work throughout their long careers. The lines of influence, in these cases, worked both ways, from voluntary associations to public service and back.

To the task of drawing plans for comprehensive social security Roosevelt called those he knew had been working with the infinitely intricate problems of insurance for many years. Witte and Altmeyer came with backgrounds of more than a decade's pioneering in Wisconsin on unemployment compensation and related programs. Business and labor were represented on the Advisory Council to the President's Committee on Economic Security; among those who had been active in social reform movements were Paul Kellogg, editor of the *Survey* magazine; Belle Sherwin, former president of the National League of Women Voters; Grace Abbott of the Children's Bureau; George H. Nordlen of the Fraternal Order of Eagles; Josephine Roche, business woman, public servant, and member of the Consumers' League; and Mary Dewson. On Paul Kellogg's urging, Helen Hall and Joel D. Hunter, the latter general superintendent of the United Charities of Chicago, were added to the council; at Witte's suggestion, after it was noted that no Catholic had been named, Roosevelt appointed John A. Ryan. Acting in a technical advisory capacity were such social insurance pioneers and experts as William R. Leiserson, Murray W. Latimer, Aubrey Williams, Bryce Stewart, Barbara N. Armstrong, Meredith B. Givers, Eveline Burns, Ewan Clague, Grace Abbott, Katharine Lenroot, and many others. Neither Abraham Epstein nor Isaac Rubinow was formally involved in the deliberation, the latter because of ill health.[5]

The gross sense of insecurity that accompanied the depression undoubtedly created a climate favorable to social security legislation; the political threat of the Townsend movement made action on old-age security eminently expedient; the determination of F. D. R. and of Frances Perkins to give social security one of the highest priorities brought imaginative leadership to its accomplishment. Two additional vital factors were present: the existence of a small group of experts, learned and experienced, to give shape and substance to the act; and the momentum of agitation that reformers and welfare leaders supplied. Without the pioneer studies and propaganda of Epstein, Rubinow, Andrews, Commons, and Douglas would the nation have been prepared for social security in 1935? The experts provided the requisite technical knowledge and contributed to a favorable environment, in which there was readiness to accept a principle and a program that western Europe and nations of the Commonwealth had inaugurated many years earlier.

Before an overflow audience of social workers at their national conference in June 1933, Harry Hopkins brought the word they had been waiting to hear. Everyone was expected to pitch in and do the best he could to provide relief; certainly the federal government was eager to experiment, and if some of the expedients did not work, well, "the world will not come to an end." The need for action was urgent: "We propose to see that the unemployed get some relief."[6] With equal bluntness he announced to the American Public Welfare Association, a year later when the desperate emergency had passed, that the need was now for "regular and orderly assistance" — pensions for the aged without regard to need, widows' pensions, special provisions for the unemployable. Compulsory health insurance was desirable, so was the planning of public works — parks, forests, roads, housing. In all these programs — which aimed at security, the good life, freedom from fear — social workers had been leading the way for years.[7] Looking back upon eight years of New Deal experience, Jane Hoey, who had done as much as anyone within the ranks of federal government to develop its programs of public assistance, proclaimed that the New Deal carried through principles for which social workers had labored — the dependence of political democracy upon social and economic democracy; "the assumption by government of a continuing responsibility for promoting the general welfare"; the provision of "regular income" for all families through private employment, public work, social insurance, and public assistance. In the administration of public assistance programs the New Deal had accepted the social workers' insistence upon fair hearings, "unrestricted and unconditional cash payments," and the confidential nature of all records.[8]

It is understandable that those who had labored in the dry seasons rejoiced when reforms, long-agitated, came into their own in the fullness of time. Julia Lathrop and Florence Kelley died in 1932, before they could see the harvest of their recent efforts. But Lillian Wald, testifying in 1935 that she was "very much for Roosevelt," expressed gratification that many reform goals were being fulfilled that she had feared would be such a long time coming.[9] Others knew what a thankless task theirs had been, and was. And so rarely, wrote Elisabeth Christman, had the "chief beneficiaries" of reforms been among those "most eager and active in bringing them about."[10] To little Agnes Nestor, fatigued from years of seeking to organize her fellow workers into unions and to wrest welfare measures from callous legislatures, it seemed, in 1936, that things went painfully slowly and sometimes seemed "not to move at all. But we are making progress and I suppose that is the way we have to move." She hoped that many reforms for which she and others had worked would now be won, but she reminded Margaret Dreier Robins, to whom she was writing, of a poem that Alice Henry had sent to them some years earlier — "'We shall not

travel by the roads we make.' We may not," she concluded, "but someone else will and someone made roads for us."[11]

Florence Kelley had never been one to stand aside. The waters
parted where she wished to go. As an associate recalled of living with
Mrs. Kelley in New York City and crossing the hectic traffic of its
streets: "She behaved like Moses crossing the Red Sea. And the traffic
behaved like the Red Sea. It simply dammed up on both sides
while Florence Kelley and I walked through an empty lane."[12] But even
Florence Kelley knew the hard resistance of society to new ideas. "Inch
by inch" were women's rights in industry formulated and won; only by
unceasing, "grinding, nagging patient" efforts was any reform achieved.[13]
Isaac Rubinow testified to the same point: first came the setting forth
of a new idea or program by a "professional 'reformer'"; then came
research and agitation and the proposal of model bills; then the appointment of legislative commissions for study; if the facts could not be
denied, finally a bill might be passed (after the needful compromises
had been struck, of course); other states might then be persuaded to
follow suit. So went the progress of reform, step by painful step.[14]

The professional reformer had his cause to promote (and his salary
to justify, critics were quick to add). But however extravagant the
claims of influence might be — and they were usually surprisingly
modest — there was uncommon good sense in John B. Andrews' asser-
tion that without the voluntary association, composed of citizens with
no direct self-interest to push, the general welfare suffered. They did
the hard research without which understanding and viable solutions
to problems were impossible. By constant publicity they brought their
analyses and their proposals before groups of influential citizens. They
talked to politicians and testified before commissions.[15]

Not many of these organizations exercised crude political power,
however. The tactics so often employed by the Anti-Saloon League, or
the Farm Bureau, or the American Medical Association, or the National
Association of Manufacturers, or the CIO were not often available to
the Consumers' League, or the Association for Social Security, and
certainly not to the National Federation of Settlements. The latter
groups were not bound by self-interest; they represented no coherent
bloc of voters in a politician's constituency; they operated on tight
budgets and with limited staff. (Abraham Epstein complained, in 1938,
that he didn't have the price of a railroad ticket to Washington.[16])

There were many associations that exercised influence on social and political events in the postwar years of the twenties — associations of businessmen, preachers, farmers, and veterans; the American Legion, Rotary, and the Ku Klux Klan were perhaps more representative of the main streams of American life in those years than the Child Labor Committee and the Women's Trade Union League; there is no doubt that they commanded more money and larger memberships. The National Consumers' League operated with an annual budget of from twenty to thirty thousand dollars in these years. The Child Labor Committee did better, far better than most, with an annual budget of around a hundred thousand dollars; but the Women's Trade Union League scrimped along often with no more than twenty thousand dollars, although in some few years that sum was doubled. The WTUL, moreover, faced the financial embarrassment of being forced to accept large cash gifts from philanthropic donors because the unions could not or would not underwrite their efforts. "[A]re we not inconsistent in accepting large anonymous gifts from persons whose names would not find favor in trade union ranks?" the financial secretary asked the Executive Board in 1925.[17] John Andrews' budget for the American Association for Labor Legislation ran around forty thousand dollars.

It is impossible to estimate how many citizens were actively involved. Letterheads provide notoriously unreliable indices of personal commitment beyond the lending of one's good name. These associations typically listed as many vice presidents as even the most inflated insurance corporation table of organization could ever boast; and the suspicion is well justified that their executive staffs did most of the work. Annual or biennial conferences were as often used to stimulate local activity and to inform the local units as they were occasions for the delegates to shape policy for the national organization. Reliance upon overlapping membership and interlocking directorates was notorious; the same names show up on the executive committees and boards of directors of one group after another.

The surpassing influence of New York City leadership and funds is notable. Except for the Women's Trade Union League, which maintained its central office in Chicago until the mid-years of the 1920's when it moved to the nation's capital, associational headquarters were located either in New York or in Washington. Chicago provided leaders and money, but it was in New York that day-by-day direction was asserted, and this by a relative handful of leaders all of whom knew each other intimately (if not always with affection). The strongest local associations were to be found in New York, Massachusetts, Connecticut, Pennsylvania, Ohio, Illinois, Wisconsin, and California, states most highly industrialized and urbanized, states in which the old progressive surge toward public welfare and service had been strongest. They enjoyed scattered strength in other states; but save to the Child Labor Committee the South rarely made contributions. It was, finally, in New York that national policies were formed, and at the very center of this circle of influence stood Paul Kellogg and the Survey Associates, whose outreach comprehended both agitation for social reform and the practice of professional welfare services.

The influence of these associations can hardly be traced to financial resources or mass membership. They could rarely consider intervention in political campaigns. They had to rely on more subtle means — persuasion and cajolery rather than coercion. Perhaps they finally made an impact because they had influence in the right places at the right times, on that saving remnant of the citizenry that was both concerned and powerful. Robert Wagner, Fiorello La Guardia, Herbert Lehman, Edward Costigan, George Norris, Robert La Follette, Jr., Franklin Roosevelt did not depend upon their efforts either to gain or to stay in office. But these legislators and executives counseled and listened and learned; they called upon the reformers for technical advice and appointed them to administrative offices; and they responded to and borrowed from the theories and programs that the reformers pioneered. The associations provided social laboratories in which new policies and programs could be initiated and tried out. They provided the institutional means through which all the pressing issues of society could be explored; not ultimately effective until politicians took up their causes, they sharpened the issues at a time both parties had defaulted from that essential task; in so doing they offered constructive alternatives in an age of political drift.

Their task was never an easy one; it required perseverance quite beyond what common prudence would seem to dictate and the mastery of complex details as well. A contemporary welfare leader, Eveline M. Burns, who knew from personal experience the costs of social pioneering, drew the lesson from the careers of Jane Addams, Florence Kelley, John A. Ryan, and the Abbott sisters that "courageous and dedicated

individuals and groups can effect change." They evidenced not concern alone but dedication, "devotion to a cause," a "zeal for social
justice." But before they arose to positions of national leadership, they
had to spend "years of pretty discouraging activity on a small scale: of
addressing hundreds of dreary little meetings in small communities
where the chairman apologizes for the absence of half the audience;
of long hours spent in composing letters to the press that never get
published or preparing testimony for hearings before boards and local
and state legislatures only to find one is allowed to speak less than
five minutes; of organizing groups and individuals to bring pressure to
bear on some local bigwig who, despite the convincing arguments one
has mustered, votes the other way." [18]

The function of the Survey Associates may be taken as representative of all those associations, causes, and services it publicized and promoted. With a circulation ranging from fifteen to twenty thousand
throughout these years, the Associates' publication, the *Survey*, depended upon special contributions, for it was, as Paul Kellogg wrote
to one generous patron, "an educational, not a commercial enterprise."
Its purpose was "to report and interpret social movements," a member
of the staff explained to Jane Addams, to find "principles of social action which in many cases will be as revolutionary and foreign to accepted practice as were some of the preventive social movements twenty
or thirty years ago." [19]

Like social reform and social welfare movements generally, the *Survey* relied upon facts, "the clear and honest reporting of actual conditions, that will inform or convince public opinion," as Ray Stannard
Baker phrased it. But, the editors added, empirical evidence was not
to be collected for its own sake — that would represent merely the
"synthesis of sterile data"; the facts were rather to be gathered so that
constructive "judgment and action" would proceed from sound understanding. The emblem chosen by the Survey Associates — a gallant
galleon under full sail, charting unknown seas and exploring distant
lands and "new frontiers" — may be taken as symbolic of the whole
enterprise which the *Survey* so ably captained.[20]

As for the professional social workers with whom the social reformers
were so often and intimately allied, their commitments were to service and assistance to the individual in need, and to a reconstruction
of the environment within which the client lived. To provide assistance

so that the client, and his family, could move away from need and dependence upon others toward independence and self-direction was, in these years, a fully accepted principle of welfare work, particularly in the casework field. Care, and the removal of the causes of dependency, required financial support, provision of health or recreational services, vocational guidance, family counseling. The focus of such work was upon helping the client to help himself, to see him through a time of crisis when his own resources (financial or psychological) were inadequate to the demands placed upon him (and poverty was but one form of dependency), to give him opportunities to enrich his life, and to assist him in making satisfactory adjustments to his environment.[21]

During these same years, professional social work evidenced a persisting concern for the general welfare of society as for the health of the individual client. When the limits of personal assistance were reached, then social-work leaders accepted the obligation to promote measures, through political and social action, that would lighten the handicaps and create opportunities for fuller and richer lives for all. Helen Hall, whose study of unemployment set forth the human consequences of hard times, put it in the specific terms with which settlement workers habitually dealt: It was acceptable casework method, she said in 1936, to assist a torn and deprived family to get out of objectionable quarters for the sake both of health and morale. "But in the long run," she continued, "it is both poor case work and poor health work merely to move particular families and do nothing toward changing the conditions out of which you have taken them and into which others will move." Social workers must drum up support for housing reform, slum clearance, and public housing, and must assist other groups to work effectively toward these ends. "Social action for social change and advance is inescapable," she concluded, "unless we are willing to drift along eternally patching up the consequences of social neglect and industrial breakdown."[22]

Family agencies emphasized the inward factors of adjustment during the 1920's, when the exciting new possibilities of psychiatric social work were just beginning to provide new tools of diagnosis and treatment. But even in casework, reported Leonard W. Mayo in retrospect, the voluntary agencies "saw at first hand the effects of bad housing, lack of recreation, the blight of tuberculosis, the adverse effects of child labor; and they gave voice to the resulting needs and became articulate concerning the causes of such disorders and defects in society." [23]

Perhaps a metaphor borrowed from organized religion will sharpen the point a bit. A minister may be priest or prophet; at best he is both, but rarely are these talents combined in one holy person. As priest, as shepherd, he serves, he counsels, he comforts, he reconciles, he listens, he accepts, he judges not, he bears witness to a transcendent concern. As prophet, as preacher, he has a harder, more demanding, and more lonely role to play. In the world, if not of it, he holds up absolute standards against which the sins of man and the shortcomings of the world may be measured, and judged; his cry is less for charity and compassion than for justice; he is not content merely to stand and to serve; repentance and reform or doom is his prophecy. Without pushing the metaphor too far, it may be safe to say that the dedication of professional social work was to both the priestly and the prophetic qualities of its calling, to both service and reform. The vast majority of social workers were properly engaged in what we may call priestly functions. The actionists, the prophets if you wish, were the exceptional leaders — impatient with ameliorative measures, demanding social justice through social reform. [24]

Social workers in the early depression years may not have played exactly the same role that pioneers had back in the days of progressive reform before the war when the line between social reform and social work was blurred, but they performed similar functions in sometimes different ways. The role of direct agitation was often left largely to voluntary reform associations, to politicians, to labor leaders (playing an aggressive role in the New Deal years that had rarely been countenanced in the days of Gompers); social workers were more often, in the 1930's, found working in and through government, on the staffs of numerous commissions, committees, bureaus, and agencies, than as voices crying in the wilderness. They labored, each in his own way, within and without government, in season and out, for social security, slum clearance and public housing, adequate standards of relief, public works, industrial minima, and the right of labor to organize and bargain collectively.

If not as imaginative and creative perhaps (although the measuring stick is perforce rather subjective and flexible) as literature (Hemingway, Fitzgerald, Cummings, and Pound), or the visual arts (John Marin, Marsden Hartley, Arthur Dove, Georgia O'Keefe), or the movies (Charlie Chaplin, Robert Flaherty), or social and literary criticism (Harold Stearns, Joseph Wood Krutch, Walter Lippmann, Edward Sapir, Malcolm Cowley, H. L. Mencken), social-welfare and social-service movements from 1918 to 1933 possessed a vitality too, and one that has been little noted or appreciated. We have taken the reformers too much at their own word. We have fallen too easily into the generalization that the decade from armistice to panic was marked by one prolonged and uninterrupted slump in reform thought and determination, when the processes were more subtle and more complicated than that. Through frustration there persisted an unending search for new ways to meet problems both old and new when old ways fell short or (as was as often the case) when perfectly reasonable means of legislative action were overruled by hostile judicial rulings.

Particularly in the actions of voluntary associations dedicated to reform causes was the field never surrendered to the forces of reaction. Beleaguered and beaten back, these social-reform movements recruited new leaders and enlisted new soldiers, somehow scraped up the money to keep at least a token force well armed, experimented with new field tactics and in time evolved new strategies.

At the same time, like all voluntary efforts, these lacked coherence and unity; their objectives were frequently confused, their actions at cross-purposes. Often they failed for lack of focus, attempted too much, or relied too heavily on the efficacy of exhortation and fine resolutions. Mrs. Elizabeth Tilton confided to her diary the fatigue and weariness that weighed down her life as a reformer. "I am no longer the enthusiasm of youth," she put down in January 1921. "I am the seasoned worker of fifty, who knows it is just hitch and drudgery." The futility of her efforts she often sensed, and the absurdity of presuming to alter the course of the nation or the world by words and resolutions, however well intentioned. After one long day of speaking before public gatherings in favor of education, health, and child-welfare measures then being considered by the state legislature, she mustered the strength to attend an afternoon tea for the cause of world peace. At home that night she recorded her fatigue and her bemusement with the futile gestures of her tea companions. "Rose Nichols sat in front running true to form — sewing placidly as she disarmed the nations." [25]

An understanding of where progressivism led and an appreciation of whence the New Deal derived require study of reform associations and movements in these years. In voluntary action progressivism survived in the decade of normalcy and reaction, even if it did not triumph. In the National Consumers' League and the Women's Trade Union League, in the National Child Labor Committee, the Association for Old Age Security, the American Association for Labor Legislation, and the League of Women Voters, the reform impulse was kept alive. In the arena of professional social work, in the Child Welfare League and the National Federation of Settlements, in the National Conference of Social Work and the American Association of Social Workers, new ways of social amelioration and of social action were being pioneered. In many cases the leaders were directly out of prewar progressivism — Jane Addams, Lillian Wald, Graham Taylor, John L. Elliott, Lillie Peck, Mary Simkhovitch, John B. and Irene O. Andrews, Florence Kelley, Owen Lovejoy, Samuel McCune Lindsay, Margaret Dreier Robins, Paul Kellogg. Other leaders had been fed on progressivism, but did not really come into their own until the interwar era — John R. Commons, Bruno Lasker, Abraham Epstein, Edward Clopper, Elisabeth Christman, Felix Frankfurter, Isaac Rubinow, Gertrude Vaile, Eduard Lindeman, Porter R. Lee. Still others were relative newcomers on their way to positions of much greater influence in the 1930's: Mary Dewson, Paul Douglas, Harry Hopkins, Frances Perkins, Aubrey Williams, Helen Hall, Helen Alfred, Edwin E. Witte, Arthur J. Altmeyer, Hilda Smith, Mary Anderson, Jacob Billikopf, Harry Lurie, Jane Hoey, and a host of others whose names have recurred in this narrative. Rooted in progressivism and on their way (unwittingly) to the New Deal, social reformers and social servants evidenced a remarkable vitality and imagination during the years that lay between the armistice and the inauguration of Franklin Roosevelt.

With the inauguration of Roosevelt, in the depths of the depression, the opportunity for reconstructive measures presented itself. While the New Deal never offered fully valid solutions to the economic problem of depression (as the persistence of mass unemployment attests), it did initiate measures that provided built-in stabilizers of substantial efficacy, and it did afford a larger measure of social justice and a more equitable distribution of income and social power than the previous generation had known. If progressivism, from which it drew inspiration, was more hardheaded than many historians have recorded, the New Deal was laced more heavily with moral purpose than most critics believed. From progressivism and from reform movements in the postwar decade it drew both its methods of analysis and its spiritual inspiration.[26]

The New Deal was eclectic in both theory and program. It provided no logically consistent, perfectly coherent, formal system of social thought. What Clinton Rossiter has written of the political theory of the Revolutionary generation might well apply, on a lower level of brilliance one fears, to the consensus of the 1930's. The leaders of the American Revolution, he writes, were "makers of history with a flair for speculative generalization, not philosophers in single minded search of ultimate truth." The philosophy they pieced together was "earnest faith rather than ordered theory." Its genius was evident in its capacity to fashion real institutions for the implementation of popular ideas.[27] Hyde Park was not Monticello, to be sure; yet the similarities cannot be denied.

Out of pressing need the New Deal evolved a program; from the past it drew its inspiration. The inventiveness of the New Deal operated more in the arena of program than abstract policy. That it was not devoid of lively and viable theories, however, is abundantly clear. It succeeded, where it did succeed, not only because it was administered by clever politicians, not only because it proposed real, if always partial, answers to real and present problems; it succeeded also because its idiom drew from a tradition still revered in the American heart. It owed a profound debt to those reform and welfare leaders who had pioneered new programs and kept alive the tradition of humane liberalism in the years of normalcy.

Grace Abbott was right, it was uphill all the way; yes, to the very end. And it did offer great rewards, not only to those who enlisted in the long, hard struggle, but to the whole nation as well.

NOTES

IN THE interests of simplicity I have confined my footnote citations to direct quotations, to close paraphrases, and to specific points of interpretation I have drawn from other scholars. I have strained to eliminate all but the most vital "see also" citations. In my Bibliographic Essay I set forth the primary materials and discuss critically the vast literature of both general and specific significance for my own study. Readers interested in securing precise, paragraph-by-paragraph citations are invited to correspond with me.

In the footnotes I have used the following abbreviations:

AALL . . . . American Association for Labor Legislation
AAOAS . . . . American Association for Old Age Security
AASS . . . . American Association for Social Security
NCCC . . . . National Conference of Charities and Correction
NCL . . . . National Consumers' League
NCLC . . . . National Child Labor Committee
NCSW . . . . National Conference of Social Work
NFS . . . . National Federation of Settlements
WTUL . . . . Women's Trade Union League (materials at Library of Congress)
WTUL (Radcliffe) . Women's Trade Union League (materials at Women's Archives, Radcliffe)
Addams Papers . . . . Jane Addams (Swarthmore)
Anderson Papers . . . Mary Anderson (Radcliffe)
Blaine Papers . . . . . Anita McCormick Blaine (Wisconsin Historical Society)
Breckinridge Papers Sophonisba Breckinridge (Library of Congress)
Commons Papers . . . John R. Commons (Wisconsin Historical Society)
Dewson Papers
(F. D. R. Library) . Mary R. Dewson (F. D. R. Library)
Dewson Papers
(Radcliffe) . . . . Mary R. Dewson (Radcliffe)
Epstein Papers . . . . Abraham Epstein (Columbia University)
Evans Papers . . . . . Elizabeth Glendower Evans (Radcliffe)
Folks Papers . . . . . . Homer Folks (New York School of Social Work)
Gilman Papers . . . . Catheryne Cooke Gilman (Minnesota Historical Society)
Hamilton Papers . . . Alice Hamilton (Radcliffe)
Hopkins Papers . . . . Harry Hopkins (F. D. R. Library)
Hull House Papers . Hull House Papers (Swarthmore)
Knox Papers . . . . . . Maryal Knox (Radcliffe)
Lehman Papers . . . . Herbert Lehman (F. D. R. Library)
McDowell Papers . . Mary McDowell (Chicago Historical Society)
Nestor Papers . . . . . Agnes Nestor (Chicago Historical Society)

Eleanor Roosevelt
Papers .... Eleanor Roosevelt (F. D. R. Library)
Smith Papers ...... Hilda Smith (Radcliffe)
Survey Associates
Papers .... Survey Associates (New York School of Social Work)
Taylor Papers ..... Graham Taylor (Newberry Library)
Tilton Papers ..... Elizabeth H. Tilton (Radcliffe)
Vaile Papers ...... Gertrude Vaile (New York School of Social Work)
Van Waters Papers . Miriam Van Waters (Radcliffe)
Wald Papers ...... Lillian Wald (New York Public Library)
Williams Papers .... Aubrey Williams (F. D. R. Library)

Preface

[1] Donald Richberg, "We Thought It Was Armageddon," *Survey*, 61:11 (1 March 1929), pp. 723–724, 762.

[2] John Haynes Holmes, "What Is Worth Fighting For in American Life?" *Survey*, 57:9 (1 February 1927), p. 605.

[3] "Where Are the Pre-War Radicals?" *Survey*, 55:9 (1 February 1926), pp. 556–566.

[4] Arthur S. Link, "What Happened to the Progressive Movement?" *American Historical Review*, 64:4 (July 1959), pp. 850–851.

[5] John E. Tsouderos, "Voluntary Associations, Past — Present — Future," *Adult Leadership*, 6:10 (April 1958), p. 267.

[6] Herbert Rusalem, "Early Education in Voluntary Welfare," in Alfred De Grazia, editor, *Grass Roots Private Welfare* (New York: New York University Press, 1957), p. 281. In the Bibliographic Essay I have summarized the literature on voluntary associationalism.

[7] Robert A. Woods and Albert J. Kennedy, *The Settlement Horizon; A National Estimate* (New York: Russell Sage Foundation, 1922), p. 59.

Chapter 1. Great Expectations: Hopes Deferred

[1] Lewis Mumford, *Faith for Living* (New York: Harcourt, Brace, 1940), pp. 221–222.

[2] Frances Perkins, review of Josephine Goldmark's *Impatient Crusader*, in *New Republic*, 128 (8 June 1953), p. 18.

[3] Florence Kelley to John A. Fitch (26 March 1925), NCL, Box 8.

[4] Frances Perkins, "My Recollections of Florence Kelley," *Social Service Review*, 28:1 (March 1954), p. 19. See also Florence Kelley to Frances Perkins (17 January 1929), and Frances Perkins to Florence Kelley (30 January 1929), NCL, Box 8.

[5] Mary R. Dewson to Mrs. Ramona T. Mattson (1 April 1954), Dewson Papers (F. D. R. Library), Box 12.

[6] Florence Kelley to Mary Rozet Smith (22 May 1919), Addams Papers, Box 8.

[7] Mary R. Dewson to Mrs. Ramona T. Mattson (1 April 1954), Dewson Papers, Box 12. Here and in many places that follow I have drawn on Josephine Goldmark's *Impatient Crusader: Florence Kelley's Life Story* (Urbana: University of Illinois Press, 1953).

[8] Executive Committee Minutes (21 November 1918), pp. 1–6, NCL, Box 8.

[9] Resolutions of 20th Annual Meeting, NCL, Box 15; "A Ten Years' Program," *Survey*, 43:7 (13 December 1919), p. 227.

[10] Margaret Dreier Robins to Agnes Nestor (5 April 1921), Nestor Papers.

[11] Quoted in Mary N. Hilton and Mary Elizabeth Pidgeon, *Toward Better Working Conditions for Women* (Women's Bureau Bulletin 252, 1953), p. 1.

[12] Quoted from 1911 Convention Handbook of WTUL in *ibid.*, p. 28.

[13] Carbon typescript of Samuel Gompers' welcoming address to WTUL Conference (26 March 1905), WTUL, Box 25.

[14] This reconstruction program was drawn up early in 1919 by the league's Board of Directors. Accounts may be found in WTUL (Radcliffe), Boxes 1 and 2; *Life and Labor,* 9:3 (March 1919), pp. 51–53.

[15] Proceedings of 1919 Convention in WTUL Papers, Box 14.

[16] "A Program of Principles and Standards for Protective Labor Legislation in America," *American Labor Legislation Review,* 9:1 (March 1919), p. 159. The entire issue is devoted to these matters.

[17] General sources on the NCLC may be found in the Bibliographic Essay. Specifically on these points see Minutes (1916–1919), NCLC, Box 7; Reports, NCLC, Box 8; Scrapbooks, NCLC, Box 54; Conference Proceedings, NCLC, Box 13.

[18] John A. Lapp, Summary Report (1929), NCLC, Box 8.

[19] Address of Felix Adler before NCLC Conference (16 December 1929), in which he recalled his own concern for the "promise of divinity" in every child, in *Proceedings* (1929), pp. 61–65, NCLC, Box 13.

[20] Editorial, *American Child,* 2:2 (August 1920), p. 118. In addition to other official NCLC accounts, see Lillian Brandt, "A Program for Child Protection," *Survey,* 41:11 (14 December 1918), pp. 338–342; letters of Edward Clopper, of the NCLC staff, to Anita McCormick Blaine (1918–1919) in Blaine Papers.

[21] My own interpretation differs somewhat from his, but I am indebted — for a brilliant cross-sectional analysis of the early settlement leaders — to Allen Davis, "Spearheads for Reform" (Doctoral dissertation, University of Wisconsin, 1959), Chapter 1.

[22] Jane Addams, carbon typescript of notes for an address at Berkeley Lyceum (1905), in WTUL, Box 25.

[23] Woods and Kennedy, *Settlement Horizon,* p. 168.

[24] *Ibid.,* p. 57. Mary K. Simkhovitch, *The Settlements and Religion* (New York, 1915).

[25] Woods and Kennedy, *Settlement Horizon,* p. 58.

[26] Robert A. Woods, *The Neighborhood in Nation-Building* (Boston: Houghton Mifflin, 1923), pp. 268, 275.

[27] Jane Addams, *Newer Ideals of Peace* (New York: Macmillan, 1907), p. 182.

[28] Woods and Kennedy, *Settlement Horizon,* p. 58.

[29] *Ibid.,* p. 161.

[30] *Ibid.,* p. 61.

[31] Graham Taylor, Address (May 1915), in Conference Reports, NFS Office Archives.

[32] Jane Addams, *Twenty Years at Hull House* (New York: Macmillan, 1911), p. 310.

[33] Mary K. Simkhovitch, quoted in James W. Linn, *Jane Addams* (New York: Appleton-Century, 1935), pp. 330–331.

[34] Robert A. Woods quoted in Eleanor H. Woods, *Robert A. Woods, Champion of Democracy* (Boston: Houghton Mifflin, 1929), p. 317.

[35] Telegram from Alfred G. Clark to Jane Addams (15 November 1918), Addams Papers, Box 8.

[36] Charles C. Cooper to Jane Addams (undated, probably spring 1920), Addams Papers, Box 9A.

[37] Bulletin of NFS (November 1920), Hull House Papers, Box 5B; Proceedings of Conference, 1920, and Bound Minutes of Executive Committee (October, November 1920), NFS Office Archives.

[38] Lillian Wald to Albert J. Kennedy (20 December 1919), Wald Papers, File 1, Drawer 1.

[30] Edward T. Devine, "Between War and Peace," *Survey*, 41:7 (16 November 1918), pp. 183–184.

[40] Edward T. Devine, "The Reconstruction of Social Agencies," *Survey*, 41:18 (1 February 1919), p. 619, and "A Nation-wide Drive for Social Reconstruction," 41:22 (1 March 1919), p. 785.

[41] "Social Reconstruction," *Survey*, 42:10 (7 June 1919), pp. 402–409; see also "The Conference on Demobilization, 29–30 November 1918," *Survey*, 41:10 (7 December 1918), pp. 287–323.

[42] "The Church and Social Reconstruction," *Survey*, 42:18 (2 August 1919), pp. 685–688.

[43] "The Church and Social Reconstruction," *Survey*, 42:14 (5 July 1919), p. 549.

[44] "Catholic Reconstruction," *Survey*, 41:21 (22 February 1919), p. 727, and (20 March 1920), pp. 759–760.

[45] "Social Justice Program," *Survey*, 44:19 (1 September 1920), p. 654.

[46] Lillian Wald to Harriet West Knight (28 April 1919), Wald Papers, File 1, Drawer 1.

[47] Lillian Wald, correspondence with Julius Rosenwald and William L. Chenery, Wald Papers, File 1, Drawers 1 and 3; *Survey*, 43:2 (25 October 1919), pp. 35–42, 45–46, and 43:4 (15 November 1919), p. 105; Robert L. Duffus, *Lillian Wald: Neighbor and Crusader* (New York: Macmillan, 1938), pp. 214–219.

[48] League of Women Voters of New York, "Report and Protest," reprinted in *American Labor Legislation Review*, 10:1 (March 1920), p. 104.

[49] Lillian Wald to Lavinia Dock (16 August 1919); to K. G. Waters (3 September 1919); to Robbins Gilman (23 October 1919), Wald Papers, File 1, Drawer 1.

[50] Dwight Waldo, Address before NCLC Convention in *Proceedings* (1918), NCLC, Box 13.

[51] John A. Fitch, reported in *American Labor Legislation Review*, 10:1 (March 1920), p. 61.

[52] Anna F. Davis, "Roots of Restlessness," *Survey*, 43:19 (6 March 1920), p. 670.

[53] Jess Perlman, "Unfilled Pledges," *Survey*, 43:19 (6 March 1920), p. 671.

[54] Elizabeth H. Tilton, "Journal" (1 January 1922), Tilton Papers, Box 10; "Autobiography," pp. 427–428, Tilton Papers, Box 9.

Chapter 2. The Crusade for Children

[1] John A. Lapp, Report to National Child Labor Committee (1929), NCLC, Box 8.

[2] Owen R. Lovejoy in *The Humanitarian*, 19 February 1919, p. 5, reprint in NCLC, Box 25; Minutes (5 March 1919), NCLC, Box 7.

[3] Raymond G. Fuller, "The New Humanitarianism," *American Child*, 1:1 (May 1919), pp. 29–32.

[4] Gertrude Folks, reprint from an article in *Practical Educator*, January 1920, in NCLC, Box 26.

[5] Raymond G. Fuller, Press Release (28 December 1920), NCLC, Box 27.

[6] Raymond G. Fuller, Statement to Press (December 1920), NCLC, Box 27.

[7] Raymond G. Fuller, "Next Steps in Child Labor," *Survey*, 45:15 (8 January 1921), pp. 535–536; Raymond G. Fuller, unpaged carbon typescript (July 1921), NCLC, Box 27; Raymond G. Fuller, in *Life and Labor*, 11:1 (January 1921), pp. 18–21.

[8] Owen R. Lovejoy, Report in Minute Book (30 September 1922), NCLC, Box 8.

[9] Julia Lathrop, Remarks in Minute Book (29 May 1922), NCLC, Box 8.

[10] Florence Kelley's modes of action are discussed in letters from Mary R. Dewson to Mrs. Blumberg (14 July 1958) and to Mrs. Ramona T. Mattson (11 April 1954), Dewson Papers (F. D. R. Library), Box 12.

[11] Florence Kelley to Newton D. Baker (23 May 1922), NCL, Box 8.

[12] Paraphrases from letter from Florence Kelley to Robert Szold (7 June 1922), NCL, Box 10.

[13] Florence Kelley to Mrs. Maud Wood Park (5 June 1922), to Felix Frankfurter (8 June 1922), to Edward P. Costigan (3 July 1922), NCL, Box 10.

[14] Alice Hamilton to Florence Kelley (6 October 1922), and Florence Kelley to Alice Hamilton (13 October 1922), NCL, Box 11.

[15] Florence Kelley to Senator Medill McCormick (17 January 1923), NCL, Box 10.

[16] Florence Kelley to Minnie Fisher Cunningham (15 June 1923), NCL, Box 10.

[17] Minute Book (25 October 1923), NCLC, Box 8.

[18] Samuel McCune Lindsay to Anita McCormick Blaine (21 December 1923), Blaine Papers.

[19] Untitled promotional leaflet (undated, c. 1923), NCLC, Box 29.

[20] Florence Kelley, Report to Board of Directors (6 March 1923), NCL, Box 8.

[21] Florence Kelley to Mary Carroll (4 June 1924), NCL, Box 13.

[22] *Survey*, 52:6 (15 June 1924), p. 342.

[23] Alonzo B. See to Jane Addams (10 July 1924), forwarded to Florence Kelley, NCL, Box 10.

[24] Florence Kelley to Jane Addams (11 October 1924), Addams Papers, Box 12.

[25] Minute Book (6 February 1924), NCLC, Box 8.

[26] Eduard C. Lindeman, Address (27 May 1924), *Proceedings*, pp. 33–34, NCLC, Box 13.

[27] Untitled pamphlet (August 1924), NCLC, Box 29.

[28] Folder, Organizations Associated for Ratification, NCLC, Box 1.

[29] Particularly here, but at many other points of analysis throughout this chapter, I am indebted to Grace Abbott, *The Child and the State* (2 vols.; Chicago: University of Chicago Press, 1938), I, 533–555; Aaron I. Abell, *American Catholicism and Social Action* (Garden City, N.Y.: Hanover House, 1960); Sam Beal Barton, "Factors and Forces in the Movement for the Abolition of Child Labor in the United States" (Doctoral dissertation, University of Texas, 1938); Robert Bremner, *From the Depths: The Discovery of Poverty in the United States* (New York: New York University Press, 1956); Elizabeth H. Davidson, *Child Labor Legislation in the Southern Textile States* (Chapel Hill: University of North Carolina Press, 1939); Jeremy Felt, "Regulation of Child Labor in New York State, 1886–1942" (Doctoral dissertation, Syracuse University, 1959); Philip J. Funigiello, "Dr. John A. Ryan and the Fight for Social Justice of Labor, 1924–1937" (Unpublished paper, University of California at Berkeley, 1962); Josephine Goldmark, *Impatient Crusader*; Vincent A. McQuade, *The American Catholic Attitude on Child Labor since 1891* (Washington, D.C.: Catholic University of America, 1938); Rowland L. Mitchell, "Social Legislation in Connecticut, 1919–1939" (Doctoral dissertation, Yale University, 1954); Ned Weissberg, "The Federal Child Labor Amendment" (Doctoral dissertation, Cornell University, 1942).

[30] Felix Adler, "The Child Labor Panic," *Survey*, 53:10 (15 February 1925), pp. 565–567.

[31] William L. Chenery, "Child Labor — The New Alignment," *Survey*, 53:7 (1 January 1925), pp. 379–382, 425–426.

[32] Minute Book (9 December 1924), NCLC, Box 8.

[33] Florence Kelley to Frances Perkins (4 December 1924), NCL, Box 11.

[34] Florence Kelley to Mrs. Laura C. Williams (7 January 1925), NCL, Box 11; folder on Amendment in New York, NCLC, Box 1. Mrs. Kelley never forgave Governor Smith, and continued to attribute, rightly or wrongly, his position to the influence of Cardinal O'Connell: Florence Kelley to Mrs. Kohn (28 September 1928), NCL, Box 11.

[35] Pringle's letter is quoted in Grace Abbott, "Federal Regulation of Child Labor, 1906–1938," *Social Service Review*, 13:3 (September 1939), pp. 421–422.

[36] NCLC, Press Release (6 February 1925), in Wald Papers, File 3, Drawer 3.

[37] William A. White, statement in *Woman Citizen*, 21 February 1925, p. 10.

[38] Samuel McCune Lindsay to Owen R. Lovejoy (9 March 1925), NCLC, Box 8.

[39] Owen R. Lovejoy, carbon typescript of Remarks before an Adult Bible Class (9 June 1925), NCLC, Box 31.

[40] Florence Kelley, Report to Board (29 November 1926), NCL, Box 8.

[41] Florence Kelley, Reports to Board (15 October 1925, 13 May 1926, 29 November 1926, 7 February 1927, 31 October 1927), NCL, Box 8; Florence Kelley, Correspondence Files (1925–1927), NCL, Boxes 8, 10; Florence Kelley to Lillian Wald (April 1927 and 7 December 1927), Wald Papers, File 1, Drawer 4; Lillian Wald to Mrs. Le Boutillur (28 March 1927), File 1, Drawer 1.

[42] Ethel Smith, Report to Board (1 June 1925), WTUL, Box 3.

[43] Quoted in Report of Illinois Child Labor Committee (15 October 1926), Blaine Papers.

[44] *Survey*, 57:8 (15 January 1927), p. 494.

[45] *The Doctor Looks at Child Labor* (Printed pamphlet, 1929), pp. 18, 22, in NCLC Scrapbook, Box 60.

[46] Quoted in News Release (17 January 1925), NCLC, Box 31.

[47] Poem by Charlotte Perkins Gilman printed in *Bulletin* of Philadelphia Women's Trade Union League (no date, probably issued in the mid-1920's), WTUL (Radcliffe), Box 1.

[48] "Idle Men — Working Children," *Survey*, 63:8 (15 January 1930), p. 453.

[49] Dorothy Canfield Fisher closed a radio appeal (February 1929) with its recitation, NCLC, Box 36. Miss Cleghorn's poem had long been a staple of NCLC propaganda, but it seems to have been used but rarely during the 1920's until the failures to ratify the child-labor amendment had become clear.

[50] Wiley Swift, "The Changing Order in Child Labor Work," *American Child*, 9:9 (September 1927), p. 2.

[51] Lillian Wald to Grace Abbott (30 October 1926), Wald Papers, File 1, Drawer 1; Grace Abbott to Lillian Wald (7 April 1927), Wald Papers, File 1, Drawer 4.

[52] Gertrude Folks Zimand, Editorial, *American Child*, 10:10 (December 1928), p. 2.

[53] Florence Kelley to Grace Abbott (7 April 1927), NCL, Box 8.

[54] Owen R. Lovejoy, "The Faith of a Social Worker," *Survey*, 44:6 (8 May 1920), pp. 208–211.

[55] Children's Bureau, *Children's Year Working Program* (Publication 40, 1918), *Standards of Child Welfare* (Publication 60, 1919), and *Children's Year* (Publication 67, 1920).

[56] Francis Tyson, "Family Protection through Supplemental Income," *Annals*, 121 (September 1925), p. 34.

[57] William H. Matthews, "Breaking the Poverty Circle," *Survey*, 52:2 (15 April 1924), pp. 96–98.

[58] Florence Kelley to Grace Abbott (15 January 1927), and Grace Abbott to Florence Kelley (15 January 1927), NCL, Box 8.

[59] Florence Kelley, manuscript memorandum (no date, c. 1929), NCL, Box 12; Grace Abbott to Lillian Wald (25 November 1929), Wald Papers, File 1, Drawer 4.

[60] Grace Abbott, "Looking Fore and Aft in Child Labor," *Survey*, 63:6 (15 December 1929), p. 334.

[61] William Cooper, Address (16 December 1929), NCLC *Proceedings* (1929), NCLC, Box 13.

[62] Children's Aid Society, *The Crusade for Children* (New York: Children's Aid Society, 1928), p. 49.

[63] Children's Bureau, *Courts in the United States Hearing Children's Cases* (Publication 65, 1920), p. 7.

[64] For an evaluation of this work I am indebted to Phyllis Rochelle, "Words and Action: The Care and Treatment of Juvenile Delinquents, 1912–1932" (Unpublished paper, University of California at Berkeley, 1962).

[65] Sophonisba P. Breckinridge to Grace Abbott (22 May 1931), Breckinridge Papers, Box 1.

[66] Julia Lathrop, "Child Welfare Standards a Test of Democracy," NCSW *Proceedings* (1919), pp. 5–9.

[67] "Notes and Comments," *Social Service Review*, 25:3 (September 1951), p. 384.

[68] Children's Bureau, *Unemployment and Child Welfare* (Publication 125, 1923), pp. 3–4.

[69] Grace Abbott quoted in Dorothy E. Bradbury, *Four Decades of Action for Children* (Children's Bureau, Publication 358, 1956), p. 34.

[70] Grace Abbott quoted in *Proceedings* (16 December 1929), NCLC, Box 13.

[71] Grace Abbott quoted in *Proceedings* (May 1929), WTUL, Box 15.

[72] Francis Tyson, *Annals*, 121, p. 33.

[73] Neva R. Deardorff, "Research in the Field of Child Welfare since the War," *Annals*, 151 (September 1930), pp. 195–206.

Chapter 3. The Campaign for Women's Rights

[1] Helen Glenn Tyson, "Mothers Who Earn," *Survey*, 67:5 (1 December 1926), pp. 275–279.

[2] Nelle Swartz, review of *Mothers in Industry*, in *Survey*, 67:6 (15 December 1926), pp. 400–401.

[3] Resolution in *Proceedings* (1924), pp. 336–337, WTUL, Box 15.

[4] Frances Perkins, "Do Women in Industry Need Special Protection? Yes," *Survey*, 55:10 (15 February 1926), pp. 529–531.

[5] Monthly Labor Bulletin of Massachusetts WTUL (January 1928), in WTUL Local Bulletins (Radcliffe), Box 1. Box 3, in same collection, contains comments of factory girls to an investigator of the Connecticut Consumers' League.

[6] Florence Kelley, "The Inescapable Dilemma," *Survey*, 41:25 (22 March 1919), p. 885.

[7] Executive Board of the New York WTUL, Minutes (6 June 1921), in WTUL (Radcliffe), Box 2.

[8] The stories in Massachusetts and New York may be traced in WTUL, Box 15; NCL, Box 20; Dewson Papers (F. D. R. Library), Box 17.

[9] Dr. George W. Webster quoted in "The Woman's Work Day," *Survey*, 46:4 (23 April 1921), p. 121.

[10] Report of Rose Schneiderman, Julia S. O'Connor, and Matilda Lindsay (8 November 1925), WTUL, Box 3.

[11] Florence Kelley to Adolf A. Berle, Jr. (31 January 1923), NCL, Box 8.

[12] Florence Kelley to Mildred Chadsey (8 March 1923), NCL, Box 11.

[13] Felix Frankfurter, *Felix Frankfurter Reminisces* (New York: Reynal, 1960), pp. 101–104.

[14] Felix Frankfurter and Mary R. Dewson, *District of Columbia Minimum Wage Cases* (New York: Steinberg, 1923); *Adkins v. Children's Hospital*, 261 U.S. 525 (1923).

[15] Mary R. Dewson to Isador Lubin (April 1957), Dewson Papers (F. D. R. Library), General Correspondence, Box 18.

[16] "The Minimum Wage — What Next?" *Survey*, 50:4 (15 May 1923), pp. 215–222, 256–258, 263; Francis B. Sayres, "The Minimum Wage Decision," *Survey*, 50:3 (1 May 1923), pp. 150–151, 164, 172; Florence Kelley to Mrs. John Blair (1 May 1923), NCL, Box 10.

[17] Typescript of Stenographic Report of Minimum Wage Conference (20 April 1923), NCL, Box 10.

[18] Mimeographed Report on Conference in Tilton Papers, Box 3; Press Releases, WTUL, Box 25; Correspondence, WTUL, Box 2; Florence Kelley to Edward P. Costigan (31 May 1923), NCL, Box 10.

[19] John R. Commons, Notes for Speech (9 November 1923), NCL, Box 8.

[20] Florence Kelley to Amy C. Maher (17 March 1923), NCL, Box 11.

[21] Jeanette Rankin, Report to Executive Board (25 October 1923), NCL, Box 8.

[22] James A. Haight to Florence Kelley (19 December 1925), NCL, Box 11.

[23] "Highlights of a Speech Made by Florence Kelley in 1923," in Massachusetts Consumers' League (Radcliffe), Drawer 1.

[24] Florence Kelley to Board of Directors (12 June 1923), NCL, Box 11.

[25] Felix Frankfurter to Florence Kelley (19 October 1923), NCL, Box 10.

[26] Felix Frankfurter to Florence Kelley (25 October 1925), NCL, Box 10.

[27] Roscoe Pound to Florence Kelley (22 October 1923), NCL, Box 10.

[28] Zechariah Chafee to John R. Commons (1 April 1924), NCL, Box 11. See also Florence Kelley's correspondence, 1923–1924, with Charles Beard, Ernst Freund, Charles Warren, Ethel Smith, Newton D. Baker, Edward P. Costigan, NCL, Boxes 10 and 11.

[29] Florence Kelley to Felix Frankfurter (25 June 1924), NCL, Box 11.

[30] Correspondence in regard to conference (1 July 1924) that broke up with no agreement having been reached, NCL, Box 11.

[31] Florence Kelley to "Dear Sister Dewson" (8 April 1924), NCL, Box 8.

[32] Florence Kelley to John R. Commons (13 April 1927), NCL, Box 8.

[33] Women's Bureau, *Fact Finding with the Women's Bureau* (Bulletin 84, 1931).

[34] Mrs. Peake Faxon[?] to Leonora O'Reilly (no date, c. 1919), O'Reilly Papers (Radcliffe), Box 7.

[35] Florence Kelley, "The New Woman's Party," *Survey*, 45:23 (5 March 1921), pp. 827–828.

[36] Florence Kelley to Newton D. Baker (3 June 1921), NCL, Box 13.

[37] Mary Anderson, *Woman at Work: The Autobiography of Mary Anderson as Told to Mary N. Winslow* (Minneapolis: University of Minnesota Press, 1951), Chapter 16.

[38] A carbon copy of Dean Acheson's letter to Ethel M. Smith (8 September 1921) found its way into the files of the NCL, Box 13.

[39] Florence Kelley to Mrs. C. J. Evans (16 December 1921), NCL, Box 13.

[40] Alice Hamilton, draft of letter to Mrs. Hooker (16 January 1922), Hamilton Papers, Box 1. There is no evidence that the letter was ever sent, but it reflects the feelings of the amendment's opponents.

[41] Mabel Leslie to Maud Swartz (4 May 1926), WTUL, Box 3.

[42] Mary Anderson, *Woman at Work*, pp. 171–172.

[43] Quotation from official statement of the Bryn Mawr School for Working Women (1921 and 1923), in Hilda Smith, *Women Workers at the Bryn Mawr Summer School* (New York: American Association for Adult Education, 1927), p. 7. Papers, bulletins, reports, memoranda of the school, 1921–1933, may be found in Smith Papers, Boxes 2, 3, and 16.

[44] Mary Anderson, *Woman at Work*, Chapter 25.

[45] Eleanor Roosevelt, Address (24 October 1933), quoted in Hilda Smith, "Autobiography," Smith Papers, Box 16.

[46] Research folder on Minimum-Wage Legislation, Commons Papers, Box 9.

[47] Ethel M. Johnson, "Fourteen Years of Minimum Wage in Massachusetts" (Typescript, 1927), WTUL (Radcliffe), Box 3.

[48] Elizabeth Brandeis to Florence Kelley (20 June 1929), NCL, Box 10.

[49] "What Girls Live On and How," *Survey*, 64:6 (15 June 1930), p. 277.

[50] Leaflet of New York Consumers' League (1927) in Dewson Papers (Radcliffe), Box 2; Florence Kelley, Report to Board of Directors (27 September 1929), NCL, Box 8.

[51] Newton D. Baker, Preface to Maud Nathan, *Story of an Epoch-Making Movement* (Garden City, N.Y.: Doubleday, 1926), pp. xii–xiv.

Chapter 4. The "Cause" and "Function" of Social Work in the 1920's

[1] Porter R. Lee, "The Future of Professional Social Work," *Compass*, 7:11 (July–August 1926), p. 2. Much of this chapter originally appeared as "Creative Effort in an Age of Normalcy, 1918–33," *The Social Welfare Forum, 1961* (New York: Columbia University Press, 1961), pp. 252–271.

[2] Seven-page typescript of a speech by Frank J. Bruno to the Minnesota Committee on Social Legislation, 1925, in Gilman Papers, Box 48.

[3] "Social Research," *Survey*, 64:4 (15 May 1930), p. 179.

[4] Elizabeth Healy, " 'Get Your Man,' " *Survey*, 64:4 (15 May 1930), pp. 202–203, 207.

[5] Eveline M. Burns, "Social Welfare Is Our Commitment," *The Social Welfare Forum, 1958* (New York: Columbia University Press, 1958), p. 3.

[6] Abraham Flexner, "Is Social Work a Profession?" NCCC *Proceedings* (1915), pp. 576–590.

[7] Gilman Papers, Box 35.

[8] J. B. B., "The Challenge to Social Workers," *Survey*, 45:5 (30 October 1920), p. 164.

[9] Abraham Epstein, "The Soullessness of Presentday Social Work," *Current History*, 28:3 (June 1928), pp. 390–395. See also Donald S. Howard, "Social Work and Social Reform," in Cora Kasius, editor, *New Directions in Social Work* (New York: Harper, 1954), p. 165.

[10] Porter R. Lee, "Social Work: Cause and Function," NCSW *Proceedings* (1929), pp. 3–20.

[11] Gertrude Vaile, NCSW *Proceedings* (1926), pp. 3–11.

[12] Karl de Schweinitz, "The Past as a Guide to the Function and Pattern of Social Work," in W. Wallace Weaver, editor, *Frontiers for Social Work* (Philadelphia: University of Pennsylvania Press, 1960), p. 85.

[13] Dr. Richard C. Cabot to Gertrude Vaile (27 May 1926), Vaile Papers.

[14] Mary Ross and Paul U. Kellogg, "New Beacons in Boston," *Survey*, 64:8 (15 July 1930), p. 341.

[15] Isaac M. Rubinow, "Can Private Philanthropy Do It?" *Social Service Review*, 3:3 (September 1929), p. 369.

[16] John A. Fitch quoted by Ross and Kellogg, *Survey*, 64:8 (15 July 1930), p. 343.

[17] A. J. Muste quoted in *ibid.*, p. 344.

[18] Geddes Smith, "Behemoth Walks Again," *Survey*, 56:6 (15 June 1926), pp. 360–363.

[19] Mary E. Richmond, "Possibilities of the Art of Helping," in Joanna C. Colcord, editor, *The Long View* (New York: Russell Sage Foundation, 1930), p. 586; the paper dates originally from 1925.

[20] Isaac M. Rubinow, "Social Case Work; a Profession in the Making," *Journal of Social Forces*, 4:2 (December 1925), pp. 286–292.

[21] Penciled copy of speech at Kansas State Social Work Conference, 1921, in Vaile Papers.

[22] Homer Folks, "Prevention Succeeds," NCSW *Proceedings* (1923), p. 3.

[23] Leonard W. Mayo, "The Changing Role of Voluntary Agencies," *Social Work Journal*, 36:3 (July 1955), p. 96.

[24] Gertrude Vaile, NCSW *Proceedings* (1926). Some of Miss Vaile's private papers suggest that the phrase "a more abundant life" referred less to material prosperity than to Christ's promise of "a life more abundant."

[25] Jane Addams, "Charity and Social Justice," NCCC *Proceedings* (1910), pp. 2–3.

[26] Robert W. Bruère, "The Main Business of Industry," *Survey Graphic*, 50:3 (1 May 1923), pp. 135, 171.

[27] Mary Van Kleeck to Lillian Wald (11 October 1930), Wald Papers, File 1, Drawer 4.

[28] John A. Lapp, "Do Prosperity and Welfare Work in America Make Unnecessary the Establishment of Protective Labor Standards?" *American Labor Legislation Review*, 17:3 (September 1927), p. 232.

[29] Typescript of Address (7 November 1928), Folks Papers.

[30] Typescripts in Folks Papers: "The Human Costs of War" (10 October 1919), "Jungle Rule or Golden Rule" (23 October 1925), untitled Address on Family Care Programs (c. 1926); Address to the State Committee on Public Health (1 June 1927).

[31] Howard W. Odum, "Newer Ideals of Public Welfare," *Annals*, 105 (January 1923), pp. 1–6.

[32] I am particularly indebted here (and at other points as well) to Gisela Konopka, *Eduard C. Lindeman and Social Work Philosophy* (Minneapolis: University of Minnesota Press, 1958).

[33] William Ernest Hocking, "Osmosis: The Object of Social Work," *Survey*, 55:6 (15 December 1925), pp. 361–362.

[34] Miriam Van Waters, typescript of introduction to social work course at the University of Southern California (September 1924), Van Waters Papers, File Drawer 2.

[35] "Where Are the Social Engineers?" *Survey*, 52:10 (15 August 1924), pp. 542–543.

[36] Homer Folks, "Prevention Succeeds," NCSW *Proceedings* (1923), pp. 3–9.

[37] Bruno Lasker, "What Has Become of Social Reform?" *American Journal of Sociology*, 28:2 (September 1922), pp. 129–159.

[38] Bruno Lasker, typescript of Address to YWCA Foreign Secretaries (4 June 1925), Working Notebooks II (Columbia University); "Notes for LDW; the Future of Social Work" (25 January 1927), five-page typed memorandum for use of Lillian D. Wald in Working Notebooks, IV.

[39] Robert W. Kelso, "The Transition from Charities and Correction to Public Welfare," *Annals*, 105 (January 1923), p. 21.

Chapter 5. The Settlements in Service to Their Neighbors

[1] From the extensive materials surveyed in my Bibliographic Essay, three studies are particularly valuable to an understanding of the early settlement movement: Allen Davis, "Spearheads for Reform" (Doctoral dissertation, University of Wisconsin, 1959); Louise Carroll Wade, "Graham Taylor, Social Pioneer, 1851–1938" (Doctoral dissertation, University of Rochester, 1954); and Margaret Blumberg, "Social Settlements in the Interwar Era" (Unpublished paper, University of Minnesota, 1961). Woods and Kennedy, *The Settlement Horizon*, offers by far the best general account of the settlement movement down to World War I.

[2] Jane Addams, "The Subjective Necessity for Social Settlements," and "The Objective Value of a Social Settlement," in *Philanthropy and Social Progress* (New York: Crowell, 1893).

[3] Quoted in Vida Scudder, *On Journey* (New York: Dutton, 1937), p. 136.

[4] *Ibid.*, pp. 84, 139. 140, 109.

[5] Kenneth E. Boulding, "Alienation and Economic Development," *Neighborhood*

Goals (New York: National Federation of Settlements, 1958), pp. 61–71. Richard Hofstadter has explored these hypotheses in *The Age of Reform* (New York: Knopf, 1955).

⁶ Jane Addams, "The Subjective Necessity for Social Settlements," in *A Centennial Reader* edited by Emily C. Johnson (New York: Macmillan, 1960), pp. 10–14.

⁷ An account, tinged with irony, of the comparative role of civic reformers and machine politicians on these issues is in Jane Addams, *Democracy and Social Ethics* (New York: Macmillan, 1902), pp. 221–277.

⁸ Helen Hall in National Federation of Settlements, *Neighborhood Goals*, p. 12.

⁹ Jane Addams, carbon typescript of notes for Berkeley Lyceum meeting (1905), WTUL, Box 25.

¹⁰ Woods and Kennedy, *Settlement Horizon*, p. 174.

¹¹ *Ibid.*, p. 198.

¹² Davis, "Spearheads for Reform," Chapter 5; Jane Addams, *The Second Twenty Years at Hull House* (New York: Macmillan, 1930), pp. 290–291; Howard E. Wilson, *Mary McDowell: Neighbor* (Chicago: University of Chicago Press, 1928).

¹³ My notes from the rambling reminiscences of Albert J. Kennedy in an address before the National Federation of Settlements (Minneapolis, May 1961).

¹⁴ Lea Taylor, "The Social Settlement and Civic Responsibility," *Social Service Review*, 28:1 (March 1954), pp. 31–40.

¹⁵ Graham Taylor, *Religion in Social Action* (New York: Dodd, Mead, 1913), pp. 142–143.

¹⁶ Mary Simkhovitch, "The Settlement and Religion," reprinted from the [Episcopal] *Churchman* (n.d., c. 1915).

¹⁷ Jane Addams, *Newer Ideals of Peace*, pp. 24–25.

¹⁸ Quoted in Eleanor Woods, *Robert A. Woods, Champion of Democracy*, pp. 309, 317.

¹⁹ Catheryne Cooke Gilman, "Neighbors United" (Typescript in Minnesota Historical Society, 1950), pp. 771–772.

²⁰ Vida Scudder, "The Doubting Pacifist," in *Yale Review*, 6:4 (July 1917), quoted in *On Journey*, p. 287.

²¹ *Ibid.*, p. 300.

²² Jane Addams, *Second Twenty Years*, pp. 153–155.

²³ John Elliot to Charles Cooper (30 August 1927) and Cooper to Elliot (2 September 1927), Hull House Papers, Box 9A.

²⁴ Charles Cooper to Graham Taylor (27 January 1921) and Taylor to Cooper (14 February 1921), Taylor Papers.

²⁵ Minutes of Business Meeting (14 June 1931), NFS Office Archives; Alice Hamilton, *Exploring the Dangerous Trades* (Boston: Little, Brown, 1943), pp. 274–277.

²⁶ Graham Taylor in remarks to Executive Committee (1920), NFS Office Archives.

²⁷ Minutes (26 May 1926), NFS Office Archives.

²⁸ Mary K. Simkhovitch, *Twenty-Five Years of Greenwich House, 1902–1927* (New York: Greenwich House, 1927), unpaged.

²⁹ Social Activities Committee of Henry Street, Minutes (16 November 1932), Wald Papers, File 2, Drawer 1.

³⁰ Louis J. Bing in *Neighborhood*, 3:3 (6 June 1930), pp. 124–127.

³¹ Mary Simkhovitch, Annual Report of Greenwich House, 1921, p. 13, in Hull House Papers, Box 9A.

³² Gaynell Hawkins, *Educational Experiments in Social Settlements* (New York: American Association for Adult Education, 1937), p. 3.

³³ Sidney Hollander, Jr., "Trends in the Relationship of the Settlement to Its Neighborhood" (Typescript report, 1936), Taylor Papers; although the date is 1936, the references are clearly to trends underway since the end of the Great

War. A. J. Kennedy, "Social Settlements," *Social Work Year Book, 1929*, pp. 425–426.

[34] Quoted in obituary clipping from *New York Herald Tribune* (6 November 1955) in Knox Papers, Box 1.

[35] Catheryne Cooke Gilman, "Neighbors United," pp. 99–100.

[36] Robbins Gilman quoted in *ibid.*, p. 871.

[37] Minutes (September 1922), pp. 9–11, NFS Office Archives.

[38] Albert J. Kennedy, "Social Settlements," *Social Work Yearbook, 1933*, p. 481.

[39] Vida Scudder, *On Journey*, pp. 164–165.

[40] Helen Hart, untitled mimeographed report (undated, c. 1931), Wald Papers, File 3, Drawer 3.

[41] Albert J. Kennedy, editor, *Settlement Goals for the Next Third of a Century: A Symposium* (Boston: National Federation of Settlements, 1926).

[42] Isabel Taylor, in "Settlement Faith and Practice: A Symposium," *Neighborhood*, 3:3 (September 1930), p. 118, and "New Settlement Leadership," *Neighborhood*, 1:3 (July 1928), pp. 19–24; Jane Addams, "The Settlement as a Way of Life," *Neighborhood*, 2:3 (July 1929), pp. 139–146.

[43] Lena Cain, summer playschool director, Henry Street Settlement, Report (1932), Wald Papers, File 2, Drawer 1.

[44] Statement of Music Division, NFS, Minutes (February 1925), NFS Office Archives.

[45] Quoted in William Hodson and Neva Deardorff, "Preface," *Neighborhood*, 4:1 (March 1931), p. 7.

[46] Robbins Gilman, Address to Board of Welcome Hall St. Paul (1933), quoted in Catheryne Cooke Gilman, "Neighbors United," p. 549.

[47] Albert J. Kennedy, mimeographed copy of speech in my possession (4 June 1953), p. 19.

[48] Helen Hart, "The Changing Function of the Settlement under Changing Conditions," NCSW *Proceedings* (1931), p. 291.

[49] Jane Addams, "The Settlement as a Way of Life," *Neighborhood*, 2:3 (July 1929), pp. 139–146.

[50] Paul U. Kellogg, "The Unsettling Settlements," *Survey*, 60:4 (15 May 1928), p. 218.

[51] Paul U. Kellogg to Albert J. Kennedy (17 February 1928) and Kennedy to Kellogg (7 April 1928), in Kennedy folder, NFS Office Archives.

[52] Minutes (22 November 1930); Lillie Peck Folder in NFS Office Archives.

Chapter 6. The Settlements' Drive for Social Action

[1] Bruno Lasker, Preliminary Working Memorandum (3 October 1923), Working Notebooks, I, pp. 121–122.

[2] Bruno Lasker, Address to Race Relations Department, Community Council of St. Louis (1927), Working Notebooks, IV, p. 144.

[3] Minutes of Business Meeting (1920), NFS Office Archives.

[4] Conference Report (1920), NFS Office Archives; Memorandum of NFS Conference (1920), Hull House Papers, Box 9A.

[5] Minutes of Executive Committee (31 October 1920), NFS Office Archives.

[6] Folder on Public Committee of Fifty on Housing (1921), Taylor Papers; McDowell Papers, Folder 14; Catheryne Cooke Gilman, "Neighbors United," pp. 873–879.

[7] Jane Addams to Anita McCormick Blaine (18 April 1926), Blaine Papers.

[8] Minutes of Business Meeting (8 September 1922), NFS Office Archives; mimeographed summary of conference, Hull House Papers, Box 9A.

[9] Lillian Wald to Herbert Lehman (21 February 1929), Wald Papers, File 1,

Drawer 2. Here, and at many places that follow, I am indebted to Timothy L. McDonnell, *The Wagner Housing Act: A Case Study of the Legislative Process* (Chicago: Loyola University Press, 1957).

[10] Katharine Faville to Lillian Wald (7 December 1933), Wald Papers, File 2, Drawer 2.

[11] David Rosenstein, "Social Settlements after the War," *School and Society*, 9:234 (21 June 1919), pp. 727–735; Minutes of Executive Committee (24 June 1924), NFS Office Archives.

[12] Graham Taylor to Mrs. R. W. MacDonald (23 February 1928), Taylor Papers.

[13] Minutes of Executive Committee (26 May 1926), NFS Office Archives; Account in Hull House Papers, Box 5B.

[14] Martha Bensley Bruère, *Does Prohibition Work?* (New York: Harper, 1927), pp. 275, 285, 304. Marie Waite, "Prohibition Survey of the Stockyards Community" (Typescript survey, c. 1926), 32 pages in McDowell Papers, Folder 7.

[15] Letter to social workers sent out over the signatures of Lillian Wald and John L. Elliott (29 September 1928), Wald Papers, File 1, Drawer 4. The strategy was directed by Mary Van Kleeck, Katherine Lindsay, Walter West, and William Hodson. Lillian Wald to Mary McDowell (27 September 1928), Wald Papers, File 1, Drawer 2; Katherine Lindsay to Lillian Wald (5 October 1928), Wald Papers, File 1, Drawer 4.

[16] Letters to Lillian Wald (October 1928), File 1, Drawer 4.

[17] Elizabeth H. Tilton, "Journal" (entries for 28 June and 18 July 1928), pp. 170–171, and "Memoir," Book IV, Chapter 2, pp. 21–30, Tilton Papers.

[18] Lea Taylor, Speech before NFS Conference, Boston (April 1928); "Unemployment Discussion of Adelphi Club of Boys" (Winter 1928); Chicago Commons, "Summary Report on Unemployment" (no date, c. 1928) – all in Taylor Papers. Graham Taylor to Anita McCormick Blaine (27 June 1928), Blaine Papers; Graham Taylor, *Chicago Commons through Forty Years*, pp. 180–182, 212–214; Paul U. Kellogg, "The Unsettling Settlements," *Survey*, 60:4 (15 May 1928), pp. 250–251. Paul U. Kellogg to William M. Matthews (20 April 1928), Survey Associates Papers: "The settlements seem to be about the only group of social agencies which have the ginger in a collective way to tackle some of these hot pokers."

[19] Minutes of Executive Committee (15 April 1928), NFS Office Archives. Helen Hall and Irene H. Nelson, "How Unemployment Strikes Home," *Survey*, 62:1 (1 April 1929), pp. 51–53, 84–86.

[20] Helen Hall Papers, Box 1, Folder 1. Helen Hall to Lillian Wald (23 May 1933), Wald Papers, File 2, Drawer 2.

[21] Executive Committee, Minutes (22 June 1929), NFS Office Archives.

[22] *Ibid.* (12 November 1928).

[23] Clinch Calkins, *Some Folks Won't Work* (New York: Harcourt, Brace, 1930), pp. 21, 163.

[24] Helen Hall, *Case Studies in Unemployment* (Philadelphia: University of Pennsylvania Press, 1931), pp. xli, xliv, xlv, xxxiii, xxxvi.

[25] Rough notes for Minutes, Executive Committee (12 November 1928), NFS Office Archives.

[26] Zona Gale, "Great Ladies of Chicago," *Survey Graphic*, 67:9 (1 February 1932), p. 482.

[27] Graham Taylor, "The Social Settlement, Religion, and the Church," in Jerome Davis, editor, *Christianity and Social Adventuring* (New York: Century, 1927), p. 172. Graham Taylor to Mr. Stead (8 March 1918), to "all my fellow-residents" (28 January 1922), to Mrs. C. H. Ainley (4 May 1927), to Homer Folks (26 February 1923), Taylor Papers. Wade, "Graham Taylor," pp. 600–626, provides an incisive criticism of Taylor's religious beliefs.

[28] Graham Taylor, *Pioneering on Social Frontiers* (Chicago: University of Chi-

cago Press, 1930), p. 444. Graham Taylor to Lea Taylor (9 April 1925), Taylor Papers.

[29] Mary McDowell, "How the Living Faith of One Social Worker Grew," *Survey*, 60:1 (1 April 1928), pp. 40–43, 57–60. "Social Service in Chicago" (Typescript, c. 1925), McDowell Papers, Folder 3b.

[30] Mary McDowell, "Settlements and Their Outlook," *First International Conference of Settlements* (London, July 1922), pp. 79–80.

[31] Mary Simkhovitch, *The Settlements and Religion*, unpaged.

[32] Catheryne Cooke Gilman, "The Philosophy of the Settlements" (13 October 1920), Gilman Papers, Box 20. Algernon Black, "Settlement Faith and Practice: A Symposium," *Neighborhood*, 3:3 (September 1930), p. 102.

[33] Helen Phelan, "Settlement Faith and Practice: A Symposium," *Neighborhood*, 3:3 (September 1930), p. 113.

[34] Robbins Gilman quoted in Catheryne Cooke Gilman, "Neighbors United," pp. 545–547.

[35] George Bellamy, Address (26 May 1926), in NFS mimeographed bulletin, pp. 3–8, Hull House Papers, Box 5B.

[36] Graham Taylor, Address (23 May 1918), in NFS Office Archives.

[37] Paul U. Kellogg, "Semi-Centennial of the Settlements," *Survey Graphic*, 24:1 (January 1935), p. 30.

[38] Catheryne Cooke Gilman, "Neighbors United," p. 634.

Chapter 7. The Search for Security

[1] Louis Brandeis, "Workingmen's Insurance – the Road to Social Efficiency," NCCC *Proceedings* (1911), pp. 156–162. The sentences quoted here are from Brandeis' original presentation as cited and also from "The Right to Work as Formulated Long Since by Louis D. Brandeis," in *Survey*, 62:1 (1 April 1929), p. 5.

[2] Henry R. Seager, *Social Insurance: A Program of Social Reform* (New York: Macmillan, 1910).

[3] Isaac M. Rubinow, *Social Insurance* (New York: Holt, 1913), p. 501.

[4] Isaac M. Rubinow, *Standards of Health Insurance* (New York: Holt, 1916).

[5] John L. Elliott, Address (13 May 1915), Bulletin, NFS Office Archives.

[6] Mary K. Simkhovitch, *The City Workers' World in America* (New York: Macmillan, 1917), Chapter 9.

[7] Mabel Louise Nassau, *Old Age Poverty in Greenwich Village* (New York: Revell, 1915).

[8] Frank J. Bruno, *Trends in Social Work* (New York: Columbia University Press, 1948), pp. 230–232; Isaac M. Rubinow, "Needed: A Social Insurance Revival," *Survey*, 56:4 (15 May 1926), pp. 233–234, 283.

[9] The Bibliographic Essay discusses the literature on this subject; especially useful is Maurice B. Hamovitch, "History of the Movement for Compulsory Health Insurance in the United States," *Social Service Review*, 27:3 (September 1953), pp. 281–287.

[10] The New York League of Women Voters in a report carried in the *American Labor Legislation Review*, 10:1 (March 1920), p. 73.

[11] Isaac M. Rubinow, *The Quest for Security* (New York: Holt, 1934), p. 210.

[12] William J. Norton, "What Is Social Work?" NCSW *Proceedings* (1925), p. 7.

[13] John A. Lapp, "Justice First," NCSW *Proceedings* (1927), pp. 3–13.

[14] Isaac M. Rubinow, "The Status of Social Insurance," *Survey*, 56:4 (15 May 1926), pp. 242–244.

[15] Rubinow, *Quest for Security*, p. 429.

[16] John B. Andrews, "Two Decades in Industrial Insurance," NCSW *Proceedings* (1930), pp. 258–265; Paul H. Douglas, *Social Security in the United States* (New York: McGraw-Hill, 1936), pp. 3–5; Abraham Epstein, *Insecurity: A Challenge to*

America (New York: Smith and Haas, 1933), pp. 659, vii, 660; AASS, *Record* (1934), p. 8.

[17] John B. Andrews in *American Labor Legislation Review*, 14:4 (December 1924), p. 287; Homer Folks in *ibid.*, p. 283.

[18] Lucile Eaves, "The 'Aged Citizens' of Massachusetts," *Survey*, 55:10 (15 February 1926), pp. 554–556; James H. Maurer in *American Labor Legislation Review*, 14:4 (December 1924), pp. 292–300.

[19] Flyer of Massachusetts Committee for Old Age Security (no date, c. 1930) in Evans Papers, Box 7.

[20] Pamphlet reprinted in Lamar T. Beman, editor, *Old Age Pensions* (New York: Wilson, 1927), p. 241.

[21] Elizabeth Glendower Evans, typescript of Address to Massachusetts Federation of Labor, 1930, in Evans Papers, Box 7.

[22] Associate editor to William H. Matthews (25 February 1927), Survey Associates Papers.

[23] Isaac M. Rubinow, "The Modern Problem of the Care of the Aged," *Social Service Review*, 4:2 (June 1930), p. 178.

[24] Isaac M. Rubinow, "Conflict of Public and Private Interests in the Field of Social Insurance," *Annals*, 154 (March 1931), p. 113.

[25] Alton A. Linford, *Old Age Assistance in Massachusetts* (Chicago: University of Chicago Press, 1949), pp. 21–33. I am indebted here and elsewhere to David S. Patterson, "The Old Age Pension Movement" (Unpublished paper, University of California at Berkeley, 1962), and to Joseph Charles Dougherty, Jr., "The Genesis of the Social Security Act of 1935" (Doctoral dissertation, Georgetown University, 1955).

[26] Abraham Holtzman, "The Townsend Movement" (Doctoral dissertation, Harvard University, 1952), pp. 20–22.

[27] Abraham Epstein, *Facing Old Age* (New York: Knopf, 1922).

[28] Robert A. Hoffman to Helen Alfred (10 October 1929), and Alfred to Hoffman (16 October 1929), Epstein Papers.

[29] Leo Hartman, associate editor, to Abraham Epstein (10 October 1928); see also Paul Blanshard, of the *Nation*, to Epstein (24 December 1928), Epstein Papers.

[30] Abraham Epstein to George Soule (4 January 1929), Epstein Papers.

[31] Abraham Epstein to Mrs. Willard Pope (4 December 1931), Epstein Papers.

[32] Eleanor Roosevelt to Mrs. Alida Miller (22 March 1930), Eleanor Roosevelt Papers, Correspondence, 1929–1933, Box 6.

[33] Memorandum of Massachusetts Committee for Old Age Security, Women's Educational and Industrial Union Papers (Radcliffe), Box 7.

[34] Helen Alfred to Joseph G. Wolber (4 March 1931), Epstein Papers.

[35] Epstein, AAOAS *Proceedings* (1931), p. 31.

[36] Stephen Wise, *ibid.*, p. 83.

[37] Benjamin Glassberg, *ibid.*, p. 59.

[38] Herbert Hoover, Address (26 September 1921), in *American Labor Legislation Review*, 11:4 (December 1921), pp. 302–303.

[39] Warren G. Harding quoted in *Survey*, 47:2 (8 October 1921), p. 42.

[40] William L. Chenery, "Unemployment at Washington," *Survey*, 47:2 (8 October 1921), p. 42.

[41] Otto T. Mallery, Letter to Editor, *Survey*, 47:7 (17 November 1921), p. 255.

[42] Press Release (22 September 1921), NCLC, Box 28.

[43] WTUL *Proceedings* (1922), pp. 296–300, WTUL Papers, Box 14.

[44] Florence Kelley to Allen Forsberg (23 August 1924), NCL, Box 13, and to D. J. Richard (31 July 1924), NCL, Box 10.

[45] Sidney Hillman quoted in *American Labor Legislation Review*, 11:1 (March 1921), p. 28.

[46] John B. Andrews in *ibid.*, pp. 233–239.

[47] AALL Leaflet, written by John B. Andrews (c. 1929) in Blaine Papers.

[48] A summary of Commons' career can be found in Joseph Dorfman, *The Economic Mind, 1918–1933* (New York: Viking, 1959), IV, 377–395.

[49] Quotations are from an unsigned typescript summary of arguments for the Huber Bill in Commons Papers, Series A, Box 3. The date is apparently 1923, and the summaries, presumably, were drawn up by Commons or under his direction or for his use. For the whole Wisconsin story, see also Roger S. Hoar, *Unemployment Insurance in Wisconsin* (South Milwaukee: Stuart Press, 1932), and Irving Bernstein, *The Lean Years; A History of the American Worker, 1920–1933* (Boston: Houghton Mifflin, 1960), pp. 498–501.

[50] The Bibliographic Essay may be consulted for extensive documentation of this part of the narrative. Of special helpfulness was Harry Malisoff, "The Emergence of Unemployment Compensation," *Political Science Quarterly*, 54:2 (June 1939), pp. 237–258; 54:3 (September 1939), pp. 391–420; and 54:4 (December 1939), pp. 577–599. A useful contemporary analysis is Dale Yoder, "Some Implications of Unemployment Insurance," *Quarterly Journal of Economics*, 45:4 (August 1931), pp. 622–639.

[51] John R. Commons to NCL meeting in New York City (29 January 1925), in Minutes (5 February 1925), NCL, Box 8. The development of voluntary plans is briefly summarized in Bernstein, *The Lean Years*, pp. 488–491.

[52] Leo Wolman in *American Labor Legislation Review*, 13:1 (March 1923), pp. 39–45, and 18:1 (March 1928), pp. 81–84.

[53] John B. Andrews in *American Labor Legislation Review*, 18:1 (March 1928), pp. 65–75; Andrews, "Why Are We Idle?" *Survey*, 59:12 (15 March 1928), pp. 743–744; Margaret D. Meyer in *American Labor Legislation Review*, 18:2 (June 1928), pp. 153–162.

[54] A. J. Muste, "The Tug of Industry," *Survey*, 59:5 (1 December 1927), pp. 281–284, 344.

[55] Daisy Lee Worthington Worcester, "This Amazing Prosperity," *Survey*, 41:3 (1 November 1928), pp. 120–124, 183.

[56] Karl de Schweinitz, "Are the Poor Really Poor?" *Survey*, 59:8 (15 January 1928), pp. 517–519.

[57] James Couzens, "The Senate Takes Stock," *Survey*, 62:1 (1 April 1929), pp. 7–8; Edward D. Lynde, "The Responsibility of the Case Working Agency," NCSW *Proceedings* (1929), pp. 317–328.

[58] Paul U. Kellogg, "Unemployment and Progress," NCSW *Proceedings* (1929), pp. 80–102.

[59] Frank Morrison, Address (May 1929), WTUL, Box 15; William Leiserson, "Unemployment, 1929," *Survey*, 62:1 (1 April 1929), pp. 9–10, 77–78.

[60] Solomon F. Bloom, in AASS *Record* (1934), p. 9.

[61] Samuel Gompers, *Labor and the Employer* (New York: Dutton, 1920), p. 18; F. D. R., Acceptance Speech, 27 June 1936, in *Public Papers*, V, 233; F. D. R., Fireside Chat, 14 April 1938, *ibid.*, VII, 236–247; F. D. R., State of the Union Address, 11 January 1944, *ibid.*, XIII, 40–41.

Chapter 8. The Unemployment Crisis

[1] Lillian Wald to Mrs. Frederick Nathan (3 November 1931), Wald Papers, File 1, Drawer 2; to Henry Morgenthau (14 January 1931), *ibid.*; Press Statement (5 July 1932), *ibid.*; to "Beloved Musseys" (5 October 1931), *ibid.* Wald, *Windows on Henry Street* (Boston: Little, Brown, 1939), Chapter 10.

[2] Lillian Wald, "What Keeps the Nurses Going?" *Survey*, 68:16 (15 November 1932), pp. 590–591.

[3] Typescript Reports of Special Emergency Fund, Chicago Commons, 1931, Taylor Papers.

[4] Graham Taylor, draft of solicitation letter, 1931, Taylor Papers.

[5] Lea Taylor to Board of Directors, NFS (10 December 1932), NFS Office Archives.

[6] Copy of letter of Leo Wolman to Colonel Arthur Woods (9 December 1930), in folder marked "Herbert Hoover (Relief)," Hopkins Papers.

[7] Homer Folks, Address to Protestant Episcopal Churches of New York City (30 October 1932), Folks Papers.

[8] Beulah Amidon, "Toledo: A City the Auto Ran Over," *Survey*, 63:11 (1 March 1930), pp. 656–660; Paul U. Kellogg, "Outflanking Unemployment," in paraphrase and in agreement with Judge Julian W. Mack, *Survey*, 64:3 (1 May 1930), p. 146.

[9] The Bibliographic Essay provides extensive commentary on sources; especially valuable here is Margaret E. Rich, *A Belief in People* (New York: Family Service Association of America, 1956), Chapter 7.

[10] Gertrude Springer, "The Challenge of Hard Times," *Survey*, 66:8 (15 July 1931), pp. 380–383.

[11] Statement of Commission on Unemployment of the American Association of Social Workers, Neva R. Deardorff, Chairman (2–3 January 1932), in *Compass*, 13:4 (December 1931), pp. 1–2.

[12] C. M. Bookman, "The Social Consequences and Treatment of Unemployment," NCSW *Proceedings* (1932), pp. 3–24; People's Lobby *Bulletin*, 2:2 (June 1932), pp. 9–10.

[13] Virginia P. Robinson, *A Changing Psychology in Social Case Work* (Chapel Hill: University of North Carolina Press, 1930), p. 3; Josephine C. Brown, *Public Relief, 1929–1939* (New York: Holt, 1940), pp. 13–17.

[14] Lillian Brandt, *et al.*, *An Impressionistic View of the Winter of 1930–31 in New York City* (New York: Welfare Council, 1932), p. 23.

[15] Linton B. Swift, "Community Chests and Relief," *Survey*, 64:12 (15 September 1930), pp. 502–503.

[16] Dorothy Kahn, *Unemployment and Its Treatment in the United States* (New York: American Association of Social Workers, 1937), chart, p. 16. (I have rounded off the figures to the nearest million dollars.)

[17] "Tightening the Belt," *Survey*, 64:12 (15 September 1930), pp. 512–513; "Summer and the Unemployed," *Survey*, 64:10 (15 August 1930), pp. 419–420; Sumner Slichter, "Doles for Employers," *New Republic*, 65:839 (31 December 1930), pp. 181–183. Two graduate studies were particularly useful to me here and elsewhere: James J. Hannah, "Urban Reaction to the Great Depression" (Doctoral dissertation, University of California at Berkeley, 1956), and Albert U. Romasco, "American Institutions in the Great Depression" (Doctoral dissertation, University of Chicago, 1961).

[18] The semiofficial story of the Woods Committee is told by one of its members, E. P. Hayes, *Activities of the President's Emergency Committee for Employment (October 17, 1930–August 10, 1931)* (Concord, N.H.: Rumford Press, 1936). Of the secondary accounts, Bernstein's *The Lean Years*, pp. 302–310, is the most useful.

[19] Mollie Ray Carroll, eight-page mimeographed report in McDowell Papers, Folder 16.

[20] C. M. Bookman, "Community Organization to Meet Unemployment Needs," NCSW *Proceedings* (1931), pp. 385–399.

[21] Homer Folks, Report to Lt. Governor Herbert Lehman (June 1931), Lehman Papers, Box 48.

[22] William H. Matthews, *The Story of the Emergency Work Bureau, New York City* (New York, 1933), copy in Wald Papers, File 3, Drawer 3.

[23] William Hodson in *Survey*, 67:3 (1 November 1931), pp. 144–145.

[24] William H. Matthews, Report (August 1932), copy in Wald Papers, File 2, Drawer 1.

[25] Gifford Pinchot, "The Case for Federal Relief," *Survey*, 67:7 (1 January 1932), pp. 347–349, 389–390.

[26] Walter S. Gifford, "Cities, Counties, States Can Handle the Situation," *Survey Graphic*, 67:9 (1 February 1932), p. 466.

[27] Editorial (9 November 1932), quoted in Mary B. Gilson, *Unemployment Insurance* (Chicago: University of Chicago Press, 1933), p. 6.

[28] Summary Report of Conference (1932) in McDowell Papers, Folder 16.

[29] U.S. Senate, 71st Congress, 2nd Session, Hearings on Unemployment (March–April 1930), pp. 7–12, 27–57.

[30] U.S. Senate, 72nd Congress, 1st Session, Hearings on Unemployment Relief (December 1931–January 1932), VII, 10–56, 73–77, 133–138.

[31] *Ibid.*, pp. 111–123.

[32] *Ibid.*, pp. 64–73, 79–104, 123–133, 143–145, 256–270, 211–223.

[33] *Ibid.*, 309–333.

[34] U.S. Senate, 72nd Congress, 2nd Session, Hearings on Federal Aid for Unemployment Relief (January–February 1933), VI, 5–21.

[35] *Ibid.*, VI, 380–396, 37–46, 64–77, 79–86, and V, 83–90, 23–35.

[36] *Ibid.*, VI, 246–258.

[37] Again, my primary reliance is upon Bernstein, *Lean Years*, Chapter 14.

[38] Convention Proceedings (May 1929), pp. 173–174, WTUL, Box 15.

[39] Agnes A. Sharp in *Life and Labor Bulletin*, 8:6 (May 1930), p. 1.

[40] The work of Foster and Catchings is analyzed in Dorfman, *The Economic Mind*, IV, 339–352.

[41] Leo Wolman, *Planning and Control of Public Works* (New York: National Bureau of Economic Research, 1930), especially Chapter 10; Philip Klein, *The Burden of Unemployment* (New York: Russell Sage Foundation, 1923), especially Chapter 3.

[42] Robert Wagner, Address (30 December 1930) in *American Labor Legislation Review*, 21:1 (March 1930), pp. 11–16.

Chapter 9. Demands for Federal Action

[1] Report of Mrs. Richard Hogue in AAOAS *Proceedings* (1932), pp. 1–2; Abraham Epstein, *ibid.*, pp. 2–7.

[2] The Bibliographic Essay presents the general literature on this subject. Of special weight, here and elsewhere, is Edwin E. Witte, *Development of the Social Security Act* (Madison: University of Wisconsin Press, 1962). I am also indebted throughout this chapter to Dougherty, "The Genesis of the Social Security Act of 1935," especially pp. 1–94.

[3] Lillian Wald to Rose Rosenberg (10 December 1930).

[4] Lawrence H. Fuchs, *The Political Behavior of American Jews* (Glencoe, Ill.: Free Press, 1956); Alfred Kutzik, *Social Work and Jewish Values* (Washington, D.C.: Public Affairs Press, 1959); Harry Lurie, *A Heritage Affirmed* (Philadelphia: Jewish Publication Society, 1961); Herman D. Stein, "Jewish Social Work in the United States, 1654–1954" (Doctoral dissertation, New York School of Social Work, Columbia University, 1955); Morris D. Waldman, *Nor by Power* (New York: International Universities Press, 1953), especially Section III.

[5] Maynard Krueger, "Economic Planning," *Neighborhood*, 4:3 (September 1931), pp. 220–225; Minutes of Business Meeting (11 June 1933), NFS Office Archives.

[6] Joanna C. Colcord, *Community Planning in Unemployment Emergencies* (New York: Russell Sage Foundation, 1930), pp. 74–84.

[7] Testimony of Jacob Billikopf (6 November 1931) in U.S. Senate, 71st Congress,

1st Session, Hearings on Unemployment Insurance, pp. 280–292; "The Social Duty to the Unemployed," *Annals*, 154 (March 1931), pp. 65–72; "What Have We Learned about Unemployment?" NCSW *Proceedings* (1931), pp. 25–50.

[8] Porter R. Lee, "Social Workers: Pioneers Again," in *Social Work as Cause and Function, and Other Papers* (New York: Columbia University Press, 1937), pp. 177–200. The paper was originally presented before the Association of the New York School of Social Work, 1933.

[9] Paul H. Douglas and Aaron Director, *The Problem of Unemployment* (New York: Macmillan, 1931), p. 485. Douglas' career is summarized in Dorfman, *The Economic Mind*, V, 526–534.

[10] Abraham Epstein, *Insecurity: A Challenge to America* (New York: Smith and Haas, 1933); testimony before U.S. Senate, 71st Congress, 1st Session, on Unemployment Insurance (13 November 1931), pp. 430–437.

[11] Isaac M. Rubinow, "The Conflict of Public and Private Interests in the Field of Social Insurance," *Annals*, 154 (March 1931), p. 108.

[12] Rubinow, *The Quest for Security*, pp. 19–20; "Stabilization *versus* Insurance?" *Social Service Review*, 5:2 (June 1931), pp. 199–312. The story of unemployment insurance in Ohio may be traced in Bernstein, *The Lean Years*, pp. 496–498.

[13] Helen Hall in Minutes (29 January 1932), NFS Office Archives. See also Bernstein, *The Lean Years*, pp. 490–492.

[14] William Leiserson in *Life and Labor Bulletin*, 8:7 (June 1930), p. 1.

[15] Elisabeth Christman to Secretaries of Local Leagues (29 December 1931), WTUL, Box 5.

[16] Matilda Lindsay to Executive Board (5 February 1932), WTUL, Box 5.

[17] My primary reliance on the role of organized labor in these years is Bernstein, *The Lean Years*, pp. 347–354. See also Hannah, "Urban Reaction to the Great Depression," especially pp. 154–166; and James O. Morris, *Conflict within the AFL* (Ithaca, N.Y.: Cornell University Press, 1958), pp. 138–140, 271.

[18] Morris, *Conflict within the AFL*, pp. 124–135; "A Better Way with Unemployment," *New Republic*, 65:839 (31 December 1930), pp. 176–178.

[19] *Unemployment Insurance*, Report of the Select Committee to Investigate Unemployment Insurance (Report No. 964, 72nd Congress, 1st Session, June 1932). Senator Wagner's views were argued briefly in the official report and were set forth more extensively in "Rock-Bottom Responsibility," *Survey*, 68:5 (1 June 1932), pp. 222–224, 256. See also Bernstein, *The Lean Years*, pp. 501–503; and Thomas R. Byrne, "The Social Thought of Robert F. Wagner" (Doctoral dissertation, Georgetown University, 1951), pp. 110–118.

[20] See issues of People's Lobby *Bulletin* for 1931 and 1932.

[21] Frances Perkins, "Unemployment Insurance," *Survey*, 67:3 (1 November 1931), pp. 117–119, 173; Frances Perkins, *People at Work* (New York: John Day, 1934), pp. 119–120. See also Bernstein, *The Lean Years*, pp. 492–496.

[22] Fiorello La Guardia in AASS *Record* (1933), pp. 72–76.

[23] Warren Jay Vinton in AASS *Record* (1934), pp. 56–59.

[24] The position of the AALL may be traced in the *American Labor Legislation Review* for these years. See also commentary on these and related developments by Herman A. Gray in AASS *Record* (1934), pp. 19–25.

Chapter 10. Toward the New Deal

[1] Paul U. Kellogg to Graham Taylor (15 September 1932), Taylor Papers.

[2] Alice Hamilton, *Exploring the Dangerous Trades* (Boston: Little, Brown, 1943), p. 65.

[3] Abraham Epstein, typescript of speech (Fall 1934), Epstein Papers.

[4] Florence Kelley to Amy G. Maher (29 October 1920), NCL, Box 8.

[5] Elisabeth Christman, Report to Affiliate Leagues (July 1924), WTUL Papers, Box 3; Correspondence (1931), Box 5.

[6] The item on Rubinow is in Bernstein, *Lean Years*, p. 498.

[7] Mary Anderson to Margaret D. Robins (7 November 1930), Anderson Papers, Box 2.

[8] This latter is the sound thesis set forth in Donald C. Swain, "The Role of Federal Government in the Conservation of Natural Resources, 1921–1933" (Doctoral dissertation, University of California at Berkeley, 1960).

[9] Fannia Cohn to Miss Penn Shelton (27 September 1923), WTUL, Box 26.

[10] Bernstein, *Lean Years*, pp. 1–13, is particularly effective on these points. For contemporary observations see Gerald Johnson, "Behind the Monster's Mask," *Survey*, 50:1 (1 April 1923), pp. 20–22, 55–56; Jennings J. Rhyne, *Some Southern Cotton Mill Workers and Their Villages* (Chapel Hill: University of North Carolina Press, 1930); Tom Tippett, *When Southern Labor Stirs* (New York: Cope and Smith, 1931).

[11] Margaret Dreier Robins to Elisabeth Christman (11 October 1926), WTUL, Box 3.

[12] Report of Matilda Lindsay (5 October 1928), and Report of Elisabeth Christman (24 April 1928), WTUL, Box 4.

[13] Bernstein, *Lean Years*, pp. 13–40, tells the story in some detail. See Margaret Bowen, UTW representative in Elizabethton, Report (1929), WTUL (Radcliffe), Box 5; Florence Kelley, "Our Newest South," *Survey*, 62:6 (15 June 1929), pp. 342–344.

[14] Matilda Lindsay, Report (through 1 July 1930); Francis J. Gorman in Minutes of Executive Board (26–28 September 1930); Elisabeth Christman to Executive Board (6 September 1930), WTUL, Box 5.

[15] Elisabeth Christman, Report (5 December 1931), WTUL, Box 5.

[16] I have relied here upon the analysis of James O. Morris, *Conflict within the AFL* (Ithaca, N.Y.: Cornell University Press, 1958), pp. 124–135.

[17] Donald R. McCoy, *Angry Voices* (Lawrence: University of Kansas Press, 1958), pp. 4–20.

[18] Donald B. Meyer, *The Protestant Search for Political Realism, 1919–1941* (Berkeley: University of California Press, 1960); Paul A. Carter, *The Decline and Revival of the Social Gospel* (Ithaca, N.Y.: Cornell University Press, 1954); Robert M. Miller, *American Protestantism and Social Issues, 1919–1939* (Chapel Hill: University of North Carolina Press, 1958).

[19] "National Economic Objectives for Social Work," NCSW *Proceedings* (1933), pp. 639–651; Gertrude Springer, "Partners in a New Social Order," *Survey*, 69:7 (July 1933), pp. 243–250.

[20] President's Research Committee on Social Trends, *Recent Social Trends in the United States* (New York: McGraw-Hill, 1933), I, xxxii–xxxiii, xii–xiii, xv.

[21] *Ibid.*, xxxii, liv, lxxiv.

[22] Anne O'Hare McCormick, report dated 16 August 1931 in *The World at Home* (New York: Knopf, 1956), pp. 75, 82.

[23] Margaret Dreier Robins to Mary Anderson (12 November 1930), Anderson Papers, Box 2.

[24] Paul U. Kellogg to Lillian Wald (29 March 1930), Wald Papers, File 1, Drawer 4.

[25] Lillian Wald to Mrs. Bertram Crowley (19 March 1931), Wald Papers, File 1, Drawer 2.

[26] Aubrey Williams, draft for first chapter (typescript reminiscences), pp. 25–26, Williams Papers.

[27] Grace Abbott to Lillian Wald (6 December 1931), File 1, Drawer 4.

[28] Press Release from Democratic State Committee (19 October 1930) citing sup-

port of committee of forty-seven social workers, chaired by Lillian Wald, Wald
Papers, File 1, Drawer 4; Wald to Naomi Deutsch (17 March 1931), and to Alice
Crowley (27 July 1932), File 1, Drawer 2; Maud Swartz to Eleanor Roosevelt (18
December 1930), Eleanor Roosevelt Papers, Correspondence, 1929–1933, Box 7.

[29] Alice Hamilton to Lillian Wald (21 October 1932), File 2, Drawer 1.

[30] Lillian Wald to Lavinia Dock (24 October 1932), File 1, Drawer 2.

[31] Sophonisba Breckinridge statement (2 September 1932) in Wald Papers, File
2, Drawer 1.

[32] Mary Anderson to Margaret Dreier Robins (28 November 1932), Anderson
Papers, Box 2.

[33] Rose Schneiderman to Lillian Wald (5 July 1933), Wald Papers, File 2,
Drawer 3.

[34] Edith Abbott, "Grace Abbott: A Sister's Memories," *Social Service Review*,
13:3 (September 1939), pp. 351–407.

[35] Marshall E. Dimock, "The Inner Substance of a Progressive," *Social Service
Review*, 13:4 (December 1939), p. 578. See also Helen R. Wright, "Three against
Time," *Social Service Review*, 28:1 (March 1954), pp. 44–47.

[36] Grace Abbott to Lillian Wald (11 April 1933), File 2, Drawer 2.

Chapter 11. "Uphill All the Way"

[1] Arthur M. Schlesinger, Jr., was one of the first historians to note the significance
of Mary Dewson's career. See also Mary R. Dewson, "An Aid to the End"; Eleanor
Roosevelt and Lorena A. Hickok, *Ladies of Courage* (New York: Putnam, 1954),
Chapter 2; Dewson Papers (F. D. R. Library), Box 12; Dewson Papers (Radcliffe),
Box 1.

[2] The materials here are scattered, but see especially Josephine Goldmark, "50
Years — The National Consumers' League," *Survey*, 85:12 (December 1949), pp.
674–676.

[3] Bruno Lasker, Oral History Project (Columbia University), p. 196.

[4] Louis H. Pink, Oral History Project, pp. 6–10.

[5] Witte, *Development of the Social Security Act*, Part I.

[6] Harry Hopkins, "The Developing National Program of Relief," NCSW *Proceedings* (1933), pp. 69–70.

[7] Harry Hopkins, "Social Planning for the Future," *Social Service Review*, 8:3
(September 1934), pp. 397–407.

[8] Jane Hoey, "The Contribution of Social Work to Government," NCSW *Proceedings* (1941), pp. 3–17.

[9] Lillian Wald to Judge Ben Lindsay (November 1935) quoted in Duffus, *Lillian
Wald*, pp. 318–19.

[10] Elisabeth Christman in Catherine Filene, editor, *Careers for Women* (rev. ed.;
Boston: Houghton Mifflin, 1934), p. 359.

[11] Agnes Nestor to Margaret Dreier Robins (undated, c. January 1936), Nestor
Papers. This was in reply to a deeply pessimistic and nostalgic letter from Mrs.
Robins (8 January 1936).

[12] Lucy Sprague Mitchell, *Two Lives* (New York: Simon and Schuster, 1953),
p. 209.

[13] Florence Kelley, AAOAS *Proceedings* (1928).

[14] Rubinow, *Quest for Security*, pp. 276–277.

[15] John B. Andrews, "A Social Adventure Invites Your Cooperation," *American
Labor Legislation Review*, 18:4 (December 1928), p. 331.

[16] Abraham Epstein to William J. Ellis (21 November 1938), Epstein Papers.

[17] Report of Financial Secretary (12 September 1925), WTUL, Box 3.

[18] Eveline M. Burns, "Social Welfare Is Our Commitment," *Public Welfare*, 16:3
(July 1958), pp. 147–154.

[19] Paul U. Kellogg to Mrs. Anita McCormick Blaine (28 February 1926), Blaine Papers; Bruno Lasker to Jane Addams (9 January 1923), Addams Papers, Box 12.

[20] *Survey*, 44:13 (26 June 1920), p. 426, and 47:5 (29 October 1921), pp. 184–185; "The Story of the Survey," *Survey*, 43:22 (27 March 1920), pp. 788–796.

[21] Here and in the paragraphs that follow I am drawing from my own study, "Social Service and Social Reform: A Historical Essay," *Social Service Review*, 37:1 (March 1963), pp. 76–90.

[22] Helen Hall, "The Consequences of Social Action for the Group-Work Agency," NCSW *Proceedings* (1936), pp. 235, 237.

[23] Leonard W. Mayo, "The Changing Role of Voluntary Agencies," *Social Work Journal*, 36:3 (July 1955), p. 96.

[24] I am indebted here to the Reverend William H. Mead, "Voice of Prophecy" (Sermon delivered at Episcopal Church of St. John the Evangelist, St. Paul, Minnesota, 1961).

[25] Elizabeth Tilton, "Journal" entries for 10 and 21 January 1921, Tilton Papers, Box 10.

[26] For a full elaboration of this view see my "FDR, Pragmatist-Idealist," *Pacific Northwest Quarterly*, 52:2 (April 1961), pp. 50–55.

[27] Clinton L. Rossiter, *Seedtime of the Republic* (New York: Harcourt, Brace, 1953), p. 439; Rossiter, "The Political Philosophy of F. D. Roosevelt," *Review of Politics*, 11:1 (June 1949), pp. 87–95. Frances Perkins' twofold commitment to social intelligence and moral principles is clearly demonstrated in "What Is Worth Working for in America?" NCSW *Proceedings* (1941), pp. 32–40.

BIBLIOGRAPHIC ESSAY

IT WOULD be foolhardy — and probably gratuitous — to attempt to list every letter and report, every article, every monograph from which I have drawn raw evidence, valuable leads, and interpretative ideas or organizing principles. The footnote citations attest to some of the specific kinds of materials I used. I intend here to select and to discuss merely those materials, primary and secondary, that were most useful to me and presumably would be most helpful to the serious reader.

Personal Papers

The Jane Addams Papers (Swarthmore College Peace Collection) include correspondence, drafts of speeches, reprints of articles by and about the settlement pioneer, and clippings; the incoming correspondence is far more extensive than the outgoing, and for the period 1918–1933 the collection is far stronger in material on international peace than on domestic reform. The Hull House Papers (in the same collection) are neither as extensive nor as well organized, but they do include correspondence, reports, and memoranda on the settlement movement in these years not easily available elsewhere.

The Anita McCormick Blaine Papers (McCormick Collection, Wisconsin Historical Society) run to eighty-four four-drawer file cabinets. (I used the collection selectively!) For the years 1918 to 1933 they include correspondence with such representative leaders as Lillian Wald, Margaret Dreier Robins, Paul Kellogg, Agnes Nestor, Grace Abbott, and Julia Lathrop, and with such organizations as the Consumers' League, the Child Labor Committee, the American Association for Old Age Security, and the Chicago Council of Social Agencies. The solicitation letters often included detailed descriptions of agency or associational work and offer insights into the financial problems of reform and welfare organizations and into their inner workings as well.

The Sophonisba Breckinridge Papers (Library of Congress) are weak for the period of the 1920's, but they do include lengthy, revealing correspondence with Grace Abbott.

The John R. Commons Papers (Wisconsin Historical Society) offer, in addition to two boxes of correspondence for this era, several boxes of research files, speeches, and papers which deal with the issues of unemployment insurance, minimum wages, child labor, and industrial relations.

The Abraham Epstein Papers (Columbia University Library) cover the years 1918–1942 with special concentration upon the decade of the 1930's. When I used them in the spring of 1960 they were jammed in unarranged form into a series of unnumbered boxes; although this is potentially an extraordinarily rich collection, including correspondence, press releases, mimeographed reports, and printed flyers, I could but sample the ore.

The papers of Mary (Molly) R. Dewson are located in the F. D. R. Library, Hyde Park, and in the Women's Archives, Radcliffe. The former collection includes a typescript autobiography, "An Aid to the End," correspondence, and scrapbooks; the latter collection, while smaller, is strong in materials on the Consumers' League in the 1920's.

The Catheryne Cooke Gilman Papers (Minnesota Historical Society) tell the story of the Northeast Neighborhood House of Minneapolis during the years that she and her husband, Robbins Gilman, played a vital role in the life of the community, 1914–1948. They include a three-volume typescript autobiography and ninety-three boxes of correspondence, speeches, clippings, and the files of the Women's Cooperative Alliance; they contain extensive raw material on settlement activities and on child welfare, public health, women in politics, race relations, immigration, prostitution, and developments in professional social work.

The New York School of Social Work of Columbia University holds the papers of Homer Folks, Helen Hall, Mary Richmond, Gertrude Vaile, and the Survey Associates. The latter collection, potentially the richest single deposit of primary materials on social reform and social work during the first half of the twentieth century, had not yet been put in order when I used it in 1960; I could not, therefore, do more than dip here and there into its wealth of evidence.

In the Chicago Historical Society are located the papers of Mary E. McDowell, 1894–1936, and of Agnes Nestor, 1880–1948. The former contain materials vital to an understanding of the work of the University of Chicago Settlement and touch upon such issues as prohibition, juvenile delinquency, recreation, housing, health, and unemployment. The Nestor Papers, containing approximately six thousand items, throw light on her career in the Women's Trade Union League and on the movements for minimum-wage and maximum-hour legislation in Illinois and in the nation; they also illustrate the trade union phase of the league's program.

The Graham Taylor Papers (Newberry Library, Chicago) contain Taylor's own extensive personal correspondence files, typescripts, and newspaper clippings, and some of the personal papers of his daughter, Lea Taylor, as well; in addition to these there is a substantial body of working papers of Chicago Commons, including minutes of staff meetings and other official records.

The single most useful settlement collection, however, is the Lillian Wald Papers (New York Public Library). For the years 1918 to 1933 there are three file cabinets of four drawers each. Here is correspondence with all manner of persons and associations dealt with in this study: Paul Kellogg, Rose Schneiderman, Jane Addams, Margaret Dreier Robins, Lavinia Dock, Helen Hall, Mary R. Dewson, Julia Lathrop, John B. Andrews, Alfred E. Smith, Stephen A. Wise, Mary K. Simkhovitch, Mary Van Kleeck, Edward T. Devine, Eleanor Roosevelt, Grace Abbott, and Florence Kelley (to cite only the most prominent of the people). The letters and other papers are especially valuable for an understanding of the problems of the early depression years, and of the role of social-work and settlement leaders in the realm of political action.

In the Franklin D. Roosevelt Library, Hyde Park, I used the correspondence that seemed to bear on my subject from the office of the governor (F. D. R.), from the office of the lieutenant governor (Herbert Lehman), and from the papers of Morris L. Cooke, Harry L. Hopkins, Eleanor Roosevelt, and Aubrey Williams.

The Women's Archives, Radcliffe College, contain the personal papers of many of the reformers in whose careers I was interested: Corinne M. Allen (Utah Congress of Mothers and the Parent-Teachers Association); Mary Anderson (chief of the Women's Bureau, 1919–1944); Elizabeth Gardiner Evans (social work, minimum wages, child labor, old-age security); Alice Hamilton (public health, civil rights, reform); Ethel M. Johnson (assistant commissioner of the Massachusetts Department of Labor and Industries, 1919–1932); Maryal Knox (New York settlement leader); Harriet Laidlaw (New York League of Women Voters, white slavery, political action); Maud Nathan (scrapbooks dealing with the Consumers' League and the Women's Trade Union League among other movements); Mary K. O'Sullivan (Women's Trade Union League and Massachusetts conditions of labor); Belle Sherwin (Ohio Consumers' League and League of Women Voters); Hilda Worthington Smith (Bryn Mawr Summer School for Women Workers, 1921–1933, and other labor education materials); Elizabeth H. Tilton (including her journals and typescript autobiography, and some correspondence, dealing with the National Congress of Mothers, child labor, prohibition, prison reform); Miriam Van Waters (juvenile delinquency, penal institutions for women and girls); and Eva Whiting White (settlements, professional social work, education).

The Oral History Project at Columbia University contains transcripts of interviews with leaders in many fields related to my study. These reminiscences provided background material and occasional insights of value to this study, but they tended to focus on time periods other than 1918 to 1933 or on issues peripheral to my own concern: Ralph Albertson, William H. Allen, Ella Boole, Henry Bruère, Haven Emerson, Homer Folks, Louis Pink, Lawson Purdy, William Jay Schieffelin, Norman Thomas, Eva MacDonald Valesh, and Lawrence Veiller. Of particular significance was the three-volume reminiscence of Bruno Lasker (settlement worker, friend and adviser of Lillian Wald, associate editor of the *Survey*, member of the Inquiry); attached to his transcript were his working notebooks for the years 1923 to 1933 which contained conference minutes, committee reports, typescripts of articles and speeches, and research notes on industrial relations, education, housing, race relations, and social work activities.

Associational Archives

In the Manuscript Division of the Library of Congress are the official papers of the National Child Labor Committee, the National Consumers' League, and the National Women's Trade Union League. The NCLC collection contains typed, mimeographed, and printed reports and surveys on child labor in field, mine, and mill; proceedings of national conferences; minute books; press releases; and scrapbooks of news clippings. Save for a folder of form letters, the correspondence files are not included in this otherwise valuable collection. The papers of the Consumers' League are the most extensive and presumably the most complete. They include the minutes of executive board and executive committee meetings and the proceedings of national conferences, manuscript studies and reports, printed pamphlets and leaflets, scrapbooks, clippings, and research folders, and also a good deal of correspondence. Without the candid, revealing letters of Florence Kelley in these papers many points of analysis would have remained obscure. The Women's Trade Union League Papers, twenty-nine boxes strong, contain official reports, minutes, proceedings, and correspondence.

The Women's Archives, Radcliffe College, contain some papers of the National Consumers' League; it also holds extensive papers (minutes, proceedings, pamphlets, and some correspondence) of the Connecticut and Massachusetts leagues. There is one box of bulletins circulated by affiliate members of the Trade Union League in Boston, Chicago, New York, Philadelphia, Pennsylvania, New Jersey, and Washington, D.C.; five boxes of National WTUL materials have many items not included in the Library of Congress collection.

The Office Archives of the National Federation of Settlements (226 West 47th Street, New York City) contain correspondence files of officers and others, minutes of executive committees and annual meetings, conference reports, bulletins, printed pamphlets, conference announcements and programs.

Periodical Materials

The official journal of the American Association for Labor Legislation was the *American Labor Legislation Review*, which appeared quarterly during this period. Founded in 1910 by John B. Andrews, it ceased publication in 1942; the March edition each year contained proceedings of official business, together with transcripts of the major speeches and papers delivered at the association's annual conference.

The house organ of the American Association for Old Age Security (after 1933 the American Association for Social Security) was variously titled: *Bulletin* (1927–1929), *Old Age Security Herald* (1930–1933), *Social Security* (1934–1942). Its editor was Abraham Epstein; it varied in size from two pages to twelve pages depending upon the financial health of its sponsoring association.

In *The Compass*, the official publication of the American Association of Social Workers (1920–1947), professional social workers had a medium for the "exchange of ideas, of information, and of common experience." Although it concerned itself primarily with technical and procedural matters it occasionally addressed itself to matters of broad social policy, particularly after 1929. The *Bulletin* of the Child Welfare League of America (1922–1933) contained news and analyses of the whole range of child-welfare issues — child labor, infant mortality, dependency, delinquency, health, education, and detention.

The National Child Labor Committee changed the name of its official publication from *Child Labor Bulletin* to *The American Child* in 1919. Appearing monthly, it ranged in size from four to eight pages and touched upon all aspects of child welfare with special attention to the problems of working children. Its editors during this period included Owen R. Lovejoy, Agnes Benedict, and Gertrude Folks Zimand.

For a brief time, 1929 to 1935, the National Federation of Settlements published a settlement quarterly, *Neighborhood*, which included abbreviated minutes of the federation's annual conference and of its executive committee meetings together with articles by leading settlement workers around the country. The December 1931 edition was devoted entirely to a "Bibliography of Settlement Literature, 1920–1931."

The official journal of the Women's Trade Union League was *Life and Labor* (1911–1921); it discontinued publication briefly in the winter and spring of 1921–1922 because of insufficient funds, and when it began publication again in August of 1922 its title was changed to *Life and Labor Bulletin*. Its pages were devoted to the affairs of the league, of course, to trade unionism and women's rights movements, and, in the 1920's at least, to the cause of world peace. *The Woman Citizen*, originally part of the woman-suffrage movement, carried news on the activities of the League of Women Voters during the postwar years and on issues of welfare, family, education, employment, industrial conditions, etc. Retitled *The Woman's Journal* in 1928, it ceased publication in 1931.

In the *Annals* of the American Academy of Political and Social Science issues were regularly devoted to the welfare measures and reform movements with which this study deals. Of particular value were "Child Welfare," volume 98 (November 1921); "Public Welfare in the United States," volume 105 (January 1923); "New Values in Child Welfare," volume 121 (September 1925); "The Legal Minimum Wage in Massachusetts," supplement to volume 130 (March 1927); "Postwar Progress in Child Welfare," volume 151 (September 1930); "The Insecurity of Industry," volume 154 (March 1931); "Social Insurance," volume 170 (November 1933).

Articles in varied issues of the *Nation*, the *New Republic*, the *Arbitrator*, the *People's Lobby Bulletin*, the *Journal of Social Forces*, and the *Social Service Review* were consulted, but the single most important periodical source was (as the footnotes abundantly testify) Paul U. Kellogg's *Survey* and *Survey Graphic*. With a circulation of around twenty-five thousand in the postwar years that are the period of my study the *Survey* aimed at two primary audiences — professional social workers and an informed lay public interested in the issues of social welfare, social service, and social reform. There was not an issue of the magazine that did not yield indispensable evidence for this study.

Proceedings of the Consumers' League, the Child Labor Committee, and the

Women's Trade Union League appeared as separate publications in the official papers of those organizations. The official proceedings of the American Association for Old Age Security (and the American Association for Social Security) appeared under various titles, 1928–1942: *Old Age Security* (1928–1929), *Old Age Security Progress* (1930–1931), *Old Age Security in the United States* (1932), and *Social Security in the United States* (1933–1942). Of special importance, of course, were the *Proceedings* of the National Conference of Charities and Correction (to 1916) and the *Proceedings* of the National Conference of Social Work (1917–1949). Each annual volume contained the most significant papers and speeches delivered at these conferences of persons engaged in professional social work. Informal and extensive accounts of these conferences can be found annually in the relevant issues of the *Survey*.

Miscellaneous publications of the Childern's Bureau and of the Women's Bureau provided facts and analyses particularly useful for Chapters 2 and 3 of this study. The official story of the Children's Bureau is Dorothy E. Bradbury's *Four Decades of Action for Children: A Short History of the Children's Bureau* (Children's Bureau Publication No. 358, 1956).

Autobiographical Accounts

The settlement movement produced many articulate leaders who felt compelled to record their experiences and their ideas. Jane Addams' two personal accounts have become classics: *Twenty Years at Hull House* (New York: Macmillan, 1911), and *The Second Twenty Years at Hull House* (New York: Macmillan, 1930). Among many other memoirs the following were especially helpful: Esther G. Barrows, *Neighbors All: A Settlement Notebook* (Boston: Houghton Mifflin, 1929); Alice Lewisohn Crowley, *The Neighborhood Playhouse* (New York: Theater Arts Books, 1959); Alice Hamilton, *Exploring the Dangerous Trades: The Autobiography of Alice Hamilton* (Boston: Little, Brown, 1943); Vida Scudder, *On Journey* (New York: Dutton, 1937); Mary K. Simkhovitch, *Neighborhood: My Story of Greenwich House* (New York: Norton, 1938); Graham Taylor, *Chicago Commons through Forty Years* (Chicago: Chicago Commons Association, 1936), and *Pioneering on Social Frontiers* (Chicago: University of Chicago Press, 1930); and Lillian Wald, *Windows on Henry Street* (Boston: Little, Brown, 1934).

Important social-worker memoirs include Edward T. Devine, *When Social Work Was Young* (New York: Macmillan, 1939); Alexander Johnson, *Adventures in Social Welfare* (Fort Wayne, Ind., 1923); Morris D. Waldman, *Nor by Power* (New York: International Universities Press, 1953), particularly Section III; and Daisy Lee W. Worcester, *Grim the Battles: A Semi-Autobiographical Account of the War against Want in the United States during the First Half of the Twentieth Century* (New York: Exposition Press, 1954).

Notable reform leaders of the 1920's who set down their thoughts include Mary Anderson, *Woman at Work: The Autobiography of Mary Anderson as Told to Mary N. Winslow* (Minneapolis: University of Minnesota Press, 1951); John R. Commons, *Myself* (New York: Macmillan, 1934); Francis J. McConnell, *By the Way: An Autobiography* (New York: Abingdon-Cokesbury, 1952); and Maud Nathan, *The Story of an Epoch-Making Movement* (Garden City, N.Y.: Doubleday, 1926).

Biographical Accounts

Friends and associates often turned to biography to make their point. Thus Jane Addams wrote an insightful account of *My Friend, Julia Lathrop* (New York: Macmillan, 1935); while Josephine Goldmark, who had given her life to the cause of reform, wrote an affectionate but not uncritical story of the *Impatient Crusader: Florence Kelley's Life Story* (Urbana: University of Illinois Press, 1953); and

Eleanor H. Woods put together the life story of her husband, *Robert A. Woods, Champion of Democracy* (Boston: Houghton Mifflin, 1929). Lillian Wald found two friendly biographers in Robert L. Duffus, *Lillian Wald, Neighbor and Crusader* (New York: Macmillan, 1938), and Beryl W. Epstein, *Lillian Wald: Angel of Henry Street* (New York: Julian Messner, 1948). Other settlement biographies include James W. Linn, *Jane Addams* (New York: Appleton-Century, 1935), and Howard E. Wilson, *Mary McDowell: Neighbor* (Chicago: University of Chicago Press, 1928).

Social-work leaders and reformers had their stories told in Jean Burton, *Katharine Felton and Her Social Work in San Francisco* (Stanford, Calif.: J. L. Delkin, 1947); Mary Dreier, *Margaret Dreier Robins, Her Life, Letters and Work* (New York: Island Press Cooperative, 1950); Gisela Konopka, *Eduard C. Lindeman and Social Work Philosophy* (Minneapolis: University of Minnesota Press, 1958); and Burton J. Rowles, *The Lady at Box 99: The Story of Miriam Van Waters* (Greenwich, Conn.: Seabury Press, 1962). Chapter 2 of Eleanor Roosevelt and Lorena A. Hickok, *Ladies of Courage* (New York: Putnam, 1954), presents a lively, if sympathetic, account of the career and character of Mary R. Dewson.

The number of biographical articles and essays is legion, but of particular value for my study were Edith Abbott, "Grace Abbott: A Sister's Memories," *Social Service Review*, 13:3 (September 1939), pp. 351–407; Marshall E. Dimock, "The Inner Substance of a Progressive [Grace Abbott]," *Social Service Review*, 13:4 (December 1939), pp. 573–578; Norris C. Hundley, "Katherine Philips Edson and the Fight for the California Minimum Wage, 1912–1923," *Pacific Historical Review*, 29 (August 1960), pp. 271–285; Emma O. Lundberg, "Pathfinders of the Middle Years [leaders in child welfare]," *Social Service Review*, 21:1 (March 1947), pp. 1–34; Frances Perkins, "My Recollection of Florence Kelley," *Social Service Review*, 28:1 (March 1954), pp. 12–19; Helen R. Wright, "Three against Time: Edith and Grace Abbott and Sophonisba P. Breckinridge," *Social Service Review*, 28:1 (March 1954), pp. 41–53. Obituaries in the *Survey* and in the *Social Service Review* were invariably detailed and helpful.

Other Primary and Secondary Materials

VOLUNTARY ASSOCIATIONS

Some of my original formulations on the role of voluntary associational activity in American life, particularly in the realms of social reform and social welfare, I drew from Alfred De Grazia, *Grass Roots Private Welfare* (New York: New York University Press, 1957); Arnold M. Rose, *Theory and Method in the Social Sciences* (Minneapolis: University of Minnesota Press, 1954), pp. 50–72; W. Lloyd Warner, "Associations in America," Chapter 9 of *American Life: Dream and Reality* (Chicago: University of Chicago Press, 1953).

Periodical articles that provided hypotheses and empirical evidence included Wendell Bell and Maryanne T. Force, "Social Structure and Participation in Different Types of Formal Associations," *Social Forces*, 34:4 (May 1956), pp. 345–350; Floyd Dotson, "Patterns of Voluntary Association among Urban Working-Class Families," *American Sociological Review*, 16:5 (October 1951), pp. 687–693; Lawrence K. Frank, "What Influences People to Join Organizations?" *Adult Leadership*, 6:8 (February 1958), pp. 196–200, 219; Howard Freeman and Morris Showel, "Differential Political Influence of Voluntary Associations," *Public Opinion Quarterly*, 15:4 (Winter 1951–1952), pp. 703–714; Ronald Friedman, "Who Belongs to What in a Great Metropolis?" *Adult Leadership*, 1:6 (November 1952), pp. 6–9; C. Wayne Gordon and Nicholas Babchuk, "Typology of Voluntary Associations," *American Sociological Review*, 24:1 (February 1959), pp. 22–29; Luther Gulick, "Voluntary Organizations That Promote Better Government and Citizenship,"

Annals, 105 (January 1923), pp. 71–75; Mirra Komarovsky, "The Voluntary Associations of Urban Dwellers," *American Sociological Review,* 11:6 (December 1946), pp. 686–698; Arnold M. Rose, "Voluntary Associations under Conditions of Competition and Conflict," *Social Forces,* 34:2 (December 1955), pp. 159–163; John Scott, "Membership and Participation in Voluntary Associations," *American Sociological Review,* 22:3 (June 1957), pp. 315–326; John E. Tsouderos, "Voluntary Associations, Past – Present – Future," *Adult Leadership,* 6:10 (April 1958), pp. 267–269, 282; John E. Tsouderos and F. Stuart Chapin, "Formalization Observed in Ten Voluntary Associations: Concepts, Morphology, Process," *Social Forces,* 33:4 (May 1955), pp. 306–309.

GENERAL BACKGROUND

Recent general surveys of political and social developments in the 1920's include most notably John D. Hicks, *Republican Ascendancy, 1921–1933* (New York: Harper, 1960); William E. Leuchtenburg, *The Perils of Prosperity, 1914–32* (Chicago: University of Chicago Press, 1958); and Arthur M. Schlesinger, Jr., *The Age of Roosevelt: The Crisis of the Old Order, 1919–1933* (Boston: Houghton Mifflin, 1957). Schlesinger's interpretations are sometimes a bit extravagant, but he was among the first to suggest the significant role played by social reformers in the 1920's in anticipating much that was later essential to the New Deal. The most useful general account of the economy is still George Soule, *Prosperity Decade; From War to Depression: 1917–1929* (New York: Rinehart, 1947). Indispensable to an understanding of the careers and works of leading economists, both professional and amateur, are Volumes IV and V of Joseph Dorfman, *The Economic Mind in American Civilization, 1606–1933* (New York: Viking Press, 1959); I have drawn helpful leads and summaries from his work at many points.

The social role of organized religion in these years is traced in Aaron I. Abell, *American Catholicism and Social Action: A Search for Social Justice, 1865–1950* (Garden City, N.Y.: Hanover House, 1960); Paul A. Carter, *The Decline and Revival of the Social Gospel: Social and Political Liberalism in American Protestant Churches, 1920–1940* (Ithaca, N.Y.: Cornell University Press, 1956); Donald B. Meyer, *The Protestant Search for Political Realism, 1919–1941* (Berkeley: University of California Press, 1960); and Robert M. Miller, *American Protestantism and Social Issues, 1919–1939* (Chapel Hill: University of North Carolina Press, 1958).

Political progressivism in the decade of normalcy is analyzed in Oscar Handlin, *Al Smith and His America* (Boston: Little, Brown, 1958); D. Joy Humes, *Oswald Garrison Villard, Liberal of the 1920's* (Syracuse, N.Y.: Syracuse University Press, 1960); Kenneth Campbell MacKay, *The Progressive Movement of 1924* (New York: Columbia University Press, 1947); Arthur Mann, *La Guardia, A Fighter against His Times, 1882–1933* (Philadelphia: Lippincott, 1959); and Howard Zinn, *La Guardia in Congress* (Ithaca, N.Y.: Cornell University Press, 1959).

The backgrounds of Roosevelt's ideas and programs have been surveyed in Bernard Bellush, *Franklin D. Roosevelt as Governor of New York* (New York: Columbia University Press, 1955); Frank Freidel, *Franklin D. Roosevelt* (3 vols.; Boston: Little, Brown, 1952–1956); and Daniel R. Fusfeld, *The Economic Thought of Franklin D. Roosevelt and the Origins of the New Deal* (New York: Columbia University Press, 1956). John D. Hicks, *Rehearsal for Disaster: The Boom and Collapse of 1919–1920* (Gainesville: University of Florida Press, 1961), demonstrates the ways in which the failure to meet economic problems of the early panic prepared the way for the greater disaster of 1929.

For general accounts of labor in the 1920's Volumes III and IV of John R. Commons, *History of Labour in the United States, 1896–1932* (New York: Macmillan, 1935), are still useful; along the same line is John R. Commons and John B.

Andrews, *Principles of Labor Legislation* (2nd ed.; New York: Harper, 1927). Philip Taft's two volumes, *The A. F. of L. in the Time of Gompers* and *The A. F. of L. from the Death of Gompers to the Merger* (New York: Harper, 1957 and 1959), provide a traditional institutional history of labor. More useful for my study is James O. Morris, *Conflict within the AFL* (Ithaca, N.Y.: Cornell University Press, 1958). By far the most exciting and most thorough social history of labor in these years, however, and the account to which I am most indebted, particularly in those sections of my study which bear explicitly on the problems of labor, is Irving Bernstein, *The Lean Years; A History of the American Worker, 1920–1933* (Boston: Houghton Mifflin, 1960).

Helpful for establishing the historical context of social work and social welfare are the pioneering anthology by Ralph E. and Muriel W. Pumphrey, *The Heritage of American Social Work; Readings in Its Philosophical and Institutional Development* (New York: Columbia University Press, 1961), and Vaughn Davis Bornet, *Welfare in America* (Norman: University of Oklahoma Press, 1960).

Unpublished studies from which I have drawn leads and insights include Thomas R. Byrne, "The Social Thought of Robert F. Wagner" (Doctoral dissertation, Georgetown University, 1951); Robert P. Kaufman, "The League for Industrial Democracy, 1921–1931" (Seminar paper, University of California at Berkeley, 1962); Rowland L. Mitchell, Jr., "Social Legislation in Connecticut, 1919–1939" (Doctoral dissertation, Yale University, 1954); Robert A. Shanley, "The League of Women Voters — A Study of Pressure Politics in the Public Interest" (Doctoral dissertation, Georgetown University, 1955); James H. Shideler, "The Neo-Progressives: Reform Politics in the United States, 1920–1925" (Doctoral dissertation, University of California at Berkeley, 1945); Donald C. Swain, "The Role of the Federal Government in the Conservation of Natural Resources, 1921–1933" (Doctoral dissertation, University of California at Berkeley, 1960); and William B. White, "The Philanthropies of Anita McCormick Blaine" (Master's thesis, University of Wisconsin, 1959).

CHILD LABOR AND CHILD WELFARE

The movement to regulate or prohibit child labor is told in three unpublished accounts: Sam Beal Barton, "Factors and Forces in the Movement for the Abolition of Child Labor in the United States" (Doctoral dissertation, University of Texas, 1938); Jeremy Felt, "Regulation of Child Labor in New York State, 1886–1942" (Doctoral dissertation, Syracuse University, 1959); and Ned Weissberg, "The Federal Child Labor Amendment: A Study in Pressure Politics" (Doctoral dissertation, Cornell University, 1942). A sympathetic explanation of the position of the Roman Catholic community in regard to this issue is Vincent A. McQuade, *The American Catholic Attitude on Child Labor since 1891* (Washington, D.C.: Catholic University of America, 1938). The official story of the New York Child Labor Committee is told by Frederick S. Hall, *Forty Years, 1902–1942: The Work of the New York Child Labor Committee* (New York: New York Child Labor Committee, 1942). Other studies by proponents of more severe regulation of the evils of child labor are Elizabeth H. Davidson, *Child Labor Legislation in the Southern Textile States* (Chapel Hill: University of North Carolina Press, 1939); Forest C. Ensign, *Compulsory School Attendance and Child Labor* (Iowa City, 1921); Katherine D. Lumpkin and Dorothy W. Douglas, *Child Workers in America* (New York: McBride, 1937). Studies for the National Child Labor Committee and its local affiliates were done by Sara A. Brown, Edward N. Clopper, Raymond G. Fuller, Charles E. Gibbons, Claude E. Robinson, and Gertrude Folks Zimand.

The Children's Bureau regularly published analyses of child labor and its consequences throughout this period. See, for example, *Administration of the First Federal Child Labor Law* (Bulletin No. 78, 1922); *Child Labor* (Bulletin No. 93,

1924); *Children in Agriculture* (Bulletin No. 187, 1929); and *Child Labor: Facts and Figures* (Bulletin No. 197, 1930). Grace Abbott, "Federal Regulation of Child Labor, 1906–1938," *Social Service Review*, 13:3 (September 1939), pp. 409–430, is an informed history by one who was there.

Documentary materials on fields of family and child welfare are gathered in Grace Abbott, editor, *The Child and the State* (2 vols.; Chicago: University of Chicago Press, 1938); and Sophonisba Breckinridge, *The Family and the State* (Chicago: University of Chicago Press, 1934). Various aspects of child welfare are touched upon in Children's Aid Society, *The Crusade for Children* (New York: Children's Aid Society, 1928); Helen I. Clarke, *Social Legislation — American Laws Dealing with the Family, Child, and Dependent* (New York: Appleton-Century, 1940); Harold C. Coffman, *American Foundations: A Study of Their Role in the Child Welfare Movement* (New York: Association Press, 1936); and Emma O. Lundberg, *Unto the Least of These: Social Services for Children* (New York: Appleton-Century, 1947). A useful unpublished study is Phyllis Rochelle, "Words and Action: The Care and Treatment of Juvenile Delinquents, 1912–1932" (Seminar paper, University of California at Berkeley, 1962). Children's Bureau publications were many, but see especially *Children of Wage-Earning Mothers* (Publication No. 162, 1926). Developments in the mothers' pension movement are traced in Grace Abbott, "Recent Trends in Mothers' Aid," *Social Service Review*, 8:2 (June 1934), pp. 191–210.

Official accounts of the White House Conference are found in Ray Lyman Wilbur, *et al.*, *White House Conference, 1930: Addresses and Abstracts of Committee Reports* (New York: Century, 1931), and in more than thirty reports published under as many titles. The administration's side of the story is told in Ray Lyman Wilbur, *Memoirs* (Stanford, Calif.: Stanford University Press, 1960), pp. 522–528, and in Ray Lyman Wilbur and Arthur Mastick Hyde, *The Hoover Policies* (New York: Scribner, 1937), pp. 58–67.

WOMEN'S RIGHTS

Because of the crucial role played by the Consumers' League in the crusade for protective legislation for working women, Josephine Goldmark's biography of Florence Kelley is indispensable. Gladys Boone, *The Women's Trade Union Leagues in Great Britain and the United States of America* (New York: Columbia University Press, 1942), provides many leads and useful information. Bernstein's *Lean Years* is an important book for this chapter, as it is for others.

The dependence here, however, is essentially on primary archival and printed materials, including the bulletins and briefs written for the Consumers' League by Josephine Goldmark, Mary R. Dewson, Florence Kelley, Felix Frankfurter, John R. Commons, and others. Three hardheaded analyses from within the ranks of those who were seeking reform are Edith Abbott, *Women in Industry: A Study in American Economic History* (New York: Appleton, 1928); Alice Henry, *Women and the Labor Movement* (New York: Doran, 1923); and Hilda W. Smith, *Women Workers at the Bryn Mawr Summer School* (New York: American Association for Adult Education, 1929).

Studies made by the Women's Bureau under the general direction of Mary Anderson, its chief, provided both empirical data and closely reasoned arguments to justify the concern of the state with hours, wages, and conditions of labor for women workers. See, for example, *The New Position of Women in American Industry* (Bulletin No. 12, 1920); *The Family Status of Breadwinning Women* (Bulletin No. 23, 1922); *The Occupational Progress of Women* (Bulletin No. 27, 1922); *The Share of Wage-Earning Woman in Family Support* (Bulletin No. 30, 1923); *The Development of Minimum Wage Laws in the United States, 1912–1927* (Bulletin No. 61, 1928); *Effects of Labor Legislation* (Bulletin No. 65, 1928); and

Toward Better Conditions for Women: Methods and Policies of the National Women's Trade Union League (Bulletin No. 252, 1953).

Amy G. Maher, "The Employment of Women," *Social Service Review*, 5:1 (March 1931), pp. 28–36, is a brief summary by a loyal member of the Consumers' League. See also a publication by the Bureau of Labor Statistics: Rudolph Broda, *Minimum Wage Legislation in Various Countries* (Bulletin No. 467, 1928).

PROFESSIONAL SOCIAL WORK

For some time the field of professional social work attracted the interest of few historians, but in recent years a vigorous interest has been evidenced in many places. Robert Bremner, *From the Depths: The Discovery of Poverty in the United States* (New York: New York University Press, 1956), is a model study of social welfare confined largely to the Progressive Era, although parts of it are helpful for an understanding of the postwar era. Two professional social-work educators have essayed surveys of the field: Frank J. Bruno, *Trends in Social Work as Reflected in the Proceedings of the National Conference of Social Work, 1874–1946* (New York: Columbia University Press, 1948); and Nathan Edward Cohen, *Social Work in the American Tradition* (New York: Dryden, 1958). Special works include John M. Glenn, *et al.*, *The Russell Sage Foundation, 1907–1946* (2 vols.; New York: Russell Sage Foundation, 1947); Harry L. Lurie, *A Heritage Affirmed: The Jewish Federation Movement in America* (Philadelphia: Jewish Publication Society of America, 1961); Elizabeth G. Meier, *A History of the New York School of Social Work* (New York: Columbia University Press, 1954); Margaret E. Rich, *A Belief in People: A History of Family Social Work* (New York: Family Service Association of America, 1956); Herman D. Stein, "Jewish Social Work in the United States, 1654–1954" (Doctoral dissertation, New York School of Social Work, 1958). A concern for social-welfare history is evidenced in the articles and monographs of Vaughn Bornet, Merle Curti, Roy Lubove, Gisela Konopka, Ralph and Muriel Pumphrey, and Karl de Schweinitz.

Important studies published during the 1920's include Richard C. Cabot, editor, *The Goal of Social Work* (Boston: Houghton Mifflin, 1927); Richard C. Cabot, *Social Service and the Art of Healing* (rev. ed.; New York: Dodd, Mead, 1928); Jerome Davis, editor, *Christianity and Social Adventuring* (New York: Century, 1927); Karl de Schweinitz, *The Art of Helping People Out of Trouble* (Boston: Houghton Mifflin, 1924); Porter R. Lee, *Social Work as Cause and Function, and Other Papers* (New York: Columbia University Press, 1937); William J. Norton, *The Cooperative Movement in Social Work* (New York: Macmillan, 1927); Stuart A. Queen, *Social Work in the Light of History* (Philadelphia: Lippincott, 1922); Margaret E. Rich, editor, *Family Life To-Day* (Boston: Houghton Mifflin, 1928); Mary E. Richmond, *The Long View: Papers and Addresses* (New York: Russell Sage Foundation, 1930); Virginia P. Robinson, *A Changing Psychology in Social Case Work* (Chapel Hill: University of North Carolina Press, 1930); and Amos G. Warner, *et al.*, *American Charities and Social Work* (4th rev. ed.; New York: Crowell, 1930).

THE SETTLEMENTS

Three unpublished studies present the best historical surveys of the origins and development of the settlement movement: Allen Davis, "Spearheads for Reform" (Doctoral dissertation, University of Wisconsin, 1959); Louise Carroll Wade, "Graham Taylor, Social Pioneer, 1851–1938" (Doctoral dissertation, University of Rochester, 1954); and Margaret Blumberg, "Social Settlements in the Interwar Era" (Seminar paper, University of Minnesota, 1961).

The classic account of the settlement movement down into the 1920's by two of its most articulate leaders is Robert A. Woods and Albert J. Kennedy, *The Settle-*

ment Horizon; A National Estimate (New York: Russell Sage Foundation, 1922). An earlier summary by the same team is the *Handbook of Settlements* (New York: Russell Sage Foundation, 1911). See also Robert A. Woods, *The Neighborhood in Nation-Building* (Boston: Houghton Mifflin, 1923); Albert J. Kennedy, editor, *Settlement Goals for the Next Third of a Century, A Symposium* (Boston: National Federation of Settlements, 1926); and Albert J. Kennedy and Kathryn Farra, *Social Settlements in New York City: Their Activities, Policies, and Administration* (New York: Columbia University Press, 1935).

Mary K. Simkhovitch never ceased recording her experiences in the settlement movement; see particularly her books: *The City Workers' World in America* (New York: Macmillan, 1917); *The Settlement Primer* (Boston: National Federation of Settlements, 1926); *Twenty-Five Years of Greenwich House, 1902–1927* (New York: Greenwich House, 1927); *Group Life* (New York: Association Press, 1940); *Quicksand: The Way of Life in the Slums* (Evanston, Ill.: Row, Peterson, 1942); and *Here Is God's Plenty* (New York: Harper, 1949).

Special studies include Gaynell Hawkins, *Educational Experiments in Social Settlements* (New York: American Association for Adult Education, 1937); Arthur C. Holden, *The Settlement Ideas: A Vision of Social Justice* (New York: Macmillan, 1922); and Janet Schenck, *Music, Youth, and Opportunity* (Boston: National Federation of Settlements, 1926). Official reports sponsored by the NFS include Martha Bensley Bruère, *Does Prohibition Work?* (New York: Harper, 1927); Clinch Calkins, *Some Folks Won't Work* (New York: Harcourt, Brace, 1930); and Helen Hall, *Case Studies of Unemployment* (Philadelphia: University of Pennsylvania Press, 1931).

OLD-AGE SECURITY

Historical surveys of various aspects of the old-age pension movement can be found in Abraham Holtzman, "The Townsend Movement: A Study in Old Age Pressure Politics" (Doctoral dissertation, Harvard University, 1952); Alton A. Linford, *Old Age Assistance in Massachusetts* (Chicago: University of Chicago Press, 1949); David S. Patterson, "The Old Age Pension Movement in the United States" (Seminar paper, University of California at Berkeley, 1962); and Lawrence Shulman, "Changing Attitudes and Approaches of the Field of Social Work towards Problems of the Aged" (Master's thesis, University of Minnesota, 1959).

Classic studies by proponents of old-age assistance include Lucile Eaves, *Aged Clients of Boston Social Agencies* (Boston: Women's Educational and Industrial Union, 1925); Abraham Epstein, *Facing Old Age* (New York: Knopf, 1922), and *The Challenge of the Aged* (New York: Vanguard, 1928); Harry Carroll Evans, *The American Poorfarm and Its Inmates* (Des Moines, Iowa: Loyal Order of Moose, 1926); Mabel Louise Nassau, *Old Age Poverty in Greenwich Village* (New York: Revell, 1915); Isaac M. Rubinow, editor, *The Care of the Aged* (Chicago: University of Chicago Press, 1931); and L. W. Squier, *Old Age Dependency in the United States* (New York: Macmillan, 1912). A debaters' handbook on the subject was compiled by Lamar T. Beman, *Old Age Pensions* (New York: Wilson, 1927).

UNEMPLOYMENT INSURANCE

The best historical account of the origins and early stages of the unemployment insurance movement is Harry Malisoff, "The Emergence of Unemployment Compensation," *Political Science Quarterly*, 54:2 (June 1939), pp. 237–258, 54:3 (September 1939), pp. 391–420, and 54:4 (December 1939), pp. 577–599.

Primary printed documents are John B. Andrews, *Unemployment Reserve Funds* (New York, 1930); Paul H. Douglas, *Wages and the Family* (Chicago: University of Chicago Press, 1925), and *Standards of Unemployment Insurance* (Chicago: University of Chicago Press, 1933); Allen B. Forsberg, editor, *Selected Articles* on *Unemployment Insurance* (New York: Wilson, 1926); Mary B. Gilson, *Unemployment Insurance* (Chicago: University of Chicago Press, 1933); Roger S. Hoar, *Unemployment Insurance in Wisconsin* (South Milwaukee: Stuart Press, 1932); and Bryce M. Stewart, *Unemployment Benefits in the United States: The Plans and Their Setting* (New York: Industrial Relations Counselors, 1930).

SOCIAL SECURITY

The historical backgrounds of the social insurance movement leading up to the Social Security Act of 1935 are given in Grace Abbott, *From Relief to Social Security* (Chicago: University of Chicago Press, 1941); Joseph Charles Dougherty, Jr., "The Genesis of the Social Security Act of 1935" (Doctoral dissertation, Georgetown University, 1955); and Paul H. Douglas, *Social Security in the United States* (New York: McGraw-Hill, 1936). Historians have, of course, narrated the story of the immediate genesis of the Social Security Act in general histories of the New Deal; no account is better, in this literature, than Arthur M. Schlesinger, Jr., *The Coming of the New Deal* (Boston: Houghton Mifflin, 1959), pp. 301–315.

Primary printed materials of special note are Barbara N. Armstrong, *Insuring the Essentials* (New York: Macmillan, 1932); Abraham Epstein, *Insecurity: A Challenge to America* (New York: Smith and Haas, 1933); Isaac M. Rubinow, *Social Insurance, with Special Reference to American Conditions* (New York: Holt, 1913), *Standards of Health Insurance* (New York: Holt, 1916), and *The Quest for Security* (New York: Holt, 1934); Henry R. Seager, *Social Insurance: A Program of Social Reform* (New York: Macmillan, 1910); and U.S. Federal Security Agency, *Social Security in the United States* (Washington, D.C.: Government Printing Office, 1935). In 1936, when events were still fresh in his mind, Edwin E. Witte, executive director of the President's Committee on Economic Security, 1934–1935, set down the full inside story that was not published until 1962: *The Development of the Social Security Act: A Memorandum on the History of the Committee on Economic Security and Drafting and Legislative History of the Social Security Act* (Madison: University of Wisconsin Press, 1962). Other inside views are given by Frances Perkins, *The Roosevelt I Knew* (New York: Viking, 1946), pp. 106–108, 278–301; and Rexford G. Tugwell, *The Democratic Roosevelt* (Garden City, N.Y.: Doubleday, 1957), pp. 334–341.

THE IMPACT OF THE DEPRESSION

General historical accounts are James Joseph Hannah, "Urban Reaction to the Great Depression in the United States, 1929–1933" (Doctoral dissertation, University of California at Berkeley, 1956); Broadus Mitchell, *Depression Decade: From New Era through New Deal, 1929–1941* (New York: Rinehart, 1947); Albert U. Romasco, "American Institutions in the Great Depression, the Hoover Years" (Doctoral dissertation, University of Chicago, 1961); and Harris G. Warren, *Herbert Hoover and the Great Depression* (New York: Oxford, 1959). Bernstein in *The Lean Years* catches brilliantly the impact of the early depression years upon the working man and the union movement. President Hoover's story is told in *The Memoirs of Herbert Hoover: The Cabinet and the Presidency, 1920–1933* (New York: Macmillan, 1952), Volume II, and in William Starr Myers and Walter H. Newton, *The Hoover Administration: A Documented Narrative* (New York: Scribner, 1936).

The human consequences of the depression are revealed in Robert C. Angell, *The Family Encounters the Depression* (New York: Scribner, 1936); Lillian Brandt, et al., *An Impressionistic View of the Winter of 1930–31 in New York City* (New York: Welfare Council of New York City, 1932); Clarence J. Enzler, *Some Social Aspects of the Depression, 1930–1935* (Washington, D.C.: Catholic University, 1939); Mirra Komarovsky, *The Unemployed Man and His Family* (New York: Dryden, 1940); Jennings J. Rhyne, *Some Southern Cotton Mill Workers and Their Villages* (Chapel Hill: University of North Carolina Press, 1930); Tom Tippett, *When Southern Labor Stirs* (New York: Cape and Smith, 1931); James M. Williams, *Human Aspects of Unemployment and Relief* (Chapel Hill: University of North Carolina Press, 1933). A cross section of all phases of American society in the early years of the depression is presented in the President's Research Committee on Social Trends, *Recent Social Trends in the United States* (2 vols.; New York: McGraw-Hill, 1933).

REFORMS PROPOSED TO MEET THE DEPRESSION

Historical surveys of public welfare policies including programs for the relief of the unemployed are Edith Abbott, *Public Assistance: American Principles and Policies with Select Documents* (Chicago: University of Chicago Press, 1940); Sophonisba Breckinridge, *Public Welfare Administration in the United States: Select Documents* (2nd ed.; Chicago: University of Chicago Press, 1938); Josephine C. Brown, *Public Relief, 1929–1939* (New York: Holt, 1940); and Leah H. Feder, *Unemployment Relief in Periods of Depression: A Study of Measures Adopted in Certain American Cities, 1857 through 1922* (New York: Russell Sage Foundation, 1936).

Studies made in reaction to earlier and lesser depressions than 1929 are John L. Gillin, *Poverty and Dependency: Their Relief and Prevention* (New York: Century, 1921); Robert W. Kelso, *The Science of Public Welfare* (New York: Holt, 1928); Philip Klein, *The Burden of Unemployment* (New York: Russell Sage Foundation, 1923); and Leo Wolman, *Planning and Control of Public Works* (New York: National Bureau of Economic Research, 1930).

Studies of the problems arising out of unemployment and their amelioration, prevention, or cure are Joanna C. Colcord, *Community Planning in Unemployment Emergencies* (New York: Russell Sage Foundation, 1930); Joanna C. Colcord, *et al.*, *Emergency Work Relief as Carried Out in Twenty-Six American Communities, 1930–31* (New York: Russell Sage Foundation, 1932); Paul H. Douglas and Aaron Director, *The Problem of Unemployment* (New York: Macmillan, 1931); Helen Hall, *Shall We Stick to the American Dole?* (New York: National Federation of Settlements, 1931); Dorothy Kahn, *Unemployment and Its Treatment in the United States* (New York: American Association of Social Workers, 1937); Rose Porter, *The Organization and Administration of Public Relief Agencies* (New York: Family Welfare Association of America, 1931); Margaret E. Rich, *The Administration of Relief in Unemployment Emergencies* (New York: Family Welfare Association of New York, 1931); and Harriet E. Anderson and Margaret E. Rich, *Care of the Homeless in Unemployment Emergencies* (New York: Family Welfare Association of America, 1930).

In *Permanent Preventives of Unemployment* (Baltimore, Md.: Belvedere Press, 1931) are recorded the proceedings of the Conference on Permanent Prevention of Unemployment, 26–27 January 1931, sponsored jointly by Protestant, Catholic, and Jewish groups. The semiofficial story of the Woods Committee is told in Erving P. Hayes, *Activities of the President's Emergency Committee for Employment* (Concord, N.H.: Rumford, 1936). A definitive account of housing reform is Timothy L. McDonnell, *The Wagner Housing Act* (Chicago: Loyola University Press, 1957).

INDEX

Abbott, Edith: and NCL, 5; and social settlements, 109; mentioned, 48, 261

Abbott, Grace: and NCL, 5; and leadership of NCLC, 46; fights for extension of Sheppard-Towner Act, 51; proposes U.S. Public Health Service, 55; and Children's Bureau, 57, 76; and child-labor amendment, 57; and unemployment problem, 57, 201; settlement background of, 109; supports civil rights groups, 132; supports Fair Labor Standards Act, 203; mentioned for secretary of labor, 246; on F. D. R., 247; career and personality of, 249–250; on New Deal, 250; and social insurance, 257; mentioned, 47, 48, 104, 261, 267, 300

Accident insurance: WTUL and, 10; AALL and, 11; church organizations and, 22, 23; supported in NCCC platform, 88

Acheson, Dean: and minimum wage, 72; on Supreme Court changes, 75; and equal rights for women, 77

Addams, Jane: Florence Kelley's devotion to, 5; and NCL, 5; and AALL, 11; on residency for settlement workers, 15; on urban problems, 16, 113; on social insurance, 18; pacifist convictions of, 18; and reconstruction after World War I, 19; and civil liberties, 20, 132; backs Progressive party, 89; on constructive over preventive measures, 100; quoted on process of democracy, 108; and Hull House, 109, 110; on aims of settlement movement, 112, 113, 116; supports Amalgamated Clothing Workers of America, 115; and cause of world peace, 120; and housing reform, 135; supports Hoover, 140; political position in 1932, 248; papers of, 295; mentioned, 38, 48, 97, 104, 127, 261, 266, 299, 300

Adkins, Jesse C., 70

Adkins decision, 36, 68, 72, 76, 230

Adler, Felix, 13, 29, 32, 33, 42

Agricultural Marketing Act, 236

Alfred, Helen: and housing reform, 137, 253; supports Thomas in 1928, 140; and old-age security, 165; mentioned, 266

Alger, George W., 44, 255

Almy, Frederic, 89, 140

Altmeyer, Arthur J., 174–175, 256, 266

Amalgamated Clothing Workers, 115, 166, 176

American Association for Labor Legislation (AALL): founded, 10; and workmen's compensation laws, 11; leaders of, 11, 14; program of, 11; and child labor, 11, 40, 42; and health insurance, 12, 156–157; and old-age security, 12, 160, 166; and employment security, 12, 170, 204–205, 219; and minimum wage, 67, 71; budget for, 260; journal of, 297–298; mentioned, 21, 25, 266

American Association for Old Age Security (AAOAS), 164, 169, 211–212, 266, 298

American Association for Organizing Family Social Work, 87

American Association for Social Security (AASS), 169, 225, 298

American Association of Social Workers (AASW), 92, 190

American Association of University Women, 76, 233

American Child, The, 14

American Child Health Organization, 51, 52

American Civil Liberties Union, 21, 117

American Farm Bureau Federation, 39

American Federation of Labor (AFL): and child labor, 13, 34, 35, 36, 44; political programs in 1920's, 232; union drive in South, 239; asks reforms in 1932, 242–243

American Medical Association, 55

SELECTED ANN ARBOR PAPERBACKS

works of enduring merit

For a complete list of Ann Arbor Paperback titles write:

THE UNIVERSITY OF MICHIGAN PRESS / ANN ARBOR